973.0496 JAM

3 സ:ശ

✓ KT-599-940

FIGHTING RACISM IN WORLD WAR II

FIGHTING RACISM IN WORLD WAR II

by C.L.R. James
George Breitman, Edgar Keemer
and others

PATHFINDER
New York   London   Montréal   Sydney

Edited by Fred Stanton

Library of Congress Catalog Card No. 80-82043
ISBN 0-913460-82-6 paper; ISBN 0-913460-81-8 cloth
Manufactured in the United States of America

First edition, 1980
Second printing, February 1991

Cover photo: Rally in New York City for Black rights called by the March on Washington movement, 1942. Odell Waller, a Virginia sharecropper, was a victim of a frame-up and legal lynching that year. *Courtesy of New York Public Library*

Cover design by Toni Gorton

Distributed by Pathfinder
410 West Street, New York, NY 10014, U.S.A.
  Pathfinder distributors around the world:
Australia (and Asia and the Pacific):
  Pathfinder, 19 Terry St., Surry Hills, Sydney, NSW 2010
Britain (and Europe, Africa, and the Middle East):
  Pathfinder, 47 The Cut, London, SE1 8LL
Canada:
  Pathfinder, 6566, boul. St-Laurent, Montréal, Québec, H2S 3C6
Iceland:
  Pathfinder, Klapparstíg 26, 2d floor, 121 Reykjavík
New Zealand:
  Pathfinder, 157a Symonds Street, Auckland
Sweden:
  Pathfinder, Vikingagatan 10, S-113 42, Stockholm
United States (and Caribbean and Latin America):
  Pathfinder, 410 West Street, New York, NY 10014

CONTENTS

DATES AND EVENTS

1939

March	Spanish civil war ends with fascist victory. Germany seizes Czechoslovakia.
April	Senator Theodore C. Bilbo introduces bill to deport Blacks to Africa. Italy seizes Albania.
July	Socialist Workers Party adopts its first comprehensive program for Black liberation.
August	Stalin-Hitler nonaggression pact is signed. Communist International drops demand for "collective security" alliances between USSR and "democratic" imperialists against fascist imperialists; Communist parties in the "democracies" campaign against imperialist war.
September	Germany invades western Poland. Britain and France declare war. USSR seizes eastern Poland.
November	USSR invades Finland to gain territory Moscow needs for defense of Leningrad.

1940

April	SWP convention reaffirms policy of defense of USSR against imperialist attack despite Stalin's crimes; a large minority splits away. National Negro Congress splits, with A. Philip Randolph heading pro-Allied forces and CP heading opponents of war; Randolph quits and Stalinists take control of shell of NNC.
May-June	Germany crushes France.
June	Italy enters war.
August	Leon Trotsky is assassinated by Stalinist agent. Italy occupies British Somaliland.
September	U.S. draft law is passed.
October	Roosevelt announces that proportion of Blacks in military will be same as proportion in whole population, but opposes desegregation of armed forces units; U.S. military remains Jim Crow throughout war.
November	Roosevelt wins third term.

1941

January	Randolph calls for march on Washington July 1 against discrimination in employment and armed forces.
February	Italian army in Africa collapses; German army intervenes.
April	Black workers support United Auto Workers strike against Ford; May victory wins first union shop agreement in auto industry. Germany attacks Greece and Yugoslavia.

June	U.S. government breaks North American Aviation strike with troops. Germany invades USSR. CP drops opposition to imperialist war and demands U.S. intervene on side of USSR. Roosevelt issues Executive Order 8022 establishing Fair Employment Practices Committee. March on Washington is cancelled. FBI raids SWP headquarters in Minneapolis.
July	Government indicts twenty-nine SWP leaders under Smith Act.
August	Sixty Black soldiers persecuted by racists in Arkansas go AWOL, returning to their former base in Michigan.
October-November	Sedition trial of SWP leaders is held in Minneapolis. CIO convention resolves to organize the South.
December	Japan attacks Pearl Harbor, Philippines, Malaya, Hong Kong. U.S. declares war on Axis powers. Eighteen SWP leaders are sentenced to twelve- and sixteen-month terms. German army pulls back from Moscow as USSR counteroffensive begins.

1942

January	Over 3,000 Black soldiers are arrested after violent confrontation in Alexandria, Louisiana.
February	Mob of 1,200 armed whites prevents three Black families from moving into Detroit housing project. Roosevelt signs Executive Order 9066, leading to internment of 110,000 Japanese-Americans.
June	March on Washington movement holds mass rallies in New York and Chicago.
July	Government imposes wage controls.
August	Axis forces sweep into Egypt.
September	Siege of Stalingrad begins.
October	Roosevelt issues executive order freezing wages. Britain routs German army in North Africa.
November	Allies invade Algeria.

1943

February	German army at Stalingrad surrenders; USSR wins pivotal battle of war.
March	Post office revokes *Militant*'s second-class mailing rights.
April	Ten thousand demonstrate against racism in Detroit.
May	Alabama Dry Dock and Shipbuilders Company in Mobile instigates walkout and riot of 20,000 white workers against hiring of Blacks.
May-October	United Mine Workers strikes defy U.S. government and break wage freeze and no-strike orders.
June	Racists rampage in Los Angeles, Detroit, and Beaumont, Texas.

July	March on Washington movement holds convention. Allies invade Sicily. Mussolini is ousted and Marshal Badoglio forms new Italian government.
August	Black uprising in Harlem is triggered by police brutality and discrimination. USSR begins to drive out German army. U.S. launches campaign on Pacific islands.
September	Allies invade Italy. Italian government surrenders but Germany continues war in Italy.
November-December	Western Allies at Tehran summit conference pledge to open second front against Germany.
December	Roosevelt announces end of New Deal. Eighteen SWP leaders go to prison.

1944

January	Roosevelt calls for labor conscription law.
March	*Militant* regains second-class mailing rights.
May	U.S. Communist Party is dissolved; Communist Political Association is formed.
June	Allies take Italy. Second front is opened with invasion of Normandy (D-Day).
June-July	USSR takes Finland, Latvia, Estonia, Lithuania.
August	Troops run public transportation in Philadelphia, Pennsylvania, after white workers strike against hiring of Blacks.
November	Roosevelt wins fourth team with backing of labor leaders. Major Black newspapers oppose him because Democratic Party platform does not call for laws against poll tax, lynching, or military discrimination.
December	U.S. retakes Philippines. Allies win Battle of the Bulge in Europe. British troops battle Greek partisans.

1945

January	SWP leaders are released from prison.
February	Yalta summit conference is held.
April	Roosevelt dies; Truman becomes president. Mussolini is executed. Hitler commits suicide.
May	Germany surrenders. Japan approaches USSR for peace terms.
June	U.S. troops mop up in Pacific; Japan's cities are in ruins; 40 percent of Tokyo has been destroyed.
July	Funds to FEPC are cut. Atom bomb is tested in New Mexico.
July-August	Potsdam summit conference is held.
August	Hiroshima and Nagasaki are destroyed by U.S. atom bombs; over 200,000 are killed or maimed, and radiation causes disease and deaths for generations. Japan accepts surrender terms.
September	Japan signs surrender pact.

A Note on Authors and Pen Names

Authors' names are listed in footnotes on the first page of each article as they appeared in the original text. The following are the pen names and the real names of the authors:

J. R. Johnson—pen name of C. L. R. James (see Glossary).

Albert Parker, Philip Blake—pen names of George Breitman (see Glossary).

Joe Andrews—pen name of Jules Geller (1913-   ), an SWP leader and CIO activist during the war.

Ernest Williams—pen name of Myra Lesnik, an SWP activist in Harlem.

Jeff Thorne—an SWP member and union activist in Flint.

Abe Stein—an SWP member in New York.

George Schraum—an SWP member and union activist in Cleveland.

David Ransom—pen name of Abe Stein.

John Saunders—pen name of Arthur Burch (1897-1979), SWP branch organizer in Detroit during the war.

Art Preis (1911-1964)—labor editor of *Militant* for many years and author of *Labor's Giant Step* (Pathfinder Press: 2nd ed., 1972).

Charles Jackson—pen name of Dr. Edgar Keemer (see Glossary).

F. J. Lang—pen name of Frank Lovell (1913-   ), an SWP leader and merchant seaman during the war.

Robert Chester (1912-1975)—an SWP leader and union activist in San Francisco.

Louise Simpson—SWP candidate for New York City Council from Harlem in 1945.

INTRODUCTION

This is a collection of articles, pamphlets, letters, and resolutions from the press of the Socialist Workers Party (SWP) during World War II. It is divided into two parts. The first begins with the outbreak of the war in Europe in September 1939 and goes to the Japanese bombing of the American fleet at Pearl Harbor in December 1941. The second part extends from that point, when the U.S. government formally entered the war, until the Japanese surrender in September 1945. A table of dates helps to identify the major events referred to, and a glossary supplies information about people and groups discussed in the text.

The material in this book illuminates aspects of history usually omitted in books about the war: what Blacks and Marxists thought and said about wartime racial conditions in this country, North and South, military and civilian; what disputes were waged in the Black, labor, and radical movements over strategy, tactics, and theory; what struggles were waged to change conditions during the war, which undoubtedly laid the ground for the civil rights movements of the 1950s and 1960s. It also documents what the SWP, the only consistently antiwar party in that period, did and tried to do in the fight against the oppression of Blacks.

Younger readers will undoubtedly be surprised by some of this material, and most readers will be struck by how much conditions have changed—and how much they have not changed—in the last forty years. To facilitate their understanding, a few remarks are offered here as background.

Between the end of Reconstruction in the 1870s and the start of World War II in 1939, American Blacks were stripped by force and by law of the democratic rights they had won after the Civil War; they were oppressed economically, politically, and socially. They were confined to the lowest-paying and hardest jobs; excluded from or segregated in most unions; restricted to the worst housing; denied equal educational opportunity; discriminated against in public services and facilities; and lynched with impunity. In 1939 the median income of Blacks was 40 percent that of whites. And in twelve southern states, only 2 percent of voting-age Blacks were qualified to vote.

Racist ideology and vilification prevailed almost without challenge in the press and schools. No federal civil rights bill had been passed since 1875, and in the 1940 presidential elections the Democratic and Republican candidates hardly made a pretense that they would pass any if elected. There was only one Black member in the whole Congress.

There were 13 million Blacks out of a population of 131 million. Of the Blacks, 74 percent lived in the South, and 52 percent in rural areas. This was to change dramatically during the war, with migration to the cities and the North under the stimulus of wartime labor shortages. This migration, which was not planned by anyone and occurred only because it suited the needs of capitalism, was one of the most far-reaching changes of the twentieth century. It had begun on a smaller scale in World War I, was interrupted by the depression, but then resumed on a massive scale during and after World War II, effectively reducing the isolation of a formerly rural people in a pretelevision era and undercutting the ability of the government and the white population to ignore what was happening to Blacks.

When the Great Depression began in 1929, Blacks were in a poor position to counteract the growing assaults on their jobs and living conditions. In the 1920s millions of Black Americans had responded to one degree or another to the Black nationalist appeals of Marcus Garvey and his Universal Negro Improvement Association. But by the depression, the government had indicted and imprisoned Garvey, and his movement had dwindled into a small sect, incapable of providing leadership. Nor was there any other Black or civil rights organization on the scene that was capable of organizing the Black masses. They lost a disproportionate share of the jobs in the country and suffered even deeper cuts in their living standards than the millions of white unemployed. Blacks now were systematically driven out of what the racists called "nigger work" so that those previously unwanted jobs could be occupied by whites.

The most positive development of this decade was that the Congress of Industrial Organizations (CIO) came into existence and distinguished itself from the conservative and discriminatory American Federation of Labor (AFL) by opening its doors to Black workers and actively soliciting their participation in the unionization of the basic industries, then still unorganized. Blacks responded well to this invitation once they were convinced that the CIO meant what it said on this score, and from the beginning they were an important component of the new CIO union in the steel industry. Nevertheless, the number of Blacks in industry as a whole was quite low before September 1939, and they did not begin to play a major role in the unions until the war industries began to expand.

Even that did not occur immediately. At first most of the war plants simply refused to hire Blacks, not even bothering to conceal what they were doing. At the same time, most of the government-financed training programs for workers refused to accept Blacks on the ground that the war plants would not hire them, so why waste the training? Meanwhile, public works programs were being phased out and welfare appropriations were being slashed on the ground that unemployment was falling—although Blacks had to rely disproportionately on these programs because they were excluded from the "new prosperity."

In March 1942, a full two years after rearmament began, Blacks were only 2.5 to 3 percent of all workers in war production. But as the wartime boom continued, this began to change. By November 1944, this figure had risen to over 8 percent. Between April 1940 and April 1944, the total number of Black workers increased by one-third, from 4.4 million to 5.9 million. However, four-fifths remained at unskilled jobs, and there was widespread discrimination on the job.

The same pattern was seen in the armed forces. At first, the army and navy were reluctant to accept Black enlistees or draftees even on a segregated basis. In 1940, there were less than 5,000 Blacks and only 2 Black officers in an army of 230,000—that is, a little more than 2 percent. By September 1944, however, there were 702,000 in the army, 165,000 in the navy, 17,000 in the marines, and 5,000 in the coast guard. All together, around one million Black men and women served in the armed forces during the war, half of them overseas. However, they were segregated into all-Black units, usually under white officers, or were assigned to be cooks, porters, laborers, or servants. They also faced racist harassment by white military police. It was not until 1948 that the armed forces were officially desegregated.

It is not at all surprising, therefore, that Blacks were less enthusiastic about the war than most of the American population. Patriotism was fueled by government rhetoric about democracy and the "four freedoms,"* but among Blacks this rhetoric often had a result unexpected by its proponents—it had a politicizing, even a radicalizing, effect. Blacks began to demand some freedom for themselves.

*Roosevelt proclaimed the "Four Freedoms" as a goal of American foreign policy in an address to Congress in January 1941. They were: freedom of speech and expression, freedom of worship, freedom from want, and freedom from fear.

Another influence on Black thinking was the nature of the war itself. Fundamentally, Washington's role in World War II, as in World War I, was that of a contestant in a war between imperialist powers for redivision of the world. Britain and France, which had the largest empires, were being challenged by newer imperialist powers—Germany, Italy, and Japan. The United States, already the most powerful imperialist country, was also a latecomer in the seizure of colonies; its rulers hoped to pick up the spoils all around, especially in Asia.

Many Blacks were aware that America's allies, Britain and France, were the chief oppressors of Africa, Asia, and the Middle East. Moreover, the U.S. itself was supporting repressive regimes throughout Latin America and the rest of the colonial world so as to better economically exploit these countries.

The U.S. had several direct colonies—among them Puerto Rico, the Philippines, the Virgin Islands, and Hawaii—and had intervened militarily dozens of times in other countries to impose its policies.

The true aims of the U.S. and its allies were reflected not only in their fight to continue exploiting colonial peoples, but also in their response to the rise of fascism in Europe. When fascist governments were formed in Italy, Spain, and Germany, rather than opposing these regimes, the rulers of the imperialist democracies made fortunes selling them war materiel. And after the Germany army defeated its French counterpart, the French capitalists collaborated with the occupation and used it to drive down wages and attack the workers' movement.

The rulers of the capitalist democracies knew that German fascism was not simply the product of Hitler the individual; it grew out of methods used to defeat the working class when it rebelled in the face of the capitalist economic crisis. Unable to make concessions to stop a powerful workers' movement, the German capitalists had backed Hitler in order to retain their power and to regiment the country in preparation for a war of colonial conquest. The French, British, and American capitalists would themselves not have been opposed to turning to fascist forces in their own countries if this was needed against a challenge by the working class.

The Allied war effort was accompanied by nationalist and racist calls to kill "Krauts" and "Japs." Deliberately hidden was the fact that the German workers were victims of Nazism and were a force that could overthrow Hitler along with the capitalists who supported him. The Allies would countenance no effort to aid the German workers to rise up against Hitler. On the contrary, they took measures calculated to have the opposite effect. Saturation bombing against German cities by the Allies was directed against the German workers.

Above all, the democratic imperialists wanted to ensure the survival of capitalism after the war, even though that meant keeping in power the German capitalists who backed Hitler.

Another aspect of the war was the hostility of all the capitalist powers to the Soviet Union. The U.S. rulers hoped that the war between Germany and the USSR would weaken both countries and make it easier to restore capitalism in the Soviet Union at some point in the future. It was the Soviet Union that absorbed the brunt of the German attack, and the U.S. government did everything it could to keep it that way. Even at the height of the U.S. war effort in Europe, over 80 percent of the German forces were directed against the Soviets. The USSR lost over 20 million people in the war.

The U.S. military effort was focused not in Europe but in the colonial world—especially in Asia, where Japan was blocking U.S. economic expansion.

The nature of the U.S. war effort was reflected in other ways. The U.S. refused to open its borders to the Jewish refugees, and anti-Semitism was part of the arsenal not only of fascist groups in the U.S. but of the employers as well (the Fair Employment Practices Committee reported that 6 percent of the complaints of discrimination in employment during the war involved anti-Semitism). To put the U.S. on a war footing to win "democracy" abroad, the government resorted to police-state measures at home: it drove Japanese-Americans into concentration camps, used federal troops against striking aircraft workers and miners, censored the press, and jailed draft resisters and antiwar labor leaders.

Another indication of the nature of the war was what happened afterwards. The U.S. emerged as the undisputed victor in the war. Washington's dream of an "American Century" was ushered in with the atomic bombing of Hiroshima and Nagasaki, a nightmarish atrocity. The goal of this act was to serve notice on the world—especially the USSR—that the U.S. was now boss.

Washington became the world policeman for capitalism. In the decades after World War II, the United States played the central role in attempting to defeat or contain the struggles of the colonial peoples. Overt and covert military intervention has been used in every corner of the world. In Korea and Vietnam the death toll was in the millions. The U.S. dropped many times more bombs on Vietnam than were used by all sides in the Second World War.

The United States installed or backed the most brutal and

criminal regimes in the world: the shah in Iran, Somoza in Nicaragua, Pinochet in Chile, Suharto in Indonesia, the racist regimes in Southern Africa—to name only a few. Many of the torture techniques used against dissidents by these regimes—methods often taught them by the CIA—were originally devised in Hitler's concentration camps. These techniques, it should be added, were often "improved" upon by the U.S. instructors.

The very nature of the U.S. as an imperialist power meant that its military effort in World War II could not be a war for freedom and democracy. Its strengthened position after the war put a new burden on the backs of the masses around the world—including working people and Blacks in the United States, who have gone through McCarthyism, antilabor measures, and other attacks on their rights.

Nor was the threat of fascism eliminated with the defeat of Hitler. In reality the danger of fascism will exist as long as the capitalist system that breeds it.

World War II and its effects put the existing organizations of American Blacks on the spot. As the contradiction between the racist treatment of Blacks and the declared aim of the war as a fight for freedom became obvious, pressure mounted for an organized struggle to improve the situation of Blacks. In 1939 there were three important national Black groups. First was the thirty-year-old National Association for the Advancement of Colored People, which grew during the war from 85,000 to 530,000 members. Its main activity was legal and educational, and its main appeal was to middle-class and white-collar elements, not to the Black masses. Second was the twenty-eight-year-old National Urban League, a small social service agency largely funded by white philanthropists, which did not pretend to lead Black struggles and relied on compromise and conciliation. And third was the three-year-old National Negro Congress, which began as a coalition of about five hundred civil rights and church groups, and was gradually taken over by supporters of the Communist Party; when the war came, the Stalinists foisted their then-"antiwar" line on the NNC, which led to a split and the departure of the non-Stalinists, leaving the NNC a CP front organization with declining influence.

The failure of these organizations to provide leadership to Black people in the new situation produced by the war created the conditions for the emergence of a new type of organization, one that would base itself on the Black masses' militancy and willingness to fight for change. This set the scene in 1941 for the March on Washington movement (usually called the March on

Washington Committee during its first year), which was organized and led by A. Philip Randolph, union leader, former socialist, and president of the NNC before the CP captured its empty shell. The NAACP and the Urban League gave a certain amount of cooperation to the March on Washington movement (MOWM) during its first year, but then they withdrew from it altogether; the NNC never supported the MOWM at all. The all-Black MOWM never achieved most of its aims, but it forced concessions from the government and had a progressive impact on the labor movement. It held its last national conference in October 1946 and dissolved in late 1947. It was certainly the most important Black movement since the heyday of Garveyism, and one of the most promising in all of American history. It was the first large Black organization in which trade unionists played the leading role.

The war was also a test for political parties claiming to represent the interests of working people. It was a time of tremendous political pressure—a patriotic war hysteria; attacks on civil liberties and union rights of workers in general; and direct government persecution of those whose ideas or actions interfered with the drive of American capitalism to defeat its imperialist competitors.

The Socialist Workers Party made significant headway against these obstacles. It expanded its work in the Black struggle, sent the bulk of its membership into the unions, organized a broad defense of democratic rights, and was able to win many Blacks and other workers to its banner. While it was never large enough to have a decisive impact on events on a national scale, it set an example of principled revolutionary work under very unfavorable conditions.

The SWP had no more than a thousand members throughout the country when the war started, including a few dozen Blacks. In some cities—most notably Minneapolis—the party exercised influence in the labor movement through its leading role in union struggles. But its work in the Black struggle was more limited: although its members had participated in local and regional struggles against racism, it had little experience on a national level and adopted its basic theoretical program for Black liberation only two months before the war began.* It had to learn as it went along.

*For transcripts of discussions about this program held in Mexico between Leon Trotsky and SWP leaders, and for the text of the resolutions adopted at the July 1939 convention of the SWP in New York, see *Leon Trotsky on Black Nationalism and Self-Determination* (Pathfinder Press, 1978).

The SWP had been founded at the start of 1938 by people who were active previously in the Communist and Socialist parties and other radical groups. While most of its members were in their twenties or late teens, they had the benefit of a group of older leaders whose political experience in working-class movements dated back to the early years of the century. The party was affiliated to the Fourth International, an international organization which was founded in 1938 by Leon Trotsky and his co-thinkers in several countries.* Their revolutionary socialist program called upon the workers in the imperialist countries to oppose the war politically, striving in wartime as in peacetime to win power from the capitalists and create a new world free of militarism, fascism, and economic crisis. Despite their opposition to the U.S. war aims, SWP members served in the armed forces when drafted, as did most workers, and attempted to defend the interests of the soldiers. The SWP counterposed to capitalist militarism a policy of universal military training for working people, under the control of the unions.

At the same time, the SWP favored defense of the Soviet Union against imperialist attack, calling on working people and workers' organizations around the world to aid the Soviet war effort. Although the SWP opposed the Stalinist bureaucracy, it supported the gains of the Russian revolution—the planned economy that had enabled the USSR to avoid the mass unemployment of the world capitalist depression. In addition, the SWP supported the struggles of the peoples of China, India, Ethiopia, and other colonial and semicolonial countries to free themselves from imperialist domination of both the fascist and "democratic" variety.

These policies were not popular in the World War II period. During the Stalin-Hitler pact (August 1939–June 1941) the American ruling class used every propaganda resource to brainwash people into believing that Marxism was the twin of fascism. The pressure of this anti-Soviet barrage led to a split in the SWP in 1940, reducing the party to 600 members.

The government did not rely on propaganda alone to silence the SWP. It intervened in the unions to get SWPers expelled or

*For an account of the background of the tendencies that joined together to create the SWP in 1938, see *The History of American Trotskyism* by James P. Cannon (Pathfinder Press, 1972). At the end of 1940 the SWP voted to formally disaffiliate from the Fourth International because the U.S. Congress adopted a reactionary law severely penalizing the members of international organizations, but the party remained in political solidarity with the Fourth International and vigorously supported its revolutionary goals.

fired. It unleashed FBI informers and agents provocateurs. And it brought twenty-nine leaders of the SWP and the Minneapolis Teamsters to trial for sedition in 1941 under the Smith Act and imprisoned eighteen of them during the final period of the war. The government was also able to interfere with circulation of the party's newspaper, the *Militant,* by destroying some issues, delaying others in the mail, and revoking the paper's second-class mailing privileges.

Despite these adverse conditions, the SWP was able to take some steps forward. It refused to be silenced, fighting tenaciously and successfully to preserve its legality, telling the truth in every way possible—through the *Militant,* in leaflets and pamphlets, through election campaigns, on the radio, and in political discussions in the plants, union halls, and army barracks. Through its courageous defense of civil liberties in the Minnneapolis trial, the party succeeded in building a protest campaign against the convictions that involved over 600 labor, Black, and civil liberties organizations representing over five million members.

The party began to grow during the later war years, winning hundreds of Black and working-class members and reaching a size of about 1,500, overwhelmingly composed of industrial workers. More and more people were open to socialist ideas as the war went on. There was growing ferment in the factories and mines as the war economy brought the workers speedup, inflation, and wage freeze while the capitalists made superprofits. Sentiment in favor of forming a labor party also grew, and the end of the war brought the biggest strike wave in U.S. history.

The Fourth International expected a wave of revolutions to follow the war, as had happened after World War I. This was an accurate prediction not only for the colonial world but for Europe as well, where there were revolutionary mobilizations throughout Eastern Europe and in Greece, Italy, and France. It was only the intervention of Stalin, using the Soviet army and the Communist parties, together with the efforts of U.S. imperialism, including the Marshall Plan, that prevented revolutions in Western Europe and held them back for several years in Eastern Europe while Stalin tried to maintain his wartime alliance with the imperialist powers.*

---

*In Greece, Italy, and France the Stalinists led partisan movements which were the main armed forces in those countries after the defeat of the fascists; instead of leading socialist revolutions, they disarmed the workers and helped reestablish capitalist regimes. In Czechoslovakia, Poland, Hungary, and Bulgaria, where Soviet occupation troops were

The failure of the Western European revolutions and the economic predominance of the U.S. internationally enabled American big business to make wage concessions to workers in this country, end the strike wave, and, in collaboration with the union bureaucrats, impose a witch-hunt and begin preparations for a new war against the Soviet Union.

These factors cut off the growth of the SWP in that period; many of the Blacks and unionists recruited during and shortly after the war dropped out, and it was not until the new rise of the Black struggle and the colonial revolutions of the 1960s (especially Cuba and Vietnam) that the party began to grow again.

The Communist Party (CP) occupies a relatively large amount of space in this book, and with good reason. The CP at that time was much more influential than today. It had control of or important standing in several national unions, a Black cadre of significant size, and a reserve of sympathy in the Black community because of its role in many struggles, beginning with the Scottsboro case.

Because of its ties to Stalin's policies in the Soviet Union, the CP went through some big political zigzags. During the late 1930s, it called for "collective security" alliances between the democratic imperialist powers and the USSR against Hitler. With the Stalin-Hitler pact in 1939, the CP opposed U.S. intervention against Hitler. When Hitler invaded the Soviet Union in 1941, the CP switched again. Many of its members and friends deserted it during the period of the Stalin-Hitler pact, but it began to grow again in 1941.

When the U.S. and the USSR became allies, the CP became the most patriotic organization in this country. It hailed the government's prosecution of the SWP in the Minneapolis case and its suspension of the *Militant*'s mailing rights, complaining only that the punishments were too mild. It also denounced striking miners and protesting Blacks, demanding the arrest of A. Philip Randolph and the prosecution of John L. Lewis. As a climax, it applauded the bombing of Hiroshima and Nagasaki.

The CP paid dearly for its wartime political crimes: Its strike-breaking role cost it much of its former following in the unions, and this hampered attempts to hold back the witch-hunt of the late forties. Its justifications of prosecutions under the Smith Act helped set up its own leaders for victimization under the same

---

stationed, the Stalinists sidetracked the workers' movements into coalition governments. They did not nationalize bourgeois property or break up these coalition regimes until after the West launched the cold war and began to rebuild Western Europe. They established bureaucratized workers' states in 1948.

law in 1949. And its opposition to the wartime struggles of Blacks lost it much of its former influence in the Black community.

All the material in this book is reprinted from the SWP newspaper, which was called the *Socialist Appeal* from 1939 to 1941 and the *Militant* after that, or from pamphlets issued by Pioneer Publishers, which produced the SWP's pamphlets. The material here represents only a small portion of the total written about the Black struggles in those papers and pamphlets, and some of the articles had to be abridged or excerpted to save space or avoid inevitable repetition of points made elsewhere. In order not to distract the reader, the text does not contain signs or symbols indicating deletions from the articles as originally printed, but these abridgements in no case involved any changes in political line or substance. Stylistic changes (punctuation, spelling, etc.) have been made to achieve consistency.

The terminology of the World War II period has been left unchanged. With some exceptions, most educated Blacks (the "talented tenth") in the 1930s and 1940s preferred the term *Negro*, while in many sections of the country Black workers and farmers used the term *colored* most frequently. *Negro* and *colored* were both used at that time by the Marxist movement too, without chauvinist intentions or connotations; it was not until the 1960s that their use became universally unacceptable among opponents of racism.

Another word that requires explanation is *boys*. Today it is considered racist when applied to Blacks and paternalistic or condescending when applied to young men. But its use did not have such implications before and during World War II, either in the Black community or the radical movement. The victims in the most famous defense case of the 1930s were called the "Scottsboro Boys" not only by Marxists but by all Black organizations and newspapers. Young men of all races who served in the armed forces were usually called "our boys" by their families and the press, white and Black. Since *boys* sometimes meant young males or very young males, or soldiers and sailors, its usage was not necessarily offensive, or designed to offend, given the customs of the time. It is wise to bear this in mind when reading the literature of the past.

Note should also be taken of the way in which the term *Jim Crow* was frequently used in the World War II period. When we speak of Jim Crow today, we generally have in mind the system of racial discrimination and segregation based on local or national laws and enforced by the state through its courts and police. That was the Jim Crow system that existed in the South from the end of Reconstruction until the 1960s, when it was dismantled through the struggles led by the civil rights movement. But in an earlier period the term was often used in a broader sense by Blacks and Marxists alike: it was used as the equivalent of racism in general, of the whole racist system and not just its juridical forms. When writers spoke about killing Jim Crow they did not mean only government-sanctioned discrimination and segregation such as existed in the South. They usually meant the whole institutional system of racism, including the forms that existed in the North. On the other hand, the word *racism* did not have much currency then. Some passages in this book will make more sense if these changes in usage since they were written are remembered.

We thank the *Militant* for permission to reprint these articles. All the footnotes have been added by the editor, who is also responsible for changing titles of the original articles and pamphlets.

Fred Stanton
May 1980

PART ONE

From September 1939 to December 1941

WHY NEGROES SHOULD
OPPOSE THE WAR

"Why should I shed my blood for Roosevelt's America, for Cotton Ed Smith and Senator Bilbo, for the whole Jim Crow, Negro-hating South, for the low-paid, dirty jobs for which Negroes have to fight, for the few dollars of relief and the insults, discrimination, police brutality, and perpetual poverty to which Negroes are condemned even in the more liberal North?"

When the ordinary working Negro asks this question, what can the warmongers say to him? Nothing. Nothing but lies and empty promises of better treatment in the future.

Let us take, one by one, the arguments put forward by the warmongers. A Republican like Landon, a Democrat like Roosevelt or Hull tells everybody (including the Negro, of course) that the war now being fought in Europe is a war against aggression, a war for "democracy," for the "preservation of human liberties," and the like. They say this because, although they are talking about peace, they are really preparing the minds of the workers for war.

The average Negro lives the life of an outcast in the North. He has little enough democracy there. But go today to Memphis, Houston, Dallas, New Orleans, Jacksonville, Birmingham, Mobile, all the South, where some nine or ten million Negroes live, and tell those Negroes to fight for "democracy." Such is the "democracy" of the South that in many towns the Negroes wouldn't be able to sit in the same room with the whites to hear why they should die for "democracy." There are thousands of hotels in the South where if a Negro dared to show his nose at the front entrance, three janitors would fall on him and throw him out into the gutter, after which the police would beat him up and take him to jail. In many cities, if he went near the polling booth he would risk being beaten up and perhaps shot. He must come

---

By J. R. Johnson, a pen name of C. L. R. James (see Glossary). It was first published in ten installments in the *Socialist Appeal*, the Socialist Workers Party newspaper, from September 6 to October 3, 1939. Then it was issued as a pamphlet by Pioneer Publishers in October 1939.

out of the rear entrance of a bus in southern cities, or any white cop nearby might riddle him with bullets.

And it is the Democratic Party, Franklin Roosevelt's party, which controls the state governments in the South. Argue with these Democrats about the Fourteenth and Fifteenth amendments, which "guarantee" the political rights of the Negroes. If you insist, you will get fourteen or fifteen bullets. That is the only kind of amendment the southern Democrats have allowed Negroes for many years. So that the vast majority of Negroes in the South will tell Roosevelt and Hull, "What is this democracy I am to fight for? Where is it? Since when are Cotton Ed Smith and Senator Bilbo and the Democratic Party of Franklin Roosevelt my good friends? Why must I die for them? I am not afraid to fight. Negroes have been some of the greatest fighters in history. But the democracy that I want to fight for, Hitler is not depriving me of. I know the people who have kept me away from it for seventy-five years by rifles and revolvers, by state law and lynch law! You, Franklin Roosevelt, Cordell Hull, and Jack Garner, tell us why we must go and shed our blood for something that we have never had."

"We Americans must fight against aggression," say Franklin Roosevelt and Cordell Hull, seeking to drive American workers, white and black, into war. No wonder all of these politicians are so scared of raising the question of war directly to the Negroes. Every word they say turns to ashes in their mouths. Let us agree that Negroes must fight against aggression. But who are the aggressors against the Negroes? Hitler? Nonsense. The southerners of the Democratic Party are the greatest aggressors against the Negroes in American history, and the North is not far behind them. "Oh! but we mean aggression in foreign countries, aggression by Mussolini, Hitler, and Japan," say Roosevelt and Hull. The Negro will immediately reply, "And why, if you so hate aggression, didn't you help Ethiopia?"*

Ethiopia was the last piece of Africa left free. Mussolini decided that he wanted it. The League of Nations had sworn to defend it. Every Negro with a spark of pride knows what happened, and remembers it with justified bitterness. Not only did they *not* protect Ethiopia as they had sworn to do, but instead they prevented arms from going to her while they bargained with Mussolini. They stabbed Ethiopia in the back—Britain, France, America, these great "democracies." (And Stalin, who claims to

*Ethiopia was invaded by Italy in 1935 and was still occupied by Italian imperialism when World War II began. Haile Selassie was restored to his throne in 1941.

be a friend of Negroes, sold oil to Italy all through the Italian campaign.) Now Roosevelt comes running to tell all good Americans (Negroes included, of course) that they must fight against aggression.

And who is going to do the fighting against this aggression? The workers, as always. Roosevelt, Hull, and Landon are getting ready to push the workers of America into the war. These are the very men who actively collaborated with Mussolini in destroying the last independent African state.

Or again a Negro will ask, "Why should I trust you? You, who have betrayed the last African state. Am I to go fighting for Poland and to settle a quarrel between Britain and Germany? Have I nothing else to fight for? I am not such a fool as not to know that international affairs are important. If Africans in Africa are fighting for freedom as Ethiopians fought, and are still fighting, I'll do all I can to help. The Indians are an oppressed people, and when they fight to drive Britain out, I am with them. Negroes went to fight in Spain against Franco. That was a good thing for people to do who for centuries have suffered from oppression. But all imperialists are oppressors. When Czechoslovakia was cut up into pieces, it was fascist Germany, Hungary, and this same Poland that divided it.* Then Germany and Poland began fighting over one bone. Britain and France knew that this was only the beginning of a struggle for worldwide power. So they came in at once. But tell me, Franklin Roosevelt and Cordell Hull, why must I, a Negro, follow you into that?"

Then will come the last argument: "It is not a question of Germany and Poland and Danzig. But freedom, civilization, and liberty are in danger against fascist aggression, and the people of Britain, France, America, Belgium must ally themselves to fight against aggression." Now of all the big lies that are being told to push the people into war, this one about the war for civilization is the biggest.

There are today over 150 million Negroes in the world. There are 15 million in America.** They are the lowest paid, most humiliated, most despised people in the country; and in the

*The civil war in Spain (1936-39) ended with the victory of the fascist forces headed by Francisco Franco. International brigades were organized to fight the fascists, including the Abraham Lincoln Brigade from the United States, but the Spanish workers and peasants were betrayed by the class-collaborationist People's Front policy of the Stalinists. Czechoslovakia was dismembered in 1938 at Hitler's demand and with the concurrence of the British and French governments.

**The size of the Black population in 1939 is generally accepted as 13 million. The 1940 census figure is 12,866,000.

South, where four-fifths of them live, they are treated like the Jews in Germany. We know how this great "democracy" terrorizes Negroes in the South and how it discriminates against them in the North.

When Roosevelt and other so-called lovers of "democracy" protested to Hitler against his treatment of the Jews, Hitler laughed scornfully and replied, "Look at how you treat the Negroes. I learned how to persecute Jews by studying the manner in which you Americans persecute Negroes." Roosevelt has no answer to that. Yet he will call upon Negroes to go to war against Hitler.

War in defense of "democracy" and civilization? Lies. When we look at Africa we see how shameless is the lie that Belgium, France, and America will fight any war for liberty and civilization. For it is in Africa that Negroes have for years suffered and still suffer today the vilest fascist tortures. And at the hands of whom? Not Hitler and German imperialism. Germany hasn't an inch of land in Africa. That is one of the things this war is about, the partition of Africa. Hitler wants some of Africa, but up to now at any rate he has none. Japan has not an inch in Africa and today is much too busy trying to steal half of China. Mussolini controls a small number of Africans. Who is it, then, that has taken Africa from the Africans? Who else but Great Britain, with sixty million African slaves, and France, with another forty million, and "democratic" little Belgium, little in Europe, but with a large piece of Africa and twelve million Negroes under her control. These "democracies" are the thieves. And how do they treat the Africans?

All of us know how Negroes suffer in America. But you have to go to Africa to see how brutally the "democracies" treat Negroes. In South Africa, a Negro cannot even buy a stamp in the same place where a white man buys one. There is a special window for him even in the post office. He lives in a part of town that is assigned to him, and he cannot leave there after nine o'clock without a pass signed by a white man. Any white man, any dirty drunkard of an Englishman or a Boer, can sign a pass for a sober, self-respecting, hard-working Negro. But any Negro who is caught out of the Negro district after nine o'clock without his pass will be locked up by the first policeman who stops him. There are not ten colored doctors in the Union of South Africa, where over seven million Negroes live, and the imperialists have been there for 400 years. That is the culture and civilization they give to the Africans in South Africa.*

*In 1939 South Africa was still a colony of Britain.

31

In Kenya more than five people cannot meet without police permission. One day six of them went home after church for a cup of tea. In comes a policeman. "One, two, three, four, five, six. This is sedition. You are under arrest." They were taken to jail and the next day fined. Every working African in Kenya is fingerprinted and must carry the print around with him wherever he goes. Caught without it, he is sent to jail. Wages in Rhodesia and Kenya are sometimes four, sometimes ten cents a day. A Negro is no more than a dog to these people. And this is under the rule of the great "democratic" countries: Britain, France, and Belgium. He is a dirty traitor who tells Negroes that they must go to war for the "democracies" for the benefit of civilization. Aren't Negroes part of civilization?

How did the "democratic" imperialist nations get hold of Africa? They got it as Hitler got Austria and Czechoslovakia. Hitler lied, made promises and broke them, bribed, and sent armies to massacre all who resisted. In exactly the same way, these great "democracies" robbed the Africans of country after country, and hold them in chains. And now Roosevelt and his friends are preparing the workers to fight and shed their blood for the great "democracies." What will Negroes get? Win back their country? Live as free men? Not at all. They must help Britain and France fight against Hitler and Goering about Danzig and the Polish corridor and who should dominate the Chinese and Latin American markets—and who should dominate Africa.*

These imperialist bandits encouraged workers to fight in the last war with the same talk about democracy, freedom, and civilization. But after Germany was defeated, Britain, France, and Belgium simply took over the German colonies *and continued to treat the Negroes as before.* Now they are fighting another war. If the fascists win, they will take the colonies back. If the "democracies" win, they will keep them. But whether "democracies" win, or fascists win, the Africans remain slaves in their own country.

Now Republicans like Dewey and Democrats like Roosevelt, men like John L. Lewis and William Green, all the warmongers for "democracy," have never told Negroes anything about the situation of Negroes in Africa. Lewis encouraged Negroes to join the CIO and Negroes were right to join. But when Lewis tells

---

*Hitler's troops marched into and took over Austria in 1938. Nazi control of Danzig and a piece of territory called the Polish corridor were among Hitler's demands before his troops invaded Poland in September 1939.

Negroes to fight for democracy, as he most certainly will, they simply have to ask him the same questions that they will ask Franklin Roosevelt, and Lewis will be able to make no better reply.

Some people, however, Negro leaders included, state that there is a possibility of Negroes gaining their rights and participating freely in American life, if they show that they are willing to die for "democracy." Let us test this by the last war. They said then that the war was being fought for "democracy," was being fought to make the world a better place than it had been before. Also, and this is what is important, many Negro leaders told the Negroes to support the war wholeheartedly. By showing themselves good citizens, they would win the sympathy of the whites and gain all the things of which they had been deprived. That is what was said. But how did the rulers of their country actually treat the Negro soldiers?

First of all, they took many more Negroes than they should have taken. Out of every hundred persons in the population, ten were Negroes, so that, roughly, out of every hundred soldiers, ten should have been Negroes. More than that, the Negroes are the worst paid, live in the worst houses, in the worst localities, get the worst food and the poorest medical attention. Thus, taking the Negro population as a whole, the number of persons fit for military service should have been proportionately less than the number of whites. This through no fault of the Negroes, but because of the lives and conditions to which they are condemned. So that instead of ten out of every hundred of the soldiers being Negroes, we could reasonably expect that there should have been about seven or eight. But instead of some number like seven or eight per hundred there were more than ten. So that this American "democracy" seized the opportunity to kill off as many Negroes as possible as a means of helping "democracy" solve the Negro problem.*

The war was a war for "democracy," but the Negroes were segregated. There was not a single regiment consisting of white and Negro soldiers mixed. American "democracy" did not want to have even American colored officers, and it took a hard fight to have a few hundred. When they did agree, they trained Negroes as officers in a special Negro camp. And these men were informed by the State Department that when they visited the South, they should not wear their uniforms. "Democracy" was sending the

*After the passage of the Selective Service Act on May 8, 1917, 371,710 Blacks were drafted, 36 percent of those who registered. Among whites, only 25 percent of those registered were drafted.

33

Negro to fight for "democracy," but could not bear the sight of him in the officer's uniform of "democracy."

The old lynch spirit continued. The Negroes were beaten up near the camps, they were stoned and jeered as they marched along the streets. When they were on leave and attempted to enter cafes and restaurants frequented by white people, they were driven out in many places.

When they went to France, the discrimination continued. American "democracy" forced most of the black soldiers to be common laborers. Of the 200,000 Negroes who went to France, some 160,000 were used as servants and in labor battalions. Even when fighting for "democracy," the Negro was kept in his place. Negroes were made to build roads, wash clothes, cook food, clean up camps and trenches, and clean latrines, though they had enlisted as soldiers of the line.

Far from practicing any sort of democracy to Negroes, the American commanders did their best to make the French maltreat the Negroes. The French people are not as prejudiced as one would expect from their treatment of natives in Africa, and great numbers of French people in France do not make any differentiation at all between Negroes and whites. But when the American officers saw this and the friendly way in which Negro soldiers were being welcomed both by French men and women, they issued a military order, Order No. 40, instructing Negroes not even to speak to French women. For this offense against "democracy," many Negroes were arrested, though the French people, men and women, had made no complaint.

The American officers, in this war for "democracy," wrote a special document to the French commanding staff, telling them that Negroes were a low and degenerate race, that they could not be trusted in the company of white people, that although some Negroes were officers, the French officers should have nothing to do with them, except in matters relating strictly to fighting. The French, said this American order, should not eat with Negroes, nor even shake hands, and above all, they wanted the French to use their influence to keep the white women who worked in or near the camp from forming any associations with Negroes.

This was the way in which the American ruling class fought side by side with Negroes in the great war for "democracy."

The Negroes, believing that by fighting bravely and showing that they were men as good as any other, they would gain freedom from their oppression, performed feats of distinguished bravery. Of all the American soldiers in France a Negro was the first to win the croix de guerre (war cross), and one Negro regiment, the Eighth Illinois, received more decorations than any other regiment in France. Another American Negro regime, stayed a longer spell in the trenches than any other regiment in the Allied forces. No one after that could say that Negroes were inferior. They had stood the stern test of modern war and came out with a great record.

What happened to the Negroes, after this fine showing, should be branded on the forehead of any so-called Negro leader who tries to thrust them again into war. For as soon as the war was over, there was such a desperate series of race riots in America as had not been seen for many years. In Washington, in Chicago, white mobs, inspired and encouraged by American employers and American capitalist police, shot down Negroes, many of whom had lost relations in the great war for "democracy." The southern whites were so anxious to put the Negro back in his place that they lynched Negroes who dared to wear the uniform of a private. The great war for "democracy" and the bravery and the sacrifices for "democracy" of the Negro people ended with thousands of them having to fight desperately not for "democracy," but for their lives in "democratic" America.*

Now let Herbert Hoover and Franklin Roosevelt and Cordell Hull and La Guardia and some so-called Negro leaders stand up and tell Negroes that the present war is another war for democracy and that they must go again and fight in it.

If Negroes supported the war, Franklin Roosevelt, Jack Garner, Cotton Ed Smith, Senator Bilbo, and all that bunch in the Democratic Party would be able to sit back and say, "We give them the nastiest jobs, we pay them the lowest wages, millions of them are unemployed. Even in Washington here, the federal capital, we kick them out of restaurants and theaters. We lynch them whenever we think that they should be reminded of where they belong. We treated them like dogs in the last war. We lynched them after they came back. And now, when we want them to do some more dirty work for us, we just snap our fingers and whistle, and look at them! They come running to do anything we want them to do! We have only to make a few promises and they are ready to be fooled again. Truly these Negroes are the most ignorant, backward, and slave-like people in the world, and deserving of no more consideration than the scraps we throw to them."

But no, large masses of Negroes have no wish to support this war. Their memories of the last war and the great deception and

*In the summer of 1919, seventy-six Blacks were lynched and there were twenty-five race riots. In the Chicago riot, thirty-eight people were killed, twenty-five of them Blacks.

fraud which were practiced on them are too vivid in their minds.

So bitter was their disappointment after the last war, that millions of Negroes supported Marcus Garvey. They were ready to follow even the fantastic, impossible scheme of going back to Africa rather than to continue to live in the American "democracy" for which so many thousands of them had suffered and died.

What then is the Negro to do?

Before we can act we must know the forces with us and the forces against us. Many Negroes in America feel that they would be ready to shed their blood and take any steps to break the chains which bind them. Yet they feel also that their numbers are too few. They think that they would be overwhelmed by the number of the whites, their power, their authority, and their control of the means of destruction.

That, however, is a shortsighted view. Today we are dealing with an international war, and the problem is an international one.

Let us look at the last war. That also was an international war. It was fought in Europe, in Asia, and in Africa. The British armed the black man in Africa. The French armed nearly half a million Negro soldiers to fight for them. These fought not only in Africa but in Europe. There was a regiment of West Indian Negroes. Now today, the millions of Negroes all over the world are more politically conscious, more bitter against oppression and humiliation, than they were in 1914.

They have not only had the experience of the last war. They have suffered from the effects of the crisis. They have seen the rape of Ethiopia, and they know that in Africa, for instance, whether they are ruled by Italian fascism or British "democracy," their situation is the same. Their lands are stolen, their wages are often ten cents a day. They are driven away to live in segregated areas, where at night they are kept jailed as if they had committed a crime by being born with a black skin. They are thinking the same things that the Negroes in America are thinking, only more fiercely because they have more cause.

Many of them, particularly in the French and Italian colonies, have arms in their hands which they have learned how to use. Now that the war has begun, many more of them will be armed and trained in order to go and fight for their masters. But despite all the shouting about "democracy" by imperialists, the great millions in Africa need only leadership to use their guns not for British or French "democracy," but for their own independence, for a free Africa, liberated from all sorts of imperialist domination, liberated not only from fascist Italy and Germany but also from those "democratic" bandits: Britain, France, and Belgium. They outnumber by many millions the whites who keep them in subjection today. And these whites, in the course of a war, will have to arm more and more of these despised and oppressed blacks. The Africans are only waiting for the opportunity and for that powerful organization which will give them a policy and leadership. In a war fought on an international scale, the Negroes in America will have the Negroes in Africa as their allies. American Negro soldiers who may be forced by conscription to go to France to fight will be certain to meet hundreds of thousands of African soldiers there.

Contact and plans can be made for the struggle on an international scale. But there are many other allies as well. For two hundred and fifty years, the British have been squeezing the lives out of the masses of people in India. There are well over 350 million people in India today, and the large majority of them are just awaiting their chance to get arms in their hands, drive the British imperialists into the sea, and make their country their own again. The same in Burma, in Ceylon, and everywhere. So that from the Atlantic Ocean to the Pacific, you have over 500 million people, oppressed colonials, who are thinking in terms of freedom from the domination of imperialism. Imagine the enormous power which these colonials can exert for their own emancipation in the tremendous crisis which has been loosed upon all peoples in the world.

Nevertheless, even if we are agreed on the necessity of uniting the Negro masses against the war, many American Negroes will say: "I agree with the Socialist Workers Party that the 15 million Negroes in America have as their natural allies the 150 million Negroes in the world and the millions of Indians, Burmese, Ceylonese, etc. If we all join together, that would be an immense force acting on a world scale. It is true also that the imperialists are so hard pressed for men and forces that they are arming and training these millions of colonials. But nevertheless we remain only 15 million out of a population of some 130 million people. The Africans in Africa, the Indians in India will be concerned with their own struggles. We wish them well. But how can we here struggle against the vast numbers and the great power that are opposed to us?"

It is a very good question, and the answer to it brings us to the very heart of the matter. We shall have to examine this very carefully. Whenever a problem like that faces us we should examine it in all its aspects, then examine similar situations in foreign countries, look back into our own history, see where the circumstances are alike and where they differ, and then attempt a conclusion.

The best example that we can start with is what happened in America some seventy-five years ago, when the Negroes gained their freedom. If all American whites had agreed upon the fact that the Negroes should continue to be slaves, then the 4 million Negroes of that time and their descendants would have continued to be slaves until they died, for they would never have been able to free themselves against the enormous odds that were arrayed against them. But all the whites were not united. There was a great division among the whites themselves, between the merchants, the industrialists, and the bankers of the North on the one hand, and the slaveowners of the South on the other.

It was this terrific quarrel that led to the Civil War. At first Lincoln never intended to free the Negroes. Yet all men who fight a battle and wish to win it seek their allies where they can find them. So he enrolled the Negroes in the Northern army, and finally declared their emancipation from slavery. That is one of the great lessons of the Civil War—the division among the whites, and the necessity for Lincoln to seek assistance from Negroes.

Let us now look at what is happening in Europe at the present day and during the last twenty-five years. Everyone knows that a very bitter civil war has just taken place in Spain. The Spanish workers and peasants were on one side. The Spanish capitalists, the bankers, the great landlords, and their followers were on the other side. It is true that some Moors from Africa took part on the side of Franco.* But that has nothing to do with the fundamentals of the question. What we must note is that in Spain, where few Negroes live, the workers and the peasants on the one hand, all the poor, fought very fiercely against the rich owners of the country. Unfortunately the workers and peasants lost. Yet we see that in a country where all the population is of the same color the various classes can fight desperately to decide which class shall be master.

Let us take another example. The whole world has heard of

*Spain conquered Morocco in 1927. The colony became Franco's main base of operations despite the opposition of the Moors to Spanish rule. Moroccan nationalist leaders appealed to the Spanish Popular Front government to proclaim Moroccan independence, but the Republicans refused, fearing the loss of support from "democratic" imperialist governments (which did not want Moroccan independence to be an example for their own colonies). Thus some Moors were willing to fight for Franco against a "democratic" government that continued to oppress them.

how brutally the German fascists treat the German workers. The fascists murder the workers' leaders, throw them into concentration camps, beat up the workers in the streets, cut their wages down, and treat them in the most savage manner. But no Negroes live in Germany. This is a matter between whites and whites. The white capitalist class is in mortal conflict with the white workers. If there was not a single Jew in Germany, the leaders of the German workers would still be in concentration camps, and the working-class movement stamped upon.

The same thing has happened in Italy, where the workers and poor peasants have had their leaders murdered and their organizations destroyed by Mussolini and his fascists.

Let us take one final example: Russia in 1917. There the workers and peasants fought the same civil war against the nobles, landlords, and the capitalists. Only in this case, the Russian workers and peasants won. The land was divided among the peasants. The workers took over the factories and the workers' government was established.

Here, then, it is clear that during the last few years, not to mention other great examples in history, there have been developing terrific clashes in country after country where the population is all of one color. The struggle of the classes goes on, always, whatever the color of the people. So that many a white worker in Europe and America is saying to himself, "I am starving. In any case if I have a job my friend next door has none. These capitalists will crush me by fascism as soon as I begin to fight for my rights. Why should I support their war for 'democracy'? My war is against the capitalists in my country." In other words, some whites are saying the same about the war as the Negroes. Here is real help for Negroes.

Now let us look closely at America in the light of what we have just discussed. We saw that in America seventy-five years ago the division between sections of the white population in America resulted in one side calling the Negroes to join and assist them in their struggle. Through this means the Negroes gained their emancipation. Although at the present time it may seem that all the whites, or at least most of them, are against the Negroes, oppress them, and discriminate against them, yet we can take it as certain that the same struggle which we have seen working itself out in the various countries of Europe is taking place in America today. Sooner or later the workers and farmers of America who are now fighting against the landlords and capitalists in unions, on the WPA, in struggles for better relief, will ultimately be driven to the same civil war that we have seen take place in country after country during the last twenty-five years.

A Negro, therefore, who is looking at the political situation not as it appears on the surface, but is seeing into the realities of the struggle between the classes, can have confidence in the future. He will realize that all white America is not solid. There is a tremendous division, a great split opening up. We can already see the signs of it very clearly. And as this struggle approaches and then actually flares out into the inevitable civil war, Negroes can be certain that many white workers and farmers who today are prejudiced will seek Negro assistance in the same way that Lincoln did when he fought the South. Negroes in the last Civil War made one great step forward, and so, in this coming civil war, the workers' war, Negroes have a great chance to complete their journey to full freedom.

We know now that the millions of colonials in every country, those in Africa, in India, and all the other oppressed peoples, the majority of people now living, are allies. And, most important, we have seen that many white workers in all parts of the world, although they do not suffer from the special discriminations imposed upon the Negro, yet see no reason why they must shed their blood for capitalism, whether it is "democratic" or fascist. They believe that the war the workers and farmers must fight is the war of all the oppressed against all the oppressors, the war to put an end to the capitalist system, with its continual wars, its crises, and its fascist dictatorships.

BOSTON 'EEL' IS BENCHED

BOSTON—When Boston College locked horns with Florida this Saturday in an important intersectional gridiron contest, Lou Montgomery, star Boston back, watched the game from the stands. Mainstay of the team, Montgomery was yanked from the lineup days in advance.

Reason for his absence from the game is that Lou Montgomery, popularly known as the "Ebony Eel," is a Negro. Gil Dobie, Boston coach, according to the sports columnist of the *Boston Evening American,* withdrew Montgomery "as a sop to the ethnological prejudices of the Southern team."

Boston College might have resisted the "ethnological prejudices" of the Floridians by using the Negro back if only to affirm the principle of racial equality. Had the "ethnological prejudices" of the southern team risen to the point where they refused to take the field, Boston College would have won by default. Injury to

From *Socialist Appeal,* October 20, 1939.

Montgomery engineered by the chauvinist southerners would have had its desirable effect among the Boston rooters. Instead, under the increasing pressure of anti-Negro sentiment in this once classic city of abolitionism, Montgomery was taken from the lineup.

That the color of skin is enough to upset the beauties of sport is another of the lessons to be assimilated in a study of contemporary American democracy.

THE PITTSBURGH COURIER
ON THE WAR

The *Pittsburgh Courier* is one of the best of the Negro weekly sheets. It fights some valiant battles for the Negro cause. It was one of the very few Negro papers to wage a campaign on behalf of Negro entry into and support of the CIO (one of the three greatest steps forward of the Negro in American society during the last hundred years). The *Courier* has taken the lead in the struggle for the entry of Negro players into major-league baseball. It has battled for the right of Negroes to enter into the American army on the same conditions as the whites and for equal facilities in training as air pilots. The paper has a great reputation among the Negroes. It sells for ten cents, which the poorer Negroes cannot pay. It maintains a large staff and is essentially the paper of the Negro petty bourgeoisie. The *Pittsburgh Courier* has on its staff Mr. George Schuyler, one of the most brilliant journalists in America. It is not in any sense of the word a revolutionary paper.

The *Pittsburgh Courier* has naturally been commenting on the war. What it says, and still more what it does not say, is of the utmost importance for the revolutionary movement.

On March 29, the *Courier* published a cartoon on the war entitled "Ringside Seat." The cartoon showed two boxers, one labeled "Democracies" and the other "Dictatorships." The referee was a military-looking gentleman labeled "Imperialism." In

By J. R. Johnson. From *Socialist Appeal,* October 20 and 24, 1939. The *Pittsburgh Courier,* with local editions published in several large cities, was the biggest and most influential Black weekly newspaper in the country during World War II.

the ringside seats were Africans, American Negroes, Mongolians, Pacific Islanders, and Malays. The chief editorial of that issue expressed the following sentiments:

The "democracies" and the "dictatorships" are preparing to do BATTLE in the near future.

The referee is IMPERIALISM, who stands ready to award the decision to the VICTOR.

The stake is the right to EXPLOIT the darker peoples of the world.

The audience consists of the vast MAJORITY of those who happen to be NON-WHITES.

They have no FAVORITE, because it makes NO DIFFERENCE to them which party WINS the fight.

They are ONLY interested in the bout taking place AS SOON AS POSSIBLE.

Now this on the surface is a most bloodthirsty attitude. But the editorial had its very good reason for wishing this destruction: "The AUDIENCE knows that the destruction of white civilization means the EMANCIPATION of colored people, and that explains why they eagerly await the opening gong."

The editorial is anxious for the destruction of both camps because it knows that there is no essential difference as far as colored people are concerned between "democratic" imperialism and fascist imperialism. It explains this in detail:

The democracies which now CONTROL the dark world have never extended DEMOCRACY to the dark world.

THEIR meaning of democracy is for WHITE PEOPLE only, and just a FEW of them.

The dictatorships FRANKLY DECLARE that if they win THEY will do as the democracies HAVE DONE in the past.

The democracies as frankly declare that IF they win they will CONTINUE to do as they HAVE BEEN doing.

Here is an astonishingly clear characterization of the real nature of the great forces which are now tearing civilization apart. Note particularly that sentence which states that even among the whites democracy is only for a few of them.

This clear vision into the fundamental nature of modern society, this rage at its pretenses, this desire for emancipation at whatever cost, are what we mean by the revolutionary instinct of the Negroes. And this is why the Fourth International states that the place of the Negro is in the vanguard and not at the tail of the revolutionary movement.

The *Courier* editorial naturally makes a great error in thinking that the blacks can stand aside in the coming war. Colored people were compelled to fight in the last war. The Africans are being compelled to fight in this one, and if the workers of America, black and white, do not stop Roosevelt by working-class action, then the American Negroes will be compelled to fight when American capitalism goes in.

The *Courier* makes a still greater error when it thinks that emancipation for Negroes can come from the mutual destruction of the groups of white imperialists, with the people of color just stepping in to gather up the spoils. The root of this monumental error lies in the neglect of that most important fact that the editorial noted—even among the white people, "democracy" is only for the few. That is the key to the emancipation of the Negroes and the oppressed colonial peoples. The political battle is unity among both these groups who recognize that in essence capitalist democracy is a fraud for all the working people, white and black, and offers them nothing but continual crises, fascist dictatorships, and ultimately imperialist war. That is the unshakable basis of the Fourth International.

But what we must note is this. If the Negro petty bourgeois expresses himself in these drastic terms about imperialist war, we can have some conception of what are the real sentiments of the great masses of Negroes in every country who feel upon their backs the unmitigated blows of capitalism.

War broke out on September 1. On September 9 the *Courier* still takes a radical position:

> The war in Europe need not detain us because it will make no difference to us who wins. Our immediate concern should be the war in which we ourselves are engaged and have been engaged for a long time. That war is at once external and internal against the oppression and exploitation from without and against disorganization and lack of confidence within.

The war of the Negro in this country is to acquire educational facilities for children, more jobs, greater progress in business, social equality in America, and above all self-respect, discipline, and intelligent leadership among Negroes. The editorial concludes:

"Our war is no contest between dictatorship and democracy, our war is a contest between survival and destruction. When this is fully realized by all of us our progress will be much more rapid."

There are still some of the brave words of the April springtime. Neither "democracy" nor dictatorship. But gone is the idea of self-destruction by imperialism as the only way of Negroes earning full equality. The *Courier* thinks that when Negroes see things more clearly, then "progress will be much more rapid."

How can you in April see hope only when the imperialists destroy each other and in September be sure of rapid progress as soon as you realize things more fully? You realized them fully six months ago.

In the following issue, September 16, the *Courier* takes a great step backward. It notes, in an editorial article, that Roosevelt has declared the United States neutral. But it sees and says that Roosevelt and American business are not really neutral. They want to help France and Britain by sending supplies and will do so as soon as convenient. Where, asks the *Courier,* do Negroes stand on this question? The reply is astounding. Negroes made great progress in the last war. If America does not export munitions there will be a job slump (there is one on now, since 1929) and Negroes will suffer. So Negroes should support American sales to Britain and France and so assure jobs for themselves. "Oh, what a fall there was, my countrymen!" The great extermination of imperialism by which Negroes were to enter into the promised land has now shrunk into a war to help get jobs for Negroes. You never know where you are with a petty bourgeois.

For in the very next issue, September 23, the *Courier* takes a step forward. It denounces war for "democracy."

Before any of our people get unduly excited about SAVING DEMOCRACY in Europe, it should be called to their attention that we have NOT YET ACHIEVED DEMOCRACY HERE.

We cannot save what DOES NOT EXIST.

None of the hundreds of millions of COLORED PEOPLE under the Union Jack have ANY VOICE in the British Parliament.

They are ALL AT WAR with Germany, but they had NO VOTE in the matter.

None of the black people who live in the French Empire have ANY VOICE in the Chamber of Deputies except those from Senegal and Guadeloupe.

Yet they are ALL AT WAR with Germany and must supply MEN and RESOURCES.

If democracy means taxation and conscription WITHOUT REPRESENTATION, then these British and French colonials ARE living in democracies.

There are really NO DEMOCRACIES where black people are concerned, and therefore any talk about black people fighting for democracy when they are fighting for France and England is POPPYCOCK.

Black people may have a SMALL MEASURE of democracy in the United States, but a VERY small measure.

The article exposes the tricks of American capitalism in its plans on the Negro and ends: "He [the Negro] would have to have

44

some AT HOME before fighting for any ABROAD."

Our petty bourgeois is again uttering radical sentiments. There is only one point omitted. Suppose the Negro does not get "democracy" at home. What then? Fight against the withholders of democracy here? The *Courier* says nothing. Take a guess now at what will appear in the next issue. Step forward or backward? Backward you say? Absolutely correct.

The *Courier* editorial column is once more urging American capitalism to use the next war as a means of prosperity. Raise the embargo, create jobs and give some to Negroes. But what about the destruction of American imperialism? You don't destroy something by making it prosperous. That is the kind of mess you get into when you have not a clear revolutionary program, opposed to imperialism, everywhere, at all times. What the *Courier* will do tomorrow or the day after we do not know, but we can guess. Five steps backward and half a step forward. And if the workers and farmers do not prevent Roosevelt dragging this country into war, then when America enters, the *Courier* is going to call on Negroes everywhere to fight for "democracy," the "democracy" American capitalism has withheld from the Negro for seventy-five years and which will be promised after the new war is over.

How grand the beginning was in April! Let the imperialists destroy each other. Today it is a question of jobs. In our pamphlet we outline our policy on Negroes and war. But the *Courier* has no policy. It vacillates from the extreme of bloodthirstiness to using the war for jobs. There you have your petty bourgeois complete, always groping between the imperialists and the revolutionary workers. Are they lost? Not by any means. Quite a few can be won today, and though some are born traitors, many can be won for the revolution tomorrow.

But there is only one way. Build a powerful revolutionary party. Let it look as if it means business. Let it act as if it does. And when it leads the masses into action on a grand scale, we have a chance to tear the petty bourgeoisie away from the imperialists. It is power and power alone that keeps these wavering elements from wavering so much. They rush to the imperialists today. But an equal power can pull them away in time, the revolutionary power of the masses. It is up to us to build that power.

'POOR LITTLE FINLAND'

Ethiopia 1935, Finland 1939

Ethiopia 1935, Finland 1939. What is being done for "brave little Finland," and what was not done for Ethiopia, is causing some bitter reflections among Negroes. P. L. Prattis, *Pittsburgh Courier* columnist, expresses a widespread sentiment in the issue of December 16:

England is reported sending airplanes and other equipment to Finland. Did she send any to Ethiopia? . . . The United States is eager to play a hand. Recall our ambassador from Russia, our indignant leadership demands. All right. Recall the ambassador. Let us do anything we can to show our disapproval of Russia. But what did we do about the Ethiopians? Did anybody demand that we recall our ambassador to Italy? Did anybody become concerned enough to urge that we try to help Ethiopia? Indeed not!

This is his conclusion. And he began:

However hopeful dark people may try to be, things are happening every day to show us just how hopeless is our cause and plight. Nobody cares a great deal about us. That doesn't mean just in the United States nor does it mean dark people in the United States alone. It means that in the entire world in which we live the folk with dark skin aren't considered. Maybe this is obvious, but sometimes things happen that make you feel it all the more keenly. If you are looking out over the world, incidents, tragic incidents, occur which get you down.

By J. R. Johnson. From *Socialist Appeal,* December 23 and 30, 1939. Three months after World War II started, the Soviet government went to war with Finland, which had refused to yield territory Moscow considered vital for the defense of Leningrad. This "winter war" lasted 105 days (November 1939–March 1940), causing heavy casualties on both sides, and ended in an armistice that gave the USSR the territory it wanted. During this war the American ruling class and its media glorified the reactionary government of Finland as part of a virulent propaganda campaign against the Soviet Union. The main purpose of this propaganda was to undermine antiwar sentiment and promote conditions favorable to formal U.S. entry into the war.

Mr. Prattis's tears do not deserve even the loan of a dirty handkerchief. Negroes have shed many tears in the past, with good cause, but if in 1939 they are going to shed new tears whenever they have new proof of the treachery of what Mr. Prattis calls "England" and "the United States," then they had better all trek to the Grand Canyon and sit in a row on both sides. There they can appoint Prattis tearmaster and cry to their hearts' content without the risk of causing floods.

What infinite stupidity is this! Who expects England to be friendly to an African state? England is the greatest oppressor of Negroes that history has known. Today England is chief jailer of over sixty million blacks in Africa. Of the twenty billion British dollars invested overseas, five billion are invested in Africa. That is the only interest England has in Africa.

Come nearer home. Let Prattis dry his tear-filled eyes and look about him. Doesn't he read his own articles, his own paper? Has he read the history of the Negro people in America? Presumably, before he started to cry so much he used to. Did Abe Lincoln love Negroes or hate slaveowners? Prattis knows. And yet he comes weeping and wailing because the United States government didn't help Ethiopia and now helps "poor little Finland."

Let Mr. Prattis buy a copy of Aesop's fables. There are many copies for children, with large print, which he will be able to read despite his present infirmity. On page 1 he will decipher the following fable: "Once upon a time there were lots of lambs and a few tigers. Every day each tiger would eat a lamb, and sometimes the tigers would fight with each other as to who should have a fat, juicy lamb. One day one of the tigers ate a little black lamb. Whereupon another little black lamb [his name was Prattis] called all the other black lambs together and, his eyes streaming with tears, said, 'Isn't it a shame? Those tigers over there allowed this bad tiger to eat up this poor black lamb. It is because he is black. Boo-hoo.'"

England and France, by which we mean British imperialism and French imperialism, stood by and watched Italian imperialism rape Ethiopia. Why? Simply because it is the nature of imperialism to gorge its appetites on all colonial countries. What they were quarreling about was not whether the little black lamb should be eaten, but who should get the choice parts.

In 1936 a great revolution of the workers and peasants burst out, in Spain. Germany and Italy pounced on Spain, to help Franco and gain concessions for themselves. And what did the other imperialist tigers do? Chamberlain, the British Tory, declared for nonintervention. So did Blum, the French labor leader. Roosevelt, the New Dealer, clapped an embargo on arms to Spain. Stalin, the bureaucrat and murderer of Bolshevism and Bolsheviks, sold some arms to Spain—but on the condition that the workers and peasants would not abolish landlords and capitalists. You have only to look at a map to see how dangerous it was for British and French imperialism to have German and Italian imperialism dominant in Spain. But the "democratic" imperialists were prepared to allow even that, rather than give arms to the workers and peasants, who might conquer Franco and transform "democratic" Spain into socialist Spain.

Then Britain and France sold out Czechoslovakia. Suppose someone had said, "It is because the Czechs are white." Wouldn't Prattis have laughed at him as an idiot?

But by this time Germany was becoming too strong. So that these tigers, who didn't lift a finger for "poor little Ethiopia," or "poor little Spain," or "poor little Czechoslovakia," are now weeping almost as much as Prattis over "poor little Finland." Back of this there is another more fundamental cause. All imperialists (Hitler included) hate Russia. So when they yell "poor little Finland," what they mean is "Down with Russia." But one way or the other, it is all a matter of imperialist power.

And any Negro who seeks to defend Finland against Russia, along with Roosevelt, [Herbert] Hoover, Mussolini, and the rest, is making himself the ignorant tool of imperialism. That is the truth. And all the tears of Mr. Prattis will not wash out a word of it. The moment you begin to look at world politics from the point of black against white, you end up either in the imperialist camp of loot and slaughter or the Prattis camp of tears and despair.

Hoover has already sent $100,000 to the Finnish bourgeoisie. Let no Negro give one red cent to this counterrevolutionary campaign on behalf of the enemies of the Finnish workers' movement. The road for the workers is a different road—the road that should have been followed in regard to Ethiopia. That road was pointed. Preparations were made. But the working class and the Ethiopian leaders made the fatal mistake of putting their trust in imperialists.

When Italian fascism began its attack on Ethiopia, workers all over Europe felt great sympathy with Ethiopia.

In 1935, as in 1914 and 1939, the leaders of the big labor parties—Blum in France, Attlee in Britain; and the leaders of the trade unions—Jouhaux in France, Sir Walter Citrine and Ernest Bevin in Britain, Lewis and Green in America; were completely reactionary. They always support their capitalist government in any really serious struggle.

But in Britain, France, Belgium, Spain, among the second and third ranks of the leadership, and especially among the class-conscious workers, there arose a strong feeling for working-class action on behalf of Ethiopia. All the capitalists and the labor fakers were babbling about the League of Nations—in other words, looking to the League of Bandits to arrest another bandit for doing what all the bandits wanted to do themselves. But the rank-and-file workers, and the leaders nearest to them, were saying that the seamen who were carrying oil to Italy should, supported by the International Federation of Trade Unions, stop carrying that oil.

If the workers stopped carrying it, both Mussolini and his brother bandits would be in serious difficulty, for these gentlemen fear nothing so much as the independent action of the working class.

Eugene Jagot, official of the War Resisters International, a small political organization, went to the Brussels meeting of the International Federation of Trade Unions to urge the trade union bureaucrats to sanction this international workers' boycott. Naturally, Citrine, Bevin, Jouhaux did not want any such thing. But the pressure was strong, the workers were aroused. There was some possibility of at least a partial success, or even, given certain circumstances, of a great victory.

What certain circumstances? The Soviet Union had been clamoring for both action by the League of Nations and independent action of the workers. Now you cannot do both. Either the workers act by themselves, or they support some action by the ruling class or by some section of it. But the Stalinists claimed that they could support the League of Bandits and at the same time have independent workers' action. If, at this critical moment, when the Federation of Trade Unions was actually meeting, not the Soviet government but the Soviet trade unions had decided on a boycott and called on all seamen, railwaymen, miners to refuse to ship any materials to Italy, then those who were fighting at Brussels to break the resistance of the European Lewises and Greens would have been enormously strengthened. What happened was exactly the opposite.

The Stalinist bureaucracy is today and has been for many years the most dangerous enemy of the workers' revolution. Stalin and the Stalinists had been calling for this independent working-class action. This was for the record. But the moment there was a possibility of getting the millions of trade unionists moving, they sacrificed this to their alliance with Britain and France. A hasty telegram came from Moscow to Brussels, stating that under no circumstances would the Soviet Union support independent action. They would support the League of Nations, and the League alone.

With this blow from Moscow, the movement for working-class action was killed.

The masses of the workers, especially in Europe, meant well toward Ethiopia, but they were misled by the labor fakers, assisted by the Stalinist bureaucracy.

There was another attempt made to save Ethiopia by the masses of the people. As soon as the war broke out, thousands of young men, black and white, volunteered to form an international brigade, to fight with the Ethiopians against Italian fascism.

Why did it not materialize? Because the emperor of Ethiopia and particularly Mr. Martin, the Ethiopian minister in London, were tied up with the British Foreign Office officials, those imperialist bandits, and were looking to them for assistance and not to the masses of the workers. The result was that this splendid beginning, which could have been the nucleus of tens of thousands of volunteers and millions of dollars, was rejected by the Ethiopian government in order not to offend the imperialists, those same imperialists who were plotting its downfall.

So that today when these same rascals start talking about "poor little Finland," or poor little anybody, let every Negro ponder over the lesson of Ethiopia. Imperialism is on one side. We are on the other. We look always to ourselves. What was needed, what we need today, is an international revolutionary organization, which will agitate in the working-class movement for international working-class action for working-class aims— actions such as Eugene Jagot proposed. Such an organization as it grows stronger will organize international brigades, not to carry out the counterrevolutionary Stalinist policy, as was done in Spain, but to fight for the socialist revolution and the independence of the colonial countries. Such today is the Fourth International. Join it.

Not One Red Cent

"We say to our children, do not bring in a red cent for this cause."

This was the editorial advice given by the *Louisiana Weekly,* Negro newspaper in New Orleans, in condemning the attempt of the school board to force Negro students, parents, and teachers to

---

From *Socialist Appeal,* March 16, 1940.

contribute to the Hoover Finnish Aid Fund. It cites the fact that Negro education in Louisiana is twenty-five years behind that of the whites and that Negroes are in at least as dire need as the Finns. Many of the Negro teachers protested the program of the school board to have them write letters to the parents asking for money.

This is but one of many cases of resentment of the Negro press to the attempt of the Hoover Finnish Aid Fund to solicit funds from Negroes. The "Laundryman" column in the *California Eagle* (January 25, 1940), speaking of the proposed government loan to Finland, states: "It seems to me that it would be much more practical, much more rational, to shoot this $25,000,000 here in America to bolster the relief checks of thousands of undernourished, impoverished Americans."

The *Chicago Defender* in an editorial (February 3, 1940) on the League of Nations states:

Members of the League of Nations have made another gesture which should expose their utter and complete hypocrisy to the world—especially to the world of colored peoples.

The League has asked aid of Haile Selassie for Finland. Shades of Saint Peter and Paul! Was it not the same League that sold the King of Kings down the river? What colossal shamelessness.

For the Negro people to send funds to the Finnish Mannerheims and Tanners, who have forced thousands of Finns to leave their country, and to flee to America seeking democracy and freedom, would be like a Negro sending money to Cotton Ed Smith and Bilbo of Carolina and Mississippi.

Black men who fled Mississippi, wouldn't send money to help those who lynch and murder Negroes, would they?

Roy Wilkins, in his column in the *Amsterdam News* (January 13, 1940) advises the Negro people to keep their thinking straight on the main issues before the public:

The plight of Finland has provided a new screen for vicious assaults upon any progressive, liberal or radical thought. The mighty wire-pullers in America are tugging at the heartstrings of the notoriously soft-hearted American public ostensibly for the relief of the Finns, but in reality for the destruction of what few gains have been made in past years in social advancement.

This drive to "clean out the Reds" and smear anything progressive with Red paint is one of which Negroes should beware. They should ask themselves how much of liberty and of despotism they have had under these American skies. A nation which has resisted stubbornly for forty years any attempt to wipe out the shooting, hanging and burning of human beings at the stake has a lot of nerve trying to tell Negroes it is civilized and the other fellow is a heathen. A nation whose Christianity is ruled by the color line has a nerve pointing to someone else as a pagan. "By their fruits ye shall know them."

An empire with its heel on 400 million black and brown men has a nerve talking about despotism. And, closer at home to Negroes, the National Association of Manufacturers, many of whose members fight labor in open warfare with spies, tear gas and guns, and most of whose members shut the door of employment in the face of Negroes, has its nerve talking about liberty and despotism.

THE ANTILYNCHING BILL

On February 6 the antilynching bill goes again to the Senate.

Again and again this bill, or one with substantially the same provisions, has passed the House only to be blocked in the Senate by a southern filibuster. Each time there is a tacit agreement by the large majority of our senators that the bill shall not be passed. The southern contingent acts the direct role, calling on their confreres not to "sacrifice the virtue of southern womanhood and mongrelize the race" (Representative Cox of Georgia in the recent debate in the House). And others speak grandly of the necessity of maintaining "democracy" in these United States and refuse to apply the cloture rule to put a time limit to debate. "Democracy" in these United States consists not in checking mob savagery with even a grossly inadequate law, but in allowing the representatives of Southern Bourbons to shout lies until their lungs give out.

Let us anticipate some of these lies and answer them. The most

From *Socialist Appeal*, February 3, 1940. A bill to punish lynching was first introduced into Congress in 1919, and was reintroduced repeatedly from then through World War II, but it was never enacted, no matter which capitalist party controlled the government.

plausible is that the South is itself doing away with lynching and, if left alone, will entirely eliminate it in a few years more. Those who say this point, for example, to the list of lynchings, which shows a steady decline in recent years to a new low of three in 1939. Three men or women tortured by a mob and then murdered are not as unimportant as our southerner would have us believe, but, yes, it is an improvement over previous years, when fifty or a hundred lynchings were recorded annually. Or is it?

The sharp drop in the list of the NAACP, or of the Tuskegee Institute, or of any other list of lynchings has been since the year 1922. In that year for the first time an antilynching bill, the so-called Dyer Bill, passed the House after a relatively short debate. It was blocked by a Senate filibuster. But it was a sufficient threat to the right to indulge in mob sadistry to check these defenders of civilization to some extent.

Only last week, for example, two Negroes were convicted in Prentiss, Mississippi, of the murder of a former marshal, a white man. The mob was ready for a lynch spree. They milled about the courthouse and worked themselves up to a frenzy. Hilton Fortenbury and Jerome Franklin would undoubtedly have been added to Mississippi's long list of lynch victims but for one fact. The governor sent state troops to protect them. Each door of the courthouse was heavily guarded, and when the prisoners were taken to the jail they marched in the center of a cordon of troops. Why did Governor White take this "extra precaution"? He tells us, quite frankly: Because of the debate now going on in Congress on the antilynch bill.

So the sharp drop in the number of lynchings in recent years is not a reason for not passing the bill but a direct result of attempts to pass it. Moreover, the drop has to a large extent not been a real one. The old-time lynching was a community affair. Local newspapers announced it days in advance, to give the people from neighboring counties time to reach the scene. Then before a crowd of hundreds the victim would be tortured to death. This practice has not passed out. Only in 1937 at Duck Hill, Mississippi, a new refinement was introduced: blow-torches were applied to the bare bodies of the two Negroes.

But it has to some extent been supplanted by another sort of lynching, one which seldom is to be found in any of the annual lists. A group of men waylay their intended victim in some deserted spot, kill him, and fling the body into a river or swamp. Lynching has gone underground.

All sorts of evidence can be adduced to show that the list of three lynchings given by the NAACP barely scratches the surface. The International Labor Defense, the Stalinist defense agency, gives twenty-five apparently well-authenticated cases for 1939. In a recent issue of *Editor and Publisher*, southern newspapermen tell some things they omit from their papers. One man has killed no fewer than twenty Negroes, according to this article, none of which was ever in the list of lynchings. Again, William Standard, deputy sheriff in New Orleans, says he is being haunted by the ghost of Oscar Smith, a Negro he killed in January 1938. The story is in the newspaper solely because of this macabre touch; only incidental is the fact that Standard has killed six men in his life. The murder of Smith, allegedly because he was frequently in the company of a woman with whom the officer was in love, was almost recorded by the publicity director for the Southern Regional Conference as the first lynching of 1938. Because of this a grand jury investigation was started. The witnesses did not show up, and a no-true bill was returned by the jury. No action was taken against either the witnesses or Standard. The case died. But because a grand jury had been called, this was not a lynching.

The bill in Congress will never stop lynching; only the abolition of the capitalist system can do that. But the mere threat of its passage has reduced somewhat this pastime of southern gentlemen, and its passage would undoubtedly reduce it more. This time the bill has a better chance than ever before. This is an election year, and in half a dozen northern states the Negro vote holds the balance of power between the two capitalist parties. If sufficient pressure is brought to bear on the Senate, the bill will pass.

RESISTANCE TO THE KLAN

Some months ago the refusal of Miami Negroes to be frightened away from the polls by the Ku Klux Klan made national headlines in all the Negro papers and even had some attention in the capitalist press. It was only afterwards that we learned what had frightened off the Klan. The Negroes sat in their houses waiting for the Klan with loaded Winchesters across their laps. Backed by this not-to-be-despised argument, American "democracy" won a small victory.

Now a similar situation is developing in Greenville, South Carolina. Both sides are primed for civil war. The Klan is determined that the Negroes shall not vote. The Negroes are determined that they shall. They are carrying on a campaign for registration in the city elections. James A. Briar, sixty-nine-year-old head of the local National Association for the Advancement of Colored People, considered chiefly responsible for the agitation, has been arrested for illegal possession of a gun. This time Briar is defending not only "democracy" but his life. The Klan visited his house a few times in recent weeks, but he was always out. According to the *Amsterdam News* (December 23, 1939), the Klan raided the Negro area and "have beaten up men, stripped and humiliated women and destroyed some property."

This conflict has been going on for months. How does it affect the Negro? Enter your southern scientist: "Here is a situation where the Negro's uncontrollable lust for white women shows itself." William Anderson, nineteen years old, president of the local NAACP Youth Council and very active in the registration campaign, was framed some time ago for disorderly conduct and breach-of-the-peace charges by the "authorities," who insisted he had tried to date a white girl in town. There you have the kernel of lynching in the South. The "authorities" bring a case. The mob is less subtle. It tears the victim to pieces.

It is a principle of propaganda today to smear your enemy with the crimes of which you yourself are guilty. Hitler is a pastmaster

---

By J. R. Johnson. From *Socialist Appeal,* February 3, 1940.

at the art, Stalin its greatest exponent, living or dead. The South acts on the same principle. The southern gentlemen pester the Negro women with their attentions. They accuse the Negro of this, their own besetting sin.

JIM CROW TEXTBOOKS IN MISSISSIPPI

JACKSON, Mississippi—The race-haters of Mississippi are not going to allow Hitler to receive all of the laurels for inventing devices for racial segregation if they have any say about it.

Negroes all over the state and nation are protesting the Jim Crow textbook law just passed by the legislature. The civics textbooks for the Negro pupils will not contain information on voting, instructions on how to vote, matters of government and civic responsibility.

In passing the law, the legislature said that Negro children should not know those things. In the Senate, where the bill passed by a vote of 37 to 9, Senator H. L. Davis, of Oxford, stated:

"Under the Constitution the Negro is a citizen and of course we know and accept that. But he can never expect to be given the same educational and social privileges with the white man and he doesn't expect them. The best education we can give him is to use his hands because that's how he must earn his living. It always has and it always will be."

The bill provides that all books returned by the Negro and white pupils be stored in separate warehouses to prevent white children from using the same books used by Negroes. Dr. E. M. Garvin, senator for Stafford Springs, stated that the books should be stored separately so white children would not get germs from the books used by the Negro children.

From *Socialist Appeal*, February 24, 1940.

JUDGE UPHOLDS
SEGREGATION IN HARLEM

A restaurant owner doesn't have to serve Negroes if they are sitting with white friends—that's the Hitlerite ruling handed down last week by Judge Marks of Municipal Court, Manhattan.

Two Negroes, Conrad Lynn and Elsie Jackson, went to the Marianna Restaurant on West 113th Street, Manhattan, last November, to eat with two white friends. The proprietor wouldn't serve them.

In court, the proprietor testified that he would have served the Negroes if they had sat apart by themselves, but would not serve them with their friends in a "mixed party."

Under the state civil rights law, penalties are provided against restaurant owners who refuse to serve Negroes.

Judge Marks ruled, however, that a restaurant owner may rightfully refuse to serve Negroes whenever they are in the company of white friends! As long as the owner is willing to serve the Negroes at their own segregated corner of his place, Judge Marks ruled, he is within the law.

If Judge Marks's ruling is permitted to stand, it virtually annuls the provisions of the civil rights law ostensibly protecting Negroes from discrimination. For it authorizes restaurant proprietors to establish a Jim Crow section in their establishments.

At the request of the complainants, therefore, the American Labor Aid is undertaking to appeal Judge Marks's decision to the higher courts.

From *Socialist Appeal*, February 24, 1940. Conrad Lynn, a former member of the Communist Party, later became a leading civil rights attorney. The American Labor Aid was a short-lived defense organization initiated by SWP members and their friends.

TENNESSEE LYNCH LEADERS NAMED

The National Association for the Advancement of Colored People has placed before President Roosevelt and the Department of Justice a list of names of the mob who drove a number of prominent Negroes out of Brownsville, Tennessee, following the lynching of Elbert Williams, thirty-three-year-old laundry fireman, Negro leader of a "register and vote" drive.

The names of the mob leaders include two bank officials, several police officers, a state highway commissioner, and several merchants. Williams's body was found in a river near Brownsville on Sunday, June 23. There were two wounds in his chest, his head was battered and beaten to twice its normal size, his arms and feet were tied with a rope, and his body was weighted down by a heavy log tied around his neck. Two other victims, both riddled with bullets, were found later, neither as yet identified.

It is reported that eight other Negroes are missing.

Brownsville is the county seat of Haywood County, and Negroes, who constitute three-fourths of the county's population, have not voted since 1884.

The NAACP investigation shows that on the night of June 16 a group of white men, headed by Sheriff Hunter, called at Williams's home. When Mrs. Williams answered the door, Hunter told her to tell her husband to step to the door. Williams came to the door dressed in his pajamas. Hunter told him that he was wanted at the jail for questioning and led his prisoner to a waiting automobile. One of the gang upon leaving turned to Mrs. Williams and informed her: "This is the last time you'll see that n-----; we're goin' t' kill 'im!"

Fearing for her husband's life, the woman followed the automobile until it was out of sight and then went to the town jail. She was told that Williams was not there but that he would "likely turn up later." He did, dead, at the bottom of the river.

Hunter now claims that he took the prisoner to jail where, after

From *Socialist Appeal*, July 13, 1940.

three hours of questioning, Williams was released. "He started towards home; that's all I know," the sheriff claims.

Negroes have been forbidden to gather in groups in Brownsville, even for church services, and the Rev. Buster Walker of the Baptist church was chased out of town shortly after the lynchings. Walker incurred the mob's wrath by speaking favorably of Negro suffrage.

THE NEW DRAFT LAW

A couple of weeks ago, before the conscription bill was passed, two amendments were made, which were hailed by Senator Wagner of New York (and several unsuspecting and gullible Negro leaders) as "a signal victory for the forces of democracy in American life."

One amendment was supposed to prohibit discrimination in the armed forces because of color, so far as enlisted men were concerned, the other prohibited discrimination against drafted men.

But actually, in spite of the statements coming from secretaries in the White House, nothing has changed. Jim Crow still wears his stripes.

In five cities, reporters of the *Baltimore Afro-American* attempted to join the U.S. Aviation Corps. In each case, these colored men were met with flat rejections. "And in each instance the reason given was always the same—no openings for colored men."

Another reporter of the same paper tried to enlist in the field artillery, a branch of the service that has been closed to the Negro

---

From *Socialist Appeal*, October 19, 1940. Although the U.S. government still professed neutrality in the war at this time and Roosevelt campaigned for a third term as an opponent of war, a bill instituting the registration and conscription of American male youth was adopted by Congress in September 1940. Draftees were supposed to undergo military training for one year, but that was extended less than a year later, and most draftees were not released until after the war. In the first year of conscription only 2,069 Blacks were drafted, but after that the white-dominated draft boards took more than a proportional share from the Black communities—around a million Blacks served during the war.

people. "There are no vacancies for colored," was the answer he got.

Another applied for admission into the U.S. Navy this week in Washington, the capital of this great democracy. He was told that the only place open for Negroes was as mess-hands, that is, as kitchen slavies.

And so it goes, up and down the line of the different branches. The marine corps is still lily white. So is the tank corps, the air corps, the artillery, the coast guard, the engineers, the signal corps, etc. Only the infantry, the cavalry, the quartermaster corps, mess hands in the Navy, and to a very limited extent the medical corps, are open to colored people.

MILITARY POLICY AND THE NEGROES

1. Militarization of the United States, including conscription, poses before the workers in a more acute form all the problems involved in the death agony of capitalism. The main political answers and the corresponding tactical approach were outlined in the resolution on military policy adopted by the Chicago Conference of the Socialist Workers Party.

This resolution analyzed the falseness and complete bankruptcy of all the old liberal capitalist, reformist, Stalinist, and pacifist programs and movements in the face of the death agony of capitalism. It analyzed their role in weakening and disarming the workers and turning them over, tied hand and foot, to their enemies. It pointed out that "in the epoch of militarism great questions can be decided only by military means," that "the epoch of the death agony of capitalism . . . can be brought to an end only by the definitive victory of the proletariat."

By the Political Committee, Socialist Workers Party. The adoption of the new conscription law was answered by the SWP with a national conference in Chicago, September 27-29, 1940. Rejecting both capitalist militarism and pacifism, the conference adopted a resolution to fight for military training under trade union control. Not all aspects of this position were spelled out in the conference resolution, and a few weeks later, on October 28, the SWP Political Committee adopted this supplementary resolution, which was printed in *Socialist Appeal*, November 9, 1940.

2. This is true for the working class as a whole, and applies with special force for the Negro people.

As long as the bosses control military training, the Negro faces the same dangers as the white worker: that the armed forces will be used against his interests; that the officer caste may capitulate, sabotaging the struggle of the workers; that it will be used to establish a military dictatorship in wartime; that it will throw away millions of workers' lives in imperialist adventures.

In addition: The Negro faces the certainty that bosses' control will be used to maintain and further the system of Jim Crowism in the armed forces.

3. The system of Jim Crowism in the armed forces demonstrates very clearly to the Negro the hypocrisy of slogans about "war for democracy." But the ruling class maintains Jim Crowism in the armed forces. For it cannot wipe out this system in the armed forces without endangering the whole system of Jim Crowism practiced in "civilian life": in industry, in civil service, on relief, at the ballot booth, in housing, theaters, restaurants—economically, politically, socially. The capitalists fear that *no Negro trained to handle a gun would peacefully go back to the old life of discrimination, segregation, disfranchisement, and insult, after training in an army where he was treated as an equal with white soldiers.*

In the last war, when Jim Crowism was also the established policy in the forces of the United States, the general staff's fears that the Negro soldiers might become instilled with ideas of equality from their contact with French soldiers reached the point where they sent out the infamous "Secret Information Concerning Black American Troops," in which they cautioned the French not to treat Negroes as equals or with respect, since they might entertain "undesirable aspirations."

It is because of this, and because the general staff fears solidarity between black and white soldiers in the same way a boss fears such solidarity in his factory, that Jim Crow continues in the armed forces in wartime as an extension of its use in civilian life in peacetime.

Consequently, the Negro suffers everything the white soldier does, and in addition he finds the general staff adapting peacetime Jim Crow to the conditions of war and conscription as follows:

4. "The policy of the war department is not to intermingle colored and white enlisted personnel in the same regimental organizations. This policy has proved satisfactory over a long period of years, and to make changes would produce situations destructive to morale and detrimental to the preparations for

national defense," declared Commander-in-Chief Roosevelt in a recent statement.

That is, in those branches of the service where Negroes are admitted they are segregated into Jim Crow regiments, and Negro soldiers are not permitted in the same regiments as white. (This is the policy in the national defense training program of the National Youth Administration and of the Civilian Conservation Corps.)

Negroes are barred from enlisting in most of the branches of the service. This practice prevents them from exercising free choice in designating the branch of the service in which they wish training, as white enlistees are permitted to do.

Negro Engineers is only another name for labor battalions.

The few cavalry regiments of Negroes are "principally used as chambermaids for cadets' and officers' horses and equipment at the military academy and the various service schools."

Negroes are permitted in the infantry, where the greatest number of casualties occur, and, to a limited extent, in the artillery, the quartermaster corps, and the medical corps.

But they are not admitted into the air corps, the marine corps, the tank corps, the coast guard, the signal corps, or the chemical warfare service. These branches of the service are completely lily white. No colored men may enlist in them, no colored men in other branches may even transfer to them as white soldiers are often permitted to do.

In the navy, the same general policy is followed, although life aboard ship does not permit exactly the same procedure. Negroes are admitted only into the mess attendants' division, can rise no higher than officers' cook or steward, cannot become petty officers or chief petty officers. Consequently, they receive lower pay ratings and are denied the opportunity that white men have to learn and practice a trade. While others learn mechanics and other useful trades, they can learn only how to be a waiter, cook, or valet. They are not permitted to attend the naval academy at Annapolis.

Negroes in the infantry are used principally for two kinds of work: as laborers in the labor battalions, where they dig trenches, fortifications, and latrines, or as suicide squads in the most dangerous sections of the front.

Only a small percentage of the Negroes are permitted to become officers, and they are Jim Crowed too. Regiments which are all Negro are usually officered by whites, not Negroes, and white regiments are never officered by Negroes. Negroes are not wanted in the higher councils of the army, where the Jim Crow policies are formulated. Only one has ever risen higher than the rank of colonel, and this exception was dictated by the momentary political needs of the [Roosevelt] administration, not because of any fundamental change in the rule.

5. Because many Negroes have had personal experience of discrimination and segregation inflicted on them by backward workers in factories and in trade unions, a sentiment may arise in the course of the struggle for union control of military training, for the right of Negro soldiers to choose for themselves whether they shall be in mixed regiments or in all-Negro regiments. In such a case we must pledge ourselves to support the right of the Negro soldiers to determine the question for themselves.

If the question of separate regiments arises we must explain that the bosses never give the Negroes the right to determine this question for themselves—they just shunt them off on the side where they can use them for their own reactionary ends. Unlike the bosses, the Socialist Workers Party supports their right to decide this question for themselves. At the same time that we tell them we recognize their right to choose what they want, we sincerely and cordially urge them to join us in mixed regiments, free of discrimination. The very fact that we do this is additional proof that we not only consider them equal and brothers, but that we want to be side by side with them in the struggle against Jim Crowism.

In short, we differentiate between *segregation* under bosses' control, and *self-determination* under workers' control. We are against the first, we are for the right of the second. It is part of our program, but is not a field for extensive agitation at this time.

We must take the occasion, wherever possible, to show why it is that the officer caste insists on separate regiments (to keep the workers divided, to make it easier for them to assign the Negroes as a group for dirty or dangerous work, to reinforce the system of Jim Crowism in civilian life). We must point out that success in the struggle for mixed regiments can protect the Negroes from special selection as a group for dirty or dangerous work, can unite the soldiers and build up a solidarity of Negro and white, and can help to undermine the system of Jim Crowism everywhere.

6. It is clear then that all the abuses of the armed forces under control of the bosses which impel the white workers to fight for workers' control of military training apply even more acutely to the Negro.

For the Negro worker as well as the white worker then, the main question today is taking control away from the bosses and placing it in the hands of the workers, through their class organizations, the trade unions.

Since the Negro, however, has a special problem in the armed forces, just as he has in civilian life (that is, he suffers extra oppression and persecution because he is a Negro), the Socialist Workers Party must so concretize its general slogans as to express the special needs of the Negro in the struggle for union control of military training. This will make it easier for Negro worker-soldiers to join in the general struggle.

These slogans can be formulated as follows:

Abolish Jim Crow in the army and navy!

End segregation! Stop shoving Negroes into separate regiments where they can be most easily discriminated against!

Open the doors for Negroes in all branches of the service, in mixed regiments led by officers and generals of whom a proportionate share shall be Negroes!

Stop using Negroes as laborers and lackeys!

For the full right of Negroes to rise to any position in the armed forces!

For the right of Negroes, along with other workers, to elect committees to present grievances to the officers pertaining to conditions, including specific cases of discrimination and segregation!

For the right of Negroes to attend training schools for officers!

FIFTEEN SAILORS IN THE BRIG

Their Crime: Writing a Letter

A number of Negro sailors serving as mess attendants on the U.S.S. *Philadelphia,* now stationed at Long Beach, California, could not stand it any longer.

By Albert Parker, a pen name of George Breitman (see Glossary). From the Pioneer Publishers pamphlet *Defend the Negro Sailors of the U.S.S. Philadelphia,* November 1940, which was based on material in the *Socialist Appeal.* Previously, the SWP's main form of participation in defense of Black rights had been through educational activity (circulating literature, holding meetings, etc.) supporting the campaigns initiated by other antiracist organizations. The *Philadelphia* case was the first national struggle against Jim Crow in which the SWP was able to play an independent active role that had some effect on the labor and radical movements it sought to influence and mobilize.

The discrimination, insult, and abuse they suffered aboard ship because they were colored had become almost intolerable.

Fifteen of them got together towards the end of September 1940 and decided they would have to do something. They needed help, and they had learned from experience that there was no use in appealing for it to the officers commanding the ship, because they were the very ones who were responsible for what was going on. They felt they could get support only from the outside.

So they sat down and wrote a letter to the *Pittsburgh Courier*, one of the nation's leading Negro newspapers. They told the world about the horrible Jim Crow conditions under which colored sailors suffer. They appealed for all possible help in changing these conditions.

Their letter, printed in the *Courier* of October 5, tells the following story:

On enlisting, we are given the same mental and physical examination as the white sailors and were given to believe that we have the privilege of choosing any branch of the service the Navy offers. This is not true.

With three months of training in making beds, shining shoes and serving officers completed, we are sent to various ships and stations of the Navy.

The white sailor, after completing his training period, is not only eligible for the branch of service he has chosen, but he is automatically advanced in rating and his pay is increased to $36 a month without even having to take an examination.

In our case, we have to be in the service for a full year at $21 a month before we are eligible for advancement rating. It is also necessary for us to take a competitive examination. Even if we pass, it doesn't mean necessarily that we will be rated and have our pay increased to $36 a month.

On this ship, out of a crew of 750, there are 18 colored boys, ranging in ages from 18 to 25. They are fresh out of high school and some have a year of college education.

Their work is limited to waiting on table and making beds for the officers. . . .

In the last nine months there have been nine mess attendants given solitary confinement on bread and water.

Five of the nine were given brig time because of fighting and arguments with other enlisted men. From this you will probably think we are a pretty bad bunch. We are not.

With the treading on and kicking around we receive here (without being able to do anything about it), every last one of us becomes bitter enough to fight a member of our own family.

We, the mess attendants of the *Philadelphia,* are not merely stating these facts because of our own plight. In doing so, we sincerely hope to discourage any other colored boys from joining the Navy and make the same mistake we did.

All they would become is sea-going bell hops, chambermaids and dishwashers.

We take it upon ourselves to write this letter, regardless of any action the Naval authorities may take or whatever the consequences may be.

We only know that it could not possibly surpass the mental cruelty inflicted upon us on this ship.

Fred Louis, Floyd C. St. Clair, Floyd W. Owens, Theodore L. Hansborough, Byron C. Johnson, Robert Turner, Arval Perry, Otto Robinson, E. Bosley, Jesse Willard Watford, George Elbert Rice, John William Ponder, James Porter, Shannon H. Goodwin, James Edw. Ponder.

Remember, they were still in the navy. They were still under the domination of the officer caste commanding the ship, and therefore still at their mercy. The fact that they wrote and signed the letter under these conditions is the best possible indication of the desperation to which they had been driven.

It was in this dramatic way that these fifteen boys gave to the world its first open and signed picture of the degrading system of Jim Crowism that rules the navy and its ships.

The dictatorial, Negro-hating, labor-hating officers of the ship were outraged. These colored men had written a letter and mailed it to a newspaper! Mutiny! The officers moved against it with the speed and violence of a mob organizing a lynching.

All the men who had signed the letter were arrested. An "investigation" was instituted. Two of the men, Shannon Goodwin and Byron Johnson, were thrown into prison. They now face court martial.

The rest of the men are prisoners-at-large on the ship, not allowed to leave it, held for further "investigation" which the commanding officer is conducting in order to force the boys to tell who is the "brains" behind the letter.

But while they may be able to shut the mouths of the heroic *Philadelphia* boys for a time by arrests, courts-martial, and jail sentences, they cannot hide the truth. It is out, and more is being learned about the ugly picture every day as colored sailors from other ships rally to the defense of the *Philadelphia* mess men and swear to the truth of what they charged the officer caste.

All this, of course, places Roosevelt and the ruling class in an embarrassing position. They may be able to fool some workers with the idea that they are preparing us to fight a war for democracy instead of a war for Wall Street's profit, but what Negro worker would be foolish enough to believe that a Jim

Crow army and a Jim Crow navy can fight a war for real democracy?

Demand End to Navy Repression

Letters of protest, demanding the freedom of the Negro sailors on the U.S.S. *Philadelphia* and an end to the Jim Crow practices in the navy, began to pour into the offices of President Roosevelt and Secretary of the Navy Knox last week, at the same time that the government announced its intention of standing by the policy of segregating colored sailors to the mess attendants division only.

The letters from various organizations and individuals printed in the *Pittsburgh Courier* last week showed that an increasing number of people are aroused over the case of the imprisoned *Philadelphia* sailors, and are eager to express their resentment over conditions in the navy.

The National Association for the Advancement of Colored People in a letter to Secretary Knox stated that the colored people of this country "are bitter about the treatment of their men in the armed forces of the nation. . . . We wish to enter a most vigorous protest against this action and to request you, as Secretary of the Navy, to intervene."

The NAACP upheld the action of the mess attendants in bravely signing their names to the published letter of complaint, saying they had done so "in belief that they had a just complaint which ought not to be weakened by an anonymous letter."

The *Courier* also quoted from the "pointed letter" to Roosevelt and Knox by the Workers Relief & WPA Union of Newark, New Jersey, signed by George Breitman, secretary, which asked for an immediate end to the arrest, confinement to the ship for "further investigation," molestation, and inquisition suffered by the boys, "whose only 'offense' is that they complained with much cause against a brutal system of discrimination and segregation."

The unemployed union also demanded that Roosevelt and Knox use their powers to put an end to these conditions.

Another letter, for Local 32 of the Building Service Employees International Union, signed by J. Cyril Fullerton, executive

---

By Albert Parker. From *Socialist Appeal,* November 30, 1940.

manager, explained that the union has a membership of 2,000 who reside and work in Harlem, 90 percent of whom are Negroes.

"We have one aim and that is to see that justice is secured for the colored men in the Navy who are now being unjustly punished for demanding their rights as men and American citizens."

Since their arrest, the mess attendants on the *Philadelphia* have been joined by sailors from at least three other ships who have spoken out and in most cases signed their names, corroborating their testimony about treatment of Negroes in the navy.

Added to these this week were the names of Negro sailors from two other ships. Those on the U.S.S. *Brooklyn,* stationed off Mare Island, California, show that they understand what is going on behind the closed doors of the *Philadelphia* case when they write:

> They are trying to make an example of Johnson and Goodwin to try to scare the rest of us into submission. But these constant letters to you are the only hope Johnson, Goodwin and the rest of us have to get your help, that of the NAACP, and other such organizations throughout the country so that this case will not be dropped into obscurity and forgotten by our people while conditions remain the same. We, part of the messmen of the U.S.S. *Brooklyn,* . . . are prepared to sacrifice the time that we have in here and ourselves to help remedy this condition.

Ousted for Daring to Protest

Rear Admiral Nimitz, chief of the Bureau of Navigation, Navy Department, last week finally told what had happened to the fifteen Negro sailors on the U.S.S *Philadelphia* who had written a letter protesting Jim Crow conditions in the navy.

Nimitz announced, in an interview with P. L. Prattis, executive editor of the *Pittsburgh Courier,* that thirteen of the sailors had been kicked out of the navy with "undesirable" discharges, and that the other two were still in the brig, probably being held for even more drastic action.

But the case would not be closed even if all the men had been set free. Indeed, the fight must go on as long as the officer caste controls military training and has the power to Jim Crow Negroes.

This was indicated also by the *Courier* in its issue of December

By Albert Parker. From *Socialist Appeal,* December 14, 1940.

7 in the story entitled "Here Are Six More 'Chambermaids' You Can Fire, Rear Admiral Nimitz," which contained another letter, from a group of six Negro sailors of the U.S.S. *Davis,* stationed at San Diego, California.

This letter, which is the sixth signed by groups of mess attendants on as many different ships in the navy in the last two months, tells the same story that the others did, of segregation, brutal discrimination, and vicious punishment for any "back talk."

Unfortunately, like the others, the authors of this letter, while they demonstrate great courage in signing their names, make the mistake of urging as a solution "that the Negro youth of America . . . cease to enlist in the U.S. Navy."

Such a policy will not solve the problem because it is ineffective in the face of conscription; because it will not help the four thousand Negro sailors already *in* the navy; and because it does not take into consideration the need for military training of all kinds by the oppressed Negro people and the working class, if they are to be able to defeat their enemies.*

The latest developments in the *Philadelphia* case point once again to the need for the Negro people to join in the struggle for a system of military training under the control of the trade unions—take control and power out of the hands of the Jim Crow and antilabor officers and put it in the hands of the workers themselves.

*For a discussion of these points, see the article "Conscientious Objection or Militant Struggle," page 73.

POLICE TERROR IN PHILADELPHIA

PHILADELPHIA, November 30—The Negro and working-class population of this city is bitterly aroused against the mass arrest of almost six hundred Negroes, whom police seized in the streets, restaurants, and taprooms of the North Philadelphia Twentieth Ward last week.

Of those arrested, 128 who were held incommunicado in jail twenty-four to forty-eight hours without warrants for their arrest

From *Socialist Appeal,* December 7, 1940.

or formal charges being placed against them, have already started civil suits for false arrest against thirty-seven police officials and police who commanded or conducted the raids.

The police claimed they had instituted the raids in an alleged effort to "clean up" a series of petty crimes in the area.

But the arrests were really an attempt to intimidate the Negro population of Philadelphia, because of their defiance of this city's dominant Republican political machine. Most Negroes here voted Democratic in the elections.

The Philadelphia political machine is taking advantage of the present political atmosphere—war hysteria, the government drive against striking workers as "saboteurs" and "reds," the brazen Jim Crowing of Negroes in the army and navy, the refusal of corporations with military orders to hire Negroes—to force the Negroes by terror to support the local bosses in City Hall. Such an attempt would hardly be possible in "normal" times.

Of the almost 600 arrested, police were able to find only twenty on whom any kind of a charge could be put, although all spent one to two nights in jail. Finally, seven were held for "suspicion" and thirteen for "vagrancy" or carrying concealed weapons.

No warrants were used in making the arrests, nor were immediate hearings permitted, the two proceedings required by law.

A mass meeting of all Negro organizations here is to be held Wednesday, December 4, at the St. Paul's Baptist Church. Scores of those arrested will attend and testify to their treatment at the hands of the police. The meeting will be for the purpose of organizing the campaign to halt the vicious police terrorism against the Negro people and to aid the conduct of the suits against the police.

HIRING POLICY, EARLY 1941

The whole economy of the nation is being shifted to a war basis. Production of all the great and important industries is being reorganized and expanded. The factories and machinery which the bosses kept idle for over ten years when people were starving are now being opened and put to use to produce the instruments of war. The bosses and their corporations are rolling

From *Socialist Appeal,* January 11, 1941.

in profits. The cost of living is going up for everyone, but so far most of the unions have managed to boost wages along accordingly, so that the standard of living of many of the white workers is no worse than it was before.

But where are the Negroes in this busy picture?

One industry after another bars them altogether from jobs that pay even a half-decent wage. They occupy only two kinds of jobs in the vast majority of the war industries that do hire them: in the menial, nonproductive positions, or at the hardest and worst laboring jobs. The cost of living is going up for them as well as others, but because they are excluded from the better-paying jobs in the strategic industries, their income isn't able to keep up with it. The hullabaloo about the "end of unemployment" is being used as a good pretext in each state to slash the relief budget and the relief rolls far more sharply than ever before. Negroes who want to work and can't get jobs suffer from this more than white workers, because at least some of the white workers are able to escape from the need of getting relief for the time being.

In short, the Negroes are being left out in the cold. The old saying about "the last to be hired" is still true.

LOCAL 683 APOLOGIZES

The aircraft workers at Vultee (organized into Local 683 of the United Auto Workers union, CIO) deserve double thanks from the workers of this country.

First of all, they struck a blow which showed that it is not only desirable but possible to win higher wages and better working conditions in the war industries, even under a heavy barrage of attacks from the employers, their stooges, and the government.

Secondly, they have taken another action which will be greeted with enthusiasm by the workers, especially those Negro workers who are almost 100 percent barred from many important industries such as aircraft.

Here is how it happened. At the dance celebrating the victorious strike, two Negro members were asked to leave by people acting as floor managers and making the request on their own initiative.

By Albert Parker. From *Socialist Appeal*, January 18, 1941. UAW Local 683 consisted of 3,700 aircraft workers who had just won a strike at the Vultee Aircraft plant in Downey, California.

When the members of the union learned about it, there was a discussion of this action on the floor of a regular local meeting, resulting in the adoption of the following resolution:

WHEREAS: At a public dance given by the Vultee unit of Local 683, two Negro union brothers and their guests were asked to leave, and

WHEREAS: This action is in direct contradiction to the national CIO policy of no discrimination because of race, color, creed, nationality or political affiliation, and

WHEREAS: The success of our drive to organize the aircraft industry depends upon the broadest possible public support, and

WHEREAS: The Negro people, who helped on our picket line with donations of food and money in our recent successful strike, are part of that public, and

WHEREAS: We recognize that discrimination of any kind is the weapon used by the employer and his organizations to split and divide us in our struggle for a higher standard of living, therefore be it

RESOLVED: That we apologize to the Negro people for this action, and that we give our complete assurance that this action will not be repeated, and be it further

RESOLVED: That this Local 683 of the United Auto Workers, CIO, do all in its power to break down the anti-labor, racial discrimination policy in the aircraft and national defense industries, recognizing that our national defense must rest on the maintenance of our democratic principles, foremost among which is the right of every citizen to an opportunity to earn his livelihood without discrimination.

URBAN LEAGUE ON JOB BIAS

The recent report by the National Urban League, the organization most closely in touch with statistics dealing with hiring and barring of Negroes from the war industries, shows that very little progress has been made in breaking down the discriminatory practices employed by the bosses and their employment managers.

According to the report, those employers who were questioned were "practically unanimous" in claiming that they barred Negroes not because they themselves personally were opposed to them, but because they were afraid that the white workers in

From *Militant,* February 1, 1941. *Socialist Appeal* changed its name to *The Militant* starting with this issue.

their plants would resent it, and "it might lead to serious labor trouble, or at least sufficient ill will to interfere with efficient production."

In this way, the bosses who are guilty of Jim Crowing the Negro try to palm off the responsibility on the white workers—who were never consulted in a single case by the bosses about what they thought about hiring Negroes. Thus the bosses accomplish two things: they bar the Negro, and then they build up antagonism among the Negroes toward the white workers. "Divide and rule" is the motto of the bosses.

CONSCIENTIOUS OBJECTION OR MILITANT STRUGGLE?

When Ernest Calloway told a Chicago draft board last month that he wants exemption from military service because he is a conscientious objector against the Jim Crow treatment of the Negroes in the armed forces, he opened up a very important question for all those who are serious about the fight for equal rights in the army.

That question is: Should other Negroes follow Calloway's example? Should they declare that they are against being trained how to fight, and refuse military training? Can such a course of action have a decisive effect on the shameful treatment of the Negro soldiers by the officer clique in charge of conscription?

There can be no doubt here, of couse, of our attitude toward the attacks that the draft officials are going to make on Calloway. Already his local board has turned down his request for exemption, and although he is appealing their decision with the aid of the NAACP, it is pretty certain that they will prosecute and attempt to jail him if he persists in his determination not to be drafted. When the draft officials and the army bureaucrats launch their attack against him, they will do it because he has opposed their draft and has given publicity to the Jim Crow regime in the army. All workers must defend Calloway against such attacks even if they don't agree with Calloway's method.

But it is one thing to oppose Jim Crowism in the army and another thing to oppose it correctly and successfully.

We are certain that actions such as Calloway's will not have

By Albert Parker. From *Militant*, February 1, 1941.

any decisive effect on the fight for equal rights in the armed forces. It can't, because it leaves untouched the power of the officer caste to do exactly what it pleases. As long as the labor-hating, Negro-hating officers have the power to do what they want with the rank-and-file soldiers, there will be Jim Crowism in the army. Not until their complete and all-powerful control over military training is taken from them can the fight for equal rights be won.

What is wrong with Calloway's method, even if it were followed by ten other men, or a thousand, or ten thousand, is that it does not touch this main problem at all. Whether Calloway is sent to jail or whether he will be set free will not in any way affect or diminish the powers of the officer caste. They'll still have the power to Jim Crow Negroes and treat them as second-class citizens.

The second major weakness in Calloway's method (which was conceived of and proposed by a Chicago organization known as "Conscientious Objectors Against Jim Crow," headed by St. Clair Drake, who is also executive secretary of the local branch of the Stalinist-controlled National Negro Congress) is that it does not take into consideration at all the need of the Negro people to learn the military arts.

This is a world of war and revolution today. Every important question is being decided by military means. The Negro people too will be able to solve their problems only by struggle against their armed and trained enemies. Whoever denies that the Negro people must master the military arts is misleading and disarming the Negroes in the face of their enemies. Whoever says that the Negro people in this country will win their freedom in any way other than by fighting for it is miseducating and confusing the Negro people.

It is correct and necessary to maintain our opposition to conscription by the boss class, but it is useless to do so unless at the same time we present some other proposal which, while it will eliminate military Jim Crowism and antilabor practices, will also provide for training the workers in the military arts.

Since the Calloway-Drake proposals ignore both the question of *control of military training and the necessity for such training,* they cannot be accepted as a program for Negro workers.

Since the Socialist Workers Party program for trade union control of military training has the answer to both these questions, it must be pushed by Negroes as the only real and practical solution of discrimination and segregation in the armed forces.

To push this program requires not an arms-folded policy of

individual abstention, which by itself can never win anything, but militant activity to mobilize the Negroes and the trade unions to struggle against the bosses for its realization.

FORD, THE UAW, AND BLACK WORKERS

Ford's 'Strike Insurance' . . .

For a long time it has been a practice in this country for the bosses to refuse to hire Negro workers in their plants, placing the blame for this on the white workers. Thus the bosses stored up a labor force among the Negroes that could be used for union-smashing and strike-breaking when the white workers began to organize. On certain occasions, employers have brazenly referred to this policy of creating resentment between black and white as "strike insurance."

Henry Ford has played a shrewd variation of this same game. Realizing that the time would come when the unions would begin to make some headway in organizing his empire, he began to employ Negroes in his plants, to build up the idea that he was a friend and benefactor of the Negro people and deserved their support in his bitter struggles against unionization.

He established a special division of employment of colored personnel and through this began to hire Negroes in large numbers. Today it is estimated that he has 10,000 Negro employees, representing about 10 percent of his labor force. As part of his plan, Ford has also contributed to certain Negro churches, organizations, and individuals.

A highlight in Ford's antiunion campaign was a recent ban-

By Albert Parker. From *Militant*, February 15, 1941. Henry Ford resisted unionization by the United Auto Workers longer than the other auto barons, thanks in part to a hiring policy that enabled him to pose as a friend of Blacks. But when the showdown came in April 1941, the great majority of the Black workers at the River Rouge plant sided with the UAW in a strike that forced Ford to sign a UAW contract.

quet for 300 people in Detroit by Donald J. Marshall, director of colored personnel for the Ford Motor Company.

In attendance was nearly every colored minister in the city, who came at special invitation to get the free meal and to listen to Marshall's harangue against the CIO. Those Negro ministers in Detroit who have expressed sympathy for the CIO were not invited; of them it was said, "The time has come to let our unfaithful leaders know we do not need them."

"We are appealing to the ministers to try to help us keep our feet on the ground," said Marshall.

He then launched an attack on the unions in which he blamed them because Negroes are not hired in great numbers in the other auto plants.

For instance, he showed that Knudsen, now head of the National Defense Commission, had refused to let Negroes hold skilled jobs in General Motors. What follows from that, according to Marshall? That the union which Knudsen fought so bitterly is responsible for this situation which existed long before the union was founded.

He finished this attack by making a not-too-veiled hint that if the Negro workers in Ford's plants didn't support him, they would be sorry:

"The open shop of Henry Ford has two Negroes out there to see that the Negroes get at least part of their rights [meaning himself and his assistant]. The Negro will regret the day if he helps to turn the Ford shop over to the CIO."

By this he meant that if the CIO organizes the Ford plants, Ford will have no further use for Negroes and will try to get rid of them. "It will be a sad day for us if the Ford Company changes its policy," moaned the Rev. Mr. Bradby, to emphasize the point.

Horace R. Cayton, one of the authors of *Black Workers in the New Unions,* has in two articles in recent issues of the *Pittsburgh Courier* dealt with the subject in a way that could be of use to the CIO in tackling this problem.

After explaining how Ford by his financial contributions has "given substance to the myth that Ford had a sympathetic interest in the problems of the Negro," and showing that "many Negro professional men and Negro leaders who lived on the back of these Ford employees, fearful of anything which might disrupt (even momentarily) their sources of income, are violently pro-Ford and anti-union," Cayton goes on:

Ford's policy toward the Negroes, however, is one that had been born of self-interest and has not offered the Negro much except employment.

That Ford has hired more Negroes than other companies is a matter of fact. He has done this, however, to provide himself with "strike insurance."

It is the testimony of most persons familiar with the Ford plant that Negroes are definitely limited in their ability to be promoted within the Ford plant and are pretty largely confined to the lower wage income brackets.

Likewise, all workers in the Ford plant, including Negro workers, suffered from the speed up, the possibility of brutal treatment from Ford's service men, and enjoy a wage which is about ten cents an hour below that of workers in other automobile plants.

Cayton explains clearly why Negro workers are hesitant about joining the union. First of all, they're glad they've got jobs, and they're not sure that Ford would keep them on if the union won out. Secondly, the Negro is under terrific pressure from Harry Bennett's thugs and from Donald Marshall and the other "leaders." Thirdly, they don't know whether they can trust the unions, because many of them have had experiences of discrimination, or have heard of discrimination, by white workers even in the union movement.

In this situation, it is imperative that the CIO pay special attention to the Negro workers. True, R. J. Thomas, president of the UAW, has written a letter which has received some publicity, in which he promises that there will be no discrimination by the union against Negro Ford workers. He urges that those who are interested should check in the other plants that have been organized and determine for themselves whether the Negro worker has been discriminated against. "They will find upon checking that in the Detroit plants Negroes now receive more money and have better jobs than they had prior to the advent of the union. . . ."

But when the scoundrels who call themselves leaders are so active in prejudicing the Negroes against the union, it is not enough to suggest that "anyone who is concerned about such rumors [of discrimination] check in other automobile plants. . . ." Every one of the 10,000 Negro workers in Ford is very much concerned about these vicious rumors. To tell them to go and check in the other automobile plants is not very helpful. It is up to the UAW to bring them the proof that there will be no discrimination, and to spend a lot of time combatting these rumors and spreading the truth that, as Cayton puts it, "the CIO has made a desperate effort to break down color barriers and it presents the greatest hope for Negro laborers since the Knights of Labor" and that "certainly Negro workers in the Ford plant will suffer greatly, both as workers and as Negroes, in the long run if they are instrumental in defeating unionism in Ford's plants."

. . . And How It Failed

The biggest thing about the Ford strike was the miserable failure of Ford, Bennett, and Marshall to preserve the open shop by provoking a race riot between the Negro and white workers.

The fact stands out, big and proud, that the overwhelming majority of the 12,000 Negro workers in the plant, in spite of a barrage of antiunion, pro-Ford threats and promises, went with their class.

Ford found that he could not use the Negro workers to break the strike, for a good 80 percent or more of them saw through his trick, resisted the pressure of many of their "leaders," and went out with the union.

In order to preserve the remnants of this vicious plan, which would have put back the cause of the Negro workers for many years, Ford and his assistants had to depend on a comparatively small number of Negroes who were brought into the plant during the last month from the South.

These Negroes, not at all acquainted with what was going on—never having had the opportunity to hear the arguments of the union, in no way familiar with Ford's antiunion, anti-Negro scheme—were all he had to depend on when the strike actually began.

The other Negroes, the workers who have suffered under the Ford speed-up, spy system, and low wage rate for many years—the real Ford Negro workers—knew where their best interests lay: with the union.

So although Ford did have a small group of Negroes to use for his scheme, and he certainly did use them in every way he could, he could not break the strike, nor arouse the spirit of white chauvinism in the union members. Everyone involved in the situation could see that the great bulk of the Negro workers were fighting with the union, not against it.

Incidentally, those Negroes who fell for and helped to spread the pro-Ford propaganda before the strike, must have felt pretty cheap to see how Ford and the boss press consciously directed so much of their publicity toward making it appear that the strike

By Albert Parker. From *Militant*, April 19, 1941.

was a race conflict rather than a struggle of workers of all races for improved working conditions.

The Negro Ford workers did their full share in saving the day for the union at Ford. It is up to the white workers in the labor movement now to recognize that they need the full support of the Negroes in the coming struggles and to raise high on their banners the demand for full equality for their colored brothers.

RANDOLPH'S APOLOGETICS FOR BRITISH IMPERIALISM

Four or five months ago A. Philip Randolph, head of the Pullman Porters' union, issued a statement called "The Battle for Britain," which called for support by the Negro people of all aid, short of war, to Great Britain.

Randolph was immediately answered by George Schuyler, *Pittsburgh Courier* columnist, who took up each of his arguments point by point and tore them to pieces. Randolph did not try to answer Schuyler; and Randolph's statement was widely distributed by the warmongering Committee to Defend America by Aiding the Allies.

This week again Randolph, undaunted by the weakness and falseness of his arguments, has issued another statement, "England's Fight Our Cause."

"Negroes," he begins, "should support 'all out aid,' including the Lend-Lease Bill, to Great Britain, short of war, because she is fighting the cause of democracy, the only hope and salvation of minority groups."

Did Randolph ever hear about the British Empire? Does he know that it is the greatest corporation of slave colonies the world has ever seen? Does he know that it has more than 400 million colored people under its control, that the "cause of democracy" for which it is fighting is not intended to include these 400 million, that the democracy of Great Britain means oppression, exploitation, dictatorial rule, discrimination, segregation, excessive taxation, and denial of every kind of liberty but

---

By Albert Parker. From *Militant*, February 15, 1941.

the liberty to work for the lowest wages in the world or starve?

Randolph of course must know what this democracy means to the Negro, not only in the British Empire but right here in the United States, where he is Jim Crowed and discriminated against everywhere and in everything.

He continues:

> Now, of course, there are those who say that this is an imperialist war. . . . It is true . . . in the sense that Germany, Great Britain and Italy are imperialist nations, and that Great Britain has been and is an oppressor of the darker races. But it does not follow that Great Britain, Germany and Italy represent equal degrees of evil and danger to the darker races and to . . . progress and the cause of peace. . . .

Then follows an attempt to differentiate between imperialist Germany and imperialist Britain.

Hitler has shown his contempt and disdain of the Negro people in *Mein Kampf*, where he calls them half-apes and sub-human. The Nazis in France pulled down Negro statues and drove the Negroes out of the country. "In other words, Hitler preaches and practices, unashamedly, his hellish hatred of all Negroes."

Randolph then contrasts to this his version of the behavior of British imperialism. Does he say a word about the policies it is still carrying on in Africa and India and the West Indies—the denial of all rights of free speech, free press, and free assembly, the arrests of all who speak up against the war, the intensification during the war of the exploitation of the Africans to raise the money to run the war? Not a word. For then he would have to admit that while Hitler *preaches and practices* Negro oppression, England *keeps quiet and practices* it; that while Hitler *calls* the Negro inferior, England *keeps quiet and treats* him as an inferior.

Instead, Randolph points to the "co-operation Britain is giving Emperor Haile Selassie" in driving the fascists out of Ethiopia. He also points to the fact that since the raids over London, West Indian Negroes have been permitted to join the RAF [Royal Air Force]. And beyond that, he has nothing to say.

The fact that he can point to so few specific things which can be offered in England's favor is proof itself of the bankruptcy of Randolph's position.

Imperialist Britain, which was largely responsible for Italy's invasion of Ethiopia, is now described as helping to free Ethiopia today! Even Randolph knows that this is a little too much to get people to swallow, so he tries to qualify it:

> There are those who cynically remark that England's support of the freedom of Ethiopia is inspired by a selfish interest. There would be no

point in denying this. It is true. But what is wrong with it? The motivation of all great power nations is self interest. Self interest is not to be condemned if it is not anti-social and reactionary. Here, the self interest of Great Britain takes the form of fighting to help restore the independence and liberty of a smaller, defenseless nation, and thereby serves the cause of humanity and justice, though, verily, this course of action be belated.

Thus, according to Randolph, England isn't fighting Germany because these two gangs of bandits each want control of the colonies and their markets, England isn't fighting because it wants to continue its exploitation of the 400 million—it's fighting because it is interested in the freedom of Ethiopia!

"Therefore," he says, "the Battle of Britain is the Battle of America, and the Battle of America is the Battle of the Negro. . . ."

If England's fight to maintain its death grip on the colonies is the Battle of the Negro, one may logically ask, why give only aid "short of war"? Randolph's only answer, when Roosevelt and the Sixty Families* give the word, will be: "That's right, we've got to get into the war too." And again, Randolph will have no answer to those who try to point the correct path to the workers of the world: uniting Negro and white against the imperialist gangsters on both sides and taking power to set up a socialist society.

*Referring to the ruling class as the Sixty Families began with the publication of Ferdinand Lundberg's book *America's Sixty Families* in 1937. The book illustrates the economic and political power of the superrich.

WHO HELPS HITLER?

Under the title, "Beware of Disunity," printed in this week's *Pittsburgh Courier*, Edward Lawson, managing editor of *Opportunity* magazine, has written the most nonsensical and disgusting article that has yet appeared anywhere on the question of the Negro in the present war crisis.

Lawson starts off by quoting a recent statement of the National Urban League: "The Negro must guard against the possibility that, in the excitement of the nation-wide defense program,

By Albert Parker. From *Militant*, February 22, 1941. *Opportunity* was the magazine of the National Urban League.

propagandists for various groups will attempt to stir up trouble between white and colored people."

On this he comments: "Today that possibility is a reality. In the press, on the radio, in countless letters and handbills—and even more often by word of mouth—we are hearing today the cry, 'Let's solve our own problems here in the United States before we presume to interfere in the problems that beset the European nations.'" He points to recent statements of Dr. Robert Hutchins, president of the University of Chicago; Dr. Emmett J. Scott, leading Negro Republican; and John P. Davis, executive secretary of the National Negro Congress, to show that each (for different reasons) has advocated this view.

Lawson claims he doesn't want to argue about the truth of their statements about conditions in this country, that he is willing to admit them. "But also," he says in the same breath, such statements are "dangerous." And why?

> . . . because they paint for us an illusion . . . that all our problems could be solved in one brief period of readjustment. . . . because, by oversimplifying a many-faceted situation, they lead to false hope. . . . because in their logical development they would set one race against another, here in America, at a time when we need more than anything else complete unity of spirit and full co-operation. . . . because, intentionally or not, they dovetail neatly into Hitler's technique of propaganda against the democracies, which is divide and move in.

Later he asks, "Could it be that Messrs. Hutchins, Scott, Davis, et al., are helping him [Hitler] to do this little job?"

The other little nugget in this treacherous article of Lawson's is the following idea:

> If America were a totalitarian state, and if the dictator were sympathetic and fair-minded in his attitude toward minority groups, everything the Negro now desires could be accomplished overnight, by one stroke of the dictator's pen, or one sweep of his sword.
>
> Because America is a Democracy, the changes which we all desire for the betterment of our lives must come gradually through what we call the Democratic process.
>
> Those who would substitute some other process should first be required to demonstrate that their method would be more advantageous to us than the one we already have.

Now we do not mention all this because we are particularly interested in defending any of the three men whom Lawson attacks. Hutchins is an isolationist who never before showed any interest in the Negro's problems. Scott is a Republican, seeking to make political capital among the Negroes for his brand of capitalist politics. Davis is a Stalinist, interested in winning support among Negroes for Stalin's foreign policy.

But we *are* interested in defending the idea that Negroes have no reason to support this so-called war for democracy when they themselves are deprived of democracy by the capitalist class preparing this war.

What is the "disunity" that Lawson talks about? He is talking about disunity between the Negro and the bosses who Jim Crow the Negro. To Lawson, asking for equal rights for the Negro is "disunity." Beware of asking for your rights, is what he is warning the Negro people.

It is fair to ask: Whose little job is Lawson doing? Is he helping the Negro or is he helping Senators Bilbo and Cotton Ed Smith when he tells the Negro to beware of fighting for his rights? Using Lawson's own logic, one could easily assert that, "intentionally or not," he is helping the cause of white supremacy.

Lawson says, in effect, that Hitler is helped by a struggle for equal rights for Negroes. This is a lie. Hitler could never be helped by a struggle to wipe out racial discrimination; he is greatly weakened in his own country whenever the idea of racial superiority is wiped out anywhere in the entire world. On the contrary, Hitler (and the American Bilbos) are greatly helped whenever anyone tries to tone down the struggle for racial equality.

Nowhere in his entire article does Lawson advocate a struggle against Jim Crowism in the armed forces or in civilian life. This omission by a so-called Negro leader is treachery to his people.

We ask Lawson: How was the Negro emancipated? By gradualness? Or by civil war? With Lawson's method, the Negro would still be a slave. And what has happened since 1877? The policy of gradual improvement has been followed, especially as exemplified by Booker T. Washington, and with what results? The Negro doesn't have a single right more today than he had then. Thus history has tested Lawson's method.

We reject both the fairy tale about the benevolent dictator and the falsehood about the gradual method, and we stick to our own policy of Negro and white labor unity against capitalist oppression and discrimination, in peacetime and in wartime.

RUNAROUND IN NASHVILLE

A classical example of the endless circle of the runaround being given Negro labor by both the government and the bosses can be observed in the story of the Nashville, Tennessee, branch of the NAACP, which has been carrying on an active campaign to attempt to get Negroes into industry.

First the branch tried to get a defense training course from the government and the local school board so that Negroes would be able to get some training and qualify for skilled and semiskilled jobs in the Nashville plant of the Vultee Aircraft Company.

But the local school board replied that there was little chance of such a course being opened to Negro workers, because the Vultee management would not employ Negroes "in skilled capacities, even if properly trained persons were available."

The branch then turned to the management of Vultee. The reply of the industrial relations manager was that they "do not now believe it advisable to include colored people with our regular working force. We may, at a later date, be in a position to add some colored people in minor capacities such as porters and cleaners."

From *Militant*, March 1, 1941.

BLACK TROOPS AND
THE FALL OF FRANCE

Last fall, Roosevelt laid down the law that Negro soldiers are to be segregated into separate regiments in his statement:

"The policy of the War Department is not to intermingle colored and white enlisted personnel in the same regimental organizations. This policy has proved satisfactory over a long period of years, and to make changes would produce situations destructive to morale and detrimental to the preparations for national defense."

In an effort to stem the nationwide protest that arose over this, Edgar G. Brown, an Uncle Tom "leader," endorsed this policy and called for its extension.

In our criticism of Brown, printed last November, we pointed out that not only does this policy in the armed forces place a stamp of approval on Jim Crowism and segregation in civilian life, but also that it directly involved the question of the life and safety of the Negro soldier in the segregated regiments. We said then:

As long as the Negroes are separated from the white soldiers, it is very easy for the labor-hating officer caste in charge of the army to pick them out for special assignment and work: as labor battalions, digging trenches and latrines, and as suicide squads, for the most dangerous work, where men's lives are thrown away cheaply."

Now, our charge that segregated regiments means more deaths has been proved to the hilt, in the European battles of the Second World War.

In the Battle of France, the Negro soldiers in the Senegalese and other African regiments were used purely and simply as a body-and-flesh barrier against the advance of the Nazi war machine. Hundreds of thousands of their lives were thrown away

---

By Albert Parker. From *Militant,* March 1 and 8, 1941.

by the French-British army commands in an attempt to save what was left of their white regiments.

All this is demonstrated in the reports of R. Walter Merguson in his current series in the *Pittsburgh Courier,* and in the first article of a series by William Veasey in the New Jersey *Herald News.* Both have just returned from Europe, where they were able to witness many of the events they write of and to talk to the Negro soldiers who managed to survive.

Merguson tells a story which has never before been printed, the account of what happened to at least a million Negro soldiers who were drawn out of the African colonies and into the French army as shock troops to stop the oncoming Nazi war machine.

No one has written about it before only because both the French and the Germans don't want the truth to come out, says Merguson. That truth is that these Negro soldiers were mowed down in cold blood! *No prisoners were taken.* These colored soldiers are not in Germany; they are not in any part of France, occupied or unoccupied; they were never sent back to Africa.

Veasey shows how the retreat from Dunkirk was made possible only by the sacrifice of scores of thousands of Negroes who were rushed up and thrown into the breach to hold up the Nazis long enough for the British soldiers to get away.*

If there were Negroes in the United States who didn't understand what Roosevelt's Jim Crow ruling meant before, they should certainly understand it now.

*As France was falling to the Nazis, more than 300,000 Allied troops were evacuated from Dunkirk across the English Channel in May-June 1940.

VIEWS FROM THE SOUTH

Duncan Aikman reports in his series of articles on the "national defense" program currently appearing in the *Washington Post:* "I found a widespread inclination throughout the South to look upon the defense crisis as another crisis in labor relations. Southerner after Southerner, in various economic brackets, said to me substantially this:

From *Militant,* March 15, 1941.

" 'We're not going to let the colored man come out of this war on top of the heap the way he did in the last one.'

"That means, and plenty of Southerners state it specifically, no colored officers, this time; no colored skilled labor training and, if avoidable, not even any colored combat regiments."

The Negro worker certainly did not come out on top of the heap in the last war, but what these southern crackers mean was that in the labor shortage of the last war many Negroes left the South for jobs in the industries of the North.

According to a speech at Kentucky State College by Robert Weaver, Negro administrative assistant of the advisory commission to the National Defense Council, the crackers need not worry about a repetition of what happened in the last war.

For the Negro is being kept out in the cold in the present industrial boom, according to Weaver, and from present indications, he will continue to be kept there. What is chiefly required by industry today is skilled and semiskilled labor. The Negro, by and large, has been and is denied the opportunity to get skilled training.

'INCONCEIVABLE,' SAYS THE GENERAL

A Washington dispatch from the Associated Negro Press reports:

No thought will be given to assigning colored doctors, dentists or nurses to centers where they might at any time be called upon to serve white soldiers, according to an official U.S. Army announcement.

This determination to confine colored professional personnel to troops of their own race was emphatically declared by Surgeon General McGhee, Friday, during a conference with members of a committee from the National Medical Association. . . .

The general, professing to represent Northern sentiment, said that under no circumstances could he see colored and white doctors working together in the same hospital or as examiners of recruits.

Advised that colored physicians had served white soldiers in recruiting stations during the World War, he said it was inconceivable to him that colored doctors could work on an examining team with white doctors, and that no attempt would be made to integrate them into white medical teams.

From *Militant,* March 29, 1941.

BILBO'S BILL AND THE GARVEYITES

Strange bedfellows have turned up around a bill to deport all American Negroes to Africa. Senator Bilbo of Mississippi, who stands for "white supremacy" and hates the Negroes, is the author of the bill. J. R. Stewart, successor to the late Marcus Garvey as president general of the Universal Negro Improvement Association, in a speech in Chicago early this month, endorsed the bill of the enemy of the Negro people in the following words: "As a long range measure, though not through any heartfelt benevolence, Bilbo of Mississippi has a bill which would deport us to Africa (Liberia). . . . I am not for Bilbo but I am for this bill and will fight to support it. . . ."

In other words, the Garvey movement, which once attracted the hopes of so many millions of Negroes, is now acting as the tail to the kite of America's outstanding exponent of "Negro inferiority."

From *Militant,* March 29, 1941.

WILLIAM PICKENS, NAACP LEADER

He Defends Southern Congressmen

The most disgusting article of the month by any Negro was the one by William Pickens in his Associated Negro Press column, "Views of the News."

In it Pickens complains that during a recent speech someone in the audience asked a question, trying to discover how he explained the fact that the most outspoken enemies of the Negro people, the southern congressmen in Washington, were like

By Albert Parker. From *Militant,* April 12, 1941.

himself violently in favor of the passage of the Lend-Lease Bill.

Pickens attempts to dodge the question by poking names and jibes at the person who asked the question. This is easy to do, for it is true, as Pickens says, that because your enemy stands for one thing, you do not *necessarily* and *automatically* stand for the opposite.

But still, when your enemy says the same thing as you about something that concerns your fate, it is necessary to stop and think about it and figure out why. Maybe he is wrong in taking that position—and on the other hand, maybe you are.

But Pickens does not do this. Instead, in order to justify his stand, he launches into a defense of the Jim-Crow, poll-tax, lynch-mob lovers who sit in Congress as representatives of the South! He says:

> Without the almost solid South behind our defense movements, the President would never have been able to make any progress with that movement. The southerners are Americans, and it happens to be that they are American next to the Negro American himself. The rest of the country is largely European and of other more recent foreign origins. . . . The southerner is a much older American, on the whole, than are the whites of the rest of the land.
>
> When it comes to an international problem, the southern whites and the blacks, if they use their heads instead of their gall bladders, are most apt to agree together. In defense of America the Negro, when he thinks, will be second to nobody, and the whites of Texas and South Carolina will be second to no white people. There is not great room for differences; the southern whites want to keep their national freedom and their rights— even their rights to keep trying to keep the Negro down. And the Negro wants to keep his American rights—his rights to fight like the devil against being kept down. Under Hitler or any foreigner, both of these Americans would lose their good American rights—for the foreigner would keep BOTH of us down—white and black.

What does all this blather of Pickens mean? This garbage about the southern Negro-haters being the best Americans? This bosses' argument about the northern and western workers, who hate war, being of "more recent foreign origins," being aliens and so on? This fear that the southern ruling class that oppresses the Negro people may lose its rights to oppress them? This false posing of the problem that if you are opposed to helping England win the war to control the 450 million colored people now under its heel, you are automatically in favor of having Hitler win it?

It means that Pickens is so bankrupt in his politics and his defense of the war plans of the Roosevelt government that he has to throw overboard everything he has been saying for the last twenty-five years. There is no other way to account for his defense of the Southern Bourbons and his veiled attacks on the progressive workers in the North. And there is no better example of our contention that you cannot at the same time logically be for the war and against the institutions which the war is intended to preserve. Only those who oppose the war can effectively fight for full equality for the colored people.

In his article, Pickens attempts to deride the person who asked him the question by telling the story that

Booker T. Washington used to tell about the old colored man's politics in "Reconstruction" days: The old man would go down to the town square, before election times, and lean against the telegraph poles and listen slyly to the talk of the white people, to hear how they intended to vote, and when asked about that interest, he explained it thusly: "Well, you see, I'm tryin' to find out how I must vote, and when I learn how the white folks is goin' to vote, I know that I must vote agin' it."

Pickens tells the story not only to sneer at his questioner, but also to sneer at the old man in the story, who doesn't have his education and his standing as a "leader."

But the old man, in my opinion, had a better grasp of politics, instinctive as it was, in his left foot than Pickens has in his whole body.

He Takes a Government Job

William Pickens has a new job. It is with the federal government, in the Treasury Department. He has left his job as branch director of the National Association for the Advancement of Colored People.

This is not surprising to those who have been watching his development in recent years. After all, he was spending more time and energy supporting the war than "advancing" the colored people. For every word he wrote about the conditions of the Negroes in the United States this last year, he wrote ten about how much tougher it would be for them under Hitler.

It is fitting for Pickens to do what he has done. Pickens should be paid by his real masters, the powers whom he really serves.

There has been a lot of sound and fury about the appointment. The Negro Democrats who supported Roosevelt last year feel

By Albert Parker. From *Militant,* May 24, 1941.

bitter because none of them got the job, which pays a reported $6,000 salary. They feel that Roosevelt should never have appointed a man like Pickens, who was an ardent supporter of Willkie last November.

They don't seem to understand what is involved. Pickens didn't get the job because of his position in the presidential elections. He got the job because of his position on something far more important: the war. Roosevelt picked him because he supports his war plans, and certainly Pickens stands out head and shoulders above all the other Negro misleaders when it comes to warmongering. He can show the others, both Democrats and Republicans, a lot of tricks at this game.

TWO BILLS ON DISCRIMINATION

Recently two bills pertaining to discrimination against Negroes in employment were passed.

One, in New York, amends the civil rights law and penal law to "make it unlawful for any person, firm, or corporation engaged to any extent whatsoever in the production, manufacture or distribution of military or naval material, equipment or supplies for the state of New York or for the federal government to refuse to employ any person in any capacity on account of the race, color, or creed of such persons." This measure is now awaiting the signature of the governor.

The other bill, already signed by the governor and now a law, was passed by the Kansas legislature. It prohibits any labor union in the state from being certified as a bargaining agency if it "discriminates against, bars or excludes from its membership any person because of race or color."

It is not hard to make predictions about these bills. The New York bill will be signed and made a law too. But it won't mean a thing so far as getting jobs for the Negroes. The employers will just stop saying they refuse to hire Negroes; they will just not hire them. And the Negro people will still have to continue their struggle to force open the doors of industry.

The Kansas law also will not help the Negroes. It will not change the attitude of those reactionary AFL union leaders who

From *Militant,* April 19, 1941.

now bar them from admission to unions. All it will do is enable the employers, who are really responsible for the lily-white ideas of their labor agents, to divert attention from their refusal to hire Negroes. And it will offer a handle to employers to attack and break up unions.

SIDNEY HILLMAN WRITES A LETTER

After many months of receiving complaints from Negro and labor organizations about the Jim Crow bars that keep Negroes from getting jobs in the vital industries, Sidney Hillman, labor front for the Office of Production Management, finally has written a letter. In this letter, sent to all manufacturers receiving contracts from the government, Hillman follows his usual practice of subordinating every other consideration to that of "national defense."

He is not interested in Jim Crowism in plants financed and in many cases built by the government because of the effect it has on the Negro people, who are largely confined to menial jobs as a result, but because of the effect it will have on the war plans of the capitalist government he is serving.

First he points out that current reports "indicate skilled labor shortage in a number of fields vital to defense production." This situation has been aggravated because "in many localities, qualified and available Negro workers are either being restricted to unskilled jobs, or barred from defense employment entirely." Then he goes on with his complaint:

Such practices are extremely wasteful of our human resources and prevent a total effort for national defense. They result in unnecessary migration of labor, in high rates of labor turnover, and they increase our present and future housing needs and social problems for defense workers.

Then follow his suggestions for correcting this situation:

All holders of defense contracts are urged to examine their employment and training policies at once to determine whether or not these policies make ample provision for the full utilization of Negro workers. Every

By Albert Parker. From *Militant,* May 3, 1941.

available source of labor capable of producing defense materials must be tapped in the present emergency.

Two things stand out in this letter.

First, Hillman is interested in Negroes being employed only because he doesn't want the war plans of the government disrupted. Second, his letter is not going to change the present situation at all.

It should be noted that the letter does not emphasize the need for hiring Negroes where there is no shortage of labor. This can be interpreted to mean that employers should take them where they can't get anyone else. The employers do just that anyhow. The most rabid Negro-hating employer will hire Negroes when he can't get anyone else, because his main interest is in making profit; and to make it, he needs workers, regardless of their race or color.

Even assuming that Hillman really wants Negroes to get jobs, and that his letter is not just a face-saving device, what does it amount to? Little more than nothing. Because the letter does not provide a single hint of a measure to do something about those plants that refuse to "examine" their policies and, worse yet, refuse to hire Negro labor as long as they can get other workers.

And so, because of the weakness of the letter and its lack of threat to take action against the employers who disregard it, we can confidently predict that nothing will come of it, any more than came of the no-discrimination statement issued several months ago by Knudsen, Hillman's partner. Not a Negro will get a job as the result of it.

CLASH AT FORT JACKSON

Editor:

I have a piece of interesting news from Fort Jackson. On April 20 we were bowling at Twin Lakes, which is now part of the military reservation. One of the alley boys asked us whether we had seen the MPs (Military Police) hurrying by, armed with riot guns. The boy stated that there was a riot at the fort, but knew no more about it.

The next morning we heard all sorts of rumors about clashes

A letter to the editor, *Militant,* May 3, 1941.

between colored and white troops. This was confirmed when the newspapers had to give the incident publicity in the form of a statement from the commanding officer.

This is the straight story as I was able to gather it from reliable eyewitness sources.

A few Negro soldiers were swimming in a pond on the reservation which is devoted to their exclusive use (one form of segregation practiced in the army of "democracy"). Some white CCC boys, who were in camp near the fort, began to use this pond and seized and ducked one of the Negro soldiers and almost drowned him. A fight immediately ensued.

The other Negro soldiers, being greatly outnumbered, sent for aid, and truckloads of colored soldiers shortly arrived on the scene. The fracas became very hot, but was finally broken up through intervention of a commanding officer.

When the officer's back was turned, the white CCC boys hurled rocks at the Negro soldiers and the fight began all over again.

A regiment of white Georgia national guardsmen had heard of the fight and had been told that eight white men had been killed. Without confirming this information, they all grabbed their arms and marched to the place where the Negroes were stationed and immediately took up battle formation.

The national guardsmen had two machine guns and opened fire with these and their rifles. Although they were under armed the undaunted Negro soldiers defended their lives, set up barricades, and returned the fire. The National Guard colonel tried to intervene and stop the fight, but was shouted down. I have it from absolutely reliable authority that the guardsmen were led by some of their officers.

Upon the threat that the entire Thirtieth Division would march on them, both sides ceased firing. Fortunately, no one was seriously hurt.

The significant part of this incident is the courageous spirit of the Negro soldiers. That they fought back in the deep South is astounding. It will give the general staff something to think about. There will probably be an "investigation" of the matter and the National Guard will be exonerated.

A Soldier

ARMY BREAKS AVIATION STRIKE

J. H. Kindelberger, president and general manager of North American Aviation, Inc., who last week said of the strikers in his plant, "I don't have to pay any more to my workers because most of them are young kids who spend their money on a flivver and a gal," is the same man who recently stated about the North American plant being built in Kansas City:

"Under no circumstances will Negroes be employed as aircraft workers or mechanics"—and that they would be hired only as janitors "regardless of their training as aircraft workers."

This is also the man of whom Secretary of War Stimson declared last week: "There are not enough like him. We do not want to do injury to such a man."

There were no Negroes employed by North American Aviation before the strike, when Kindelberger and the bosses were running the place. Now, when the government's army is running it, there are still no Negroes there and there is little likelihood that Roosevelt's army will permit Negroes to get jobs there during the period that they remain in control. It won't be until the workers themselves control the plants through democratically elected committees from the ranks of labor that Negroes will be able to secure employment in industry on a truly equal basis.

From *Militant*, June 21, 1941. On June 9 Roosevelt sent 3,500 federal troops to smash UAW picket lines at the Inglewood, California, North American Aviation plant. Management had provoked the strike when it refused to raise the minimum wage from forty to seventy-five cents an hour. The first U.S. military engagement of the war thus was fought on American soil against American workers.

THE MARCH ON WASHINGTON

Building the March

A committee of prominent Negroes headed by A. Philip Randolph, president of the Brotherhood of Sleeping Car Porters, is now engaged in furthering a march on Washington, which is scheduled to take place July 1.

Ten thousand Negroes, it is planned, will join in the march, demanding an end to Jim Crowism and discrimination in the armed forces and industry.

Certainly, if ever there was a time for the Negro people to take action against Jim Crowism and discrimination, this is the hour.

Never before has the plight of the Negro stood out so sharply against the national scene, now loud with talk about democracy and the rights of minority groups—somewhere else. Not even in 1917, just before this country entered the First World War, was there such a contrast between the treatment of the Negro and the high and shining words used to describe the advantage of living under capitalist democracy.

And now, as in 1917, there are misleaders who say that this is not the time for action, that the Negro people should wait.

By Albert Parker. From the Pioneer Publishers pamphlet *The Negro March on Washington*, June 1941, which was based on material in the *Militant*. A. Philip Randolph first called for the march in January, and definite plans for it were issued in May. The May 1 "Call to Negro America to March on Washington for Jobs and Equal Participation in National Defense on July 1, 1941," was issued by the Negroes' Committee to March on Washington for Equal Participation in National Defense, whose members were: Walter White, secretary of the NAACP; Rev. William Lloyd Innes; Lester B. Granger, executive secretary of the National Urban League; Frank B. Crosswaith; Layle Lane; Richard Parrish; Dr. Rayford W. Logan, history professor at Howard University and head of the Committee on National Defense; Henry K. Kraft; and A. Philip Randolph. Rev. Adam Clayton Powell, Jr., was later added to the committee.

"Wait," they say, "wait until later; don't take advantage of the crisis; let us show them how loyal we are, and they will treat us differently after the war is over."

But to do what these Uncle Toms urge would be to close our eyes to what happened last time. In 1917 the Negro people followed this advice, with tragic results. A larger proportion of Negroes than whites went into the army. They gave up their lives; they suffered insult and discrimination both in the American training camps and abroad in the AEF [American Expeditionary Forces]. And when it was all over, they were forced back into the same old Jim Crow straitjackets, Negroes who dared to continue wearing uniforms were lynched, and the Negro people did not have a single right or privilege in addition to those they had before the war.

Maybe the Negro misleaders can afford to wait—those who have soft jobs in the government, or are angling for them as a reward for their advice to sit and wait, or—that small top layer of Negroes who live well.

The Negroes dare not wait. The condition of the average Negro worker is getting worse. Nobody has all the figures—no government agency is anxious to collect them—but everyone knows that Negroes just aren't getting jobs in any numbers or of any importance in the booming war industries.

The old saying "last hired, first fired" applies as much as ever in the present expanding industrial picture. Most of the comparatively few jobs which Negroes are getting are the lower-paid occupations abandoned by workers getting employment in the strategic industries. Those jobs Negroes do get in the big industries are limited to the menial categories. The heads of big corporations controlling airplane and similar production have openly stated they refuse to hire Negroes except as janitors and similar categories. Most of the other corporations, more discreet, say nothing, but follow the same policy.

This would be bad enough for the Negro at any time, but it is critically serious because of the economic background against which it is taking place.

The cost of living is going up. As a result of profiteering and curtailed production of consumers' goods, food, shelter, and clothing cost more. The increased taxes to raise more money for the war machine hit the Negroes; before long these taxes will include sales taxes on everything workers use and income taxes on practically everyone working. All this is a heavy burden for the workers lucky enough to have halfway decent jobs. For the Negro people it is truly crushing.

Relief and WPA appropriations are being slashed. The argument that some workers have gotten jobs is being used to justify cuts in the individual relief allowances of those who aren't getting jobs. The argument that there is less unemployment is being used to justify discontinuance of most WPA projects, although they employ the people who haven't been able to get jobs. Since Negroes were the group that suffered the most in the depression, and since they find it hardest to get jobs today, these reductions in relief and WPA hit them the hardest.

In addition to being denied work, Negroes are being denied the right to learn how to work at skilled and semiskilled jobs. The usual argument of the officials in charge of the training schools is that there is no use in "wasting the training" when Negroes won't be able to get jobs afterward to utilize the training. To complete this picture, it should be remembered that one of the many alibis of employers who are put on the spot is that they can't find Negroes "qualified to handle skilled work."

In short, because the Negro is locked out of the war boom and because at the same time he is being forced to share the costs of the war program, his plight doesn't remain the same but grows constantly worse.

They won't take the Negro into the factories, but they take him into the armed forces. But not as an equal. He can die for democracy but he can't have it in life.

In the army, Negroes are separated off in segregated regiments. Roosevelt has said that it is in the interests of "national defense" that the Negro should be segregated this way; apparently he feels that a Jim Crow army can best carry on the kind of war for democracy that he wants.

Segregated regiments mean separate eating quarters, separate sleeping quarters, separate seats at the theaters; no Negro officer in command of white soldiers, practically no Negro officers in command of even Negro troops.

In the navy, the Negro is segregated too—into the kitchen. He can serve only as a mess attendant or cook or flunky. Regardless of his training or his inclinations, these are his only field of operations in the navy.

And if he objects, if he even writes a letter to the Negro press protesting the Jim Crow treatment he receives, as fifteen sailors on the U.S.S. *Philadelphia* did a few months ago, then he is thrown into the brig and faces court-martial and discharge "for the good of the service." This is what has already happened in peacetime; in wartime such a mild protest would be called mutiny and would almost certainly be punished with execution.

Negroes long clamored for admission into the air corps; finally they got—a segregated all-Negro squadron. Negro doctors asked admission into the army; they were admitted—but limited to attend to Negro troops. Other branches of the services, such as the marines and coast guard, are still closed to the Negro. If the government should open them, it would be on the same Jim Crow basis as the others.

The Uncle Toms have their little piece to say about this too: "Why fret about this?" they ask. As F. D. Patterson of Tuskegee Institute put it:

> We are asking for a lot of things that are not of immediate importance though they aim at noteworthy ideals. One that is of apparent import to a lot of people is that we should be integrated in companies and regiments with white soldiers, claiming that the discrimination of the nation's soldiers on the grounds of color and race is a breach of democratic procedure. All that is admirable, but what we should be concerned with at the moment is an opportunity to serve in any capacity. . . .

Scoundrels like Patterson try to make it appear that full equality is a "noteworthy ideal," but certainly not "of immediate importance." This is where they do their most treacherous work. Because full equality in the armed forces is an *immediate* necessity if the lives and safety of the Negro soldiers are not to be thrown wantonly away.

Segregation in the army serves a double role. First, it serves to remind the Negro soldier at every moment that although he is learning how to handle a gun, he is still regarded as a second-class citizen and is still considered not good enough to mingle with white soldiers.

Secondly, it lays the basis for life-and-death discrimination against the Negro soldier. Negroes in separate regiments can more easily be assigned to dirty work or extremely dangerous work than they could be if they were with white soldiers in mixed regiments. It is much easier to pick out a Negro regiment as a "suicide squad" than to pick the same number of individual Negro soldiers out of several mixed regiments for the same job.

The story of the fall of France is full of cases where the French general staff threw away the lives of the Negro colonial troops. They were thrown into the breach to die by the thousands when the general staff wanted to save the lives or the morale of white soldiers.

In short, unless the Negro wins full equality in the armed forces, his condition will not remain the same, but get worse.

Since the present war crisis began, numerous attempts by Negro leaders have been made to secure an end to Jim Crowism in industry and the armed forces.

Postcards have been mailed. Telegrams have been sent. Petitions have been signed and delivered. Fine speeches, loud speeches, have been made. Conferences have been held, many of them. Committees have gone to Washington, where they have seen the president and they have seen the congressmen. Congressional and state legislative investigations have been demanded. Bills abolishing discrimination in industry have been presented in Congress and passed by state legislatures. Orders have been issued by the heads of federal departments abolishing discrimination. The National Defense Council, under Knudsen, banned discrimination by employers executing government contracts. The Office of Production Management, through Hillman, has written a letter to all such employers urging the end of racial discrimination in hiring. Negro gentlemen, supposedly to protect the interests of the Negro masses, have been appointed to serve in advisory capacities in several governmental departments.

In spite of all this expenditure of time, energy, money, and effort by protesting Negroes, and all the government gestures, nothing substantial has been accomplished. The Negro people suffer from Jim Crowism as much as they ever did.

Nor need any Negro be surprised that this is so. Requests for improvement in the status of the Negro have been overlooked or stalled or rejected because the ruling class and its representatives in Washington felt that they had nothing to fear and nothing to lose if they did not grant the requests.

Washington saw that the leaders of these Negro committees and conferences and organizations were willing to do most of their fighting around a table, were not trying to involve the masses of Negroes in action or struggle, and were promising in advance that, regardless of what happened, they would always be loyal to American democracy, including its continued Jim Crowism.

Since that was the case, the rulers of the country were neither afraid of the petitions and the speeches and the resolutions, nor ready to take any steps outside of vague promises and the appointment of more Negro "advisors" to act as a front for their Jim Crow agencies.

It is against this picture that we can best understand and evaluate A. Philip Randolph's recent series of articles in the Negro press, calling for a march on Washington of ten thousand Negroes to protest against Jim Crow conditions; the establishment of the Negroes' Committee to March On Washington For Equal Participation In National Defense; the "Call to Negro America" issued by this committee; and the march itself.

That Randolph should write such a series of articles—which state substantially the facts we have outlined above—is an important sign of the depth of the crisis confronting the Negro people. In the last year Randolph has spent more time and energy speaking and writing in favor of all-out aid to Britain than he has spent on anything else. If he now turns to devoting some time advocating a march which by its very being constitutes an annihilating indictment of the democratic pretensions of the American imperialists, the rising tide of resentment among the Negroes must be high indeed.

Randolph has correctly described the national industrial and military situation:

> The whole National Defense set-up reeks and stinks with race prejudice, hatred and discrimination. . . .
> Responsible committees of Negroes who seek to intercede in behalf of the Negro being accorded the simple right to work in industries and on jobs serving National Defense and to serve in the Army, Navy and Air Corps, are given polite assurance that Negroes will be given a fair deal. But it all ends there. Nothing is actually done to stop discrimination.
> It seems to be apparent that even when well-meaning, responsible, top government officials agree upon a fair and favorable policy, there are loopholes, and subordinate officers in the Army, Navy and Air Corps, full of race hatred, who seek its contravention, nullification and evasion.

Randolph has had to recognize the impotence and weaknesses of the current Negro leadership and their methods even though he has many words of praise for them: "Evidently, the regular, normal and respectable method of conferences and petitions, while proper and ought to be continued as conditions warrant, certainly won't work. They don't do the job."

And, on the same theme, in another article: "Negroes cannot stop discrimination in National Defense with conferences of leaders and the intelligentsia alone. While conferences have merit, they won't get desired results by themselves."

Randolph states the need for organization and action by the Negro masses: "Power and pressure do not reside in the few, the intelligentsia, they lie in and flow from the masses. Power does not even rest with the masses as such. Power is the active principle of only the organized masses, the masses united for a definite purpose."

And then he calls for action in the form of a march of ten thousand Negroes to Washington:

> On to Washington, ten thousand black Americans! Let them swarm from every hamlet, village and town; from the highways and byways, out of the churches, lodges, homes, schools, mills, mines, factories and fields. Let them come in automobiles, buses, trains, trucks and on foot. Let them come though the winds blow and the rains beat against them, when the

date is set. We shall not call upon our white friends to march with us. There are some things Negroes must do alone. This is our fight and we must see it through. If it costs money to finance a march on Washington, let Negroes pay for it. If any sacrifices are to be made for Negro rights in national defense, let Negroes make them. If Negroes fail this chance for work, for freedom and training, it may never come again. Let the Negro masses speak!

The Socialist Workers Party, the Trotskyist movement in this country, was among the first to hail the progressive character of the proposal to march on Washington. We stated our position as follows:

A militant march on Washington, the national capital of Jim Crowism, a march made up of thousands of Negroes who will be able to get there only because hundreds of thousands of others support the march morally and financially—this would really strike fear into the hearts of the administration and the bosses. It would really put a spoke in their wheel at the time they are shrieking about "national unity" (at the expense of the workers) and taking the last steps prior to full entry into the war. It would give a real jolt to all the propaganda about a war "for democracy," put the issue of Jim Crowism on the high plane where it belongs, and organize the forces for a finish fight for full social, economic and political equality.

Correctly carried out demonstrations would also establish the Negroes as a force to be reckoned with by the conservative leaders of trade unions in the AFL, who are guilty of Jim Crow practices and could be used as a wedge for breaking down bars against Negro membership in those sections of the labor movement wherever they still exist.

Nor should it be forgotten that a correctly carried out struggle of this kind, even if *actively* supported at the start by only a minority of the Negro people, would be an inspiration and a source of new hope and courage to millions of other Negroes; would help to deepen and extend the local struggles of the Negroes throughout the North; and would undoubtedly serve to set off in the direction of organized struggle millions of Negroes in the South who are awaiting action from their brothers in other parts of the country, and who need only an inspiring example from the rest of the working class to set them into action on a wide scale at last. [*Militant,* May 17, 1941]

It should be obvious from this that our support of a march on Washington does not depend on any of Randolph's ideas at all. We support a militant action, not Randolph's reasons for it. We do this in the same way that we would support a strike of the union of which Randolph is president, in spite of our sharp differences with Randolph on many basic questions.

That is to say, our support of the march, while full and

wholehearted, is not uncritical. We feel it our duty, as part of our fight for full social, economic, and political equality for the Negroes, to indicate mistakes and shortcomings where we see them, and to urge Negro militants to correct them.

It is in this sense that we make our criticisms of the committee organized to put Randolph's proposals into effect, its "Call to Negro America," and its general policy.

Randolph says again and again in his articles: "Let the masses speak." But the masses had nothing to say about the composition of the committee or its functions. This committee has taken on itself the sole right of determining the slogans to be used and the work to be done in Washington.

A representative conference should have been called together before the final plans were adopted. At such a conference, representatives of different organizations that want to participate in the march could have worked out policy and strategy and elected a leading committee. This would have enabled participating organizations to help work out the policy, instead of putting them in a position, as Randolph has done, where they have only the choice of carrying out the Randolph committee's decisions or just not participating. Such a conference would not only have increased the publicity for the march, but it would also have improved the morale of those participating. The Negro workers would then really have felt that this was *their* march; something that is not truly accomplished by the mere device of excluding white workers.

Nor can Randolph object that "there wasn't time for that; we'd have wasted valuable time." This is not true. There was plenty of time for it between the time Randolph first presented the proposal in January and the time the handpicked committee issued the call in May.

Furthermore, at the time this is written, during the first week in June, less than a month before the march is to take place, there is no evidence that the masses, even on the eastern seaboard, have yet been reached and aroused by the organizers of the march. Most workers haven't even heard about it.

It is to be hoped that, in spite of the slow beginning, the masses and especially the workers in the trade unions will be mobilized to support the march during the weeks that still remain. The Socialist Workers Party is doing what it can to influence advanced workers to participate in this action. But if the march fails because of lack of support from the workers, it will be directly attributable to the bureaucratic organization of the whole affair.

In spite of many militant words and phrases, the "Call To

Negro America" suffers from the same half-heartedness that has characterized the other attempts by "respectable" Negro leaders to win concessions.

Certainly one of the key questions to be faced by any movement is the question of the war and the capitalist demand for "national unity." The exploiters mean that the workers should stop asking for higher wages and better conditions until the war is over. For the Negroes, "national unity" means suspension of the fight for equal rights until after the war is over.

The Randolph committee has no forthright answer to this question. Instead, it says:

But what of national unity? We believe in national unity which recognizes equal opportunity of black and white citizens to jobs in national defense and the armed forces, and in all other institutions and endeavors in America. We condemn all dictatorships: Fascist, Nazi and Communist. We are loyal, patriotic Americans, all.

But, if American democracy will not defend its defenders; if American democracy will not protect its protectors; if American democracy will not give jobs to its toilers because of race or color; if American democracy will not insure equality of opportunity, freedom and justice to its citizens, black and white, it is a hollow mockery and belies the principles for which it is supposed to stand.

Why all those ifs? Don't the committee's members know very well what is going on? Is there any real doubt in their minds as to exactly what is happening to the Negro? Hidden behind the ifs is a potential surrender of the fight for the rights of the Negro people. The bosses will think: "Never fear; this is only another bunch of people who are urging us to be good, but who are pledging their loyalty in advance."

Because the committee is afraid to take an out-and-out position on this key question, it weakens the effectiveness of the march. There can be only one correct answer to "national unity"; unity of the Negroes with the white workers against their common enemy and exploiter.

This is not the only instance of the call for the march making concessions to ideas looked on with favor by the ruling class. In another place it says:

However we sternly counsel against violence and ill-considered and intemperate action and abuse of power. Mass power, like physical, when misdirected, is more harmful than helpful.

We summon you to mass action that is orderly and lawful, but aggressive and militant, for justice, equality and freedom.

Crispus Attucks marched and died as a martyr for American independence. Nat Turner, Denmark Vesey, Gabriel, Harriet Tubman and Frederick Douglass fought, bled and died for the emancipation of Negro slaves and the preservation of American democracy.

Our criticism of this section of the call should not be mistaken to mean that the Socialist Workers Party is in favor of "ill-considered and intemperate action" or anything of the kind. Not at all.

But who is served by this reassurance that everything is going to be nice and respectable and within the "lawful" bounds established by the ruling class and its antilabor, Jim Crow legislatures and courts?

If we are going to talk about history, let us talk about it correctly. Did King George think that Crispus Attucks's action was "lawful"? Did the slaveholders of Virginia think that Nat Turner was "orderly"?

The trouble is that the Randolph committee members are too much concerned about what the powers that be may think about them. And as long as that is true, they lead a half-hearted fight, in spite of all their talk about aggressiveness and militancy.

Considerations such as these may seem trivial on first glance, but they help to determine the character of the entire march, and those who want a successful and meaningful march must think about and correct them.

The central demand of the committee is that Roosevelt issue an executive order abolishing discrimination in all government departments, the armed forces, and on all jobs holding government contracts. This Roosevelt will be asked to do when he is asked to address the marchers. The local demonstrations are supposed to ask their city councils to memorialize the president to issue such an order.

To fully understand this proposal, one should read the article written by Randolph himself, explaining the theory behind this demand. Printed in the April 12 *Afro-American,* it began this way:

"President Roosevelt can issue an executive order tomorrow to abolish discrimination in the Army, Navy, Air Corps, Marines, and on all defense contracts awarded by the Federal Government, on account of race or color, *and discriminations against colored people would promptly end"* (our emphasis).

If Randolph's statement means anything at all, it means that discrimination and segregation continue to exist in the government, the armed forces, and in industry, only because the president hasn't issued an order abolishing discrimination and segregation.

Can Randolph really believe that? He must know that Jim Crowism does not depend for its existence on the lack of executive orders abolishing it. Jim Crowism exists because it serves the interests of the capitalist ruling class to keep the working class divided along racial lines.

We are ready to support the Randolph committee's demand for President Roosevelt to issue an executive order abolishing discrimination. To force him to issue such an order would be a step forward in the struggle for abolition of racial discrimination. But only a step. Roosevelt's executive order would not be so very much more weighty than the laws and rulings and orders already on the books prohibiting discrimination. In spite of them, Jim Crow rides high.

Randolph should recall one of the statements he made when he first called for the march: ". . . even when . . . top government officials agree upon a fair and favorable policy, there are loopholes, and subordinate officers in the Army, Navy, and Air Corps, full of race hatred, who seek its contravention, nullification and evasion."

How can Randolph square his January statement with his statement in April that a presidential decree would "promptly" end discrimination?

He can't, and he doesn't try to. He ignores this very important point, which means that he ignores the facts that touch the heart of the problem:

Industry is in the hands of an employer class which fosters and strengthens anti-Negro prejudices in order to be able to more easily exploit workers of all races.

Military training is in the hands of a hardened antilabor and therefore anti-Negro bureaucratic military caste which is dedicated to the maintenance in military life of every form of racial discrimination that exists in civilian life.

The government is in the hands of a warmongering administration that is notorious for its indifference to the needs and desires of the Negro people. The two big capitalist parties take turns when they are in power in kicking around legislation such as the antilynch bill and the poll tax bill.

In other words, far more important than the question of a presidential order which would merely echo other ignored laws and rulings, is the question of *control*.

An executive order abolishing discrimination would remain

largely on paper, as long as control of industry, military training, and the government remain in the hands of the enemies of the Negroes.

A movement that denies these facts or tries to ignore them cannot successfully lead the struggle for full equality. A movement that shuts its eyes or refuses to open them is good only for sleeping.

Negroes must fight for more than a presidential executive order. They must fight for a program that will take control out of the hands of the enemies of the Negro people.

Employers controlling the war industries won't hire Negroes? Then have the government take those industries over, and let them be managed and operated without discrimination by committees elected by the workers.

Negroes need military training in this epoch when all major questions are decided arms in hand. But the army bureaucrats are bitterly anti-Negro and determined to "keep them in their place." Therefore, Negroes must join the fight for military training, financed by the government but under control of the trade unions, based on full equality for the Negroes.

The government and the capitalist parties aid the bosses in segregating and discriminating against the Negro people, refusing to pass such elementary legislation as punishing lynching and granting the Negroes in the South the right to vote. Therefore, aid in the formation of an independent labor party pledged to carry on the Negroes' struggles. An independent labor party pledged to establish a workers' and farmers' government that would create a new society that would forever abolish poverty, war, and racial discrimination.

Such a program, aimed at putting control of their destiny into the hands of the workers themselves, black and white—in military training, in industry, in politics—this *must* become the program of the militant Negro workers. This is the road to jobs and equality.

The Negro misleaders will say that this program is impractical and utopian. That is what Uncle Tom said about freedom for the slaves.

But the fighting program we propose is infinitely more realistic than expecting Roosevelt—the partner of the southern Democrats and ally of the British Empire which oppresses Negroes on every continent—to abolish discrimination.

The Socialist Workers Party supports the march on Washington. We call on the Negro workers to bring forward in the march a really militant program. If this is done, the march on Washington, whatever its immediate results, would serve to be an important stage in the fight to change the world.

Answering the Courier's Attack

The July 1 march on Washington to demand the abolition of discrimination against the Negro people in employment and the armed forces is a project worthy of the support of every Negro and white worker. It is worthy of support in spite of the fact that its organizers (A. Philip Randolph and his friends) have not done too good a job of arousing and mobilizing the Negro masses behind it, and in spite of the fact that its demands are not formulated very well.

The march is worthy of support because essentially it is an *action* against the system of Jim Crowism that segregates and discriminates against Negroes wherever they go.

The Negro masses themselves have had no difficulty in seeing this. Everywhere, the local March on Washington Committees report the workers, whenever they have been reached, have dug into their pockets and donated and volunteered for the march— and the questions they have asked have not been "Should we support the march?" but "How can we make this march more successful?"

But while the Negro masses have grasped the need for the march immediately, some sections of the Negro intellectuals have been unable to do the same. A typical example is the editorial writer of the *Pittsburgh Courier* this week, who says:

> Nothing is going to be accomplished by the crackpot proposal of A. Philip Randolph and his associates to stage a march on Washington in protest against color discrimination in national defense.
>
> Marches on Washington have always failed of their purpose because Congress has regarded them merely as nuisances organized by publicity hounds, job-hunters and addle-pates, and consisting of the mob-minded and misguided. . . .

In order to justify this language, exactly the same language that will be used by the Negro-hating poll tax Democratic

By Albert Parker. From *Militant,* June 21, 1941.

legislators in Washington on July 1, the *Courier* editorial writer continues:

Led by the *Pittsburgh Courier,* which has spent thousands of dollars during the past four years in enlightening public opinion about color discrimination in national defense, colored people have so flooded their Congressmen, Senators and the President with protests that not a single official in Washington is unaware of the evil.

Can a parade tell them anything they do not already know?

Randolph's group is loudly claiming that they will have between 50,000 and 100,000 Negroes parading in Washington on July 1, 1941.

This will be a great boon to the railroad companies and to the oil and gas stations in Washington and vicinity, but it will certainly be a hardship on the marchers.

The most effective way of influencing Congress and the Administration is by personal letters and telegrams from individuals, societies, church congregations, clubs and fraternities; by memorials and resolutions sent to both Houses and by intelligent personal representations.

And the rest of the editorial is devoted to the fact that even one thousand Negroes would swamp the eating and housing facilities in Washington, and to the prophecy that because of the heat and other difficulties, "there will be far less than the heralded 50,000 Negroes present on that date."

A parade will not tell the Washington administration anything they do not already know about the evil effects of Jim Crowism on the Negro people. If all the parade were intended for was to make the congressmen "aware of the evil," it would indeed be a waste of time. But this line of argument, as the *Courier* editors know well enough, doesn't really touch the point of the march.

A successful and gigantic demonstration in Washington that presented a militant set of demands on the administration, a demonstration that showed that the Negro people are ready to do more than send telegrams, that showed they are ready to fight. Jim Crow—that would certainly tell Washington something it doesn't already know!

The *Courier* editorial writer describes "the most effective way of influencing Congress and the Administration." What has come of this "most effective way"?

What good have all the resolutions, letters, telegrams, memorials, and "intelligent personal representations" done so far? Has it gotten any jobs in the war industries? Has it diminished by one inch the segregation in the armed forces? If that is really "the most effective way," then there isn't much hope.

But the masses know that isn't the most effective way at all. They know from their own daily experiences that you don't get anything unless you're ready to put up a fight for it, that you don't get higher wages by writing a letter but by organizing your fellow workers and putting up a united, militant struggle against your exploiters. Those who exaggerate the difficulties of a fight usually are not around when it takes place.

And this *Courier* editorial writer certainly has a nerve saying that the march "will be a great boon to the railroad companies and to the oil and gas stations." Using this kind of logic, one could easily condemn the *Courier* and its methods of fighting Jim Crow as a great boon to the telegraph companies, the post office, and the ink manufacturers.

The Socialist Workers Party rejects the defeatist, nonstruggle policies of the *Courier*'s editorial writer, and calls on all workers to join and to build the march on Washington into a powerful manifestation of the Negroes' intention to fight to the death against all forms of Jim Crow.

The same day that the *Courier* broke its silence on the march to come out against it, the *Daily Worker* and the Communist Party broke their silence to come out in critical support of the march.

The long silence of the Stalinists on the question indicated that they would have been glad to duck it altogether. That this was so was shown by the hands-off attitude of the local Stalinists wherever the march was being organized.

However, their failure to find a reason to justify nonsupport of the march, and the pressure they must have felt from those Negro workers with whom they are in contact, must have driven them at the last moment to a declaration of qualified support. Just what else they will do besides this remains yet to be seen.

Pressure from the White House

As the day of the July 1 Negro march on Washington draws closer, numerous attempts are being made to exert pressure on the organizers of the march to call it off. These attempts include "advice" and hardly veiled threats from so-called friends, government officials, and Negro misleaders.

The coming march on Washington has the government worried. It will be a strong and telling condemnation of the hypocritical talk about saving the world for democracy. The refusal to grant the just and simple demands of the marchers will be a real

By Albert Parker. From *Militant*, June 28, 1941.

eye-opener to hundreds of thousands of Negroes as to the true character of the Roosevelt administration and the war it is preparing.

The main gun in this drive to stifle the march was fired by Roosevelt himself, in his memorandum to the OPM on Negro employment.* Roosevelt hoped that this memorandum would satisfy the leaders of the march and persuade them to call it off. But the leaders of the march just could not do this, when so little had actually been offered by Roosevelt.

A. Philip Randolph declared: "The statement of the president is one which was expected ten months ago. It has no teeth in it and it's not a proclamation or executive order which would give assurance of discontinuance of discrimination. Therefore the mobilization effort for the march on Washington is being redoubled."

Walter White of the NAACP stated that "the president's statement is about six months late. What Negroes want now is action, not words."

Later in the week, unfortunately, both Randolph and White began to give in a little under the pressure of Washington, but both still asserted that the march would go through as planned. Randolph said: "It is not only the president who must be impressed with the gravity of the Negro situation. . . ." White said: "The president's memorandum, sound and democratic in principle, is too little when one considers the areas it leaves untouched, and comes too late to convince the committee that a mass demonstration isn't needed to dramatize race discrimination in the nation's life." After all, Randolph and White were also under pressure from the Negro people who want the march.

An example of how the masses responded to the cry that the Roosevelt memorandum was a victory was shown in the statement by one of the rank-and-file members of the Harlem march committee who said: "Even if this is a victory, that's no reason why we can't hold a victory demonstration in Washington!"

The administration did not content itself with utilizing the

---

*Roosevelt's memorandum on June 15 merely approved the action of the Office of Production Management in sending a letter to all employers in April asking them to "examine whether or not" their employment policies "make ample provision for the full utilization of available and competent Negro workers." The memorandum was greeted with blazing but inaccurate headlines in the Black press. For example, the *Pittsburgh Courier*: "JOBS FOR ALL—ROOSEVELT: Nation's Chief Executive Orders OPM to Halt Discrimination in All U.S. Defense Industries." As though to clinch the matter, the *Courier* head on the continuation of the story says: "Roosevelt Ends Industrial Bias."

services of the male half of the family. After all, while Roosevelt has kept quiet on all these questions for years, his wife has built herself quite a reputation as a "friend of the Negroes." So she too went into action.

First she wrote a letter to Randolph:

> I have talked over your letter with the President and I feel very strongly that your group is making a very grave mistake at the present time to allow this march to take place. I am afraid it will set back the progress which is being made, in the Army at least, towards better opportunities and less segregation.
>
> I feel that if any incident occurs as a result of this, it may engender so much bitterness that it will create in Congress even more solid opposition from certain groups than we have had in the past. . . .

This was followed by a surprise visit by Mrs. Roosevelt to New York, where, in La Guardia's office, she and the Little Flower attempted to persuade Randolph and White in person.

Randolph and White were not convinced, they said afterwards, but they certainly did not help the march any when they issued Mrs. Roosevelt's letter a little later with the brief statement that the march would produce beneficial results, but presenting her letter as the expression of "an important point of view from not only an influential person in American affairs but a strong and definite friend of the Negro. There is no question that can rise in the minds of the Negroes about the fact that she is a real and genuine friend of the race."

By not answering point for point what she had said, and by characterizing her as a "friend of the race," Randolph and White weaken the fight.

Eleanor Roosevelt's letter is not that of a friend, but that of an enemy disguising herself as a friend. For what is her letter but a half-threat? A half-threat that the march will "set back the progress which is being made, in the Army at least" (what progress?).

What is this talk of hers about an "incident"? Who will create the incident? Not the marchers. If any incident occurs, it will be brought about by the administration or its underlings. All Roosevelt need do to prevent any incidents when the marchers arrive in Washington, is grant their demands. It is significant that when Mrs. Roosevelt spoke to her husband, she evidently did not try to persuade him that he should do this, and thus avoid incidents.

It is just because she has the reputation of being a friend that Randolph and White should have taken extra steps to expose her letter and her attitude, and to explain that if she were a friend of the Negroes she would spend more time trying to convince her husband to grant the demands of the Negroes and less trying to convince the Negroes to withdraw their demands.

Congressman Arthur Mitchell, the only Negro member of Congress, chimed in and attacked the march too. The effects of this, of course, will be little, inasmuch as Mitchell has completely discredited himself before the Negroes by his endorsement of Roosevelt's appointment of Negro-hating Senator Byrnes to the Supreme Court.

The official cabinet members and their "family" followed up with telegrams to Randolph, urging him to come to Washington to meet with Stimson and Knox. The *Chicago Defender* states: "Though the purposes of the conferences were not mentioned in the invitations, it was expected that both secretaries would offer to correct some of the abuses which have angered Negroes if the parade plans are abandoned."

Thus, better than anything the March on Washington Committee might have said or done, the true significance of the march is being revealed in the frantic efforts of the Roosevelt administration to stifle it.

The March Is Cancelled

The Negro march on Washington, scheduled for July 1, has been called off.

Thousands of Negroes preparing to leave for the demonstration, with the promises of the official march leaders still ringing in their ears, at the last minute heard A. Philip Randolph over the radio Saturday night declare that "the march is unnecessary at this time" and therefore the committee in charge has called it off.

Thus ended a hectic ten-day period during which the Roosevelt administration had used every ace it had up its sleeve and which ended in the march being called off only because the Randolph-White leadership was willing to "compromise" and call it off if they were offered something they could use to save face before the thousands who insisted on the march going through until all their demands were granted. Roosevelt finally granted them this face-saving device in his executive order of June 25.

Last week the *Militant* reported that the leaders of the march were being subjected to all kinds of pressure from their "friends" in the administration, but that they were forced to resist it

By Albert Parker. From *Militant*, July 5, 1941.

because nothing concrete had been offered them as a bribe to call off the march. Then Randolph and Walter White were called to Washington.

Here, at a conference attended by many government officials, Roosevelt condescended to give his own views on the march.

He declared that the march was bad and unintelligent. He said that the march would give the impression to the American people that Negroes are seeking to exercise force to compel the government to do certain things and that this attitude would do more harm than good. (What the Negroes are really trying to get the government to do is to live up to the laws of the United States, the Constitution, and the Bill of Rights, which are supposed to guard all races against discrimination.)

Although Randolph pointed out that the demands of the marchers were completely just and reasonable, Roosevelt persisted that it was a grave mistake and would not accomplish the object sought, but on the contrary might create serious trouble. He did not state what this serious trouble was, nor who would create it. "What would happen if Irish and Jewish people were to march on Washington?" was the kind of argument he used.

Roosevelt refused to speak to the marchers, claiming that it is his policy not to talk to any groups who come to Washington. White replied that the president had spoken before the American Youth Congress a little over a year ago. Roosevelt became a little confused and said, "And you see what happened, too," referring to the fact that he had been booed by part of his audience.

When it was pointed out to Roosevelt that Negroes in the navy are permitted to serve only in the most menial and low-paid capacities, his reply was that the stokers on the ships performed even more menial work than the messmen. He deliberately avoided the point that white men who serve as stokers can also serve elsewhere, while Negroes are not permitted to serve anywhere but in the mess department.

Roosevelt then rose to go, saying that he wanted to see discrimination against Negroes eliminated in the war industries, and that he wanted the conference to continue without him. He suggested that perhaps much could be accomplished along these lines if a board were set up which would receive and investigate complaints of discrimination in industry.

Sidney Hillman claimed progress was being made by his office in breaking down discrimination. He was then asked if his office would withdraw a contract from a business concern that practiced discrimination. He evaded the question by saying that there are many factors involved and that "national defense has to come first."

In other words, the preparations for a fake war for democracy abroad are more important to him than the question of democracy at home.

Knudsen stated that he did not think an executive order necessary, that "more can be done through persuasion and education than through force."

This is the administration's attitude when it comes to dealing with the employers, but not when it comes to dealing with the workers, as was shown in the governmental strikebreaking at Inglewood, California.*

Then Secretary of the Navy Knox said he wanted to ask Randolph a direct question and that he hoped he would receive an honest reply. "Do you take the position that Negro and white sailors should be compelled to live together on ships?" Randolph replied in the affirmative, and Knox stated lamely that "in time of national defense, experiments of this kind cannot be carried on."

Here, better than anything else, is an indication of where the administration really stands on Jim Crowism. For if the head of the navy believes that it is a dangerous experiment for Negro and white to work together on ships, how can anyone expect the administration to be sincere in its efforts to see to it that Negro and white work together in the factories?

A committee headed by La Guardia was finally set up to make recommendations to Roosevelt, but as the conference ended it was still clear that no gains had been made, and Randolph again issued a statement that the march was still to be held.

The march leaders were under pressure not only from Roosevelt, but also from the masses supporting the march and insisting that it be carried out unless their full demands were granted.

On the evening of June 25, as the important Harlem march committee was making its final preparations for the march and a demonstration at New York City Hall before that, a telegram arrived from Randolph proclaiming "victory" and ordering the march to be held up.

Instead of securing the agreement of the local committees to calling off the march, Randolph went on the radio Saturday evening.

In his address, entitled "A Pledge of Unity," he declared that the march was "unnecessary at this time" and then referred to and quoted an executive order issued by Roosevelt on June 25. He explained that the committee had been intent on going through

*See page 95.

with the march until they got something with "teeth in it." Now they had the executive order.

In the order Roosevelt says:

I do hereby reaffirm the policy of the United States that there shall be no discrimination in the employment of workers in defense industries or government because of race, creed, color, or national origin; and I do hereby declare that it is the duty of employers and of labor organizations, in furtherance of said policy and of this order, to provide for the full and equitable participation of all workers in defense industries, without discrimination because of race, creed, color, or national origin.

And it is hereby ordered as follows:

1. All departments and agencies of the Government of the United States concerned with vocational and training programs for defense production shall take special measures to assure that such programs are administered without discrimination. . . .

2. All contracting agencies of the Government of the United States shall include in all defense contracts hereafter negotiated by them a provision obligating the contractor not to discriminate against any worker because of race, creed, color, or national origin.

3. There is established in the Office of Production Management a Committee on Fair Employment Practice consisting of five members to be appointed by the president. The Committee shall receive and investigate complaints of discrimination in violation of the provisions of this order and shall take appropriate steps to redress grievances which it finds to be valid.

It does not require great study of this document to understand that while it certainly is an executive order, it is not the executive order demanded by the marchers.

The most obvious shortcomings in the document are that it refers only to "defense" industries; it does not say a word about discrimination and segregation in the governmental departments and in the armed forces. Even Randolph had to recognize this in his speech.

But Randolph says nothing about the fact that the order refers only to contracts "hereafter negotiated" and thus leaves untouched the fifteen billion dollars worth of contracts already negotiated.

But even this is not the main point.

The order provides that future contracts must have a provision obligating the contractor not to discriminate. That is all right. But the question is—and this goes to the heart of this particular problem—suppose the contractor gets the contract containing this provision, and continues to practice discrimination?

What will happen then?

The answer is: The contract will not be withdrawn. This was

what was asked of Roosevelt. The fact that he didn't include it in his order is proof that contracts won't be withdrawn.

We could understand, although we would not agree to it, calling off or postponing the march for tactical reasons, after winning a partial victory that would meanwhile build up and maintain the morale of the Negro people.

But nothing was won, nothing at all, except a recognition by Roosevelt that a problem exists and an executive order that changes nothing basic and sets up the eighty-eighth committee to investigate and recommend.

Everything Randolph and White said a week ago about the memorandum still applies today. "It is not a proclamation or executive order which would give assurance of discontinuance of discrimination." "What Negroes want now is action, not words."

Randolph last week said: "Let the masses speak!" But now he says, "I'll decide the questions, not you." Randolph said, "Let the masses march!" Now he says, "It is unnecessary at this time." Randolph stands condemned by his own words. If there is anyone who still doubts this, let him go back into the files and read the statements Randolph made when he declared the march was necessary.

Partly in order to cover up his own betrayal of the march, Randolph has called "upon the Negro March on Washington Committees in various sections of the country to remain intact in order to watch and check how industries are observing the executive order the President has issued."

We of the Socialist Workers Party also want to warn the members of the local committees that their job is far from done.

Do not disband your committees but, on the contrary, build them stronger and larger. Get more members, more organizations, more trade unions to join in the fight. The mere threat of a march frightened Washington half out of its wits. Further organization, careful study of the problems involved, greater militancy will bring real concessions.

And in addition to building the committees, rank-and-file Negroes must take some steps to see to it that they are not again sold out. This movement does not belong to Randolph and Company. It belongs to the Negro masses, to those who contributed their time and their money to building up the movement—without which Randolph would not have been permitted to enter even the back door of the White House.

The movement belongs to the masses, and it is they who must decide its policies. This time Randolph cannot complain that there is no time for such things. Let the masses decide the policies of the movement, and let them select its leaders, let them appoint people whom they can trust to follow out their directions and aspirations.

'Second Emancipation Proclamation'?

A. Philip Randolph and a few others consider Roosevelt's executive order on Negroes and the war industries a "second Emancipation Proclamation." But apparently Roosevelt doesn't. He didn't speak about it over the radio; you won't see him reading the order in the newsreels; he didn't even hold a press conference on the matter, as he does on almost everything else, small or big.

The capitalist press gave the order practically no publicity.* (It would be interesting to find out how many newspapers south of the Mason-Dixon line even mentioned it.)

Randolph had to speak about the order over the radio since Roosevelt wouldn't. Hillman had to hold the press conference. Negroes had to wait for the Negro press to explain what the order was about, and those papers didn't do a very good job at it either.

All this indicates very clearly how important Roosevelt considers this so-called second Emancipation Proclamation.

Randolph had no trouble in getting his handpicked national committee in charge of the march to approve its "postponement, but not cancellation." But the national youth committee, which was not handpicked but was made up largely of delegates of different youth organizations, had a different attitude, and one which really represented the feelings of 95 percent of the rank-and-file supporters of the march.

At a meeting called to consider Randolph's report on why the march was being called off, the youth committee "voted 44 to 1 to repudiate the action of the national executive committee and to demand that the march be staged within 90 days" (*Pittsburgh Courier*).**

---

*The New York Times printed its report on page 12 (June 26, 1941).

**The meeting, held in New York on June 28, asked that local committees be consulted on such important decisions and urged that the march be rescheduled. Randolph charged that their attitude was "the inevitable outcome of manipulation by an artful and aggressive fraction that religiously follows the Communist Party line." He allowed no youth divisions in the later development of the March on Washington movement.

By Albert Parker. From *Militant,* July 12, 1941.

The *Chicago Defender* tells of a typical rank-and-file supporter of the march: "In Florida, a 77-year-old woman sold a member of the Office of Production Management staff a 'jobless march button' and swore that she was going to take part in the parade. She had money enough to carry her only as far as Savannah, Ga., which is about six or seven hundred miles short of her goal, but she was determined to get the rest of the distance and vowed she would make it if she had to walk."

What a far cry this is from the attitude of some of the leaders of the march, who had only to get into a Pullman train or a plane, and who were just as determined to see that the march did not go through!

Horace R. Cayton, labor editor of the *Pittsburgh Courier,* one of the speakers at the NAACP conference in Houston, describes a stirring speech by Robert Ming on the Negroes and the armed forces, and then says:

In one very real sense it was a pity that they did not stop the meeting then, for A. Philip Randolph followed Ming. Randolph made an apologetic statement which finally led up to the fact that "they" (I don't know who "they" were) had called off the march to Washington. His argument concerning the reason for calling off the march, as I understood it, was because the President had issued an executive order setting up a board for the purpose of integrating Negroes into the defense program. . . .

It sounded pretty thin when he stated it in the Good Hope Baptist Church; it sounds even worse when I write it today. Randolph has a lot of explaining to do, and so have all the rest mixed up in the direction of the march—and he didn't do it down here. Walter White, in the last mass meeting on Friday night, expressed his own dissatisfaction with the President's order and pointed out its weaknesses. He also, however, justified the calling off of the march.

First Effects of Executive Order

Since the Negro march on Washington was called off, the government has done nothing to implement Roosevelt's executive order which was supposed to do so much to end racial discrimination in the war industries. Yet most of the Negro "leaders" and papers have continued to shout themselves hoarse about the great significance of that executive order.

By Albert Parker. From *Militant,* July 19, 1941.

The reaction of neither the government nor the Negro leaders is half so significant, however, as the reaction of the big businessmen and industrialists who have until now continued to refuse Negroes employment in their factories.

Sam Lacy in the *Afro-American* last week reported on a hearing on housing problems held in Baltimore *after* the issuance of Roosevelt's order, in the course of which Glenn L. Martin, president of the big aircraft corporation bearing his name, was asked some very direct questions regarding the problem of employing Negroes, something his company has refused to do up to the present time.

For some reason Congressman Osmers of New Jersey, who was conducting the questioning, sought to get a statement from Martin with regard to the effects of the president's order.

Osmers began by asking Martin, to his great embarrassment, what the employment policy of his company was, whether it used Negro labor. Martin replied that it did not, and when asked why, explained as follows: "Because we have not been able to find a sufficient number of colored men skilled or being trained in the work in which they might be used. And because wherever vocational courses are being conducted in Baltimore there are not enough colored persons taking the courses to justify our consideration of them as likely prospects." (Lacy points out that the Martin plant has several thousand people taking training courses on the grounds and that the company refuses to admit Negroes to these courses as well as employment.)

Osmers asked Martin if lack of trained colored men was the only reason, and Martin replied: "Well, there are some other factors perhaps. I, personally, have nothing against the colored race, but if I hired them I would be forced to segregate them."

Pressed for an explanation of this, he said: "Because I'd be compelled to do so by policy. It is the policy of the State of Maryland to segregate colored people. They go to different theaters, different churches and different schools. They're segregated all over the State, therefore, I'd have no alternative."

But it was obvious that there was a real contradiction at this point. Even if Maryland practiced Jim Crowism, President Roosevelt had just issued an order which said there was to be no further discrimination in employment. Martin was trying to justify his vicious policies by pretending that he was only abiding by the laws of the state. But how could he justify that if the federal government had ordered that discrimination must be stopped? Was he "law abiding" only so far as the *state* went? Could he justify disregard of a federal order by reiterating his desire to abide by the state's laws?

Osmers then rushed to Martin's aid with a "leading question": "Is it a fact that should you place colored help in your plant you will face an immediate stoppage of work?"

Martin pounced on that excuse: "There would be an immediate stoppage of work. We know that. It couldn't be avoided."

Here we see the pretext that will be used by Martin and all the other bosses to justify disregard of the president's order. It is not they who want to keep Negro workers out of work, oh no, it is the workers who are responsible! And much as the bosses dislike it, they can't do anything because, after all, they are concerned only with "producing" for "national defense," aren't they?

Negroes must not be deceived by maneuvers of this kind. They must continue their struggle against the bosses, the government, and the Uncle Toms until they win full equality.

White workers must see through Martin's schemes too. By organizing militant unions that accept Negro workers as brothers and fight for their rights too, the white workers can defeat these attempts to fasten the blame for Jim Crowism on themselves, unite the ranks of the working class, and go forward to better conditions for all of labor.

THE NAZI INVASION OF THE USSR

Class conscious American Negroes must defend the Soviet Union against its imperialist enemies as part of their own struggle to abolish the system that starves, lynches, disfranchises, and Jim Crows them in this country.

We do not pretend that the Soviet Union is an ideal country, where all problems have been solved, where socialism has been reached. Not at all. But it is a workers' state, where power has been taken out of the hands of the employers and the landlords, where capitalist bosses no longer run the factories for their own profit, where the foundations for a better life have been laid.

By Albert Parker. From *Militant,* July 5 and 12, 1941. Germany's invasion of the Soviet Union on June 22, 1941, was a major turning point in the war. With the Stalin-Hitler pact destroyed and the Soviet Union in a desperate situation, the American Communist Party made a 180-degree turn and gave full support to Roosevelt's war drive. In the process, the CP tried to subordinate all social struggles, including that of Blacks, to support of the war.

The Soviet Union is like a large trade union, a workers' organization, which has fallen under the control of a group of reactionary bureaucrats who are concerned about the welfare not of the union, but of themselves. These bureaucrats often make deals with the bosses behind the backs of the workers; they don't permit the workers to determine the policies of the union; they don't fight properly to raise wages and better conditions of the rank and file; they expel and even beat up militant workers who take the floor to oppose their policies.

In such a situation it is the job of advanced workers to seek the support of the majority of the members of the union to replace the conservative leadership of the union with a militant leadership that will restore democracy in the union and lead it in struggles against the bosses.

The bosses attack the union; and the bureaucrats, who will have no job if there is no union, are forced in self-defense to declare a strike against the bosses. What should be the attitude of all the members of that union, and of all other unions?

Their attitude must be to defend the union against the bosses, in spite of their sharp differences with the union bureaucrats. The main enemy is the bosses. If the bosses win, there will be no union and there will be no chance for the rank and file to improve their union and their conditions. If the bosses win, not only will the bureaucrats be kicked out, but the union and the whole labor movement will be weakened.

In the same sense, advanced workers, Negro and white, must call for the defense of the Soviet Union. If the imperialist powers win, they will carve up the Soviet Union in the same way the bosses would break up a union.

We must never forget this principle: wherever a workers' organization comes into conflict with a capitalist state, wherever a workers' organization comes into conflict with the bosses, wherever an oppressed people come into conflict with their oppressors, we must support and defend the workers' state, the workers' organization, the oppressed people.

It was more or less along the lines of this principle that advanced workers supported and defended the recently called-off Negro march on Washington against its enemies and critics. We did not trust the leaders of the march, the Randolphs and Walter Whites, and we warned the masses that they would not conduct the march in the militant, independent manner required. We pointed out the weaknesses in their program and the bureaucratic way they had organized the march.

Nevertheless we supported the march and called on all workers to do the same. For essentially, in spite of its leadership, the march was a struggle between the Negro people with their labor allies on the one side, and the capitalist government protecting and sponsoring Jim Crowism on the other. If we hadn't supported the march, or if we had been neutral and indifferent, we would only have played into the hands of Jim Crow.

By defense of the Soviet Union, it must be understood first, we Trotskyists do not mean the same thing at all that the Stalinists do. They don't defend the same things we do, and they don't defend them in the same way.

What they defend in the Soviet Union first of all is Stalinism: the power and privileges and theories of the corrupt bureaucracy that has seized control of the state. What *we* defend is the remains of the greatest revolution of all time, the nationalized property relations, the economic foundation which if extended will lead to socialism and a new kind of society.

For example, a month ago, the Stalinists, feeling that the United States when it entered the war would probably be in an alliance directed against the Soviet Union, spent all their time denouncing the war preparations of the U.S. government and trying to keep it from entering the war with full military steps. As part of its propaganda, the Communist Party dealt with the Negro question and Jim Crowism, showing how false are Roosevelt's slogans about "a war for democracy."

Then came the Nazi invasion of the Soviet Union. And now the policy of the Stalinists in this country is not to "get out and stay out of the war," but to get into it as quickly as possible. As a result, almost every single correct argument the Stalinists used a month ago has today been thrown overboard. In order to get an alliance between Stalin and Roosevelt, the Stalinists are ready to drop everything else, including the struggle against Jim Crowism.

A concrete example of the change in their approach to the Negro problem is the recently called-off Negro march on Washington. Before the invasion of the Soviet Union, the Stalinists bitterly criticized the leaders of the march because they were tied to Roosevelt's war machine, because their demands were inadequate, because they did not demand that the government support the antilynch and anti-poll tax bills, because they did not demand that the government stay out of the war, etc. When the Roosevelt administration began to put pressure on Randolph and White and the other leaders of the march, in an attempt to get it called off, the *Daily Worker* warned the Negroes to be careful that they did not submit to the pressure and call off the march.

Then came the invasion. A few days later Randolph gave in to Roosevelt and, in return for a face-saving executive order which granted very little, called off the march. If this had happened a week earlier, the Stalinists would have raised holy hell, attacking and condemning Randolph. But since the Stalinists now had a new line, they uttered not a single word of criticism that the march had been called off. True, they saw what they called a few "loopholes" in Roosevelt's executive order, but their National Negro Congress called it "a great step forward."

We want to warn Negroes who watch the developments of the Stalinist line not to expect a complete and open reversal overnight. If they did this, they would quickly lose all the influence among the militant Negroes which they now have. They will not drop their demand for the passage of an antilynch bill, for instance. After all, many liberals who also support the imperialist war, still think it would be good to pass such a bill. But the Stalinists will no longer make much of a point of it, and certainly will support Roosevelt's war plans despite his refusal to back the antilynch bill.

As opposed to the Stalinist line, the Socialist Workers Party finds no contradiction between revolutionary defense of the Soviet Union and continuation of militant struggle for labor and Negro rights.

Class conscious Negroes must continue their struggle against Jim Crowism. Together with their white brothers, they must help to substitute for the present system of exploitation and discrimination, a system of socialist brotherhood which will help to solve our problems here and to defend the Soviet Union at the same time.

ROOSEVELT ATTACKS THE SWP

The Socialist Workers Party is under attack from the war-monger Roosevelt and his Gestapo-FBI because of our opposition to the war.

In the indictments against the twenty-nine defendants handed down by the St. Paul grand jury last week, it was charged that they were trying to get "members of the military and naval forces of the United States to become undisciplined, to complain about food, living conditions and missions to which they would be assigned, to create dissension, dissatisfaction and insubordination among the armed forces. . . ."

In other words, the government is trying to find a scapegoat to blame for the fact that black and white workers are dissatisfied with the present antilabor, Jim Crow regime in the army and navy.

But every Negro who is at all acquainted with the way Negro soldiers and sailors are segregated and discriminated against in the armed forces will quickly understand what the government is up to. This attack on the Socialist Workers Party, which has consistently fought for the rights of all workers, is also an attack on the right of the workers to seek equal and just treatment in the armed forces. For if the Socialist Workers Party can be indicted and suppressed because the party fights for an end to Jim Crowism in the armed forces, so can everyone else.

That is why Negro workers must rally to the defense of the twenty-nine defendants.

Roosevelt may attempt to suppress the activities of the Socialist Workers Party because of its consistent opposition to his war plans and its demand for military training under the trade

---

By Albert Parker. From *Militant,* July 26, 1941. In July 1941 the government got indictments against twenty-nine members of the SWP and the Teamsters union in Minneapolis. They were accused of conspiracy to overthrow the government, advocating the overthrow of the government, and distributing publications which "advised, counseled and urged" insubordination in the armed forces. In response, the SWP launched a major defense campaign.

unions—but that will not remove the smallest part of the dissatisfaction that now exists, any more than it will prevent our continued struggle against war, fascism, Jim Crowism, and unemployment.

ROOSEVELT PICKS SIX

After the Uncle Toms who condoned calling off the march had finished praising and extolling Roosevelt for his great "states-manlike" act, a behind-the-scenes struggle took place as to the composition of the five-man committee which would "investi-gate" all complaints of discrimination and "recommend" punitive and corrective steps to be taken.

Exactly what took place behind the scenes has not been revealed to the Negro people, whose welfare is involved. All that leaked out was that it had developed into a fight over the question: Should there be two Negroes on this committee, or only one?

In the end, Roosevelt solved the problem by appointing six men to the five-man committee—and among the six, two Negroes.

So that even if no Negroes have gotten jobs in industry as a result of Roosevelt's order, at least two of them have gotten posts with Roosevelt.

Picked to head the committee was one Mark F. Ethridge, a newspaper executive from the South, labeled a "southern liberal." This is to satisfy southern sentiment, and to assure the Jim Crow sections of the Democratic Party that they will not be "discrimi-nated" against.

The two Negroes are Earl B. Dickerson, Chicago alderman and a member of the board of directors of the NAACP, which endorsed the march on Washington when it was being organized and endorsed its being called off when Roosevelt made the request; and Milton P. Webster, vice-president of the Brotherhood of Sleeping Car Porters, of which Randolph is president.

Selected as representatives of organized labor were Philip

By Albert Parker. From *Militant,* August 2, 1941. Roosevelt's June 25 Executive Order No. 8802 established the five-person Fair Employment Practices Committee to "investigate complaints of discrimination" in war industries.

Murray, head of the CIO, which practices equality in admission and treatment of membership; and to compensate for him there was added William Green, president of the AFL, which refuses to do anything about the many affiliated international craft unions which bar Negroes from membership or admit them only to Jim Crow locals.

Representing business and industry is David Sarnoff, president of RCA. And with regard to industry and the Negro, Sarnoff certainly represents it in this case, for his own company hires practically no Negroes, with the exception of a few Negro salesmen and porters.

One thing these six men have in common: they are political supporters of the Roosevelt administration and its war program.

The committee does not have any real powers. Its job is to investigate what everybody of high school age knows, and to recommend corrective steps to a man who has shown that he doesn't want to take them.

Negroes who want job equality and who pin their faith to Roosevelt and his committee had better be prepared to live to a ripe old age before anything is done.

As always, the struggle for Negro rights continues to require mass action and mistrust in all promises, whether they come from white Jim Crow politicians or Negro Uncle Tom stooges for those politicians.

UAW CONVENTION ASKS FOR ACTION

It is clear that the United Automobile Workers, CIO, is fully awake to its responsibilities to the Negro workers, and understands that if it wants the aid of the Negro people in its struggles, it must do more than pass resolutions against Jim Crow—it must actively take up the struggle to win equality for the Negroes in the auto factories and in industry generally.

By Albert Parker. From *Militant,* August 23, 1941. The Sixth Annual Convention of the UAW was held August 4-16, 1941, in Buffalo, New York. In the main dispute at the convention, the conservative Reuther faction pushed through a constitutional amendment barring Communists (who were part of the more liberal faction led by George Addes) from holding office in the union. By this time the CP was just as prowar as Reuther, and after Pearl Harbor the UAW became the first union to adopt a no-strike pledge.

The convention of the union last week passed a resolution instructing all locals to fight for the following program:

1. Hiring of Negro workers in all departments in all auto, aircraft, and "defense" industries.

2. Equal opportunities for transfers, promotions, and training for Negro workers in all auto, aircraft, and "defense" plants.

The delegates made it clear that they wanted the officers to carry out this program without any fail.

One Negro delegate in a moving speech said, "We want to demonstrate we are men and we are brothers and we believe in the CIO." Most of the Negro auto workers have already demonstrated this. It is now up to their white brothers to understand that action on the job to fulfill the union's resolution will make the Negro workers the best and most loyal members of the union.

The convention also passed a resolution demanding abolition of the poll tax, which disfranchises millions of Negro and white workers and sharecroppers in the South.

THE CASE OF PVT. NED TURMAN

He Died Fighting for Democracy

Ned Turman, Negro draftee, died like a hero, fighting for democracy.

He did not have a hero's burial, but he joined the long list of fighters for Negro freedom and equality who were not afraid to risk everything, even their lives, in the struggle against oppression.

Like thousands of other young Negroes, Ned Turman was drafted into the United States Army and told he would be given military training to prepare him to help save the world for democracy.

But once he got into the army, at Fort Bragg, North Carolina, he found that the democracy he was being trained to defend was not supposed to include him.

He found that as a Negro he did not have the same rights and standing that other soldiers had. He found that he was not good enough to sleep in the same barracks that white soldiers used. He was not allowed to eat in the same mess hall. He could not drink

By Albert Parker. From *Militant,* August 23, 1941.

soda in the same post exchange. He was forbidden to play checkers in the same recreation hall.

He was good enough to serve as cannon fodder like white soldiers, but not together with them. He was segregated from the whites, shunted off on the side. He saw that there were practically no Negro officers, and none of these few could command white soldiers, while most of his own commanding officers were white. He saw only a handful of Negro military police. He saw that most of the MPs were deliberately recruited from among the most backward, prejudiced, southern whites—men who were accustomed to treating Negroes as so much dirt.

Ned Turman came from the South himself, from Ashton, South Carolina. Lynch mobs and persecution of Negroes because they failed to address a white man as Mister were nothing new to him. In the twenty-seven years of his life he had had plenty of chance to become acquainted with Jim Crow and oppression. He had never complained or tried to fight it before.

But now he was in the U.S. Army. He had expected things to be a little different now, to be treated halfway decently while he was in service. He had been in the army less than three months, and Roosevelt had asked for indefinite extension of the soldiers' terms. Ned Turman knew that this meant he would not be released until after the war was over.

There is no question that he, like the thousands of other Negro draftees, resented the way Negroes were being treated. In civilian life, Jim Crow is unbearable enough. But when he was being trained to die for democracy, he must have thought to himself many times that he would like to have a little of it himself, that he might just as soon die fighting for it here as anywhere else.

August 6 was payday for the men in Ned Turman's regiment, Battery C, Seventy-sixth Coast Artillery. With many others, he went to town that night, to "celebrate" in Fayetteville, to go to a Jim Crow movie house, to walk around and see the sights in the windows.

When Turman returned to the bus later that night, he was perfectly sober. Witnesses of what followed, who knew him, reported this to newspapermen from the *Pittsburgh Courier* and the *Afro-American*.

Turman entered the bus and sat down near the front. The bus driver refused to start back to the fort because he claimed that some of the men, colored and white, had been drinking and were too boisterous. He demanded MPs and the soldiers didn't like this.

They argued with him until seven or eight MPs showed up. They entered the bus and told the men to shut up. One of them,

Pvt. Mack C. Poole, continued to talk and the MPs began to savagely beat him over the head with their clubs. "It looked like the whole side of his head was caved in," one of the soldiers said later.

Ned Turman spoke up, said that Poole was in need of hospitalization, that he should be taken care of.

"Hospital, hell!" said the MP sergeant, E. L. Hargraves of Texas. "I'm going to take him to jail."

Evidently Turman repeated that he thought Poole needed medical attention. "Talking back" is what they call it in the South when a Negro tries to say something to a cracker.

Hargraves told him to shut up and struck him roughly on the shoulder. Turman threw up his hands to ward off the blow. In the South such an act is unpardonable. Crackers don't like Negroes to lift their hands to a white man, even in self-defense.

Hargraves began to club him over the head. At the same time an MP outside the bus began to strike at him through an open window. And the other MPs advanced to do their share.

Suddenly Turman broke away and produced a revolver. The *Pittsburgh Courier* reports that he cried out:

"I'm going to break up you MPs beating us colored soldiers!"

Those were his last words. He began shooting. Hargraves was killed, two other MPs wounded. When Turman's gun was empty, an MP who entered the bus from the back shot him dead.

A night of terror followed. All the five thousand Negroes at Fort Bragg were rounded up, cursed, beaten, and driven by MPs armed with sawed-off shotguns out of the camp to another nine miles away.

Ned Turman is dead. He will not receive any medals for what he did. The commanding officer at Fort Bragg has airily explained the tragedy by saying that there are always some "bad actors" in a large group of men. The MPs will be spurred on to even more savage acts by warnings of what happens when they don't shoot first.

But the Negro soldiers who saw and heard what he did say he died a hero. According to the *Courier,* "They make much of the fact that he had not been drinking and was not drunk. They thrill over his last words. . . ."

All friends of equality for the Negro people will honor the bravery of Ned Turman and defend his action against his Jim Crow defamers. But at the same time they must realize that while bravery and self-sacrifice are necessary in the struggle against discrimination and segregation, they are not enough.

Jim Crowism cannot be overthrown by individual acts, justified though these acts of protest may be. One man may be able to inspire others, but only a mass movement will actually destroy racial discrimination. And to do it, a mass movement must have the proper program.

This program must be based on unity of Negro and white workers in struggle against the creator of Jim Crowism, the system of capitalism itself that is also responsible for war and fascism and unemployment. To achieve this unity, it must fight for full social, economic, and political equality for the Negro people. It must also demand military training under control of the workers themselves to put an end to the Jim Crow practices now employed by the officer caste.

Negro workers can best honor the memory of Ned Turman and achieve the goal for which he gave his life by joining with the Socialist Workers Party around this fighting program.

The Army's Version

Finally, after three months, the office of the secretary of war has worked up and put out its whitewash version of what happened at Fort Bragg early last August when Pvt. Ned Turman, Negro draftee, was shot down for resisting brutal treatment of Negro soldiers by white military police who were following out the "treat 'em rough" policy that is applied toward Negro soldiers in the Jim Crow army that is being prepared for another "war for democracy."

About the only thing that isn't denied in the version put out by the War Department is that two men—Turman and a white MP— were shot to death. The reason they couldn't deny that was that two bodies lay there when the shooting ended, and it would be stretching it a little too far to say that they committed suicide.

All the rest of the story, with a few unimportant exceptions, flies in the face of all the previous reports given by eyewitnesses at the scene, and the daily papers and news services, the Negro newspapers, a personal investigator of the NAACP, and others.

If you believe the War Department, the white MPs did nothing wrong when they stepped on that bus on the night of August 6. All they did was push some people into seats and start to remove "one of the ringleaders." Then suddenly "a colored soldier" reached out and took the revolver out of the holster of the MP

By Albert Parker. From *Militant,* November 22, 1941.

who was later killed, and fired it six times. According to this story, the MP and Turman were both killed by this "unknown soldier"; Turman, the story goes, was not killed by the MP, Sergeant Owens, who was previously alleged to have killed Turman "in line of duty."

It is very strange how well this story serves the needs of the army officer caste, whose Jim Crow system was really responsible for the tragedy. For if you believe this story, Turman's death was an accident, and he didn't die defending his rights. Furthermore, his death was an accident caused not by the authorities, but by "a colored solider" who hasn't been caught yet, and who probably never will be caught.

The original story was very embarrassing to the army tops, but now they can say, "It wasn't our fault and it wasn't Turman's fault either." Thus they can clear their own skirts and at the same time make Negro draftees forget Turman's last words: "I'm going to break up you MPs beating us colored soldiers!" Turman becomes a victim of circumstances, and not a hero to those who thrilled at his behavior.

And thus the War Department's statement is able to say: "A noteworthy feature of the investigating officer's report is the finding that in no respect did the incident itself, or its after effects, acquire any semblance of a conflict of racial sentiments; and that the occurrence did not arise from, or cause, any tendency toward racial discrimination."

But this report is so raw, and so contradicts every report made up to now, that the War Department had to do something it hasn't often resorted to: it ordered Brig. Gen. Benjamin O. Davis, one of the few Negro officers in the army, to serve on the committee investigating the Fort Bragg affair. And of course, he arrived at the same conclusions that the others reached: everything was fine and dandy, only thing was to catch the unknown soldier who was responsible for the whole mess, and so on.

I don't know whom they expect to fool with such a whitewash report even though it is signed by a Negro general. One thing is sure: they're not fooling the hundreds of thousands of Negro soldiers who are still segregated, discriminated against, insulted, and kicked around just as they were before the report was thought up, and who know that Jim Crowism, not accidents, is responsible for Fort Bragg "incidents."

SIXTY SOLDIERS GO AWOL

Lt. Gen. Ben Lear is again having trouble with the soldiers of his command. Two months ago it was white troops who yoohooed at girls on a golf course. Now it is sixty Negro soldiers and noncommissioned officers who went AWOL from Camp Robinson, Arkansas, and attempted to hitchhike back to their home camp at Fort Custer, Michigan.

These men accepted the danger of a court-martial and long terms in military prisons rather than face the white terror recently intensified against Negro draftees throughout the South. Desertions by both white and Negro soldiers have been increasing throughout the country, but these sixty men and their brothers in the Ninety-fourth Engineer Battalion had received particularly striking demonstration of "democracy" under the fascist-minded army officers.

The Ninety-fourth Engineer Battalion is composed entirely of Negro soldiers but is officered by whites. The men were drafted mainly from Michigan, Ohio, Indiana, and Illinois, but were transferred to Arkansas to participate in the Second Army maneuvers now being conducted.

The southern bosses resented the presence of northern Negroes that "didn't know their place" and decided to teach them a few lessons.

The "lesson" is reported to have risen out of an incident in Little Rock, Arkansas, when a soldier was walking along the street with a young woman and happened to brush against a cop. The policeman immediately turned upon the Negro soldier and slapped him in the face. The soldier thereupon beat up the cop. Nothing more happened in Little Rock but the news spread throughout the area.

The following day some of the Ninety-fourth Battalion soldiers went into Gurdon, Arkansas, during their time off. They were immediately subject to abuse from the local police and state troopers. They were not only segregated in the Negro section of the

---

From *Militant,* September 13, 1941.

town, but forbidden to use most of the streets leading to and from that section. The state troopers attempted to run down the men with police cars, threatened them with guns, and yelled insulting remarks at them. Defensive action by the soldiers was prevented by the arrival of white army officers who herded the men back to camp and declared Gurdon would henceforth be off limits and no Negro would be allowed to visit it. Prescott, Arkansas, about twelve miles from camp, was then selected as "suitable" for Negroes.

That night a state trooper approached the camp and beat up a Negro sentry on duty. The sentry carried a gun but had no ammunition.

On August 13 the Ninety-fourth Battalion was marching in formation along a highway between Camp Robinson and Prescott when several carloads of state troopers drove up and yelled at the white lieutenants to "get those niggers off the highway." The police then began to slap and shove the soldiers into a ditch on the side of the road. The two white lieutenants in charge of the battalion protested that the police were interfering with military work. The police turned upon the lieutenants, called them "Yankee nigger-lovers," and slapped them in the face.

The soldiers were forced to continue to march in the ditch, sometimes through water kneedeep.

When the Ninety-fourth got back to camp, the soldiers demanded ammunition for their guns so that they could protect themselves from the bullets of the police. The officers told them that it was contrary to regulations, but assured them that "ample steps" would be taken for their protection.

Throughout these incidents, both in Gurdon and along the road to Prescott, white military police armed with clubs and guns were present. They never lifted a hand in defense of the soldiers.

Most of the soldiers, after leaving Camp Robinson, voluntarily surrendered themselves at northern military posts. They offered to return to Fort Custer in Michigan but begged not to be sent back to the white terror in the South.

They *were* returned to the South, however, and their commanding major magnanimously promised that they would not be considered as deserters, and would be punished "only" with extra and "less desirable" work assignments.

Major Harman then made it clear to the southern bosses that the Negroes would be more fully segregated, thus "obviating any difficulties."

Even this severity, however, did not meet with the approval of the major's superior. General Lear relieved him from command on the grounds that he had been "too easy with his men." Lear has not yet indicated just what sort of discipline he considers necessary in this case, but he has placed the entire blame for the trouble upon the Negroes and their "bad acting."

"The Ninety-fourth Engineers have disgusted me," Lear said this week. "You are the ones who started all this trouble and have disgraced the army and your race. I have watched you since you first started, and I want it all stopped now, not tomorrow, but today."

This is the same Lear who marched his white troops fifteen miles for yoohooing at girls; who sponsored an army manual which openly praised fascist ideas and methods; who recently said in a radio broadcast that *all* critics of the U.S. Army officers caste are inspired by "enemy agents."

There were a thousand Negroes in the Ninety-fourth Battalion when it was sent south. Practically all of them were drafted. There is no way of judging just how many believed that they were to be trained to defend "democracy," but they are rapidly learning what a bosses' army is like.

RANDOLPH URGES NEW MOBILIZATION

In an article printed in a number of Negro newspapers last week, A. Philip Randolph, president of the AFL Brotherhood of Sleeping Car Porters and national director of the March on Washington Committee, called for the organization of a million Negroes to fight against racial discrimination.

Negroes must no longer think in terms of little units, or small maneuvers. To this end, the March on Washington committees are out to enlist a million Negroes to increase the striking and driving power of the Negro masses for their rights.

Recent history in international and national affairs shows that it is not enough to be right. You must also be powerful. You must also build the machine with which to work and fight for justice. . . .

It was just, proper and right for the President to issue an Executive Order in the early stages of discriminations in national defense on account of race, color, religion or national origin as it was proper and just, June 25. But it never happened until the March on Washington movement was launched. . . .

A million Negroes speaking at one time behind one vital issue will

By Albert Parker. From *Militant,* September 27, 1941.

shake America and is certain to get a serious and respectful hearing.

Let the Negro masses speak through a million voices.

Randolph does not indicate whether he is just talking about something that would be nice or whether he plans to go ahead and take concrete steps to actually organize a Negro mass movement.

At any rate, his actual proposals are quite vague. Is the organization going to be democratically run? Are the masses going to have the decisive word about the organization's policies? Or is the organization to be controlled and directed from the top with a small committee not only making day-to-day organizational decisions but also the vital and fundamental decisions of policy?

All that Randolph has said on the question is this: "In it [the organization proposal] every Negro will count. The highest will be as low as the lowest and the lowest will be as high as the highest." This may be the answer in Randolph's own style. But then again it may only be an evasion of the question.

But Randolph has never asked the masses to decide *anything* of importance—the program of the march on Washington, whether the march should have been called off or carried through, the personnel on the national committee announced by Randolph after the march was called off.

Such a handling of questions is not only dangerous for the future of the proposed organization, but it also tends to hold back the initial steps. For many of the local committees will think: "If Randolph doesn't let us decide what our organization should do on a question like this, what reason do we have to believe that we will be permitted to decide policy later on? What guarantees then will we have against being sold down the river by a leadership over which we have no control?"

If Randolph's procedure in calling off the march last June had been correct—and we said before and after it happened that no greater mistake could be made—then he would not have to be coming before the people today and saying that a million Negroes are needed to be "certain to get a serious and respectful hearing" from the ruling class and its government.

We warned that nothing could come of deals with the Jim Crow forces, that Negroes must organize to fight them all the way through. Randolph's article is proof that we were correct, that his past procedure was incorrect and inadequate.

Negroes can learn much from the lessons of that march, and it is their duty to do so if they want within the proposed organization to avoid the mistakes its leaders have made in the past.

STEELWORKERS HIT MILITARY BIAS

Segregation and maltreatment of Negro soldiers in the United States army were sharply condemned by the regional conference of the Steel Workers Organizing Committee, CIO, meeting in Gary, Indiana, October 5.

The conference of 550 delegates, representing fifty-three SWOC locals in the Chicago area, unanimously passed a resolution demanding that Roosevelt take immediate action to end the vicious army Jim Crow system. The resolution also called on all CIO unions to organize action against discriminatory treatment of the Negroes in the army.

This action of the steelworkers is one further indication of the growing awareness in progressive union ranks of the undemocratic character of the army of American imperialism. It is an example also of the progressive efforts of the CIO unions, in contrast to the AFL, in fighting for the rights of the Negro workers, both in industry and the army.

It is clear from the attitude expressed by these steelworkers that there would be no Jim Crowism in military training if that training were under the control of the trade unions.

From *Militant*, October 25, 1941. The SWOC became the United Steelworkers of America in 1942.

FOR NEGRO LABOR COUNCILS

One of the great achievements of the CIO, among many others, was that it opened its doors wide to Negro workers, and especially the great bulk of them in the mass industries. This resulted not only in a more effective organization of the basic industries, but it also did much to build up a feeling of solidarity among the

By Albert Parker. From *Militant*, November 15, 1941.

white and Negro workers and to greatly increase the prounion sentiment among the Negro people generally.

Since the organization of the CIO, the Negro workers have been integrated into hundreds of local unions. They have attended their meetings in "peacetime" as well as done their full share on the picket lines in time of strike. They have been elected as officers and shop stewards and committeemen and responsible leaders in many shops, even where the Negro workers form only a small part of the membership. More and more Negroes have been selected as national organizers and representatives of their union, and sent in to organize new fields. On the whole, the Negro workers in the CIO feel that it is their home, and they belong in it.

But it would not be painting a true picture to let it go at that and say that complete and full equality for the Negro people exists in all the shops that have been unionized, even by the CIO.

By this I do not mean to say that it is the policy of the CIO or its affiliated unions to practice discrimination or segregation against its Negro members. Far from it. If in isolated instances in the CIO such Jim Crow practices are discovered, they are the exception to the rule, and should be reported and exposed and fought against, and undoubtedly the CIO national office would aid in such a fight.

But while there are no, or practically no, cases of such open discrimination in the CIO, that does not mean that there are no special problems for the Negro members in many situations. For even if the CIO does not discriminate, the employers and their managers still consider the Negro workers as "inferior" and do not hesitate to go out of their way in giving Negroes the dirtiest and lowest-paid jobs and in preventing them from advancing to better and skilled positions.

What is to be done in this situation? It is serious, for as long as it exists, many Negro workers will continue to feel that their white brothers are only paying lip-service to the idea of equality for the Negro workers, and in the end the employers may be able to turn them against the unions.

The answer is that the Negro workers in the unions—AFL as well as CIO—must get together as an organized force within the unions to bring these problems before the other workers and propose steps to correct them. They must organize Negro Labor Councils, or any other name you want to give it, which will concern themselves with the solution of the special problems facing Negro workers.

Does this mean separate unions? No. Does this mean separate Negro locals? No. Does this mean a body set up to fight against the regularly constituted locals in the various shops? No.

It simply means that the Negro workers will get together in their unions and in their cities to discuss how to best protect the interests of the Negro workers in the unions, how to bring unorganized Negroes into the unions, how to develop a more favorable attitude toward the unions among the nonunionized Negroes, and all other measures which will help to build the unions. They will not function separately from the unions, but as a matter of fact will try to get the unions to endorse their work and assist them in it.

Won't such a step antagonize many white workers? Not at all. As a matter of fact, the white workers will respect the Negroes all the more when they see that they are determined to build the unions and protect their own interests at the same time.

Is this a new idea? There is nothing new about it. For many years such a body of Jewish workers in New York did a very good job in helping to organize Yiddish-speaking workers into the unions. There have been various such groups in the history of the American labor movement. Many prominent Negroes have for a long time been advocating the formation of such councils—not to fight unionism, but to help it.

At the present time such bodies already exist in various parts of the country. Just recently there was organized a Midwest Negro Labor Council in Chicago, with representation from CIO and AFL unions. In many different local unions such bodies already exist and have done some good work.

What is necessary now is to spread and extend the formation of such councils everywhere. Negro delegates to the CIO convention in Detroit this week should discuss the matter and bring it before the convention for its approval. Such approval would be a real impetus to formation of these councils.

CIO VOWS TO UNIONIZE THE SOUTH

In spite of the strong prowar stand of the CIO convention and the general political retreat of the leadership, the discussions and decisions at Detroit dealt in a progressive way with many important and crucial problems of the American workers. The outstanding organizational decision of the convention was the firm resolve to organize the South.

The resolution unanimously adopted on this point put the CIO invasion of the reactionary, poll-tax, and open-shop South as point number one on the CIO agenda for the coming year.

Other militant resolutions which gave the convention a progressive aspect, such as attacks on the poll tax system, against Negro discrimination, against lynching and the like are linked with an all-out campaign to crack the vigilante Bourbon dictatorship in the South.

The CIO, with its ability to inspire all the exploited, has already made its first successes in the South. The victory of the United Mine Workers in abolishing the wage differential in southern mines, served to bring a ray of hope to southern workers, black and white, who have been given the dirty end of the stick in this country. The closed-shop contract achieved by the historical Ford strike victory established the CIO in Dallas. Cities such as Memphis, Birmingham, Atlanta, and Norfolk have been successfully opened up for organized labor by the CIO victories in mining, auto, and steel.

Sounding the tocsin for this drive to bring industrial unionism to the white and Negro workers in the South, President Philip Murray said to the CIO delegates, "That is your job. . . . Nobody

By Joe Andrews, a pen name of Jules Geller. From *Militant,* December 6, 1941. The fourth convention of the CIO was held in Detroit November 17-22, 1941. It ended just fifteen days before the bombing of Pearl Harbor, which led to Washington's formal entry into the war. The fine resolution and splendid words about organizing the South were all laid aside as the leaders of the CIO joined with the government and the capitalist class in subordinating everything to the winning of the war.

else is going to do it. Yes, the slogan of the National CIO for the ensuing year is going to be one of organizing the . . . great South . . . the great South must be organized before this convention meets next year!"

Murray further said, "Insofar as the CIO is concerned, there is not going to be anything to stand in our way of organizing the South during the current year. We have to do it, we are going to do it."

Delegate after delegate rose to his feet to support this bold slogan. And many CIO organizers, who had fought the union fight the hard way, during the past couple of years in the South, recounted tales of antiunion brutality equalled only by the labor-smashing violence of Hitler's storm troopers.

Delegate Mitch, of the Steel Workers Organizing Committee, formerly of the Mine Workers, told of the Mine Workers campaign in Alabama, in which organizers were shot and killed, where companies had their gunmen stationed at every mine in the state. He pointed out that it was the poll tax senators in Congress, representing those areas where the workers were unorganized and terrorized, who were the strongest advocates of vicious anti-labor legislation.

"When we talk about democracy," said Mitch, "we are not getting democracy here in our own country. We want democracy here . . . and we want to whip Hitler . . . but we want to whip these other Hitlers in this country. . . ."

Although a start has been made, the Deep South is today largely unorganized. It is still the domain of low wages, lynching, intimidation, and antilabor terror, ruled with an iron hand by the southern employers and landlords. As one delegate pointed out, "In the South there are millions of workers in textile, furniture, woodworking, and in farm labor that have had no chance to join the fold of the CIO. We are going to be confronted with a migration of northern industry into the South if something is not done to bring organization to those workers."

Delegate Baldanzi of the Textile Workers pointed out, "It must be a double-barrelled campaign. We must carry on the fight against the poll tax, we must carry on a fight for legislation, we must see to it our organizers are not beaten up and tarred and feathered. The workers in the South are ready for freedom, if we can provide leadership."

This delegate hit upon the kernel of the problem of organizing the South. That it is the most important organizational problem confronting the labor movement is unquestionable. But the full implications go far beyond an ordinary organizational campaign.

Any serious struggle to smash the open-shop rule of the

southern land and industrial barons will inevitably lead to a clash with the whole apparatus of the United States government, including President Roosevelt himself.

The whole apparatus of the Roosevelt administration is loaded down with labor-baiting poll tax congressmen from southern states; these congressmen are in the forefront of the current campaign in Congress to shackle and manacle the labor movement, and their purpose is above all to keep the labor movement out of the South.

The Roosevelt party's firmest base is these southern Democrats, who for years have been the most powerful force in that party's apparatus. Roosevelt has refused to push the antilynch bill in Congress, because he has feared a revolt on the part of these poll tax Democrats, whose support is so necessary for his war program. A CIO drive in the South would mean, therefore, opposition from the Roosevelt administration, in response to the demands of the southern congressmen and industrialists.

Added to this fact, the CIO will face in the South the same antilabor campaign under the guise of "national defense" which has characterized every major struggle to bring bargaining rights and union conditions to war industries in the recent period.

The steel, aircraft, munitions, and ordnance industries are spreading throughout the South precisely because the big-business interests seek out the sections which offer low wages, the open shop, and the protection of openly reactionary, terroristic state and municipal governmental agencies.

The southern workers are more than ready for the CIO campaign. Just as the Ford workers, who lived under the whip for so many years, answered the CIO campaign by flooding the ranks of the CIO and by conducting a brilliant militant fight for unionism, the southern workers, Negroes and whites alike, will spring into the battle for unionism at the first sign of a real campaign by the CIO.

But no half measures will succeed in the South. A fight to organize the South means a battle with the government; it means militant action to defend the very lives of the workers in the union; it means a struggle with Standard Oil, whose agents patrol the streets of southern cities, guns in hand, ready to murder the organizers and members of the union.

But the militant membership of the CIO demands that the task be done, and it is equal to the task. The southern millions, deprived of their economic and political liberty, are equal to the task.

The most uncertain factor bearing on the ultimate success of this drive is the political tie of the CIO leadership to the Roosevelt administration and its war program. This political attitude confronts the CIO leaders with a fundamental contradiction. In the showdown fight that must ensue in any effective union organization drive in the South, they will in all likelihood meet the opposition of the government. The CIO has the choice of successfully organizing the South and smashing the greatest reservoir of open-shop strength, thus facing a break with the administration, or watering down the drive and retreating on the basis of the CIO leadership's political commitments.

PART TWO

From December 1941 to September 1945

IRONY AT PEARL HARBOR

An eyewitness account of the Pearl Harbor battle, published in the December 22 *New York Times,* tells how "a Negro mess attendant who never before had fired a gun manned a machine gun on the bridge [of the sinking battleship *Arizona*] until his ammunition was exhausted."

We cite this story not simply to show that Negroes have heroic fighting qualities. The Negro people have demonstrated such qualities in fullest measure through all the centuries of their struggle against slavery and racial oppression and in every war in which this nation has participated.

Rather we point to this incident of the Negro mess attendant on the U.S.S. *Arizona* as an example of the discriminatory treatment accorded Negroes in all branches of the American armed forces, particularly the naval division.

The thing that sticks out like a sore thumb in the *Times* account of this Negro mess attendant's action is that he "never before had fired a gun." Why? Only because this Negro and every Negro in the country is barred by the navy's Jim Crow regulations from any post other than mess attendant.

The Negro people for a long time have wondered what kind of war for democracy it is that must be fought by a Jim Crow navy. They have asked what is the difference between Hitler's treatment of the Jews in Germany and the treatment they receive here in a war that has been officially dedicated to the high principles of the "four freedoms." Perhaps wider sections of the population will begin to wonder the same thing after reading about the Negro mess attendant on the *Arizona.*

From an editorial, *Militant,* December 27, 1941. Dorie Miller, the first hero of the war, was a sharecroppers' son who enlisted in the navy in 1938. He was awarded the Navy Cross for heroism; toured Harlem to help sell war bonds; and was killed in action in the South Pacific in 1943, still a messman.

BLOOD IS SEGREGATED TOO

Many Negroes have volunteered in response to the call for blood donors—only to find their services rejected. The Red Cross has openly stated that it does not wish, nor will it accept, Negro blood.

The aim of the Red Cross is to collect a blood bank for use by the army and navy. The blood is contributed by healthy volunteers, and a large supply is stored for use during wartime. Of course there is no limit to the amount that will be necessary as the war progresses.

Protests arose, it is said, from the Southern Bourbons against the use of Negro blood. In spite of the scientific fact that there is absolutely no difference between the blood of whites and Negroes, these prejudiced southerners insist on interfering in an important phase of defense work.

The army and navy then issued a memorandum saying that only blood of white people would be acceptable and that if a Negro soldier needed blood and did not wish to use the white blood which was stored in the bank, then live Negro blood would be provided. The Red Cross then issued its statement, repeating the same sentiment.

The Red Cross has just been put on the spot. Its excuse for refusing Negro blood donors who volunteered to give their blood for wounded soldiers and sailors had been that it was acting on instructions from the army and navy.

But the U.S. Navy has just denied that it ever requested the American Red Cross to refuse the blood of Negro donors. A public statement to this effect was made by Rear Adm. Ross T. McIntire, surgeon general, in answer to an inquiry about the refusals made by the National Association for the Advancement of Colored People.

McIntire stated that all Negro applicants were told that their contributions would be accepted, and were referred to the Red Cross.

By Ernest Williams, a pen name of Myra Lesnik, an SWP activist in Harlem. From *Militant*, January 1 and 31 and February 7, 1942.

This question of blood for wounded soldiers and sailors has still not been satisfactorily settled by any means. The Red Cross has finally retreated under pressure, and announced that it will accept donations from Negro blood donors. But—and there seems to be some but—the blood plasma of Negroes, after it is dried and stored, will be segregated! Although even the Red Cross admits that there is absolutely no scientific difference, the cans of plasma will be labeled "white" and "colored." Plasma from whites will be given to wounded whites, and plasma from Negroes will be given to wounded Negroes.

FIGHTING IN LOUISIANA

The Jim Crow treatment of Negro soldiers in southern training camps led to open riots last week in Alexandria, Louisiana. Ever since Negro draftees, mainly from the North, were sent into the heart of the Deep South, where they face insult, segregation, and terrorism on a scale far greater than above the Mason-Dixon line, all indications have pointed to inevitable and bloody outbreaks.

Violence broke out in Alexandria in the heart of the local colored section, allegedly when a white MP arrested a Negro soldier on charges of not paying admission to a theater. It is claimed that the MP had started to beat the soldier, when several colored soldiers who were passing by, jumped into the fight.

State police were summoned by the MPs, and civilians of both races joined in the general fighting. Guns, bricks, rocks, and finally tear gas were used in the battle. It was reported that over three thousand Negro soldiers were rounded up and sent back to their camps, and an equal number of Negro civilians were dispersed. Although no official comment has been made, it has been rumored that the so-called ringleaders of the Negroes will face army court-martial.

By Ernest Williams. From *Militant,* January 24, 1942.

THE LYNCHING OF CLEO WRIGHT

In the midst of the war that is proclaimed a crusade against intolerance, racial hatred, and all other forms of injustice, the newspapers again carry the headline "Negro Lynched by Missouri Crowd."

Cleo Wright, a thirty-year-old Negro mill worker, already critically wounded by three bullets, was dragged from the city jail of Sikeston, Missouri, on January 25. According to the Associated Press report, he "offered no resistance. He was stuffed into the trunk compartment of a motor car and taken to the Negro district, where he was dragged through the streets behind an automobile. Later the body was cut loose and gasoline applied. . . . A city truck removed the Negro's body after it had been in the street several hours."

As usual in such cases, the charge against Wright was that he was "suspected of an attack on a white woman." Someone entered the home of an army sergeant and stabbed his wife, inflicting a wound in her side. After a chase across town, an officer captured Wright, according to the reports, took away a knife and put him in the back seat of his car. A struggle then ensued, during which the policeman drew his revolver and shot Wright three times.

What happened after the lynching was typical too. Apparently the so-called law-and-order enforcing agencies felt more concerned about preventing the Negro population from expressing their feelings than in capturing the members of the lynch mob. State highway patrolmen were stationed in the Negro section of Sikeston. American Legion members "guarded" streets leading into the area. "Negroes were ordered to remain indoors."

The *New York Times* of January 27, in a pious editorial discussion of the lynching entitled "Sikeston Disgraces Itself," tries to place the responsibility for this lynching solely on the people of Sikeston. In this way the *Times* editorial writer tries to absolve the whole damnable system of racial discrimination—ap-

By Ernest Williams. From *Militant,* January 31, 1942.

proved and fostered by the government and the capitalist class—
of any responsibility for the murder of Cleo Wright.

Negro and white workers who want to abolish the hellish
practice of lynching must not be taken in by the *Times* and the
other hypocrites. They only way to abolish lynching is to abolish
all forms of racial discrimination, wherever they exist.

MOB ACTION IN DETROIT

Barred from Sojourner Truth
Housing Project

FEBRUARY 3—Announcement was made in Detroit yesterday
at the office of Mayor Jeffries that the opening of the Sojourner
Truth housing project, scene of last Saturday's violent struggle to
prevent Negroes from moving into the project, will be postponed
indefinitely. Thus the latest round in this struggle has been won
by the reactionary landlords, real-estate sharks, and Ku Klux
Klan-incited gangs who have been fighting for many months to
prevent the Negro people from occupying the federal housing
project designated for their use.

On Friday night, February 27, a cross was burned in the center
of the project as a warning to the first Negro families who were to
move into their new homes the following day. A "picket line" of
hundreds of people, armed with knives, clubs, rifles, shotguns, and
stones, patrolled the project all night and grew to more than
twelve hundred by morning.

When the Negro families arrived with the trucks carrying their
furniture and belongings, the mob attacked them and prevented
them from reaching the project buildings. Scores were injured,
many of them seriously; thirty-eight people were taken to hospi-
tals, of whom thirty-three were Negroes.

When unions go on strike in Detroit, as a spokesman for the
United Auto Workers, CIO, pointed out later, the city administration "was able to have a thousand police on the job. That was to
protect employers' interests." But for this violent attack on the

---

From *Militant,* March 7, 1942. On February 28, a mob of 1,200 whites
prevented three Black families from moving in. Finally in April, twelve
Black families did move in, with 800 state troopers standing guard.

rights of the Negro people, the city administration was able to spare only two hundred or fewer police.

And from the way these police acted, one would have thought that it was the Negroes who were responsible for the fight. *PM* reports that "of 104 persons arrested on charges ranging from felonious assault to inciting to riot, 101 were Negroes." This means that the hundreds of whites who attacked the Negro people got away scot-free. If anything, the police by their arrests helped the whites in preventing the Negro people from moving into their homes.

Immediately after the riots, Mayor Jeffries ordered that the moving be held up "since I understand it would take at least 3,000 policemen to get the new tenants safely into the building." Jeffries then left for Washington—not to get aid in helping the Negroes to move into their homes, but to appeal to federal officials to postpone the opening of the project. Federal officials issued the statement Jeffries wanted.

The latest decision to postpone "indefinitely" the occupation of the homes shows that Washington officials have been only too glad to seize upon the "riot" as an excuse for preventing the Negroes from moving in.

'Protection'

If an individual is assaulted on the streets by a gangster, it is customary to arrest and punish the gangster and assist his victim. Under the impact of the "war for democracy," however, this simple concept of justice is being reversed so far as the workers, Negroes, and noncitizens are concerned.

Thus, when workers sent him protests about the bosses' war profiteering, Col. Roy M. Jones, of the procurement division of the army air corps, did nothing about the war profiteers, but sharply "warned" the workers about becoming "tools of nazism."

When a Ku Klux Klan–incited mob in Detroit attacked a group of Negro families who were moving into a government housing project built for Negro war workers, Mayor Jeffries "protected" these Negro workers and their families by ordering them to stay out of their new homes "until further notice." And when his

An editorial, *Militant,* March 7, 1942.

police got through "protecting" them, of 38 persons sent to the hospital, 33 were Negroes, and of 104 persons arrested, 101 were Negroes.

When vigilante terror broke out against persons of Japanese descent on the West Coast, President Roosevelt issued an order empowering the army arbitrarily to drive all persons of Japanese descent, citizens and noncitizens alike, from their homes and farms. Attorney General Biddle, self-styled guardian of civil liberties, hastened to approve of it as a measure for the "safety" of the threatened victims of reactionary terrorism.*

Hitler is a past master in applying this concept of "justice." Every time he undertakes a new invasion, or some other new blow at the masses, he explains that he does it "for their own good," to "protect" them.

---

*On February 19, 1942, Roosevelt signed Executive Order 9066, which gave the government authority to uproot people from "military areas." Under this order, and as part of a well-orchestrated anti-Japanese racist campaign, 110,000 Japanese-Americans, including 70,000 U.S. citizens, were herded into concentration camps. Many had their land, property, and houses stolen. Among the supporters of this action was the Communist Party.

Labor's Duty

The Detroit CIO acted quickly and wisely in declaring their solidarity with the Negro people. The unions showed that they recognized that the enemies of the Negro people are their enemies too, that a blow at the Negro people is a blow at the working class as a whole. Their prompt action did much to prevent the housing clash from developing into a bloody struggle between the races.

But the labor movement by making this expression of solidarity fulfilled only half its role. It is correct for the unions to demand of the city and federal governments that they permit the Negro families to move into their homes; but it is not correct for them to let it go at that. For what guarantee have they that the same thing that happened on February 28 will not happen again, or that the police will not act the same way they acted on February 28?

The labor movement has another task—and that is to show

An editorial, *Militant,* March 21, 1942.

that their expressions of solidarity go beyond mere words. They must show the Negro people that they back them up with action too.

The labor movement must demand that the authorities set a date for the reopening of the Sojourner Truth homes—and that it be soon. Then on that date the labor movement must organize its forces as strongly and as powerfully as they did when they fought and defeated the mighty auto barons and their goon squads and "service men." They must be present at the homes in great numbers with their picket lines and flying squadrons to see that February 28 is not repeated. If they do this, the Negro people will be able to move into their homes; the odds are that under such conditions the Ku Kluxers and fascists would not even dare to show their faces there.

In this way the labor movement could at one and the same time win the wholehearted support of the Negro people and put to rout those fascist forces that seek not only to intensify racial hatred ag inst the Negroes but also to smash the trade unions.

Lies from a Northern Congressman

In Congress recently, Representative Tenerowicz of Michigan took the floor to utter the lie that the majority of the CIO auto workers were opposed to permitting the Negro people to move into the Sojourner Truth housing project in Detroit, which had been built for them.

In this way he hoped to remove from the real-estate interests and reactionary vigilante organizations the responsibility for organizing the February 28 attack on the Negro families trying to move into their homes.

But the recent UAW conference in Detroit completely exposed Tenerowicz's filthy trick. President Thomas reported what the congressman had said, and then called on everyone in the hall who was in agreement with Tenerowicz's position to stand. Not a single delegate arose. Thomas then asked the delegates who agreed with the official UAW stand, for the unqualified right of the Negro people to move into their homes, to get up. Every one of the 1,500 delegates stood up.

From *Militant,* April 25, 1942.

MORE BRUTALITY REPORTED

The *Kansas City Call,* March 13, reveals some of the facts in the "secret lynching" in Brookshire, Texas, of Howard Wilpitz, "which never reached publication in the daily newspapers."

Wilpitz was ordered out of Brookshire, which is thirty-five miles from Houston, by a local constable. In the argument that followed, the constable hit Wilpitz over the head with his pistol and shot him in the leg when he tried to run away. Wilpitz shot back, and knocked the constable's gun out of his hand. An armed lynch mob was quickly formed, surrounded Wilpitz in the toilet behind a Negro lodge building, and riddled it with bullets until the victim fell out. They then stood over him and shot him till he was dead.

The Negroes in the town were threatened into silence. The body was held for a week and then buried secretly. Wilpitz's wife never even saw the body.

The lynching took place on February 21. No word of it was printed until the *Call* learned the story last week. How many other such cases there are which are hushed up, we do not know. But we have no doubt that there are many of them.

In the same issue of the *Call* is the report of the action by the Scott County, Missouri, grand jury on the lynching of Cleo Wright in Sikeston. Although everyone in Sikeston knows the names of the people who led and participated in the Wright lynching, the grand jury, meeting for less than two days, found no one to blame, and announced it had insufficient evidence to return a true bill. The jury was composed almost exclusively of merchants, bankers, and retired farmers. The judge, J. C. McDowell, accepted the report without comment. Apparently he was satisfied that they had obeyed his warning, given just before they opened their hearings, not to pay any attention to "outside agitation" and "radical talk."

Everybody knows who lynched Cleo Wright; the guilty parties are walking the streets of that town free and easy. Everybody knows that if anybody talks, he'll join Cleo Wright, and nothing

---

By Albert Parker. From *Militant,* March 21, 1942.

will happen to the men who murder him either. The people who lynched Cleo Wright are all-out supporters of the "second war for democracy. . . ."

The *California Eagle,* March 5, reports another army "riot" in Merced, California, on March 2. It all began when the Negro soldiers were refused service at a tavern on the fairgrounds on which they are camped. The report says:

"Negro soldiers attacked the discriminatory tavern twice. Both times they were 'calmed' by military police.

"Colored troops were armed only with sticks and clubs.

"Military police are still patrolling the business section, whether to prevent riots or prevent Negro patronage is not clear."

TWO WAYS OF NOT SKINNING THE CAT

The American ruling class seems to have two ways of approaching the problem of the growing dissatisfaction and anger of the Negro people with the way they are being treated today.

One way is that of the reactionary poll tax congressmen who charge that the Negroes are satisfied and happy, and there wouldn't be any problem if people would just stop bothering them. Their attitude is expressed by the speech made by Rankin of Mississippi in the House of Representatives on March 5:

Japanese fifth columnists have been stirring race trouble in this country for a long time. . . .

They are working through such organizations as this Civil Liberties Union and Associations for the Advancement of Colored People. In my opinion, they are behind this drive to try to stir up trouble between the whites and the Negroes here in Washington by trying to force Negroes into hotels, restaurants, picture shows, and other public places.

They know that if they can start race riots in Washington and throughout the country, it will aid them in their nefarious designs against the people of the United States. . . .

If these agitators will let the Negroes alone, we will have no trouble with them.

The white people of the South who have always been the Negroes' best friends, and who know the Negro problem, will have no trouble with the colored race if these fifth columnists and the flannel-mouthed agitators throughout the country will let them alone.

By Albert Parker. From *Militant,* March 28, 1942.

The other method is the one used by the liberals. Instead of shutting up the Negroes at a time they are boiling over with resentment, the liberals prefer to let the Negro leaders shoot off some steam. An example of this is the calling of a conference in Washington on March 20 by Archibald MacLeish, director of the Office of Facts and Figures. The conference, to which representatives of all the big Negro newspapers and organizations have been invited, will discuss the "wartime problems" of the Negro people, and develop an information program in connection with it.*

When the conference is finished, MacLeish will probably hire a few more Negroes to work in his propaganda office. The "information program" they will develop will be used in an effort to convince the rank-and-file Negro people that everything is fine and dandy, that they are making progress even if they can't see it, that they would be even worse off if Hitler wins the war, etc.

In short, the difference between these two methods is very superficial. The only way to eradicate the resentment of the Negro people is by wiping out the discrimination, segregation, insult, and brutality which create that wholly justified resentment. Both the reactionaries and the liberals are united in opposing any steps that would accomplish that.

*At this conference, delegates of fifty Black organizations told Mac-Leish that "the Negro people were cool to the war effort and that there could be no national unity nor high morale among Negroes unless they were given their rights."

WHY COMMUNIST PARTY ATTACKS 'DOUBLE V'

Stalinist treachery is not confined to the trade unions alone—it extends into and seeks to disrupt progressive struggles everywhere. Just as the Stalinists try to get the workers in the trade unions to give up the struggle for their rights, so do they try—in the name of their new-found patriotism—to soften down the struggle of the Negro people for equal rights.

The *Pittsburgh Courier,* a few weeks ago, began a campaign

By Albert Parker. From *Militant,* April 4, 1942.

known as the "Double V," which stands for "double victory for democracy at home and abroad." Several other Negro newspapers and many Negro organizations have endorsed this campaign, saying that a victory in this war will not be adequate or satisfactory unless democracy is also victorious at home.

This is certainly far from a radical or antiwar slogan. As a matter of fact, for many people it is only a cover for unqualified support of the war.

But even so, the Stalinists are opposed to it—because it places the struggle against Jim Crow in this country on the same plane as the war against the Axis!

Last week, at a symposium on the Negro press in New York, Eugene Gordon, Negro writer for the *Daily Worker,* came out against the Double V slogan because "Hitler is the main enemy" and "the foes of Negro rights in this country should be considered as secondary."

The other Negro newspapermen present—who also support the war—sharply disagreed with Gordon's position on this question. The reason for this is not that they are more radical than the Stalinists, but that they are more dependent on Negro rank-and-file sentiment than the Stalinists are.

They know how hard it would be to try to sell the Negroes a paper, claiming to represent their interests, which told them that their struggle for equality is "secondary." They know how the Negro people would repudiate a paper that tried to convince them that Hitler is their main enemy when they can still feel on their backs the oppression of the American Jim Crow ruling class.

The Stalinists, on the other hand, don't care a hang about the interests or aspirations of the Negro masses—they are in no way dependent on them. Their policies are decided for them not by what the masses want or need, but by what the Stalinist bureaucracy in the Soviet Union wants or needs. Stalin has told them to support the war and to crack down on any movement or group that conducts a struggle which might interfere with the bosses in their conduct of the war. That is why they now have the impudence to lecture the Negro people that their struggle for equality is "secondary"—a sight which must indeed gladden the hearts of the poll taxers, lynchers, and advocates of white supremacy!

FIRST BLACK TROOPS IN AUSTRALIA

The first American Negro troops to be sent abroad in this war have wound up in Australia. Australia is an all-out Jim Crow country, where Negroes are not permitted to come in time of peace. The country's war minister, Francis M. Forde, gallantly greeted them as follows: "We look upon the Negro troops as part of the United States Army and we would not be so presumptuous as to place any bar against any form of assistance to the defense of this country." Oliver Harrington cleverly summed up the situation in a *People's Voice* cartoon showing a Negro soldier being greeted by an Australian official standing in front of a sign which reads, "Colored persons not allowed in Australia." The official is saying to the Negro soldier: "Jolly glad to see you, old boy. Just ignore these bloody signs around here—for the duration." The final payoff is that the Negro troops are not to be used for combat but only as work gangs to do the dirty work.

From *Militant,* April 11, 1942.

A NEW WAVE OF VIOLENCE

A new wave of violence has broken out against Negro soldiers. On April 2 two Negro privates were shot dead and five wounded by military police in Fort Dix, New Jersey. On March 29 a Negro sergeant in Little Rock, Arkansas, was shot dead by a white policeman, aided by white MPs. A few days before that a Negro private in Houston, Texas, was shot dead by a white soldier assigned to guard him. At the same time a Negro private stationed in Georgia reported that he had been cruelly beaten by

By Albert Parker. From *Militant,* April 11 and 18, 1942.

white policemen as white MPs stood by and watched.

Military and even civil investigations and hearings are under way in most of these cases. But it is already clear that attempts will be made to whitewash the cases and gloss over the Jim Crow treatment of Negroes which is at bottom responsible for these killings. The public statement by Col. C. M. Dowell, Fort Dix post commander, that the whole case was "merely a brawl," laid down the line that will probably be followed by the authorities.

Brig. Gen. Benjamin O. Davis, ranking Negro officer and assistant to the army inspector general, has been sent to Fort Dix to supervise the inquiry, and to lend a show of "impartiality" to the proceedings. Davis has been used for such work before, notably in the case of Pvt. Ned Turman, Negro soldier who was killed at Fort Bragg, N.C., last summer, for resisting the brutal attacks of MPs.

The authorities will have to try to explain why it is that an estimated forty Negro soldiers were armed, and why they opened fire immediately after the MPs fired, and why the ammunition they were not supposed to have was already loaded into their rifles, where any routine inspection would have revealed it.

Soldiers are not in the habit of arming themselves in such large numbers against orders—for which they could be strongly punished—unless they have a very good reason, unless they feel that they have to protect themselves from something that is threatening them.

(*PM* of April 5 reports that "anti-Negro feeling had been deliberately whipped up at times" and "there have been frequent fist fights between the white and Negro troops, particularly the Southern soldiers.")

If the boards of inquiry at Fort Dix really want to know what caused the gun battle, let them find out why these soldiers felt it necessary to arm themselves. If they overlook this aspect of the question, then it can be taken for granted that nothing fundamental will be done to prevent similar tragedies of this nature.

The Little Rock case is simpler, and an even more vicious example of brutality against Negro soldiers. A Negro soldier in the Negro section of the city was accused of being drunk. White policemen came along and began to beat him up.

Sgt. Thomas P. Foster, of Company D, Ninety-second Engineers, at Camp Robinson, Arkansas, inquired of the police why they did not turn him over to the military police, who are supposed to have jurisdiction over all soldiers accused of misconduct.

White MPs standing by then attacked Foster. He tried to resist but was outnumbered and beaten helpless on the ground.

One of the white cops, named A. J. Hay, took out his gun. A bystander, Walter Johnson, pleaded with him not to shoot. Hay fired five bullets into Foster's body; he died later that night.

The army then swept into action. It rushed trucks into town and began rounding up—all the Negro soldiers!

Sweeping investigations were ordered by military and civilian authorities. A preliminary report issued by the chief of police was an outright whitewash. The military boards have been ordered to decide the following question: Did Foster die in the line of duty? Are his parents entitled to receive a pension?

In the face of all this, a letter from President Roosevelt to the Fraternal Council of Negro Churches, released on April 5, takes on a most ironic character. In effect, Roosevelt in this letter takes credit for what has been happening to the Negroes in the armed forces:

"At my direction, the armed services have taken numerous steps to open opportunities for Negroes in the armed forces of our country, and they are giving active consideration to other plans which will increase that participation."

What these other plans may be, we do not know. But unless they provide for the complete elimination of the present system of segregation and discrimination in the armed forces, they cannot prove satisfactory to the Negro people or the labor movement.

What they want, if Fort Dix tragedies are to be prevented from happening over and over again, is:

Democratic rights in the army!

The abolition of military Jim Crowism!

APRIL 14—The wave of violence against Negro soldiers claimed new victims this week, as the army officials and boards of inquiry continued to remain silent about the many attacks against Negro troops reported in last week's *Militant.*

At Camp Lee, Virginia, Pvt. James W. Martin stepped out on to the balcony on the second floor of the prison barracks. The corporal of the guard below ordered him to step back inside. When Martin did not move, the corporal ordered a sentry to shoot. Martin died from bullet wounds in his head.

The corporal and the sentry were held and a board of commissioned officers was set up to investigate the case.

In Tuskegee, Alabama, on April 3, several Negro soldiers were injured as the result of an attack on them by city cops, according to a report received by the *Pittsburgh Courier,* which was not able to secure all the details because "all news of the occurrence has been suppressed by Army authorities."

The fight began when city police arrested a Negro soldier. The police have confirmed the clash, and say that the situation is "well in hand." All Negro soldiers have been confined to their posts.

Meanwhile strong resentment over these attacks on Negro soldiers was growing among the Negro population.

New York City Councilman Adam Clayton Powell, editor of the *People's Voice,* gave clear expression to this resentment in an editorial printed in the April 11 issue of that paper, entitled "Mr. President, Just What Is It That We Are Fighting For?" Powell pointed out that "more Negro men have been killed and beaten so far this year than in any similar period of this century," and declared:

Mr. President, we lay the blame squarely at your feet. . . . You alone have the power to deal with this correctly and you must do it and do it promptly, with firmness and exactness. . . .

This you must do:

Immediately command the military police to protect by force of arms all members of the United States Army.

Order the Department of Justice to arrest immediately for trial the civilian murderers of Negro troops.

Wipe out Jim Crow in all departments of our armed forces.

If not, then what are we fighting for?

MRS. FANNIE HALL WRITES THE PRESIDENT

Conyers, Georgia, April 5, 1942

President Franklin D. Roosevelt
Washington, D.C.

Dear Mr. Roosevelt:

I am the mother of George Hall, who was killed at Fort Dix, N.J., by a group of your white MPs.

Are the Negro women of this country raising up boys to be slaughtered like hogs and beef cattle by the MPs?

My son is being buried today because of wanting to fight for his country. I have read of the death of several Negro soldiers being killed and nothing is being done about it. I would like very much

From *Militant,* April 25, 1942.

for you to make a thorough investigation of my son's death, and the death of all other Negro soldiers who died likewise.

I know that I speak in the voice of all women, when I say that I love my children, and do not want them to be killed just on account of neglect. I read in the paper where the soldiers had slipped some ammunition from the firing range. This should never have been, for I think that all firearms are supposed to be taken away from the soldiers before they leave: if this is so, there must be some neglect on somebody's part. The officer in charge should be punished for letting firearms be handled by soldiers, unofficially.

Our colored boys need better protection in the army. We don't want to labor for years bringing up our children to be respectful men and then have them killed like dumb driven cattle.

I have struggled hard for my children to get an education, and taught them to respect authority.

Please don't pass this up; I want you to promise me that you will investigate this case, not only for me, but for 3,000,000 Negro mothers.

They are burying my son today.

A heart-broken mother,
Mrs. Fannie Hall

WINNING PRODUCTION JOBS AT FLINT

FLINT, Michigan—Real headway against racial discrimination in the factories is now being made in this stronghold of General Motors, and Negroes have begun to work on war production machines, shoulder to shoulder with their white brothers in the UAW-CIO and at the same rates of pay, $1.10 an hour to start.

This first victory of its kind here, won through union militancy, has inspired not only the eight thousand colored people of Flint, but also their white brothers. As soon as the first half-dozen Negroes went to work at Chevrolet division of GM, Buick workers took the cue and began a fight to achieve the same kind of victory over industrial Jim Crow.

Only the organized and militant action of Negro leaders in the union, with much white support, made this forward step possible.

By Jeff Thorne. From *Militant,* May 2 and October 24, 1942.

The Negro militants in Chevrolet refused to sit idly by and wait for justice. In other plants, where the Negroes waited, they're still waiting, or working only as laborers, if they are working at all.

As soon as Roosevelt's executive order against discrimination was issued last June 25, the Chevrolet Negro militants began to organize to enforce it. When the corporation had failed to place any Negroes on machine jobs by July 2, the militants set out to file a discrimination grievance against the management.

At first the management offered to transfer Negroes to any jobs it might decide they were qualified for. But the Negro militants stood firm until they won what was needed—an arrangement whereby all workers, including Negroes, would be called by seniority as soon as new jobs were opened in the changeover from auto to war production, with the colored workers having the same chance as whites to prove their ability to hold the jobs.

For many years the corporation had justified its policy of discrimination on the grounds that to grant job equality would create trouble among the workers. This argument is still raised in some plants, but it was proved completely false at Chevrolet. Whites and Negroes who went to work together for the first time greeted each other with handshaking, backslapping, and hearty congratulations, despite the fact that more than 40 percent of the workers in Chevrolet are southerners and foreign-born. Extra police held in eager readiness by the management could find no pretext for using their clubs.

The Negroes in Chevrolet constitute only about 5 percent of the membership, and so it was not too easy at the beginning for them to make headway. The Negro militants not only had to push the case against the management, but they also had to assert themselves in union elections, helping remove some of the leaders who had stood in their way. Progress was much more rapid when more progressive leaders obtained union posts. The Negro workers became among the best union members, and today their union loyalty is recognized by everyone; even white workers who did not at first understand the need for supporting this fight learned that it was in their own interests to win it.

FLINT, Michigan, October 19—Auto workers of Chevrolet Plant 3, the most militant union group in Flint General Motors plants, took another big step forward last week in winning production jobs and fifteen-cent hourly increases for all Negro janitors except three or four who did not want to change jobs.

The decisive factor in this victory was militant mass action mapped out by the Negroes organized in the United Auto Workers, CIO, in support of the union negotiators. It is significant that the recently organized Flint branch of the March on Washington movement was centered mainly in that plant and its action actually forced the management to capitulate to the union demands.

In weeks and weeks of union negotiations the corporation stalled on all sorts of false and empty pretexts, through many heated meetings. Then the March on Washington group arranged for a mass march on the main office, with all the Negro supporters they could muster in the city. This same group had earlier held mass meetings of as many as 200 and 300 Negroes from this area, and Chevrolet management knew of its influence and power.

Management heard of the mass action plan in advance and tried to stall if off by personal calls on some of the leaders and promises of speedy settlement "as soon as we can hire new janitors, but we just can't find them now." The leaders were not fooled and stuck to their plans, whereupon the management capitulated entirely and immediately. Back pay of the fifteen-cent raise was promised for all the lost weeks of the negotiations, since the corporation had violated a previous agreement by placing white men with less seniority than the veteran Negro janitors.

This clear example of victory through militant methods, as a supplement to union membership, is winning favor to the March on Washington movement, not only in Chevrolet plants but throughout the city, and the leaders anticipate growth of the movement here into a mass organization to deal promptly with all such racial discrimination cases.

BIGOT EXPELLED IN TENNESSEE

In Rockwood, Tennessee, Local 579 of the International Union of Mine, Mill and Smelter Workers, CIO, which has a closed-shop contract with the Tennessee Products Company, was responsible for the discharge of an antiunion and Negro-baiting employee named Nichols. When he was asked to join the union, Nichols said, "I would not join a union and sit in the same hall with niggers, nor be obligated by a colored vice-president."

The members of the union, about half of whom are colored, had already learned while they were building the union that this kind

By Albert Parker. From *Militant*, May 2, 1942.

of prejudice helps the bosses to keep down the wages and conditions of workers of all races, and they voted to kick Nichols out. As the president of the union, a white worker, said, "We are fighting for white and colored alike, and an injury to one is an injury to all."

Remember, this happened in Tennessee, in the Deep South. That's what makes it all the more significant. There are still plenty of men like Nichols down there, workers who are miseducated and misguided by ruling-class propaganda so that they don't know who their real enemies are; but there are also plenty of white workers who are beginning to see through the fog of boss propaganda.

AFTER WAR MAY BE TOO LATE

A. Philip Randolph, president of the Brotherhood of Sleeping Car Porters, AFL, and the one who was responsible for calling off the march on Washington a year ago, has made many speeches and written many articles during the last two years in which he asserted that this is a "war for democracy." The Negro people, he said long before Pearl Harbor, must give unconditional support to the war because only by a victory for the "democratic" nations would they be in a position to secure the democratic rights which they are denied in this country.

Last week Randolph made a speech at a mass meeting in San Antonio, Texas, in which he emphasized the need for the Negro people to struggle for the abolition of the poll tax and the white primary system. "Randolph," according to the May 16 *Pittsburgh Courier*, "stated that Negroes must realize the necessity of winning the right to vote in the South before the war ends, while world opinion is watching the profession and practice of the democratic process everywhere. After the war it may be too late, he concluded." Would it be impertinent of us to ask Randolph to publicly explain what kind of "war for democracy" it is that he thinks may end with the Negro people being in a worse position to gain equality than they are in now?

From *Militant*, May 23, 1942.

GETTING IDEAS IN YOUR HEAD

John Wesley Jones, of Greenville, South Carolina, was found guilty of breaking the law two weeks ago. Judge James M. Richardson ordered him to pay a fine of twenty dollars or serve thirty days in jail. The crime with which he was charged was resisting arrest because he sat down beside a white man on a trolley car when there were no more seats in the "colored section" of the car. Said the judge: "Somebody has been talking to you and you are getting ideas in your head, and when you get ideas trouble is bound to result. You can't fight back. The law requires segregation of the races, and whether it is a good law or not, it must be carried out." That's the trouble with the John Wesley Joneses in this country—they hear all this talk about a "war for democracy" and equality and all this condemnation of Hitler's discrimination against the Jewish people, and they start getting ideas in their heads and the next thing you know they're acting just like regular criminals and outlaws, daring to sit down beside a white man, no less! It's enough to make a cracker sick at the stomach.

From *Militant*, May 23, 1942.

INDIVIDUAL ACTION AND MASS ACTION

For eight weeks Judge Philip Forman of the United States District Court tried to get Donald Wayman Sullivan, a Negro who lived in Newark, New Jersey, to reconsider his attitude toward being drafted into the army.

Sullivan had refused to go into the army because it would

By Albert Parker. From *Militant*, May 30, 1942.

segregate him into a separate Negro regiment and treat him as a different kind of person solely because his skin is darker than that of some "whites."

Judge Forman read things to Sullivan and pleaded with him and so on. He gave him Hitler's *Mein Kampf* to read, and showed that Hitler had called Negroes "half-apes." Finally, the judge, preparing to announce sentence on Sullivan, asked:

"How can you sit idly by and say 'I will not raise my finger against the man who thinks my race is only half human'?"

And Sullivan answered: "There are a lot of people over here that agree with him [Hitler]."

So the judge sentenced him to three years in a federal prison.

There were, of course, some unusual aspects to this particular case. Most judges don't spend eight weeks trying to convince people to go into the army. Furthermore, it developed in the course of the case that Sullivan had some years ago attempted on numerous occasions to enlist in the navy in any capacity other than mess attendant and that he had been repeatedly rejected because he was a Negro.

But on the whole, the Sullivan case is typical of all those involving Negroes who object to the draft because of the army's segregation-discrimination policies. It can therefore serve as the basis for a discussion of the far more important question: How can the Negro people successfully carry on the struggle to achieve full equality?

In the dispute between Sullivan and the judge representing the government, all our sympathies are, of course, with Sullivan. His act was one that showed not only courage, but the desire to make a protest against the whole vicious system of Jim Crowism. Sullivan is a thousand times right when he points out that there are plenty of people in this country who share Hitler's racial theories. As a matter of fact, he could have told the judge that the Jim Crow elements in this country practiced racial discrimination against the Negro people before Hitler was even born, and that Hitler only had to borrow and adapt the Jim Crow methods which keep the ruling class in power in the South and the Democratic Party in office in Washington. He could also have told the judge that the chief difference between Hitler and the American Jim Crow elements on this question is that Hitler openly says that the Negro people are half-human, while the Jim Crow elements treat the Negro people as though they are half-human.

Nevertheless, there is a difference between a protest and an effective protest. And we must have no illusions that Jim Crowism can be abolished in the army by a protest such as

Sullivan's. Its only immediate result is to remove a brave fighter for Negro equality from the arena of active struggle against Jim Crowism.

But, some people may say, suppose it was more than one person who did what Sullivan did? Suppose there were many who followed his example? Wouldn't that be effective?

In the first place, a realistic examination of the situation shows that there is little possibility of a mass movement of Negroes in this direction. Most Negroes are dissatisfied with the way they are treated, but for a number of different reasons they are not ready to go to jail as Sullivan did or are not convinced that such a course would help the situation any.

Second—and this is much more important—the government, if faced with such a movement, would take much stronger repressive measures and proceed to crack down with all the power at its disposal. The ruling class would undoubtedly mobilize terroristic gangs such as the Ku Klux Klan to launch a pogrom against the whole Negro people. All this would pose the question of power—who is to control the government? The government, of course, would fight to the last ditch on this question. But what about the Negro people?

Unless they were prepared to fight back with the same kind of determined struggle, they would suffer a crushing defeat, and if anything their conditions would be worse than they are now.

So you can see that a mass movement following Sullivan's example would be faced with all the questions that face a revolutionary movement. It would first of all have to recognize the decisive character of its fight, and have a clear idea of its goal: the overthrow of the oppressors of the Negro people. It would have to have an experienced revolutionary leadership. And it would have to have the support of the majority of the working class, both white and Negro, or it would go down to defeat.

Whatever else may be said about the present situation, almost everyone will agree that there is at this time no such Negro movement with a revolutionary perspective or revolutionary leadership. To undertake such a course under these conditions would be to invite sure disaster.

2,000 MARCH IN MARYLAND

BALTIMORE, Maryland, May 23—Late last month two thousand angry Negroes marched on the state capitol in Annapolis to demand of the governor an immediate end to the beatings and killings of Negroes by Baltimore police. This week official action was begun to whitewash and to "study" the charges of police brutality that have aroused so much resentment among the Negro people here.

The local police department and courts had already whitewashed the cops involved in recent sensational cases. Now, in an attempt to divert attention from themselves, the police have begun to slander the Negro people. According to them, the only reason there has been any trouble is—that the Negro people drink too much!

Fantastic as it may seem, Police Commissioner Stanton called a hearing at which witnesses, mostly cops, testified that all the unrest in the Negro districts comes from the bars, taverns, and package liquor stores. That is the way the official mind sums up the problems of 175,000 Negroes forced to live in three square miles of what is chiefly slum territory.

As for Governor O'Connor, his only answer to the march on Annapolis has been to appoint a commission to "study" the situation. Composed of a very conservative group of people, it is a sure thing that the commission's recommendations will be mild indeed, and neither the governor nor the state legislature will be under any obligations to carry them out. Militant Negroes here have no illusions about this commission, which includes the chief of personnel and employment at the Glenn L. Martin Aircraft Company, who for years has told Negroes they can't work at his factory.

Of course, no part of the administration has a word to say on the question of segregation. The crowded living conditions of this war-boom town bring disease and death to both white and Negro, but the death rate among the segregated Negroes in this city is 60 percent higher than among whites. Those responsible for continuing these conditions are killing off many thousands of Negroes more than the police department.

From *Militant,* May 30, 1942.

REVIVING THE MARCH
ON WASHINGTON MOVEMENT

25,000 Jam Madison Square Garden

NEW YORK, June 17—In the middle of the second war "to make the world safe for democracy," 25,000 militant Negro men and women jammed the huge Madison Square Garden here last night for five solid hours, to demand democracy at home for 13 million black Americans. Such a demonstration has never before had its like in peacetime or wartime America.

These Negro people weren't asking the white ruling class for their rights. They were telling the white bosses that they'd better not kick the Negro around any more. They weren't begging, they were demanding. They were willing to listen to words—the more militant, the better—but they were ready for and wanted action.

This vast outpouring of protest against Jim Crow in all its forms came in response to the call of the Negro March on Washington movement, whose national director is A. Philip Randolph, head of the AFL Pullman Porters. It is the first of a series of similar protest meetings to be held in Chicago, Washington, and other leading cities throughout the country.

While the speakers—mainly from the numerically small, more privileged strata of the Negro people—dealt briefly with the war and acknowledged their support for it, neither they nor the audience devoted a great deal of attention and enthusiasm to it. The keynote of the meeting was protest—protest against discrimination in industry, in government, in the armed forces, in every walk of life.

Of major significance is the very fact of the meeting itself and the fighting spirit of the audience. They warmed to every word that spoke of determination and militancy, and above all that gave the hint of action.

But there was one thing lacking. For all the militant words of

---

From *Militant,* June 20, 1942. Similar mass rallies were held in Chicago (16,000 on June 26) and St. Louis (9,000 on August 14).

the speakers—they had to be militant to get any response from the audience—they failed to sound that clear call for action that the Negro people are expecting and awaiting. If this meeting showed anything at all, it showed that the Negro masses want to know what action they can take now to destroy Jim Crow.

The three chief actions of the meeting were: (1) the adoption of an eight-point program demanding an immediate end to discrimination and segregation in every form, and advocating independence for colored races and the colonial peoples throughout the world; (2) the approval of a petition requesting a stay of execution and freedom for Odell Waller; (3) the initiation of a petition to President Roosevelt calling for an immediate executive order to abolish Jim Crow in the armed forces.

A disappointing aspect of the meeting for the audience was its poor organization. The efforts of the leadership to give a "respectable" tinge to the meeting induced them to load the program with too many speakers who had too little to say but insisted on saying it at great length. As a result, the meeting dragged out until the patient and enthusiastic audience became physically uncomfortable. What was to be the crowning feature of the meeting, the address of Randolph presenting the program of the March on Washington movement, was crowded into the last few minutes, with Randolph able to speak only very briefly.

In general, the eight-point program of demands, which was unanimously adopted with great applause, truly reflects the aspirations of the Negro masses. These demands include:

The abrogation of every law which makes a distinction in treatment between persons based on religion, creed, color, or national origin; legislation to enforce the Fifth and Fourteenth Amendments so that no persons may be deprived of life, liberty, and property without due process of law; enforcement of the Fourteenth and Fifteenth Amendments and passage of an anti-poll-tax bill; abolition of segregation and discrimination in all branches of the armed forces.

An end to all discrimination in jobs and job training; the withdrawal of federal funds from any agency practicing discrimination in the use of those funds; representation for Negro and minority groups on all governmental administrative agencies and on missions, political and technical, at any postwar peace conferences.

This last point was related to freedom for the colonial peoples, as was indicated in the remarks of several of the speakers. Every reference to India, China, the West Indies, or Africa which expressed support for the immediate liberation of the colonial peoples received a tremendous ovation.

172

But though the meeting was called by the March on Washington movement, and though passing reference was made by a few of the speakers to such an action, the only concrete proposal for achieving the demands of the movement was—another committee of Negro leaders to visit Washington and talk to Roosevelt.

This is the same kind of "action" which was substituted for the originally scheduled march on Washington last year when it was called off at the last minute. Then a conference was held with Roosevelt, who made all kinds of promises and issued an executive order, without any teeth, against discrimination in war industries. Today, the March on Washington movement has had to be revived, because, in the words of most of the speakers, "conditions for the Negro are as bad as ever."

Randolph himself, the leading figure of the movement, confined himself in his few brief words to telling the people who wanted to know what mass action they could take that he and a few other leaders hoped to get a hearing before Roosevelt. And that was all he proposed.

But the thing that brought out the real sentiments of the audience, that showed that they had little faith in mere conferences between a handful of top Negro leaders and Roosevelt, that what they believe in is a nationwide organized campaign of mass action, was the cheering, stamping ovation given to a play which dramatized the plight of the Negro and stressed the call for a Negro mass march on Washington.

It was this play, presented by a top-notch cast of professional actors, which truly voiced the feelings of the Negro masses and sounded the call they wanted to hear. In scene after scene—sketching the experiences of the Negro trying to get into the navy, being called before the draft board, seeking to get a job in a public hospital, asking for membership in a lily-white craft union—was expressed the fighting determination of the average Negro to beat down Jim Crowism. And each scene was summed up in the final defiant challenge, "I'm marching!"

Then the audience truly came alive. The rafters rang with their applause, their cheers.

The single line of that play which stood out and brought the house down, was the statement of the actor Canada Lee as a youth called before a draft board and told he was being inducted. When the white board agent noticed his lack of enthusiasm for fighting in the "war for democracy," and heatedly questioned him, the reply was: "Go on! Put me in the army. I ain't no conscientious objector. But I'm starting the fight for democracy beginning at Grand Central Station and right straight on through to Georgia."

Over the entire meeting—epitomizing the kind of deal the Negro has been handed in America—was the shadow of the impending execution in Virginia this Friday of Odell Waller. The only banners that greeted the audience were three, all with the same words: "Save Odell Waller." And the climax of the meeting was reached when Waller's mother, a tiny, aged, work-worn woman, stood proudly and erect before that giant crowd, and pleaded for the life of her boy. The entire audience rose to its feet to express its sympathy and support.

Despite the shortcomings of the leaders, their failure to enunciate a clear-cut program of action, the meeting in itself was profoundly important. It was a powerful demonstration of the Negro people's determination to fight for and win equality and democracy for themselves at home. They aren't begging for a few minor concessions and a couple of condescending pats on the back from Washington. They are organizing and demanding nothing less than immediate, full, and unconditional equality from top to bottom. This is a significant sign for the future. The American Negro is taking his rightful place in the front ranks of the fighters against oppression in every form, both in America and throughout the world.

Stalinists Oppose Movement

When the Communist Party shifted its line just a year ago, and went from its all-out defense of the Stalin-Hitler pact to all-out support of the war program, the *Militant* predicted that the Stalinists would also stop advocating a militant struggle against Jim Crowism.

This prediction was fulfilled in short order. Now, at the end of one year, the Stalinists have gone so far along their new treacherous road that they not only do not advocate militancy, but viciously attack and slander everyone who does. The best example of this was the approach they took to the Madison Square Garden rally held last week under the auspices of the March on Washington movement.

Until less than a week before June 16 the Stalinist *Daily Worker* remained silent about the meeting. On June 12 and June 14 appeared articles by Benjamin Davis, Jr., of the *Daily Worker* editorial board, attacking the March on Washington movement because it had taken "no sharp and clear stand on the war" and because the Trotskyists among others were supporting the

---

By Albert Parker. From *Militant,* June 27, 1942.

objectives of this movement, and stating that for these reasons, the *Daily Worker* "cannot commit itself unreservedly to the June 16 meeting."

On the morning of June 16 itself, Davis appeared with a new attack on the movement, because the Socialist Party paper, the *Call,* had endorsed the meeting. Again Davis complained that the movement's eight-point program omitted "all reference to the war—to say nothing of winning it." He asked if A. Philip Randolph, leader of the movement, has been working "to exploit the just demands of the Negro people against the war and against the best interests of the Negroes." No one could any longer doubt after this article that the Stalinists were opposed to the meeting. The meeting was held, and so well attended, despite the efforts of the Stalinists, that Davis in reporting the rally had to say "the movement represents the honest yearnings of the Negro masses, whatever may be said of Trotskyites who would ultimately wreck the movement as they would the nation" (*Daily Worker,* June 19).

Along with this admission came another attack on Randolph because he "introduced no resolution in support of the war."

The Stalinist attacks can be understood only by those who are acquainted with the different bases of support on which men like Randolph and on which the Stalinists rest.

Without the backing of the Negro masses, Randolph does not amount to two cents and he knows it. Without the support of the Negro ranks, Randolph would never be permitted into even the back door of the White House, let alone a conference with Roosevelt. Randolph supports the war, but if that were all he offered the Negro masses they would pay no more attention to him than they do to the Stalinists. To keep the mass support he wants, Randolph has to speak the language of militancy. He knows very well from the temper of the masses that this is the only language they want to hear today. He fears that if he loses leadership over the masses today, he will be unable to regain it tomorrow or after the war.

Randolph's policy then is to speak militantly because he bases himself on the support of the Negro ranks, and to fail to offer a militant program of action because he supports the war and is afraid to lead a fundamental struggle against the capitalist class. It is his illusion that by speaking militantly he can secure a number of concessions from the administration and thus maintain his leadership of the Negro movement.

The Stalinists proceed from an entirely different basis: Their line on the Negro question as on everything else is determined by the Stalin bureaucracy in Moscow, which is concerned only with protecting its own interests. Sometimes these interests seem to coincide with those of the Negro and white workers in the United States, sometimes they clearly do not; but that does not concern the Stalin bureaucracy or its stooges in this country. In this you can find the explanation for the *Daily Worker*'s attack on a movement which, despite the defects of its leadership, expresses the aspirations of the Negro people.

The Stalinist line on the Negro question today is to complain that Jim Crowism interferes with the war. (The effects of Jim Crowism on the Negro people are secondary, so far as the Communist Party is concerned.) As Davis said in the June 14 *Worker,* for the Stalinists "the winning of this war is *the primary issue* before the Negro people." Naturally, if you think that, then you won't like a movement and a meeting which says that nothing is more important than winning democracy at home, even though its leaders also support the war.

Randolph believes it is possible to win concessions for the Negro people by speaking militantly and letting Roosevelt hear it. That is why he and most of the other speakers at the meeting emphasized the point that the Negro people are not enthusiastic about the war.

The Stalinists, however, say that the way to win concessions is by supporting the war, because then the administration will be ready to reward the loyalty of the Negro masses. As Davis said in his June 14 article, the war "is a fight in and through which the Negro people will realize their just demands. With our nation needing national unity, maximum war production and the highest possible morale in the armed forces, the opportunities are greater than ever for securing the equality of the Negro people through the very prosecution of the war."

A Report from St. Louis

How to win democratic rights at home was vividly illustrated at the June 26 Chicago Coliseum mass rally, in a report given by D. M. Grant of the St. Louis March on Washington Committee.

Grant pointed out that the United States Cartridge Company, which leases and operates a plant built and owned by the federal government, and the largest of its kind in the world for the production of small arms and munitions, employs twenty-one thousand workers of whom only six hundred are Negroes and all

From *Militant,* July 4, 1942.

of these are employed as porters and common laborers. Of the nine thousand women employed, there is not a single Negro woman in the plant.

On May 20 the St. Louis March on Washington unit was organized and adopted a militant program of action. The initial action of the committee was to organize a march on the plant of the cartridge company. On June 20, over five hundred Negroes marched around the plant, which covers nearly two square miles, carrying banners condemning and denouncing discrimination in employment because of race. The daily press took pictures and ran stories about the march. Washington sent in mediators.

On the day of the march the company reannounced plans for the immediate induction of Negroes into production. Two days after the march, the wages of Negro porters were raised ten cents per hour. Four days following the march seventy-two Negro women were hired.

In addition to these results, other St. Louis war plants, heeding these actions, are taking steps to include Negroes in their plantwide employment program. No Negroes, however, as yet are on the production lines at the U.S. Cartridge Company plant. The position of the St. Louis March on Washington unit relative to all St. Louis war plants was stated in the telegram they sent to the management of the U.S. Cartridge Company after the march:

Today's demonstration before your plant was a mere token of what the Negro people think of, and how they resent discriminatory policies and anti-democratic attitudes of the U.S. Cartridge Company, all of which flagrantly violate the declared policy of the American people as expressed in President Roosevelt's Executive Order number 8802. Your discriminatory practices forced us to take this issue into the streets. We propose to keep it in the streets until it is settled and settled right. We are preparing to return to your plant and will return with constantly increasing numbers until President Roosevelt's Order 8802 has been complied with in good faith, adequately, and without any deceptive avoidance of its true spirit and import.

GOOD NEWS ON DODGE TRUCK

The most heartening news in many weeks was the firm stand taken by the United Automobile Workers, CIO, on behalf of the Negro workers in the Dodge Truck plant of the Chrysler Corporation in Detroit.

Twenty Negroes employed in the plant were entitled by the seniority provisions of the contract between the union and the corporation to receive jobs on production work, and at the insistence of the union, they were transferred to production work from the janitor tasks to which the corporation had confined them for so many years.

When these Negro union men went to work on June 2, about 350 white workers raised a protest and started a fight. The plant was shut down for a day.

But to the credit of the union, it stood fast and refused to be intimidated by this group representing only about 10 percent of the workers. Morris Field, assistant director of the union's Chrysler department, said that the Negro workers would have to be accepted. "The UAW and CIO policy calls for equal treatment of all races, and so does the American constitution. The union will abide by that policy."

It is difficult to tell whether these 350 men were acting on their own—that is, acting in line with the vicious racial prejudices they received from capitalist propaganda sources—or whether they were acting in line with a plan worked out by the corporation seeking a pretext not to transfer the Negro workers to production work.

In either case, they were acting against the interests of the working class as a whole and aiding the enemies of working-class unity against boss exploitation. In either case, a halt has been put to their scissorbill game by the intelligent stand of the union.

By Albert Parker. From *Militant*, June 13, 1942.

SIGNS OF THE TIMES

Mary McLeod Bethune, official of the National Youth Administration, has from the beginning been one of the most enthusiastic supporters of the war program in the circle of Negro government "advisers" and officials. All the more significant are her observations on Negro public opinion today, made in the June 13 issue of the *People's Voice:*

"For the past few weeks I have been asking questions, making inquiries, looking people in the eye. I asked my questions, made my inquiries, and looked into the eyes of Negroes.

"What I have found has caused me concern. . . .

"I received answers and statements and looks of doubt and question when I talked to and questioned and looked into the eyes of Negroes recently."

Mrs. Bethune explains the sources of the "questioning" as follows:

Soldiers in uniform denied food for 22 hours because no restaurant would serve them—a government worker beaten over the head because he attempted to enter a cafeteria that a guard felt should be reserved exclusively for white workers—unarmed soldiers shot on little or no provocation by civil and military police—one group of draftees being examined and inoculated in the boiler room, while other draftees are, at the same time, examined and inoculated in the immaculately clean and white clinic rooms of the induction center—

All the victims Negroes—none of the perpetrators of these insults and crimes punished!

And then Mrs. Bethune concludes on a note of near panic: "Some courageous, unprecedented steps toward the elimination of discrimination are imperative—NOW!"

Last winter a move was started to kick William Pickens out of his job as director of branches for the National Association for

---

By Albert Parker. From *Militant,* June 20, 1942.

the Advancement of Colored People, because he had praised the Jim Crow air corps setup at Tuskegee. The NAACP leadership was greatly annoyed, but there were a lot of protests, and the move fell through.

Last week, on June 8, the far-from-radical NAACP board of directors voted unanimously to kick Pickens out by refusing to continue his leave of absence to work for the Treasury Department as salesman of war bonds and stamps. This time the complaint against Pickens was that he had commended the Richmond, Virginia, *Times-Dispatch* on an editorial accusing the NAACP, its magazine the *Crisis,* the *Pittsburgh Courier,* and the *Amsterdam Star-News* of stirring up trouble, creating "interracial tension," and conducting activities in time of war that bordered on "treason."

The full meaning of this act will be understood only by those who know that Pickens is one of the old guard of the NAACP and one who, by virtue of his past organizational work and his opportunist political course, enjoys a good deal of prestige among the older Negroes and the "respectable" elements who claim that "gradually" and "peacefully" the Negro people are going to get "more and more rights."

NEW ATTITUDES AND
A SECRET SURVEY

A new situation is arising which is of the utmost importance to every fighter against Jim Crowism.

What is changing is not the conditions, but the thinking and the attitudes of the Negro masses. Of course these attitudes are changing because of the new national and international conditions. The Negro masses have never been enthusiastic about talk of a second war for democracy somewhere else. Every impartial observer could testify to this before Pearl Harbor.

After Pearl Harbor the talk of democracy and equality and four freedoms increased. So did the demands for sacrifice and blood and sweat and tears increase. No one yearns for democracy and freedom and equality more than the Negro, for he above all has been denied them in this country. No one wants to fight for them

By Albert Parker. From *Militant*, June 27, 1942.

more than he does, and no one is more ready to sacrifice for them than he is.

But the Negro masses have not forgotten what happened during the last war. Nor have they forgotten what happened to them yesterday—and what is still happening to them today. They have not yet reached the position where they are ready to institute the struggle for a revolutionary change that will do away with Jim Crowism and imperialist war by replacing capitalism with socialism. But they have just about reached the point where they are thinking:

"They tell us to fight and sacrifice and die for democracy and equality. Maybe this war will bring such things to other peoples, maybe it will not; maybe the people who are conducting the war are sincere about wanting to end oppression throughout the world, maybe they are not. But we would be fools to sit back quietly and take their word for it, as our fathers and mothers did in 1917, that this war will automatically give us here in the United States the democratic rights which have always been denied to us. What we must do now is take steps which will ensure our getting the rights which belong to us."

All these thoughts have crystallized into a slogan which the leaders of the March on Washington movement have introduced into their literature: "Now or never!" Perhaps the leaders of this movement, most of whom support the war and urge the masses to support it, do not appreciate its full significance, do not realize that it implies a strong lack of faith in the flowery promises of the ruling class about what is going to happen to Negro rights and conditions after the war.

But that is not so important as the emphasis which the slogan places on the need for action today, *now*.

We have already commented on the meaning of increasing numbers of articles on the Negro question in the capitalist newspapers and magazines. One of the longest and most significant of these was written by Richard Wilson, chief of the Washington bureau of the *Minneapolis Sunday Tribune and Star Journal*, and printed in the June 14 issue of that paper.

The article gives us some revealing information about what official Washington is worrying about:

A government survey, which is regarded as a secret document, has uncovered the information that 38% of the Negroes questioned believe it is more important to "make democracy work at home" than it is to beat the Germans and Japanese.

Only 50.5% of the Negroes questioned regard beating the Germans and Japanese as more important than "making democracy work at home."

That phrase has a diverse meaning. . . . Essentially, and to most

181

Negroes, it means the elimination of economic discrimination, the right to work and live in decency; to others, it means the elimination of segregation, and to still others complete race equality.

Negroes are restive, and what is the cause?

This same secret government survey analyzes the cause and shows that this is what Negroes feel worst about:

Discrimination in obtaining jobs—47.5%.

Discrimination in wages—22.5%.

Discrimination in housing—16%.

Segregation—9.5%.

We are not in a position to check on the accuracy of figures in a report which is kept secret. Nor do we know what kind of people were questioned in this survey—what proportion for example were government employees and what proportion were in the South, where a Negro worker or sharecropper might be putting his life in jeopardy by stating his true opinion. But we can take it for granted that if there was any exaggeration in it, it was all on the side of making things seem as rosy and cheerful as possible.

THE SHAMEFUL WALKOUT AT HUDSON

The anti-Negro walkout at the Hudson Naval Ordnance Arsenal in Detroit last week marks one of the most shameful pages in recent labor history. It was comparable in every way to scabbing, the violation of all the principles of working-class solidarity. Like scabbing, it hurts the interests of the working class as a whole and benefits only the enemies of the labor movement. For these reasons, class-conscious workers must do more than deplore it—they must also know what happened, why it happened, and what can be done to prevent it from happening again.

On the morning of June 18 the company, with the support of the United Auto Workers local in the plant, put two Negroes to work on production-machine jobs in each of the four main buildings of the arsenal. Each of these Negro workers was a member of the union, and was entitled by the seniority provisions of the union contract to be transferred from janitorial tasks to production work.

An editorial, *Militant*, June 27, 1942. During the war, there were several significant anti-Black walkouts in the plants. They were usually dealt with firmly and decisively by the unions.

Previously some workers in the arsenal had been whipping up an agitation against permitting Negroes to work alongside of white workers. Responding to their harangues, three thousand of the four thousand workers on the morning shift quit work. The afternoon shift arrived, there was hesitation and argument, the local president arrived to address them, and within an hour 90 percent of the workers on this shift had returned to their machines. The night shift went to work without any hesitation to speak of.

Meanwhile Secretary of Navy Knox ordered the men back to work and threatened to discharge those who refused and to blacklist them from all war plants. UAW President R. J. Thomas also instructed the men to return to work or face charges of violating the union constitution clause which prohibits racial discrimination. Practically all of the men returned to work the next day, and shortly thereafter the company discharged four men accused of having instigated the walkout, and union officials approved the action.

No good will come from trying to deceive ourselves; there are still many white workers who have racial prejudices against their Negro brothers. But why do white workers, even union members, do such things?

Scientists have told us—and we can easily confirm their findings—that no one is born with racial prejudices. Children of all races play with each other and treat each other as absolute equals until they become affected by the society around them. Children never have racial prejudices until they learn them from their parents, from their textbooks in school, from the motion pictures, newspapers, and prevailing sentiments of the world they live in.

The present capitalist society nurtures and breeds racial prejudice because it benefits the ruling class to have the workers divided and fighting each other instead of uniting to fight their oppressors. In a socialist society, where there will be no capitalists, where the people will be trained from childhood to understand that no man is superior to another because of the color of his skin, racial bias will disappear completely.

Thus the workers who walked out at Hudson were not only responding to the miseducation they got from capitalism, but they were also aiding capitalists to conceal the identity of those who are really responsible for racial prejudices. How happy this walkout must have made the bosses who want to keep the workers divided! How much easier it will be for them to get Negro workers who have been discriminated against, to act as strikebreakers when these same white workers go out on strike to protect their living conditions!

The government does not come into this picture with any cleaner hands than the capitalist class. For decades the government has strengthened and catered to the most reactionary prejudices. The strongest argument of the backward workers at Hudson was that Secretary of Navy Knox himself denies equality to the Negroes in the navy, compelling them to serve either as mess attendants or, in line with the new navy plan, on segregated ships. "Why," they asked the workers who were hesitant about walking out, "should we work alongside of Negroes when the government itself separates them from whites in the army and navy?"

Nor does the government propose any basic policy for eradicating racial bias in the future. Firing four workers may convince backward workers that they must be cautious about how they discriminate against Negroes, but it does not convince them that Negroes are entitled to equal rights. Only a basic reeducation can do that, and the government which itself continues Jim Crow practices is not in a moral position to do it, even if it wanted to.

It is the task of the class-conscious workers, white and Negro, to reeducate the backward workers in the principles of class solidarity. White workers are most often in the best position to approach other white workers and to explain by past history and current events how discrimination against Negroes undermines the union movement and strengthens only the employers. Revolutionary workers, in particular, must seize on every opportunity to unite the workers on the basis of class unity and equality for workers of all races.

Negro militants too have an important task to fulfill. They must first of all understand the real reason why walkouts such as this occur. They must not permit discrimination by backward workers to blind them to the fact that the solution of their problems both as workers and as an oppressed people is indissolubly tied up with the future of the labor movement.

They must fight to keep events of this kind from further embittering their less class-conscious Negro brothers and thus turning them into antiunion elements. Despite the slow progress that is being made, they must not forget that progress *is* being made and primarily in the labor movement. Only a few miles from Detroit, in certain Flint auto plants, Negroes are working side by side and in full amity with white workers, who helped them to get their new production jobs and who greeted them in the most comradely spirit as they went onto these jobs.

Nor must they forget the most important thing about the Hudson incident—that the union stood firm, despite all the pressure from backward elements. The union stood firm and insisted on the right of the Negro workers to equal treatment. This fact cannot be too strongly emphasized; it is a sign that conditions have changed in the labor movement; it is a reason for much hope in the future; and every Negro worker who blames white workers as such for discrimination must be reminded of it.

THE LEGAL LYNCHING OF ODELL WALLER

His Last Testament

Shortly before he was taken to the electric chair, Odell Waller wrote a last statement which he asked be given to the newspapers.

This unlettered sharecropper, railroaded to death because he was poor and black, penned a damning indictment of the capitalist, Jim Crow system:

Have you thought about [how] some people are allowed a chance over and over again, then there are others allowed little chance, some no chance at all. . . .

I accident[ally] fell and some good people tried to help me. Others did everything they could against me so the Governor and the coats [courts] don't no [know] the true facts.

In my case I worked from sunup until sundown trying to make a living for my family and it ended in death for me.

You take big people as the President, Governors, judge, their children don't never have to suffer. They has plenty money. Born in a mention [mansion] nothing ever to worry about. I am glad some people are that lucky.

The penitentiary all over the United States are full of people ho [who]

From *Militant,* July 4, 1942.

was pore [poor], tried to work and have somthing, couldn't, so that maid [made] them steel [steal] an rob.

Odell Waller Is Dead

After keeping him in death row for 630 days, they strapped Odell Waller into the electric chair in Richmond, Virginia, on the morning of July 2.

They burned him to death because he was a Negro, because he was a sharecropper, because he had dared in self-defense to shoot the white landlord who cheated the Waller family out of their share of the crop.

They wanted his blood because the Waller case exposed in all its rottenness the "American way of life" in the South—the system of Jim Crowism, of economic superexploitation on the land, of political oppression and discrimination through the poll tax.

They snuffed out this boy's life because they wanted to show in the most demonstrative way their bitter hatred of all those who, consciously or unwittingly, presented a threat to that "American way of life."

This legal lynching was opposed by the whole labor movement. Philip Murray, president of the CIO, said, "The execution of Odell Waller would be a gross miscarriage of justice." William Green, president of the AFL, informed the governor of Virginia that "labor throughout the nation will be grateful" if he would extend executive clemency. Numerous trade unions in both the South and the North protested against the pending execution.

The Negro people were completely united on this issue too. Every prominent Negro organization and leader appealed for Waller's life.

But the pressure of the masses, although it delayed the legal lynching for almost two years, was unable to save Waller. For on the other side, arrayed against the groups defending the sharecropper, were powerful forces, influential in both state and federal governments, who did not want to antagonize the reactionary southern powers-that-be and who gave these powers the blood which they were demanding.

Who were these people behind the switch of the Richmond electric chair?

By Albert Parker. From *Militant*, July 4, 1942.

The Virginia courts, as exemplified by judge Turner Clement of the Pittsylvania County Circuit Court. As presiding judge at the speedy two-day Waller trial, which ended on Sept. 27, 1940, he refused to disqualify himself after making prejudicial and inflammatory remarks in the presence of the jury panel. He refused to grant Waller a change of venue after evidence had been introduced showing that a lynch spirit spreading through the county would prevent Waller from receiving a fair trial there. Last month, after the *New York Times* had raised certain questions about the case, he sent that paper a letter reeking of class hatred, defending the conviction and insisting on the execution of the death sentence.

The United States Supreme Court. Twice while Waller sat in death row, appeals for Supreme Court review of the case were made by counsel for the defense. Twice this Court, which has been filled with a majority of New Deal liberals, refused to halt the execution—each time without a statement explaining its refusal. Finally, on June 27, appeals for a stay of execution were made to four individual justices of the Court, each of whom had the power to grant a stay that would have enabled the case to come before the Court when it meets again in October. Each of the four justices refused to grant the stay. The superliberal Frankfurter declared: "As a Federal judge I am unable to find any justification for summary interference with the *orderly* process of Virginia's courts of justice."

Virginia's Governor Colgate W. Darden, Jr. Elected by the poll tax, which excludes the overwhelming majority of Virginia citizens from voting, he upheld the poll tax system which denied Waller trial by a jury of his peers. Calling the viciously prejudiced proceedings that condemned Waller to death "a fair and impartial trial," he gave the go-ahead signal for the execution. Not content with that, he attacked those who were defending Waller with the statement that "the widespread propaganda campaign which has been carried on without regard for the facts in this case" was "extremely detrimental to the public interests" and resulted in sowing "racial discord at a critical time when every loyal citizen should strive to promote unity."

President Franklin D. Roosevelt. Author of pretty speeches about "the four freedoms" and "democracy," he had the power to set up a presidential commission of inquiry into the Waller case, which would have resulted in the almost automatic postponement of the execution, but refused to even answer the thousands of people who requested the establishment of such a commission. Elected with the help of the poll tax and the support of the reactionary southern Democrats, he gave the runaround to a delegation of Negro leaders who had come to Washington on July 1 to ask his intervention, and by refusing to meet with them, gave the final green light to Virginia's executioner.

And to whose wishes were the "humanitarian" president, the "conscientious" governor, and the "progressive" Supreme Court justices acceding when they callously rejected the appeals of labor and Negro organizations representing millions of workers?

To the wishes of Jim Crow and Judge Lynch; of the parasitic and brutal ruling class of the South, which rules by the rope, the torch, and the poll tax; of the capitalist class of employers and landowners, who openly stated on June 29 during the last hearing on the Waller case that if Waller escaped the chair, a wave of violence would break out against the Negroes in Pittsylvania County, and that from then on Negroes would get lynchings instead of trials.

In the eyes of this ruling class the struggle to save Waller had become a symbol. For them the murder of Waller was likewise a symbol.

The working class, Negro and white, must also regard the death of Waller as a symbol—and as a lesson.

It is a symbol of the ruling class's unrelenting hatred for all those who challenge the system where the Negro must "stay in his place" regardless of what his white masters do to him, where the sharecropper must not fight back against his landlord even in self-defense.

It teaches the lesson that the working class cannot expect anything from the capitalist courts but class injustice. That they cannot get any concessions from the capitalist class except by conducting the most irreconcilable class struggle against them. That they must prepare themselves, when they fight for their rights, to resist all the violence that the capitalists can organize.

Good-bye, Odell Waller. Take your place beside Sacco and Vanzetti, Joe Hill, the Haymarket martyrs, and the other sons of the working class who like you never had a chance for justice in the capitalist courts.

The *New York Times,* which donned a semiliberal mask in writing about your case during the last weeks of your life, took it off the day after you were killed. "Odell Waller," their editorial said, ". . . is beyond all explanations or forgiveness. . . . It will never again be of much importance to determine whether or not he intended to kill Oscar Davis, and whether or not Oscar Davis had cheated him."

Do not fear, Odell Waller. The advanced Negro and white workers will not be deceived by the attempts of the capitalist press to gloss over the significance of your case. We shall not forget you or the fact that you were killed because the bosses fear the working class.

We shall not forget you, and we shall not rest until we have avenged your death and the sufferings of the million other Odell Wallers in the South, who may die more slowly and with less publicity than you received, but who are no less the victims of the capitalist-landlord system of exploitation and oppression.

We shall avenge you, Odell Waller, by the abolition of that system and the creation of a new society where humanity will live in brotherhood and peace.

The Communist Party's Role

About the most contemptible and scablike role the Communist Party has played in a long time was in connection with the Odell Waller case.

For almost two years, while the Workers Defense League and other organizations conducted a hard uphill struggle to rally support for the condemned sharecropper and four times won him a reprieve from the electric chair, the Stalinists remained as silent as the tomb.

Then last month, when the Waller case began to receive nationwide attention, when it was clear that the Negro masses were fighting mad about the attempts to carry through the legal lynching, the Stalinists broke down and said something.

On June 18 Benjamin Davis, Jr., of the *Daily Worker* staff, devoted a whole sentence to the case—the first to appear in the *Daily Worker*. (Waller was scheduled to die the next day.) Most of this sentence was an attack on the "Trotskyite defeatists" (that is, the non-Trotskyist Workers Defense League and all the other groups fighting to save Waller's life) for their "sinister exploitation" of the case (that is, for their efforts to cheat Judge Lynch of his victim).

Another and somewhat longer article in the *Daily Worker* the next day showed that the Stalinists had adopted the formula put

---

By Philip Blake, a pen name of George Breitman. From *Militant*, July 4, 1942.

189

forth by Davis for covering up their treacherous role throughout the whole case. That formula called for paying a little lip-service to the need for defending Waller—and hurling the most damnable slanders at the defenders of Waller. This was the formula followed by the Communist Party up to and past the execution.

On June 30, the same day that poll tax Governor Darden issued his statement authorizing the Virginia executioner to go ahead with the murder of Waller, the *Daily Worker* published a story approvingly quoting Darden's attacks on the Workers Defense League for issuing a "malicious" pamphlet "filled with falsehoods" on the Waller case.

This aid from one of Waller's hangmen, the Stalinists thought, is a good way to attack the Workers Defense League, which is gaining support in many quarters for its vigorous defense campaign, and at the same time divert attention from the Stalinist failure to say anything about the case.

When their source for quotations then condemned Waller to die, the Stalinists criticized him for his "stupidity." From then on, they concentrated on one main theme: the execution of Waller is bad because it will give "the foul and hypocritical defeatists" an opportunity "to divide national unity and weaken our whole war effort" (July 2, *Daily Worker*). And after Waller was electrocuted, they continued to lament the "stupidity" of Darden and others for giving "all the politically unscrupulous elements—the unspeakable Trotskyists and their Norman Thomas bedfellows" a handle "to undermine the war effort" (July 3).

This was really their chief lament. They were worried about the bitterness of the Negro and concerned with curbing it. The Harlem CP functionary A. W. Berry announced the holding of a Waller protest rally—the first meeting they held on the case was three days after Waller's death—whose aim would be to awaken the Negro people "to their real stakes in the war."

And naturally, when the Stalinists' chief concern in the Waller case was using it as a vehicle for gaining support for the war from the Negro masses, they could not be too critical about the role of Roosevelt in refusing to meet with the delegations of Negro leaders who came to Washington to plead with him at the last moment for the establishment of a commission of inquiry that would have the effect of holding up the execution.

So Roosevelt's role was lightly glossed over by the *Daily Worker*. On this question, it is true, they used the strongest language against Roosevelt that they have employed at any time in the last year. They said: "President Roosevelt's failure to speak out and to intercede in the name of simple justice and national unity, is to be deplored."

Deplored! As long as Roosevelt has such servile tools as the Stalinists in the working class, no wonder he feels he can get away with such things.

But even so, there must have been some complaints from the Stalinist leaders about such strong language against their commander in chief.

For two days later, on a page devoted to the Waller case and the poll tax, the *Daily Worker* announced in very large type that Roosevelt too had once said he was opposed to the poll tax. Since nothing else on the page had anything to say about Roosevelt's role in the Waller case, this was obviously an attempt to whitewash the president who has three times been elected to the highest office in the nation with the aid of the poll tax and the poll taxers.

But while the editorial of July 3 "deplored" Roosevelt's "failure," the Stalinist protest rally in Harlem on July 5 did nothing of the kind, according to their own report on the meeting the next day.

And since they couldn't attack Roosevelt (for that would "harm the war effort"), they attacked—the Trotskyists. James Ford, one of the main speakers, declared that "mishandling of the case by the Trotskyists did great harm to Waller." He urged that "the errors they committed be adequately investigated."

RANDOLPH ANSWERS ETHRIDGE

There has been a great deal of comment and discussion on the statement made last month by Mark Ethridge, the southern white liberal member of the president's Fair Employment Practices Committee. And justifiably so. For it was a most significant statement, made not only at the opening of the Birmingham hearings of the FEPC, but also in the Louisville newspaper published by Ethridge.

"I believe," said Ethridge, "that it is perfectly apparent that Executive Order 8802 is a war order and not a social document. . . .

"There is no power in the world—not even in all the mecha-

By Albert Parker. From *Militant,* August 1, 1942.

nized armies of the earth, Allied or Axis—which could force the Southern white people to the abandonment of the principle of social segregation."

And then, to explain why with this view he continues to remain a member of the FEPC, Ethridge added: "If he [the decent Southern white man] is not willing to break down segregation—and he is not—he can at least see that it is not achieved on the brutal standards of a Ku Klux Klansman. He can see that it is made as painless as possible."

What Ethridge hints at when he says all the armies in the world will not be able to end Jim Crow in the South has been expressed more directly by another southern newspaperman, Hamner Cobbs, editor of the Greensboro, Alabama, *Watchman,* a man who doesn't pretend to be a liberal. On June 25, according to the *Pittsburgh Courier,* he said:

> We know that 90 percent of the white people of the South are in accord over the present system, and that's all we need to know. . . . We know that the Southern white man as strong as he is today, can repeat what he did in the 70's with hardly an effort. What disturbs us is the price, and a horrible price it will be, which so many innocent Negroes will have to pay. . . . The white man has insisted upon ruling the South, and he will keep on insisting. . . . If this disturbance [the hearings of the FEPC] continues, there will be trouble. . . . The night riders will be out again. There will be hangings, shootings, burnings.

That Cobbs speaks for the whole ruling class when he says that the fight to retain Jim Crow comes first, was demonstrated last week when the governor of Alabama, Frank M. Dixon, rejected a contract offered by the War Production Board, under which Alabama State Prison cotton mills would produce material for the army, because he considered it a "Federal attempt to abolish segregation of races in the South."

Objecting to a clause in the contract which asks that there shall be no discrimination in the performance of the work because of race, creed, color, or national origin, Dixon said:

"Under cover of this particular clause the Fair Employment Practices Committee has been operating to break down the principle of segregation of races, to force Negroes and white people to work together, intermingle with each other, and even to bring about the situation where white employees will have to work under Negroes."

At the Los Angeles convention of the NAACP, A. Philip Randolph gave a correct answer to Ethridge and all those others who share his viewpoint:

The Negro's reply to Mr. Ethridge is that Jim Crowism is wrong and undemocratic. It is of the same cloth as Hitler's Nazism, Mussolini's fascism and Hirohito's militarism and it is booked to go. . . .

The old order of Southern Jim Crow can, must and will be destroyed. He is evidently blind to the fact that the Negro has changed. The old Uncle Tom is dead and gone forever.

Mr. Ethridge should also know that if as he says all of the mechanized armies of the earth, Allies and Axis, cannot force the South to the abandonment of segregation and Jim Crow, that it is also true that all of the power of the world—not even all the mechanized armies of the earth, Allies and Axis—could force the Negro to the abandonment of his fight for the destruction of racial discrimination, segregation and Jim Crowism.

And since Mr. Ethridge feels this way about the fight of the Negro for his democratic rights, he should have the decency to resign from the President's Committee on Fair Employment Practices.

But while Randolph's answer was generally correct, it was neither complete nor adequate. For there are other conclusions to be drawn from Ethridge's statement:

1. When Ethridge emphasizes that Executive Order 8802 is a war order, he is saying that after the war, the government does not intend to continue even the small, ineffective work of the FEPC. If it is up to the government, the Negro will be in the same position he was in before the war.

2. Ethridge was appointed by Roosevelt—he was appointed as the FEPC's chairman, as a matter of fact—and no one in the administration has repudiated his statement. Is it not logical, therefore, to assume his statement of FEPC objectives—to make Jim Crow as painless as possible, while continuing it—is also the objective of the administration which is interested only in getting the Negro to support the war? Is it not also clear that more than Ethridge must go before the Negro will get his rights?

3. It is not quite true that Ethridge is "blind to the fact that the Negro has changed." Ethridge is quite well aware of it, and that's why he issued his statement. Only a few weeks before this statement, he warned: "They are more aggressive and demanding than they ever have been before; and, I think, we all ought to learn that." As long as the Negroes remained docile and "in their place," Ethridge was willing to pose as a liberal; but when he saw that they were organizing and becoming militant, he dropped his liberal mask with haste. Such is the role of all capitalist liberals.

But the important question is: What is to be done? Ethridge declares that southern Jim Crow is an unmovable object, and Randolph answers that the Negro fight for democratic rights is an irresistible force. What will happen when this irresistible force meets this unmovable object? Will the struggle end only in a stalemate? Won't the Negroes ever get their rights in the South?

We think that they will, and we think that we know the way. In the first place, the South is not an unmovable object. It is not a "solid South." The white workers of the South may not yet realize it, but their interests and those of the Negro masses are identical. They are both oppressed by the ruling class of employers and landlords. They will both benefit by the elimination of capitalist rule. The struggle in the South is a struggle to unite the white and Negro masses against their common enemy.

But even if not all the white workers in the South are brought to understand this, that does not mean the cause of Negro equality is hopeless. For the Negroes in the South have allies elsewhere—in the white and Negro workers in the rest of the country.

RACIST TERROR IN THE SOUTH

Afraid that the southern Negro people may take the talk about a "war for democracy" seriously, the ruling class of landlords, employers, and poll tax politicians is preparing a bloody reign of terror against the Negro masses in the South.

The attitude of these reactionary elements has been amply indicated by many statements in the last six weeks. Numerous attacks on Negroes in this same period have shown that the southern rulers are ready and willing to back up their "white supremacy" words with action.

Especially since the beginning of July the tempo of attacks on Negro rights has been speeded up. In the last week or so alone the following things have happened:

In Beaumont, Texas, a Negro soldier, Private Charles J. Reco, was ordered off a bus because he took a vacant seat in a section "reserved for white passengers." According to the Department of Justice, these are the facts:

That after he got out of the bus, a police officer "struck him several times with a nightstick and forced him into the back seat of a police car; that during the trip to police headquarters one of the officers shot him once through the shoulder and once through the arm. . . . Reports to the Department of Justice indicate that

By Philip Blake. From *Militant*, August 22, 1942.

Reco had caused no disturbance on the bus and that he had not resisted the police officers until after he had been struck several times."

The department has announced its intention of taking legal action against the cops. The Beaumont chief of police says he is going to "stand back" of his men.

In Georgia, Col. Lindley Camp, commander of the state guard, has issued an order instructing his subordinates to be on the alert against "racial disturbances." He declared that "suspected subversive influences" were attempting to cause race trouble in Georgia and that the same condition exists in Alabama, South Carolina, and other southern states.

His order said: "There have been reported an unusual number of assault cases and attempts to assault white ladies. Other communities have reported efforts on the part of Negro men and women to demand certain privileges which are not granted in Georgia and never will be. These occurrences are believed to be the direct result of the work of white agents and colored agents who seem to be active throughout the state."

He asserted that the army, which supervises the state guard, was "fully aware" of the order.

In a New Orleans draft office, police severely beat up a Negro draftee, Herman Lee, and his mother because he stepped out of line to say good-bye to her. In addition to beating them, the cops arrested several other Negroes who protested against the unprovoked brutality.

In Birmingham, Alabama, a mine company guard assaulted and then shot to death a Negro miner, Jack Bloodworth, when he protested against an unauthorized pay deduction by a company clerk. The next day the killing was declared "justifiable" by the coroner.

Both Negro and white workers at the mine went out on strike after the killing, and although they returned to work the next day, they threatened to go out again unless the killer and other antilabor officials were fired by the company.

Earlier this month, the Negro press reported the following events:

The arrest of six Negro soldiers in Jacksonville, Florida, by military police, civilian police, sheriff's deputies, and city police armed with submachine guns and service weapons. The soldiers were accused of "attempting to incite a riot" because they had objected to an arbitrary arrest of one of them.

Threats and acts of violence against CIO organizers and members in Birmingham, Alabama, because they had stated Negroes had the right to jobs like anyone else.

The demand by Alabama's U.S. Senator John D. Bankhead that Negro troops be taken out of the South or that northern Negroes not be trained in the South. The implication in his statement was that Negro soldiers were responsible for so-called riots and acts of violence against Negro troops.

A "new Scottsboro case" in Louisiana when three Negro soldiers were convicted on charges of "rape" after being threatened by police that they would be turned over to the Ku Klux Klan if they didn't admit guilt.

In the month of July, the following occurrences and statements were recorded:

The legal lynching of sharecropper Odell Waller in Virginia, with the "liberal" U.S. Supreme Court and the "humanitarian" president refusing to intervene.

The brutal lynching of Willie Vinson in Texarkana, Texas.

The killing of Pvt. Jesse Smith, Negro soldier, by civilian police in Flagstaff, Arizona; the exoneration of his killers; and the court-martial of five other Negro soldiers who were with Smith.

The beating and arrest of the noted singer Roland Hayes and his wife in Georgia, and the approval of this action expressed by Governor Talmadge.

The flat refusal by Alabama's Governor Dixon to accept a war contract because of his opposition to Roosevelt's Executive Order 8802, which calls for no discrimination in hiring.

The inflammatory statements by elements such as Horace Wilkinson, Alabama attorney, threatening lynch action against Negroes who ask for their constitutional rights and advocating the formation of a League to Maintain White Supremacy.

The beating of a Negro soldier, Pvt. Alfred Knox, and his mother by white MPs and civilian policemen in Houston, Texas, because he dared to use the telephone booth in the white waiting room of a railroad station. Knox, who may lose an eye because of the beating, was then arrested.

The unprovoked killing of a Negro worker, Walter Gunn, by a Jim Crow sheriff in Tuskegee, Alabama, and the terrorizing of the Negro population to prevent their testifying in the case.

The refusal by a federal grand jury to indict the known lynchers of Cleo Wright in Sikeston, Missouri, on the ground that "the facts disclosed do not constitute any federal offense."

The cold-blooded murder of a young Negro, Herman Jones, by a police officer in Suffolk, Virginia, after Jones had been arrested for an alleged misdemeanor.

Who can doubt, after examining this incomplete record of six weeks in the South, that the most important place for the Negro people to be fighting for democracy is right here at home?

THE STRUGGLE IN INDIA

How It Affects Black Americans

Every militant Negro in this country should follow the developments in the current struggle for Indian independence with the closest attention. For the cause of the Indian masses in this struggle is the cause of the oppressed toilers everywhere.

What is it that the Indian people are fighting for? The same thing that the American colonists demanded and fought for in 1776. The same thing for which the Chinese people are fighting the Japanese imperialists today. Freedom, the right to determine their own destiny.

The British rulers seem to regard this as some kind of unspeakable crime, and they react to it in the same way that the Jim Crow rulers in our southern states react when the Negro workers and sharecroppers ask for the right to vote or the right to get a job on an equal basis with other workers. But the Negro people— whose ancestors also knew what oppression was and who were shot and hanged and whipped when they organized numerous slave revolts—can have nothing but sympathy for the aspirations of the Indian masses.

There is a remarkable similarity between the arguments used by the British rulers to oppose granting independence to India now and those used by the American ruling class to deny equal rights to the Negro people now.

1. We cannot give you independence now, the British rulers say to the Indians, because it would lead to "internal strife."

By Albert Parker. From *Militant,* August 22, 1942. At the time these articles were written, India was a colony of Great Britain engaged in a struggle to win its independence. Mohandas K. Gandhi (1869-1948) was the leading figure in this movement. His philosophy of passive resistance and his compromising stance toward the British helped prevent the movement from developing in a radical anticapitalist direction. India won its independence in 1947, but capitalist oppression continued.

And the American Negroes are told they cannot have equality now because it would disrupt "national unity."

2. The struggle for Indian independence at this time leaves the way open for the "common enemy," Japan, to invade and subjugate India, say the spokesmen for British imperialism; consequently, the interests of the Indian people themselves require that this struggle be stopped at once (even if it takes bullets and whips and jails to do it).

And the fight for Negro equality while the war is going on aids the Axis powers, which will take away even those rights which the Negro people now possess, because this fight undermines "morale" and "hampers" the war effort, say the spokesmen for Jim Crow; consequently the interests of the Negroes themselves demand the discontinuation of the fight against racial discrimination (even if it takes ropes, torches, and jails to do it).

3. Besides, say the British rulers, haven't we stated that we recognize your right to eventual independence, and haven't we openly promised that when this war is over we are going to give it to you?

And besides, say the American rulers, haven't we stated that we are opposed to discrimination and haven't we promised that things will be different when we win the war?

But the Indian people are not impressed or convinced by this propaganda, just as the Negro militants are not. Like their Negro brothers and sisters in this country, the Indian masses say to their oppressors:

You talk about "internal strife" but you are the people responsible for whatever strife there is. Get off our backs, stop denying us our rights, and there will be no strife.

You lie when you say that the struggle for our rights aids the Axis. The world has seen what happened to the people of Malaya and Burma as a result of your policies and your rule, and we do not intend to have the same fate befall us. Your rule and your policies aid the Axis, and we are fighting to get rid of them so that we will really have the opportunity to defeat the fascists. Victory for our fight will inspire the peoples of Asia, Africa, and the whole world to renewed struggles against their oppressors.

You not only slander us when you say that our fight aids the fascists, but you also show how hypocritical are your claims to be fighting a war for democracy. We cannot believe any of your promises, because you have made and broken them before. Whatever your "postwar" promises are, they are worthless in our eyes, and we don't believe them any more than the promises made to us by Japanese agents.

Negro workers, the Indian struggle is yours too. You cannot remain true to the principles of your own century-old struggle in this country unless you actively help to defend the Indian masses against their defamers and to aid them against their enemies.

Randolph's Statement

On the whole, the Negro press has not thus far devoted anywhere near the amount of attention to the present struggle in India that it deserves. There have been a few short articles and some editorials, chiefly on the arrest of Gandhi and the other Congress leaders. Some papers have pointed out the difference between the talk about democracy and the treatment of the Indian people. But generally speaking, the Negro papers have not come out with a sharp, clear stand on the Indian fight.

In contrast to most of the Negro press was the statement made last week by A. Philip Randolph on behalf of the March on Washington movement which he leads. Although this statement is open to considerable criticism, as we shall show below, it is significant as the statement of a Negro whose position of leadership in the Negro movement depends upon his expressing, even though in distorted form, the aspirations and sentiments of the rank and file. The statement began as follows:

> The March on Washington movement hails the militant, noble and persistent struggle of the people of India for freedom and independence from the brutal tyranny of Great Britain.
>
> Negro people of America, the West Indies and Africa should support this grim, determined and courageous battle for freedom under the gallant, wise and dauntless leadership of Mohandas K. Gandhi for they constitute one of the great oppressed and exploited sections of the darker races of the world, seeking their liberation from ruthless British imperialism.

With this part of the statement we are in practically complete agreement. We think that it expresses the sentiments of the Negro masses. Our single objection to this part of the statement would be to the characterization of Gandhi. We fully support the struggle now going on in India, even though for the time it is

---

By Albert Parker. From *Militant,* August 29, 1942.

under the leadership of Gandhi, and we oppose the British jailing of Gandhi. But we have no illusions about Gandhi, who has often placed himself in the leadership of Indian struggles in the past only to call them off at the decisive moment and to compromise and surrender to the British rulers. In this respect, Gandhi is like Randolph, who also has often placed himself at the head of Negro struggles only to call them off in return for a shabby compromise, as he did last year when he called off the march on Washington. It is one thing to support the struggle which is being led by Gandhi, it is another and a different thing to spread illusions about him.

There are other parts in Randolph's statement which are also substantially correct. He urges Negro organizations to adopt resolutions demanding the freedom of India, to demand the freedom of the Congress Party leaders, to send expressions of sympathy to India, etc.

But while Randolph takes a much more positive stand on behalf of the Indian struggle than has been taken in any other Negro statement we have seen, it is nevertheless unacceptable. For Randolph sees the Indian struggle for independence from Great Britain as part of Great Britain's war against the Axis, and he wants Negroes to appeal to Churchill for India's independence on the grounds that this would be in the interests of Britain.

Randolph thus puts himself in the position of trying to tell "ruthless British imperialism" what is the best way for it to conduct its imperialist war. To this, Churchill and the other representatives of Indian oppression would probably reply, "Thank you, but we know how to best conduct our war and protect our imperialist interests."

The British imperialists are fighting this war to be able to maintain their hold over the colonies. So far as they are concerned, there would be no sense in fighting the war at all if they had to give up colonies like India to win it. Their conduct of the war in Malaya and Burma shows that they would much prefer to lose India to Japanese imperialism than to lose it to the Indian people, because they feel they have a better chance of getting the colonies back from their rival imperialists than they would of getting them back from the colonial people. That was why the British agreed, while they were negotiating the surrender of Singapore, that "1,000 British troops would remain in Singapore City to maintain order until the Japanese Army completed occupation" (*New York Times,* February 16, 1942).

Those who really want to support India's struggle must understand the contradiction in which Randolph and all other supporters of the imperialist war find themselves. In this struggle you are either for India fighting against Britain, or for Britain fighting against India. You cannot be for India on the ground that its freedom will aid the interests of British imperialism any more than you can be for British imperialism in this struggle on the ground that its continued domination of India will aid the interests of India.

With this viewpoint we are sure the mass of the Negro people will agree. They know what oppression is from their experiences, and they hate it whether it is imposed by fascist or "democratic" oppressors. Just as they correctly place the interests of the Negro struggle in this country above the interests of the imperialist war, so too will they support the struggle of their Indian brothers and sisters, regardless of the false arguments of those who want to preserve British imperialism. And those who try the impossible task of reconciling the interests of imperialism with the interests of the masses.

Poll Shows Solid Support

The overwhelming majority of the Negro people in this country are supporters of India's struggle for freedom, the *Pittsburgh Courier*'s Bureau of Public Sentiment concludes after making a nationwide survey and receiving replies from more than ten thousand Negroes.

The results of this survey, printed in the October 10 issue of the *Pittsburgh Courier*, largest Negro weekly, show that 87.8 percent of the Negroes included in the poll answered yes to the question, "Do you believe that India should contend for her rights and her liberty now?" Only 10.7 percent said no, and 1.5 percent had no opinion.

One of the most interesting aspects of the poll was the fact that Negroes in the South fully shared the point of view of Negroes everywhere on this issue, answering yes in 87.4 percent of the cases.

This reaction by the Negro people is all the more significant because, as the *Courier* article points out, it was registered "despite the fact that nothing more than an ominous silence penetrated through the censorship from far off India."

From *Militant,* October 17, 1942.

MARCH ON WASHINGTON MOVEMENT HOLDS NATIONAL CONFERENCE

Conference Called

NEW YORK, September 8—The Negro March on Washington movement will hold a national conference in Detroit on September 26-27 to decide if and when a march on the nation's capital will be held, the *Militant* learned last week in a special interview with B. F. MacLaurin, national secretary of the movement.

This information was obtained shortly after A. Philip Randolph, national director of the movement, announced that President Roosevelt had refused to meet with Randolph and a number of other prominent Negro leaders to discuss growing complaints of racial discrimination and attacks on Negro rights. Randolph has also issued a statement claiming that a previous announcement of his had been misinterpreted and that "The plan to march on Washington has not been abandoned; it was only postponed."

By Abe Stein. From *Militant,* September 12, 1942.

A Great Opportunity

Although the eyes of every militant Negro in the country will be turned toward the conference to be held in Detroit, it is not yet possible to predict what will happen at that conference. The chief reason for this uncertainty is that the Randolph leadership of the movement, which was never chosen democratically by the rank and file but still has their support and respect, has not indicated what proposals it will present in Detroit.

By Albert Parker. From *Militant,* September 12, 1942.

It would be foolish to assume that Randolph has overnight changed from a policy of vacillation, based on the hope that talk alone will bring concessions for the Negro people, to a policy of aggressive militancy, arising from the understanding that the Negroes will make no gains in this period except by fighting for them against both the Jim Crow capitalist class and its political agents.

At any rate, there is not yet any evidence that the proposal to hold the Detroit conference arose from such a change in policy. Rather, the decision to hold the conference seems to have resulted from two events which plainly faced the leadership of the movement with a "do or die" alternative.

These two events were the aftermath of the story in the press last month that Randolph had announced the abandonment in this period of any perspective to call a march on Washington against Jim Crowism, and the brush-off given Randolph by Roosevelt.

The reaction to the story in the press was pretty much the same among both the supporters and opponents of the movement; and it must have been strongest among the masses. If the March on Washington movement is not going to hold a march, if it is going to conduct the same kind of activities as other Negro organizations now in the field and it is going to carry on those activities in the same old way as these other organizations—then, the prevailing sentiment was, what the devil use is there in having a March on Washington movement?

Randolph waited a few weeks after this story first appeared in the press before denying it as a "misinterpretation." In that time, we can be sure, he was able to estimate the response of the members. It was his estimation of their response more than anything else which led to his vigorous denial.

The other event—Roosevelt's contemptuous refusal to meet with Randolph—also put the issue squarely up to Randolph. We must remember that ever since he revived the movement last spring, Randolph has said that the need of the day is a "frank" discussion of the Negro problem in the White House. With Roosevelt refusing to even discuss, Randolph realized that either he must take some action or lose face.

While the call for a conference does not flow from a basic change in Randolph's policy therefore—but rather from conditions over which Randolph has no control—we can be certain that even Randolph and his associates had to draw certain conclusions from Roosevelt's attitude, namely:

1. *That Negroes are not going to improve their conditions by declarations of patriotism.* Randolph hastened to assure Roose-

velt in his telegram asking for a conference that he wanted to act "in the interests of national unity, effective defense and victory for the United Nations and the cause of democracy." But Roosevelt was not at all moved by this—he still refused to let Randolph into the White House even by the back door.

2. That Roosevelt will not give the Negroes anything unless they start to fight for it. Randolph must remember that last year it was Roosevelt who was sending the telegrams and asking for conferences. The reason was that Negroes were then ready to march on Washington, and Randolph was then not merely the author of telegrams, but the representative of militants organized and ready to take action.

But whatever Randolph's motivations for calling the conference, and whether he is ready to change his policies or not, there are many encouraging signs about the coming gathering in Detroit as reported to the *Militant.*

The first is that the conference will be made up of representatives of the rank and file in the movement, as well as leaders selected from the top. Their participation in the deliberations and decisions can only have a healthy effect on the proceedings and the future of the movement.

The second is that a constitution for the movement will be drawn up. This too is all to the good, for it will strengthen the movement, put it on a sounder organizational footing, make it more democratic, and therefore attract a lot of workers who feel that the movement may be a flash-in-the-pan affair.

Third, of course, is the fact that the conference will decide if and when a march on Washington will be held, as well as other questions of policy. Needless to say, such a discussion can kindle a new enthusiasm among the Negro masses, especially if the conference adopts a militant program and authorizes a fighting alliance of the organization with the labor movement against the economic and political enemies of both Negroes and labor.

This is the opportunity for the Negro people! It may not come again during the war. The struggle against Jim Crowism cannot stand still—either the masses will push it forward to new heights, or the enemies of the Negroes will smash it back to earth.

This opportunity to go forward must not be muffed now. If advantage is not taken of it, there is every danger that frustration and defeatism will set in among the Negro ranks, and there is every likelihood that the March on Washington movement will collapse in short order. Perhaps Randolph is calling the conference as a bluff—as pressure on the White House gates; and perhaps he isn't. That isn't the important question. It is up to the Negro militants to let their voices be heard, to indicate that they are serious about wanting to press forward for full equality now.

If they do this in Detroit, and if the conference adopts a program and perspective of struggle, it may well go down in history as the most important Negro gathering of all time.

Permanent Organization Established

DETROIT, September 27—Taking a historic step forward in the struggle for democratic rights for the oppressed 13 million Negro Americans, sixty-three delegated representatives of the Negro March on Washington movement at a policy conference held here yesterday and today voted to establish a permanent national organization, based on a program of mass action, "to fight to abolish discrimination, segregation and Jim Crow now, before the war ends."

The militant delegates, representing local March on Washington Committees in New York; Chicago; St. Louis; Washington, D.C.; Detroit and Flint, Michigan; and Tampa, Florida, and New Orleans in the Deep South, set as their immediate organizational goal the mobilization of a million Negro men and women. They drafted a provisional constitution; established a provisional national executive board of thirteen; worked out a broad plan for building local units and conducting immediate mass struggles on a local scale throughout the country; and set in motion machinery for a giant national convention to be convened in Chicago the week of May 1, 1943.

The planned convention, to be composed of elected representatives from the local units, will establish a permanent organizational setup, amend and ratify the constitution, elect permanent officers, and determine if and when a national Negro mass march on Washington shall take place next summer.

The resolutions adopted at the conference, the discussion of the delegates, and the keynote statement of A. Philip Randolph, national director of the MOWM and head of the AFL Pullman Porters, gave strong testimony to the fact that the Negro masses place no hope in the promises of the Roosevelt administration to protect their rights, and reflected the tremendous pressure from the ranks of the Negro people for militant and decisive action now in an all-out fight to win full and unconditional democratic rights for themselves right here at home.

By Art Preis. From *Militant,* October 3, 1942.

Of decisive importance for the future growth and effectiveness of the MOWM was the insistence of the majority of the delegates on a democratic organization, run by the membership, and with final power resting always with the rank and file.

Randolph's keynote statement laid down the basic policies and program subsequently adopted by the conference. In general, this statement was sharp and bitter in tone, stressing the need for militant mass Negro struggle and reflecting the lack of faith of the Negro people today in achieving their rights through any means but their own organized effort in collaboration with the progressive sections of society, particularly the labor movement.*

In laying down the broad policy of MOWM on the war, he declared emphatically: "We say that the Negro must fight for his democratic rights right now, for after the war it may be too late. This is our policy on the Negro and the war."

Stressing the need for mass organization and action, he cited with enthusiasm the present struggle of the Indian people for national liberation.

Randolph particularly emphasized that while the MOWM is an all-Negro organization, it does not aim to evoke an attitude of "Black Nationalism." "Our policy is that it be all-Negro, and pro-Negro but not antiwhite, or anti-Semitic or antilabor, or anti-Catholic. The reason for this is that all oppressed people must assume the responsibility and take the initiative to free themselves. . . . because Negroes build an all-Negro movement such as the March, it does not follow that our movement should not call for the collaboration of Jews, Catholics, trade unions and white liberals. . . ."

The principal discussion and debate occurred today, after the conference yesterday was divided up into a number of committees to bring in reports on the constitution, program and strategy, resolutions, etc.

A great part of today's session was devoted to adoption of the provisional constitution. The debate on this brought out the keen desire of the Negro ranks for a completely democratic organization.

The constitution committee, which was appointed by Randolph, as were all the other committees, brought in a proposal that the national director "shall have power to act or decide on any emergency affecting the welfare of the organization."

A delegate arose immediately to demand to know whether "this gives the director the power to call off the march." This related to Randolph's action last summer in calling off the

*Several paragraphs deleted here are printed on page 224.

original march on Washington at the last moment, without consultation with the rank and file.

Others took the floor to insist that the highest power between conventions should rest in the hands of the entire executive board of thirteen. Randolph himself then expressed his approval of vesting the final authority in the hands of the executive board.

A further debate arose over the proposal that "this constitution may be amended by the National Executive Board, by a two-thirds majority vote."

The delegates argued that the constitution represents the decisions of the membership, as expressed in convention, and can be amended only by the national convention. Randolph spoke on the issue and declared that "the final authority must rest in the hands of the members, either through convention or referendum."

The first resolution to come before the conference this afternoon was a brief one calling for endorsement of "the fight of the United Nations."

One delegate, a woman, strongly opposed this resolution, arguing that "if we give a blanket endorsement to the way this war is being conducted, we weaken our own fight here at home." She insisted that any resolution on the war should include an analysis of the role and objectives of American and British imperialism, the question of India, Negro rights, etc. Her remarks drew strong applause.

However, Randolph pointedly insisted that it would be "unwise" to have "any reservations on support of the war." The resolution was finally adopted, although at no time during the conference was any enthusiastic support expressed for the war.

A significant resolution was then adopted placing the MOWM on record as "opposed to any cooperation with the Communist Party or Communist Party front organizations, although this is not to be construed as an expression of opposition to Russia in her heroic fight against Hitler's Germany." The resolution also stated, however, that this did not bar members of the Communist Party from participating as individuals in the MOWM.

The discussion on this resolution brought out the efforts of the Stalinists to sabotage the MOWM, the complete distrust that the Negro masses today have of the CP, and their recognition that the Stalinists have no interest in advancing the real cause of Negro freedom.

A couple of delegates took a pure red-baiting position on the matter, arguing that if this resolution were not passed it would leave the organization open to the charge of being "red" and that the "ultimate objective of the CP is worldwide revolution." Of course, the "red" label is attached to any group that fights for its

207

rights, and it is ancient history now that the Stalinist parties today are bitter opponents of any revolutionary movements.

The resolution was finally passed principally because the delegates desired to place on record their opposition to the Stalinists for their attacks on the MOWM and attempted sabotage of the present Negro struggle.

The role of the Stalinists was clearly brought to the attention of the conference by the St. Louis delegates, who represent a fighting militant local group of Negroes. These delegates displayed a large scrapbook containing hundreds of news clippings about their recent mass picket lines and demonstrations, which at one big arms plant won 3,500 jobs for Negro workers recently. The scrapbook also displayed a large leaflet, printed on both sides, put out by the Communist Party, which directly attacked the picket lines and demonstrations as "disrupting the war effort."

Because of the tremendous scope of the work which had to be covered in a brief time by the conference, most of the resolutions were approved without complete reading and placed in the hands of the new executive board for final editing.

However, most of these resolutions were of an extremely progressive and militant character and undoubtedly, with some minor changes, would have been overwhelmingly approved by the conference had they been read completely.

An important resolution adopted covered the question of a future mass Negro march on Washington. This resolution declared that "discrimination, segregation and Jim Crowism are spreading in this country and there is no visible effort on the part of the President or the Congress to recognize the Negroes as first-class citizens in this so-called democratic war," and concluded by calling upon the forthcoming national convention of the MOWM to "declare its approval of a March On Washington of Negroes from all over America for the purpose of pressing home to the President, the American people and the Congress that Negroes want their full democratic rights now, during the war."

Another resolution, titled "Mass Action," states that "the day of 'individualism' is past and that power only resides in the masses" and places the MOWM "on record endorsing mass-action including marches on city-halls, city councils, defense plants, public utility works, picketing and sending mass letters and telegrams to the President and Congressmen and Senators to stress the will and desires of the Negro People for their rights as American citizens."

A special resolution was adopted on the attitude of the MOWM toward organized labor, which asserts that "the free trade union movement is the bulwark of democracy and is the most fundamental and constructive institution in our contemporary society—through its principles of unity of all workers regardless of race, color, religion or national origin."

The resolution then goes on to "endorse the trade union movement and bona fide collective bargaining and calls upon the AFL and CIO to abolish discrimination, segregation, Jim Crow and the color bar in all forms and collaborate with the Negro people in their struggle for equality and freedom." It further urges all Negro workers "to join trade unions that accept them and form independent unions when rejected to continue to fight to break down the color barriers and protect their economic interests against the employers."

The conference did not fail to tie in the struggles of the American Negroes with the battles of the oppressed peoples everywhere. It passed specific resolutions calling for the immediate independence of the peoples of the West Indies and India.

The resolution on India declared the conference's support for the present struggle of the Indian masses for national independence, and demanded the release of the arrested nationalist leaders and an end to "the wanton murder of the Indian masses." The resolution stated in part that "the people of India are in a desperate struggle to achieve independence and freedom now from British Imperialism" and that "the freedom of any section of people in the world is not secure so long as any other nation is in bondage."

There is no question but that the MOWM faces a tremendous task ahead. There are many obstacles, internal and external, which will have to be surmounted.

But the basic and immediately urgent task has been undertaken: the establishment of a nationwide mass membership organization based on the principle of an all-out mass action program to battle for the rights of the Negro people right now, during the war, and every day.

The program laid out by the conference is brave and ambitious and sound. If the Negro masses rally around that program, make it their own, and carry it out in action with the support and aid of all the working people, they are certain to bring nearer the day of their full emancipation.

THE SWP'S 1942 CONVENTION

55. Far from arousing enthusiasm among the Negro people, the entry of the United States into the war has intensified their determination to utilize the crisis engendered by the war to win the struggle against Jim Crowism and for full social, economic, and political equality. Official government propaganda about fighting for "democracy" and the "four freedoms" serves only to emphasize to the Negroes that they themselves are denied the most elementary democratic rights, discriminated against in the war industries and in the armed forces. "After-the-war" promises only remind the Negroes that they got the same promises during the first imperialist war, and that none of these promises was kept. Furthermore, the Negro people today derive inspiration and self-confidence from the struggles of the colonial peoples for liberation from imperialism. While the ruling class demands postponement of the Negro struggle for the sake of "national unity," the will of the Negro masses to struggle is greater than ever. This is reflected in the fear of the petty-bourgeois Negro leadership to openly counsel the Negro masses to abandon their struggles until after the war—as they did in 1917—and above all in the emergence of the militant Negro March on Washington movement. Such an independent Negro movement has been made historically necessary by the betrayals and indifference of the trade union bureaucracies, by the failures of the traditional workers' parties and Negro organizations, and by the weakness of the revolutionary party. We support the March on Washington movement, despite the vacillations of its leadership, and seek to mobilize the whole working class in support of its objectives.

56. The struggle against Jim Crowism is as much the problem of the white workers as of the Negro people. Labor with a white skin cannot be free so long as labor with a black skin is branded. The great contribution of the Negro workers to the growth of unionism—in the auto plants, packinghouses, coal mines, steel, etc.—is but the beginning of what can be done if the workers of

From political resolution adopted by SWP national convention, held in New York, October 2-4, 1942. From *Militant*, October 17, 1942.

all races firmly unite. As one-tenth of the population, the principal oppressed minority in the United States, the Negro people cannot achieve their freedom without the active and wholehearted support of the white workers. A struggle of the Negro masses unsupported by the white workers can be deflected by the ruling class into a tragic racial clash between white and Negro workers. The cementing of a firm alliance between Negroes and white workers has been hampered by the Stalinists and other groups who speak in the name of equality but have betrayed and embittered the Negro masses time and again.

57. It is therefore above all necessary for revolutionists to demonstrate *in practice* in the trade unions and in the factories that they champion the rights of Negroes and battle against all forms of racial prejudice and discrimination. One such demonstration is worth a thousand articles and speeches on the need for unity! The principal task of the party's Negro work in this period is to build the Negro cadres of the party. These cadres will be recruited primarily from Negro unionists whose joint struggles with the white workers against the employers provides them with the necessary experiences and background for revolutionary leadership of the Negro masses.

RANDOLPH AT THE AFL CONVENTION

A. Philip Randolph breathed a little life into the annual AFL convention at Toronto by taking the floor for half an hour and denouncing the Jim Crow practices that still prevail in a number of AFL international unions.

This is not a new role for Randolph; he has been doing it every year as delegate of the Pullman Porters union. He was just as vigorous and biting this year as ever, but just as little as ever was done about it by the AFL big shots.

Randolph remarked on the many speeches about democracy that had been made at the convention. A man from Mars, he said, might have thought most of the speechmakers really believed in democracy, but when he saw that Negroes were being Jim Crowed by these same people, he would reach the conclusion that these speeches are baloney.

After outlining the various ritualistic and other devices used to

By Albert Parker. From *Militant,* October 24, 1942.

deny Negroes equal rights, Randolph called on the convention to set up a committee to investigate "various forms and cases of discrimination that may be presented to it." The CIO already has such a committee.

The well-fed bureaucrats voted down Randolph's proposal, declaring instead that the AFL deplored discrimination and making it clear that the AFL would not interfere with those unions that continue discriminating. Just as the reactionary poll taxers and lynch leaders oppose the anti-poll tax and antilynch bills on the grounds of "states' rights," so the AFL bureaucrats defend the rights of Jim Crow elements in the AFL on the grounds of "local autonomy."

The next day Daniel J. Tobin, president of the International Brotherhood of Teamsters, took the floor and viciously denounced Randolph for daring to raise the question of discrimination. No more appropriate person could have been chosen to defend the defenders of "local autonomy" than this man, who rules virtually as dictator over the Teamsters and expels and frames up all those who seek to exercise their democratic rights. He probably took it as a personal affront for anyone to get up and speak a few truths that exposed the hypocrisy of the Executive Council.

What Tobin had to say about Randolph was typical of all his relations with working-class opponents, typical too of his attacks on the Trotskyists and the leaders of Local 544 in Minneapolis: the method of slander, frame-up, and threat.

"Randolph," Tobin had the nerve to say, was helping "to light the torch of dissension and destruction among a large section of the population." In other words, Randolph—not the Jim Crow elements inside and outside the AFL—was responsible for the Negro masses' discontent with discrimination and segregation!

"Men of this type," Tobin went on in his arrogant way, "are doing more in my opinion to destroy the future progress of the black man, which we are trying to bring about, than any other section within a local constitution or international union by-law." In other words, according to Tobin, Randolph was hurting the interests of the Negroes by asking the AFL to suit its action to some of its speeches—even more than were the Jim Crow artists in leading AFL posts!

Three times Randolph tried to get the floor after this attack, and each time President William Green—who also makes speeches about democracy—refused to give it to him.

Unquestionably, the coming convention of the CIO will see an entirely different attitude toward the Negro worker. The CIO is by no means perfect in this respect, but it is miles ahead of the hidebound AFL leaders.

The bureaucrats looked all powerful at the AFL convention, but the day is coming when they will be swept aside as the labor fakers they are. The Negroes can have no expectation of getting support for their struggle from people of this kind—the only place they will find support is among the rank-and-file white union workers, who are also the object of the bureaucrats' contempt. When the Negroes and the white workers unite, Tobin and his type will get the answer they deserve—and it will be at least as vigorous an answer as the one they prevented Randolph from making.

DIRTY DEAL KILLS
ANTI-POLL TAX BILL

The bill to abolish payment of poll taxes for federal elections in eight southern states is dead. It was killed by a dirty deal participated in by both the Republican and Democratic parties and approved by the Roosevelt administration.

In fact, the whole debate on the poll tax was so dirty that the administration censored all dispatches going out of the country, refusing to permit news of it to be sent even to Britain.

The administration may hope in this way to suppress abroad the story of how the poll tax was saved—a vain hope, for such news will spread like wildfire to the oppressed peoples of the world. But it can never wipe out of the minds of millions of Americans the growing realization of the vast difference between the fine democratic ideals professed by the government and the viciously undemocratic practices which the government refuses to abandon.

For a full week the poll tax minority had refused to let the anti-poll tax bill even come before the Senate. But although they had threatened to filibuster and prevent a debate on the bill until January 2, when both the present Congress and the bill expire, the poll taxers realized that to actually conduct the filibuster for that length of time would invite such a widespread mass reaction of anger and dissatisfaction that the bill might be passed despite all their efforts.

The Republicans had promised, almost to a man, in the recent election campaign that they would vote against the poll tax. But

By George Breitman. From *Militant,* November 28, 1942.

they were far more desirous of coming to a deal with the poll taxers than of making it easier for ten million white and Negro workers and sharecroppers to vote. So they gave the nod to the poll taxers.

After this, the spokesmen of the poll tax states—who had been doing everything they could to keep the bill from coming to the floor because they were afraid that a motion for cloture (to end debate) might put an end to their filibuster—brazenly stood up and offered to let the bill be entered for debate, provided the supporters of the bill would agree to a vote on cloture within two days, and to withdraw the bill if cloture was not adopted.

Cloture requires a two-thirds vote. The poll taxers would never have requested the vote unless they had more than one-third of the vote in their vest pocket. The supporters of the bill—Barkley, Norris, Pepper, etc.—realized this.

They realized too that under these conditions the only way the bill could be passed was by prolonging the debate until the angry protests of the masses would force the non-poll tax senators to go through with a vote for cloture and the passage of the bill.

In spite of this, they came to agreement with the poll taxers in what can be characterized only as a sellout. One of the many revolting aspects of this deal was that it was committed in the name of not disgracing "the good name" of the Senate!

The bill was introduced, the motion for cloture was voted on and defeated by a vote of 41-37, and the anti-poll tax bill was withdrawn. Sixteen Democrats from non-poll tax states voted against cloture, and so did ten Republicans. The Republican minority leader, McNary, who had bragged that he was against the poll tax, led the Republicans in voting down the motion for cloture that could have led to the abolition of the poll tax.

None of the liberal or Stalinist supporters of the anti-poll tax bill have commented on the role played by Roosevelt.

The "great humanitarian" had "nothing to say" about the bill while it was being debated in the House, although last February he had briefly stated that he was against the poll tax and had "always" been against it. His silence on the matter was maintained until the time when the deal in the Senate was being arranged. In a press conference on November 20, he said that he knew nothing about the filibuster.

"Asked whether he thought the poll tax repeal bill should pass, he reiterated that he knew nothing about it, had talked to no one about it, and therefore could not express an opinion" (*New York Times,* November 21).

By this openly cynical expression of contempt for a struggle which had aroused both the labor and liberal movements,

Roosevelt no doubt thought he was very cleverly sidestepping the issue.

But actually that statement revealed his true stand on this fight. For if he "talked to no one about it," that means he talked to no one *for* it. That means he didn't use a single iota of his tremendous influence to try to get the anti–poll tax bill passed. In the present situation that can only mean that Roosevelt didn't want the bill passed.

Let the workers not be fooled by Roosevelt's stooges on this issue. When they were fighting to kill the poll tax, they were fighting the Roosevelt machine as well as the poll taxers and the Republicans and Democrats.

When Roosevelt wants legislation passed, he knows how to go about getting it. He showed this last Labor Day when he ordered Congress to give him wage-freezing and price-fixing powers by October 1, or he would take them.* And he has showed it a hundred other times when he threw the full force of his administration in motion—through the press, over the radio, in Congress—to pass what he wanted.

Roosevelt can indulge in as many wisecracks as he wishes, but they will not be able to obscure the fact that Roosevelt, by his silence if nothing else, helped to kill the anti–poll tax bill.

The workers should let the full significance of this fact sink in: The responsibility for the defeat of the anti–poll tax bill lies on all wings of the Democratic Party—the northern, southern, and Rooseveltian—and on all wings of the Republican Party, the isolationist and interventionist.

If the workers cannot depend on either capitalist party to pass such an elementary democratic measure as the abolition of poll taxes, how then can they expect the slightest assistance from these parties in the struggle to safeguard their trade unions and living standards?

The chief lesson of the fight around the poll tax is that the workers need a new party, ready to challenge the power of the capitalist parties, willing to fight without compromise, and able to sweep away the rule of capitalism and all the reactionary measures which it uses to keep itself in power.

---

*On October 5, 1942, Roosevelt issued a decree freezing wages at their September 15, 1942, level.

GENERAL DAVIS IS A BUSY MAN

Brig. Gen. Benjamin O. Davis, the first and only Negro general in the U.S. Army, seems to be the busiest officer of his rank in the armed forces.

True, he isn't seeing any active service against the Axis.

True, he isn't in command of any soldiers, either Negro or white.

But just the same he's always on the go and busy proving his value to the brass hats and Washington bureaucrats who appointed him.

For his is the job of whitewashing Jim Crow conditions in the army—and that's a full-time job for any man.

His first big assignment in this field was in the Fort Bragg case in August, 1941, when Pvt. Ned Turman died fighting for democracy in a hail of MP bullets. Davis did such a good job in whitewashing the Jim Crow conditions that are at bottom responsible for "race riots" in army camps that this became a specialty of his.

More recently, after complaints about the export of Jim Crow to Britain, Davis was sent to that country. He reported that everything had been exaggerated and that conditions in Britain were actually nothing less than fine.

And now Davis is on the scene again in Phoenix, Arizona, where brutality against Negro soldiers led to an armed struggle last week that resulted in the death of three, the wounding of a score, and the arrest of 180 soldiers.

You don't have to gaze into a crystal ball to be able to predict that Davis will soon blandly announce that, of course, Jim Crow conditions and above all segregation had absolutely nothing to do with the Phoenix clash.

Who said Uncle Tom was dead?

From *Militant*, December 12, 1942.

NONCOMS BUSTED AND TRANSFERRED

Last week's *Militant* carried a story on military Jim Crow that was revealing in very many ways. Eleven Negro noncommissioned officers at Camp Lee, Virginia, got together and drew up some recommendations to the commanding general at the camp. The recommendations dealt with measures for curbing certain discriminatory practices against Negro soldiers.

The commanding general (reported to be a southerner) acted immediately. Two of the Negro noncoms were reduced to the ranks—Reg. Sgt. Maj. Samuel Reed, formerly president of the St. Paul Branch of the National Association for the Advancement of Colored People, and Sgt. Clifford Clemmons. Reed was not only demoted to a private's rank but transferred to another camp; his friends believe that he will soon "embark for parts unknown."

As reported in last week's story, the general called a meeting of all the remaining noncommissioned officers in the regiment and told them that they would have "to stop their damn mouths, and accept the Army's policy and practice of discrimination, or be busted and shipped."

One might have thought from this reaction by the general that a revolution was taking place. Since the first story was printed, however, a copy of the recommendations has been printed in the *St. Paul Recorder* of December 4, and it is clear that the recommendations were really very mild and very respectfully presented. The noncoms explain why they were making the proposals:

"We have received numerous complaints and expressions of discontent from our men concerning certain particularly irritating evidences of racial segregation and discrimination at Camp Lee. Our inability to adjust these grievances or offer adequate explanation for their existence on this military reservation has effected a fearful slump in the morale of our men."

For this reason, they continue, they recommend that the

By Albert Parker. From *Militant,* December 19, 1942.

number of Negro military police be increased; that Negro MPs be equipped the same as white MPs while on duty; that Negro soldiers be permitted onto buses on the same basis as white soldiers and that they have the same right to take seats; that Negro soldiers have the same right as whites to camp facilities such as post exchanges, theaters, service clubs, sports centers, etc.; that the Army Air Corps and Army Glider Pilot Training School be opened on an equal basis to Negroes.

In short, these proposals asked for the elimination of certain "particularly irritating" discriminatory practices, not the abolition of the whole Jim Crow setup.

The Twin Cities branches of the NAACP have set up a "Sam Reed Committee" and decided to make the Camp Lee incident "a national issue, because it symbolized the ill-treatment of Negroes in the armed forces of the nation." In this task all workers should cooperate. Let us fight to end both Jim Crowism and the antidemocratic regime.

ADVICE FOR NORTH AFRICA

United States Army troops sent to participate in the North African invasion were given pamphlets urging them to "subordinate" whatever race prejudices they have.

The pamphlet stated: "You may bring some old race prejudices with you, prejudices of race or color or creed. If so you must remember that it's your first duty to subordinate them to the good of your country. You must take the attitude that giving away to such prejudices would amount literally to shooting Americans in the back."

But if soldiers should be urged to subordinate race prejudices in Africa, why shouldn't the same request be made of them at home? Why have the authorities consistently refused, despite repeated appeals by Negro organizations, to issue similar educational material to the soldiers in this country, requesting them to subordinate race prejudices and to treat Negroes as equals?

And why don't the authorities themselves subordinate some of

From *Militant*, December 26, 1942. The U.S. invasion of North Africa began in November 1942.

their own race prejudices and put an end to the segregation in the armed forces which results and can result only from prejudice?

POST OFFICE BANS THE MILITANT

Official Explains Why

The present activities of the Post Office in preventing the *Militant* from going through the mails are closely connected with the whole struggle to smash Jim Crowism in the United States.

The Post Office's objections to the *Militant* are not based on what we have to say about the Negro struggle alone. What the Post Office dislikes about this paper is its whole prolabor policy. But an important part of this policy is its uncompromising stand against Jim Crowism wherever it exists, including Washington.

Mr. Calvin Hassell, assistant to the solicitor of the Post Office Department in Washington, has stated that in his opinion "to urge Negroes to fight for their rights at the present moment" justifies the withholding of any issue of a paper from the mails.

Of course, Mr. Hassell and those in the administration whose orders he is carrying out do not like to have the Negro people told that they should fight for their rights in wartime as in peacetime. They don't like it when the *Militant* prints such articles. But they also don't like it when any other paper, including the Negro press, does the same.

As an example of the administration's attitude on this ques-

By Albert Parker. From *Militant*, December 5, 1942. In November 1942, the U.S. Post Office began to withhold delivery of various issues of the *Militant*. This action was taken without any explanation or advance notification by the Post Office authorities. Issues of the paper that were deemed "nonmailable" were simply not delivered through the mails from New York and were destroyed after a certain period of time, or were mailed only after a delay of several weeks, which made them practically worthless. The *Militant* editors had no way of knowing precisely what parts of the paper were objected to or what issues would be allowed to go through. Protests against this arbitrary treatment led to a hearing by the Post Office in Washington on January 21, 1943, to consider the revocation of the *Militant*'s second-class mailing rights.

tion, we reprint sections of an editorial printed in the March 14, 1942, issue of the *Pittsburgh Courier*, entitled "Cowing the Negro Press":

In view of the hysteria that seems to be the inevitable accompaniment of war, colored citizens will not be surprised to learn that their only militant spokesman, the Negro press, is being closely watched and investigated by government agents.

Offices of at least two of the largest Negro newspapers have been visited by agents of the Federal Bureau of Investigation since Pearl Harbor.

Mrs. Charlotta A. Bass, editor and publisher of the militant "California Eagle," states that FBI agents have visited her office and interrogated her about possible receipt of Japanese or German funds because her paper courageously condemned color discrimination and segregation in National Defense.

This sort of thing is an obvious effort to cow the Negro press into soft-pedaling its criticism and ending its forthright exposure of the outrageous discriminations to which Negroes have been subjected. . . .

Of course it is easy to understand why those in authority do not relish having these undemocratic practices investigated and exposed, especially when our country has assumed the role of champion and arsenal of democracy.

But Negroes feel that along with the victory for democracy abroad there must also be victory for democracy at home; and until this double victory is achieved, neither they nor their newspapers will remain silent.

Instead of trying to frighten Negro editors into silence, we suggest that the FBI investigate those forces and institutions within America that are fostering and spreading fascism and disunity by treating Negroes as second-class citizens.

Now we are not trying to pretend that the *Militant* is like the Negro press. For one thing, our paper has a more consistent policy against all the forces responsible for Jim Crow; for another, our paper advocates the only program to achieve racial equality.

But the *Militant* is like the Negro press, or a great part of the Negro press, in this respect: we both expose Jim Crow practices, and we both tell the Negro masses to fight for an end to them.

If the *Militant* can be suppressed for this "crime," isn't it obvious that the administration's next step would be to go after the more outspoken Negro papers? Wouldn't the administration consider cracking down on the activities of organizations like the March on Washington movement? Wouldn't it have the effect of making many Negro editors less likely to print things for which this paper was gagged? Wouldn't all this result in a setback to the movement for Negro equality?

The *Militant* fights for the rights of all the workers, and that is why its suppression would be a blow to the whole labor movement. It would be at least as great a blow at the struggle for Negro emancipation. That is why all workers, including the Negro workers, should protest the activities of the Post Office Department.

Excerpts from Exhibit A

(10)
The Negro Struggle

by Albert Parker
October 11, 1942, p. 3

The fact that the capitalist class does not intend to grant equality to the Negroes is only one reason why advanced Negroes should join the revolutionary movement. There is another reason that is just as valid and just as important as the one I discussed last week, and I intend to raise it here.

The Negro must fight for more than equality with the white worker. For let us suppose for the sake of argument that the Negro could win and did win this equality while the white worker's conditions remain the same as they are now, that is, under capitalism. What would the Negro worker have then?

From *Militant*, January 16, 1943. Prior to the hearing on January 21, 1943, the Post Office announced that it had acted against the *Militant* for "violations of the Espionage Act" of 1917, which had automatically been reinstated when the U.S. government declared war in December 1941. It also stated that its action had been made in collaboration with Roosevelt's Department of Justice and Attorney General Francis Biddle. And as evidence to support its claims, it released twenty-seven "objectionable" excerpts from *Militant* articles and editorials since December 1941 (Exhibit A). These showed that despite the war, the paper had remained a socialist opponent of capitalist rule, including the racist crimes perpetrated by the ruling class. Excerpt 10 was from a column on the perspectives of the Black struggle, and excerpt 24 was from a radio speech over station WPAT in Paterson by George Breitman, who was the SWP's New Jersey candidate for the U.S. Senate, on October 24, 1942.

He would have what the white worker has. Like the white worker, he would still suffer periodic depressions and unemployment, and go hungry much of the time.

Like the white worker, he would still be threatened by the oppression and brutality of fascism.

Like the white worker, he would still be driven to fight and die for imperialist wars that benefit only the bosses.

Like the white worker, he would still be kicked around by the officers in the armed forces—probably not as much as at present, but still plenty.

Like the white worker, he would still get low wages—undoubtedly a little higher than he gets now, but still too low for decency and comfort, as the worker does. . . .

(24)
How to Destroy Fascism Abroad and Prevent it at Home

by George Breitman
October 31, 1942, p. 4

. . . There are numerous other policies which prove to us that this is not a genuine war to destroy fascism or extend democracy. To mention but a few:

What kind of war to destroy fascism is it when President Roosevelt openly extends a hand of friendship to the fascist butcher of Spain, Franco, and offers to help put the Spanish fascist regime "on its feet economically"? What kind of war for democracy is it that is led by Vargas, the brutal dictator of Brazil, whose record is just as bloody as Hitler's? Are fascists cleansed of their crimes when they are neutral or allied to the United States?

What kind of war for democracy is it when the Negro people are Jim Crowed in industry and in the government's armed forces? The world is revolted by Hitler's vicious persecution of minority groups, but how much better is the ruling class's treatment of the Negro minority in this country? How much better is the theory of white supremacy than the theory of Aryan superiority? Is discrimination against color any better than discrimination against religion?

What kind of war for democracy is it that denies the Indian people the democratic right to rule themselves, a right the American people fought a revolution to obtain in 1776? If it is criminal for Hitler to subject the people of Europe to his rule, is it not equally criminal for British imperialism to subject India to its rule or for United States imperialism to subject Puerto Rico to its rule?

Excerpts from Exhibit B

Excerpts from a speech made by A. Philip Randolph, national director of the Negro March on Washington movement to a conference of that organization held in Chicago last September and printed in the October 3, 1942, issue of the *Militant,* were part of the "evidence" introduced by Post Office Department officials at the Washington hearing to consider revocation of the *Militant's* second-class mailing privileges.

The insertion into the record of the quotations from Randolph's speech was intended to show how the *Militant* had violated the Espionage Act.

Actually, however, as a reading of the excerpt will show, it proved only that the *Militant* supports the struggle for Negro equality, and that the attack on this paper constitutes the first step toward the suppression or intimidation of all independent tendencies in the labor, liberal, and Negro movements.

For if the *Militant* can be charged with violating the Espionage Act today because it printed parts of Randolph's speech, can't Randolph himself be attacked tomorrow for making such speeches? If a labor paper can be banned from the mails for quoting the remarks of the leader of a militant Negro organization, won't the next step be to attack the Negro organization itself?

The *Militant's* report of the conference told of the discussion and decisions of the delegates, and quoted and analyzed the keynote speech by Randolph which opened the conference.

It was this part of our story that the Post Office authorities selected as "evidence" that the *Militant* was violating the Espionage Act. Following is the excerpt introduced into the Washington hearing last week:

From *Militant,* January 30, 1943. At the January 21 hearing in Washington, the Post Office officials introduced more "evidence"—Exhibit B, or seventy-eight more "vicious" excerpts from *Militant* articles and editorials. One of these was taken from Art Preis's report on the national conference of the March on Washington movement in September 1942 (see page 206 in this book).

While he opened his remarks with an expression of hope "for the triumph of the United Nations," Randolph was immediately compelled to characterize, at least by implication, the true character of the war: "Unless this war sounds the death knell to the old Anglo-American empire systems, which is the hapless story of exploitation for the profit and power of a monopoly capitalist economy, it will have been fought in vain." Of course, Randolph knows well that Churchill and Roosevelt are not fighting to sound the "death knell" to American and British capitalism, but to preserve it.

Randolph was compelled, in fact, to attack the chief embodiment of the war aims of the Allied powers, the Atlantic Charter:

"We score the Atlantic Charter as expressing a vile and hateful racism and a manifestation of the tragic and utter collapse of an old, decadent democratic political liberalism which worshipped at the shrine of a world-conquering monopoly capitalism. This system grew fat and waxed powerful off the flesh and blood and sweat and tears of the tireless toilers of the human race and the sons and daughters of color in the underdeveloped lands of the world."

. . . "Hence, it is apparent that the Negro needs more than organization. He needs mass organization with an action program, aggressive, bold, and challenging in spirit. Such a movement is our March on Washington."

. . . As an example of the type of actions he had in mind, he stated:

"We must develop a series of marches of Negroes at a given time in a hundred cities or more throughout the country, or stage a big march of a hundred thousand Negroes on Washington to put our cause into the main stream of public opinion and focus the attention of world interests. This is why India is in the news. . . ."

Layle Lane's Speech

Layle Lane aroused particular interest when she touched on the struggle against Negro discrimination in her speech at the March 26 meeting of the Civil Rights Defense Committee, called to

---

By Albert Parker. From *Militant,* April 3, 1943. On March 3, 1943, Postmaster General Frank C. Walker, who was also chairman of the Democratic National Committee, issued an administrative decree revoking the *Militant*'s second-class mailing privileges. This was protested by several labor, liberal, and civil liberties groups, including the Civil Rights Defense Committee, which organized a protest rally in New York on March 26. Layle Lane, a leader in the March on Washington movement, was one of the speakers at that rally. The *Militant* was mailed by third- and fourth-class mail and the post office continued to delay and destroy selected issues until March 1944, when pressure from the labor movement forced the government to restore the *Militant*'s mailing rights.

protest the revocation of the *Militant*'s second-class mailing privileges. The reason for this is that she has a long record as a respected leader in the fight against Jim Crowism and as a militant in the March on Washington movement.

Miss Lane took up—and effectively answered—Attorney General Biddle's letter to the postmaster general in which he called for repressive action against the *Militant* on the ground, among others, that its articles include "stimulation of race issues."

"But," she said,

in my opinion the government itself is the greatest offender in this respect. For it is the government which segregates Negroes in the armed forces. It is the government which discriminates against Negroes in its government departments. Indeed, in Washington, the capital of the government, Negroes are not even able to travel freely and on an equal basis.

I don't know how anyone can do more to "stimulate race issues" than is constantly done on the floor of Congress by people like Representative Rankin who launch into the most insulting and provocative attacks upon the Negro people, or by the congressmen who refuse to pass antilynch and anti-poll tax legislation.

Miss Lane went on to demonstrate that racial discrimination as practiced by the government is not confined to Negroes alone. Referring to the treatment by the administration of Japanese-Americans as "a disgraceful blot" on this country's record, she cited figures to show economic discrimination too, as for example in the salaries of teachers in the concentration camps where the Japanese-Americans are confined: A Japanese-American teacher, she declared, received $19 a month, while white teachers doing the same work receive $150 a month.

"That is why I believe," she said in concluding this portion of her speech, "that when it comes to the stimulation of race issues, the government is unquestionably the greatest offender. And any paper which opposes such practices—as the *Militant* does—is doing a service to the people of this country."

This testimony by Miss Lane is all the more valuable because she is not a Trotskyist and because she is not in full agreement with the line of the *Militant*. It is merely the recognition by a responsible and respected Negro leader and trade unionist that the fight in defense of the *Militant* is the fight of all workers and defenders of civil liberties and democratic rights.

WOMEN SUE CLEVELAND PLANTS

Two Cleveland court cases, which ended just before Christmas, were among the most significant trials to be held in 1942. They revealed that employers are still practicing Jim Crow hiring policies and that the Negroes cannot depend on either the courts or President Roosevelt's Executive Order 8802 to put an end to these discriminatory policies.

Suit was brought against two war plants, Warner and Swasey Company and Thompson Products, charging them with refusing to employ Negro women workers solely because of their color, and demanding that this practice be discontinued. The court action was organized at the initiative of the Future Outlook League, a militant organization which has been combating job discrimination for many years, and the cases were heard before Common Pleas Judge Frank J. Merrick.

Several Negro women testified against the plants' management. They told how they had gone to training school, learned machine-shop work and in most cases been commended by their teachers for their ability, and then applied to the two companies for machine-shop work. In each case they were told that there were no jobs for them, although the companies were at that time advertising in the papers for women workers needed for machine-shop work.

At the beginning of the trial the lawyers for the employers said they would prove that no discrimination existed. But during the trial itself company executives were forced to admit that it did exist; their excuse for it was that the union or individual white workers had objected to employment of Negro women, a charge which was hotly denied by the union officials involved. At the end no one disputed the contention that the employers had never even attempted to hire a single Negro woman for machine-shop work.

The lawyers for the Negro women bringing suit also showed

By Albert Parker. From *Militant,* January 2, 1943.

that the plants had war contracts from the government and that these contracts—as provided in Executive Order 8802—stipulated that there must be no race discrimination in employment.

Nevertheless, the judge hearing the case refused to do anything about it and in effect denied that anything could be done about it through the courts.

Thus for the first time a court confirmed the often-made charge that Executive Order 8802 is completely toothless and ineffective.

Also confirmed by this court decision is the necessity for carrying on a militant struggle to force the adoption of really effective anti–Jim Crow legislation and to guarantee the enforcement of such legislation.

WHY HASTIE QUIT WAR DEPARTMENT

William H. Hastie, former federal judge and dean of the Howard University Law School, was appointed as civilian aide to the secretary of war in October 1940, when conscription went into effect. Last month he announced his resignation from his post as of February 1, and now he has explained why.

"Reactionary policies and discriminatory practices of the Army Air Forces in matters affecting Negroes were the immediate cause of my resignation," the statement begins. "The Army Air Forces are growing in importance and independence. In the postwar period they may become the greatest single component of the armed services. Biased and harmful practices in this branch of the Army can all too easily infect other branches as well." For this reason Hastie's experiences in this field can be regarded as a test of the attitude of the men in charge of the armed forces.

When Hastie took office, the secretary of war directed that all questions of policy relating to Negroes should be referred to his office for comment or approval before final action. Two months later the air forces showed Hastie a plan for a segregated training center for Negro pursuit pilots at Tuskegee.

I expressed my entire disagreement with the plan, giving my reasons in detail. My views were disregarded. Since then, the Air Command has never on its own initiative submitted any plan or project to me for comment or recommendation. . . .

Moreover, even now the Air Command views the use of the Negro as an "experiment" designed to determine whether he can do this or that in the field of aviation. This attitude is the result of wholly unscientific notions that race somehow controls a man's capacity and attitudes. . . .

The Negro program of the Air Forces began some two years ago with the organization of several so-called "Aviation Squadrons (Separate)." These units, now greatly increased in number, were organized to serve no specific military need. . . . The characteristic assignment of the "Aviation Squadron (Separate)" has been the performance of odd jobs of common labor which arise from time to time at air fields. . . .

By Albert Parker. From *Militant,* February 13, 1943.

The Air Forces also are rejecting Negro applicants who wish to become weather officers or officers in other highly specialized technical fields [although large numbers of such officers are needed] so badly that white volunteers are being solicited and accepted, despite a general policy against voluntary enlistments in the Army. . . . The same situation exists in armament and engineering, both ground specialties for which the Air Forces have been accepting cadets generally, but refusing Negroes.

To date, all Negro applicants, a number of them well and fully qualified, for appointment as Army service pilots have been rejected. . . . The simple fact is that the Air Command does not want Negro pilots flying in and out of various fields, eating, sleeping and mingling with other personnel, as a service pilot must do in carrying out his various missions. . . .

Lack of space prevents us from quoting further, although Hastie gives plenty more material along the same line. But the picture is clear enough from what we have shown.

It is not the Negroes who have made "progress" in the armed forces, but the pattern of segregation. Some Negroes are now admitted into branches of the service from which they were formerly excluded, but Hastie's statement and similar facts which are not hard to discover about other branches of the service make it clear that these are token admissions, used to answer criticism but not to change the fundamental policy, which is still to regard Negroes as "different" (that is, inferior) solely because they may have a slightly different-colored skin.

There can be no real progress against Jim Crow until the policy of segregation is abandoned. The Republicans never abandoned it when they were in power in Washington; the Democrats show no intention of abandoning it now. Only when the workers are in power, only when a workers' and farmers' government is established, will the Negro people be able to win real equality.

ALCOA VICTIMS IN CLEVELAND

CLEVELAND, February 28—The Aluminum Corporation of America, aided by the army, the WLB, and a vicious press campaign, and with the tacit approval of the Stalinist leadership of Local 755 of the Mine, Mill and Smelter Workers, CIO, is attempting to victimize several hundred Negro workers who have been putting up a valiant fight here to better their conditions.

The case is in the 3F department of the smelting plant, manned almost entirely by Negroes. Their chief grievances are that their high production quotas make bonuses nearly impossible, that no mechanical hoisting equipment is provided as it is in other departments, and that no transfers are granted to other departments when there are openings.

Five weeks ago the workers began working at a normal pace, with no attempt to make the tremendous further efforts required to make a possible bonus. The management denounced this as a slowdown and called in investigators from the army air force who observed the workers for a month, finally giving orders to fire five workers with long work records as "not sufficiently qualified, careful, efficient, or reliable."

Other workers in the department struck in sympathy until the plant was closed by the management. On February 24, the WLB ordered the strikers to return or face disciplinary action.

The Cleveland Alcoa works is notorious for its antilabor policies. Workers must depend upon bonuses based on the Bedaux system to augment their low hourly rates.*

*The Bedaux system, named after the French-born U.S. efficiency expert Charles E. Bedaux (1887-1944), was based on incentive pay for workers who produced more than a certain amount per hour. Unions have attacked it as part of a speedup and a threat to safety on the job. Bedaux moved to France in 1937; collaborated with the Nazis during the war; was arrested in Algiers during the Allied invasion of North Africa and extradited to the U.S.; and committed suicide after he was charged with treason.

By George Schraum. From *Militant,* March 6, 1943.

War expansion has forced the company to hire Negro labor, but it has given the Negroes only the most undesirable jobs. For instance, the smelting plant hires 60 percent Negro labor, which is five or six times the percentage obtaining in the plant as a whole.

While Alcoa employees are generally organized into the Aluminum Workers of America, CIO, the Cleveland works employees are in Local 755 of the MM&SW, which has suffered since its inception from the plague of Stalinist leadership. Since the latest Stalinist turn, these misleaders make a pretense of representing the workers' interests only to the extent necessary to prevent sporadic attempts on the part of the AWA, UMW, or AFL to step in and organize the plant.

As a result, there have been repeated instances where isolated departments, acting independently of the union, have had to take their own action to get an adjustment of their grievances.

Edward Radden, president of Local 755, while admitting that the men had grievances and that they had dropped out of the union in the past because their grievances were not settled, nevertheless came to the management's aid, stating, "I want to emphasize that we are not in favor of stoppages and slowdowns and that we have repeatedly pleaded with the men to continue normal production."

The Negro workers have turned for leadership to W. O. Walker, the editor of the *Call-Post* (leading Cleveland Negro paper) and a city councilman. Walker has supported these men in his paper and will do what he can, no doubt, to aid them.

However, it is very necessary to enlist the labor movement of the city in defense of these workers whose case is the most flagrant example of company and army persecution of workers in this city since the war began.*

*Production was resumed the day after this article was written, under orders by the regional War Labor Board. However, third-shift operations were suspended pending replacement of eighty-two strikers fired for ignoring previous WLB back-to-work orders.

RANDOLPH AND CIVIL DISOBEDIENCE

As was to be expected, the Stalinists and some of their friends in the Negro press dug down into their slander sewers and started throwing mud at A. Philip Randolph when he proposed that the March on Washington movement call on the Negro people to conduct "non-violent civil disobedience and non-cooperation" activities for a one-week period sometime this year. "Subversive" and "disruptive" and "appeaser" were some of the milder names they hurled at him.

We Trotskyists take an entirely different attitude toward Randolph's proposal. When a course of action against Jim Crow is proposed, we examine it solely in the light of this criterion: will it or will it not be effective in fighting Jim Crow? Our main consideration is therefore completely different from that of the Stalinists, who are concerned primarily with what effect a proposal will have on "national unity." With this made plain, let us review what Randolph proposes:

> In the South, non-violent civil disobedience and non-cooperation will take the negative form of boycotting Jim Crow cars on trains and surface lines and calling upon the parents of children to refuse to send their children to school during the week that is designated for the application of the social strategy.
>
> In the civil rights states, it will take the positive form of Negroes exercising their right to make use of agencies and enter places they do not normally make use of, such as going into the downtown sections of cities as patrons of the hotels, restaurants and places of entertainment. . . ."
> [The *Call,* Kansas City, February 5]

White advocates of equal rights for Negroes will also be asked not to enter any place or share in any privilege or right denied the Negro citizens of the country.

This, in short, is the Randolph proposal to be presented to the coming national conference of the MOWM to be held in Chicago next May.

By Albert Parker. From *Militant,* March 6, 1943.

Only a fool or a knave could attack this proposal in the terms used by the Stalinists, and generally speaking they are not fools. The real reason for their slander campaign on this issue is their desire to use every possible means of discrediting Randolph and the MOWM, which they fear may become the mobilizing center of militant Negro action in the future.

The "non-violent civil disobedience and non-cooperation" plan, as presented by Randolph himself, is only a fancy name for a peaceful protest demonstration designed to publicize the opposition of the Negro people to the many discriminatory practices and laws that bar them from equality. And of course we Trotskyists are in favor of protesting Jim Crow in every possible way.

Whether Randolph's protest plan will be effective will depend entirely on how much support it gets from the ranks of the Negro masses and the labor movement. If many people rally to it, it will be effective; if only a few handfuls of people support the plan in action, naturally it will draw little attention and will do little good. When the MOWM meets in conference in May, it should bear this in mind and determine either to organize the affair properly and on a mass scale or not at all, for a poorly organized demonstration is often worse than none at all.

At this point, however, we must emphasize an aspect of this question which we regard as most important. When we say that the carrying out of Randolph's proposal can be effective with mass support, we give that word effective a very special and limited connotation. A protest demonstration is, after all, only a protest demonstration, and it can be effective in achieving only certain things.

If successful, it can be a demonstration to the broad section of the Negro masses that they are strong and powerful, and it can serve to inspire them to further activities in behalf of their own emancipation. It can be a demonstration to the ruling capitalist class that the Negro masses are awakening to the need for militant organization and action, a sign that they do not intend to remain oppressed. As such, it may result in forcing the ruling class to grant certain concessions to the Negro masses.

But a protest demonstration, even one that lasts a week, cannot by itself solve the basic problem of Jim Crow. It cannot do that, big and militant though it may be, because when it is finished, the ruling class which is responsible for Jim Crow will still remain in power. And as long as the capitalists, who benefit from Jim Crow, remain in power in this country, equality will not be achieved by the Negro people.

Protest demonstrations are necessary, and we favor holding them whenever and wherever possible, regardless of the opposition that will be raised against them by the Stalinists and the Uncle Toms and the advocates of white supremacy. But protest demonstrations are not enough, and the coming conference of the MOWM will make a big mistake if it confines its program of action only to such demonstrations.

In addition to protest demonstrations, the militant Negroes must take the path of independent political action, aimed at replacing the Jim Crow capitalists with a workers' and farmers' government which will end Jim Crow by ending the possibility for capitalists to benefit from Jim Crow. And to help establish such a workers' and farmers' government, the Negro people must work out an alliance with the labor movement, which is also exploited by the capitalists, and must help to build an independent labor party based on the trade unions and embracing the militant Negro organizations.

IN THESE PERILOUS TIMES

A friend in Louisiana this week sent us a newspaper advertisement illustrating the progress that has been made in the South in the fields of justice and politics. The voters of East Baton Rouge Parish were to elect a district judge on March 23, and one of the candidates, named Womack, advertised for votes on the ground that his opponent had been guilty of only fining a Negro five dollars for hitting a white boy who had demanded that the Negro give him his seat in a bus. Womack proudly boasted of the fact that in such cases he has always imposed the most severe sentence possible under the law, six months in jail, and asked: "Which one of these men do you want to protect your rights, your home and your family in these perilous times?"

From *Militant*, March 27, 1943.

10,000 DEMONSTRATE IN DETROIT

DETROIT, Michigan, April 17—Over ten thousand Negro and white workers marched to Cadillac Square last Sunday afternoon to hold a mass demonstration against Negro discrimination. The march and meeting were sponsored by the Detroit branch of the National Association for the Advancement of Colored People in cooperation with other organizations including the CIO United Auto Workers and Negro fraternal groups. Chevrolet Local 235 of the UAW was represented by a band and drum corps. There was also a small contingent of Negro soldiers who spontaneously stepped into the line of march as the parade swept by a Negro USO center.

Most of the speakers protested against job discrimination in war plants, police brutality, refusal to serve Negroes in Detroit restaurants, failure to give Negro women jobs to which their skill entitles them, the defeat of anti-poll tax legislation by Democrats and Republicans, Jim Crow housing, etc. Some of the placards demanded freedom for India.

An incongruous note was struck by one of the speakers, Col. George E. Strong, chief of plant protection for the army air forces in the Michigan district, who dwelt on the heroism of Negro soldiers in battle but never mentioned the fact that Negroes are segregated in the armed forces. The speakers who followed Strong took care to denounce military Jim Crow. One drew extended appaluse when he said, "If we must fight and die together, for God's sake let's live together!"

Among the speakers were Dr. McLendon, president of the Detroit NAACP, Walter Reuther of the UAW, Leonard Strong of the United Rubber Workers, Rev. Charles Hill of the Detroit Citizens' Committee. Greetings were received from Pearl Buck, A. Philip Randolph, Roger Baldwin, and others.

From *Militant*, April 24, 1943.

THE SOUTHERN WHITE LIBERALS

The problem of the South is also the problem of the Negro; the first will have to be settled if the second is to be solved. The Negro constitutes only one-tenth of the nation's population, and he is a minority even in the South, although three-fourths of the Negroes live there. The problem of the Negro is also the problem of finding and uniting with the correct allies among the white population. The Negro leaders used to teach that the proper ally was the capitalist; that without his aid the Negro could get nowhere, and that he should line himself up with the capitalist against the white worker. This kind of advice is rarely given today, and if it were it would be little heeded.

But there are still a number of Negroes who look to the southern liberal coming from the white middle class as their friends. One of these southern liberals, Mark Ethridge, former head of the Fair Employment Practices Committee, stated at the committee's hearings in Birmingham last summer that "the Southern Negro cannot afford to drive from his side, in his march to a greater fulfillment of his rights, the Southern white men of good will who have been his chief asset and his chief aid." By southern white men of good will, Ethridge meant southern liberals. A good self-drawn picture of this species can be found in a book published last month, *The Fighting South* by John Temple Graves, and should be read by all Negroes who are unacquainted with it.

Of course the southern liberal is a lot like all the other liberals: he wishes things would be better, he hopes for justice, he sees both sides of a question, he urges moderation. But the southern liberal has certain characteristics not present in his nonsouthern brothers. Chief among these are his tendency to resent any "outside" advice about the Negro problem; to blame "outside" influences for the southern Negro's dissatisfaction with conditions; and to get mad as hell when people start talking about ending segregation in the South.

By Albert Parker. From *Militant,* May 8, 1943.

This is well illustrated in the new book by Graves, who is a columnist for the *Birmingham Age-Herald*. Take his treatment of the poll tax question. Oh, he is against the poll tax, he assures us, and he has been fighting it for many years. But the nonsouthern politicians have no right to try to force its abolition down the throat of the South. In fact, he thinks that in the Senate debate on the poll tax last fall "the greater blame for the disgraceful scene [should be placed] on the incorrigible domestic crusaders who forced the poll tax issue" and not on the filibustering senators. He asserts that chances of abolishing the poll tax in the southern states would increase if attempts to abolish it by federal law were discontinued.

Lynching? "Lynching is a crime without necessity or excuse, but it was almost extinct in the South until the war-time racial agitators provoked it again, and the realism of the matter is that a federal law would create so much Southern resentment that racial hostility and violence might actually increase."

Is that a peculiar kind of logic, blaming the opponents of lynching for lynching and the opponents of the poll tax for the continuation of the poll tax? Not if you are a southern liberal.

Graves doesn't think that southern Negroes care very much one way or the other about segregation. He says the issue had already been raised by Talmadge of Georgia when the war came. "It was not a genuine issue then. Talmadge was simply putting up a one-man show. But it became genuine when Negro leaders outside of the South made the war an occasion for intensive campaigning against any and every differential, minor or major, between white man and black." Again, you can see, it is a question of outside subversive influences.

How easy life would be for Graves and his friends if no one would interfere and "put ideas in the heads" of the Negro in the South! Then they could be liberals and "friends of the Negro" and still remain on friendly terms with the lynchers of the Negro and with the Talmadges. But since trouble intrudes—and always from the outside—why, the southern liberals are driven (to use Ethridge's term) to take sides, and naturally they wind up on the same side as the Talmadges.

War is tough on all kinds of liberals, northern as well as southern. But the southern variety has special troubles. This war is different from the last war in that the Negro masses are much better organized and have learned the lessons of the first war and the postwar promises they received then. The Negro masses are putting pressure on their official leaders and demanding action now. Graves has a lot of praise for the Uncle Toms like F. D. Patterson of Tuskegee Institute, but he doesn't like the NAACP and the March on Washington movement. He blames the leaders of these organizations, completely failing to recognize that the leaders of these groups are subject to pressure and would lose all their following among the masses if they were to preach a wait-until-after-the-war policy.

Graves quotes all the old figures about Negro progress in education, etc. He does it for the purpose of convincing the Negroes that they needn't struggle—especially during the war—to make progress. Of course if the Negroes had listened to his kind in the past, they'd be even worse off than they are now. Graves doesn't want the Negroes to struggle now because it's wartime, and he won't want them to struggle after the war either on the ground that it would create strife and give new ammunition to the Talmadges and other demagogues. If it's up to Graves, not only the Negroes now living won't achieve equality, but their grandchildren won't either.

Fortunately it isn't up to him and his kind. The future lies not in the hands of the middle-class liberals, but in the hands of the working class. Significantly enough, Graves's book—which has a good deal to say about business problems—has virtually nothing to say about the labor movement. The southern unions still have a long way to go and a good many battles to win before they are established as strongly as the American union movement as a whole, but they have already come a considerable distance. Graves says nothing about this or about the tens of thousands of southern white workers within the unions who are beginning to learn how Jim Crow threatens their own interests.

Not the liberals, but the working class and its unions are the allies of the Negro in his struggle for equality. That is the lesson to be learned from life as well as from Graves's book.

LESSONS OF MINERS' STRIKES

The delegates to the coming conferences of the National Association for the Advancement of Colored People and of the March on Washington movement can learn a good deal from the current mine struggle.

The government, the coal operators, the press, and the radio threw everything they had at the miners. They threatened them, they coaxed them, they appealed to their patriotism, they exerted every form of pressure they had at their disposal. But they did not shake the miners.

If the miners win, it will be because they asserted their independence of the government and followed a policy based on their own needs. If they had listened to all the false arguments of the administration and the press and the labor fakers and the Stalinist betrayers, if they had succumbed to the demands for "national unity" with themselves at the bottom and the coal operators on top, if they had let themselves be talked out of the use of their strongest weapons—then surely they would have gained nothing.

This is of decisive importance to every Negro fighting to achieve equality and to every organization working to abolish Jim Crow. For the enemies faced by the miners in their fight are substantially the same forces standing in the way of Negro

---

By Albert Parker. From *Militant*, May 22, 1943. The United Mine Workers carried out a series of strikes interspersed with truces from May to October of 1943, defying the War Labor Board, Roosevelt, and the Smith-Connally Act (which Congress passed during the strike). The final settlement included a pay raise from $7.00 to $8.50 per day, the first break in the wartime wage freeze. With over a half-million members, the UMW was one of the biggest unions in the country, and this was the largest single strike in U.S. history up to that time. Despite contentions by the government, some labor officials, and the CP that the miners were hurting the war effort, the country was never short of coal during this period, with at least a three-month supply above the ground at all times. The miners simply refused to let mineowners use the war as an excuse to keep wages low and profits high.

advancement. In peacetime these forces are always exerting pressure against the labor movement and the Negro people; in wartime they exert a hundred times as much pressure, and intervene more openly in the affairs of labor and Negro organizations, hoping to dominate them and stifle all militant struggles.

It isn't that Roosevelt calls Walter White or A. Philip Randolph to the White House and tells them that they can't do this or that (although he did virtually that in the case of the proposed march on Washington that was scheduled to take place in July 1941). The administrative intervention into the affairs of Negro organizations is usually a lot more subtle than that. It exerts its pressure less directly, but just as effectively.

"We must have national unity in time of war," says the administration. And while it is saying it, Negroes are being segregated in the armed forces; the Fair Employment Practices Committee is deprived of whatever little effectiveness it ever had; Negroes are being lynched and terrorized in the South, discriminated against in jobs and in housing.

What is this "national unity"? Well, if you abide by what is going on and don't do anything to change things, that's national unity. And if you denounce these things and speak with determination against them and appear to be serious about ending the second-class citizenship status of Negroes, then you are threatening national unity and you are accused of stimulating race antagonism and inciting race riots and helping the Axis and betraying your own brothers in the armed forces, and the capitalist press will call you all kinds of nasty names. (If the capitalist press forgets to call you a few names, the Stalinists will step in and supply them.)

As a result you may lose your job if you are a worker, and you may lose whatever "friends" you have in Washington if you are a leader. All of this exerts tremendous compulsion on the Negro leaders who don't want to lose influence with what they call the "humanitarian" administration in Washington. And so although Roosevelt doesn't tell these leaders what to do and even does not object to petitions and occasional demonstrations which help to blow off a little steam, there are certain things that will be frowned on and disliked in the White House, and, in nine cases out of ten, the labor and Negro leaders just don't do them.

The delegates to the NAACP and MOWM conferences will have to make up their minds. Either they will continue to permit their organizations and leaders to be subservient to the administration—or else they will assert their independence, as the miners did, and break the grip of Roosevelt's domination over their organizations and policies and activities. Either they will work out a program based on the needs of the Negro struggle and go ahead on the road to equality—or else they will permit their organizations to continue to function in such a way that Roosevelt and his southern Democratic supporters will be satisfied.

The lesson to be learned from the miners' struggle and from the state of the Negro organizations today is that the basic requirement for a successful struggle against discrimination and segregation in wartime is a policy independent of the administration's desires and unspoken dictates.

NEGROES IN THE POSTWAR WORLD

The Negro's greatest opportunity for advancing toward full equality is now, as his enemies well recognize, and if the Negro does not take advantage of this opportunity now he will find it much harder to make progress after the war, when his enemies will have disposed of their foreign rivals and will be able to devote their energy and attention toward keeping the Negro "in his place."

It is necessary to make this point and to drive it home again and again because there are so many people trying to obscure it. These people—the modern Uncle Toms, in whose ranks the Stalinists must be included—never miss an opportunity to explain how much progress is being made. Nor are they the only people addicted to the pastime of progress-shouting. Government bureaus and the capitalist press have been going in for it quite heavily since Pearl Harbor. Indeed, you might say of the capitalist press articles and reports on the Negroes that they devote two-thirds of their space to inflammatory and most often distorted accounts of crimes by Negroes and one-third to accounts of the remarkable extent of Negro progress.

The purpose behind this pointing-with-pride and viewing-with-pleasure is obvious. The Negro people instinctively want to take advantage of the present crisis to achieve the rights which have been denied them. This can be confirmed by any honest person acquainted with Negro thought today. It is hard to convince the Negro masses that this is a war for democracy when they are denied the most elementary democratic rights.

By Albert Parker. A Pioneer Publishers pamphlet, June 1943.

Just what the Negro thinks about this question has been demonstrated in the polls of the *Pittsburgh Courier*'s Bureau of Public Sentiment, the most reliable and thorough index of Negro opinion in this country.

On October 24, 1942, it asked: "Do you believe that the Negro should soft-pedal his demands for complete freedom and citizenship and await the development of the educational process?" The answers were:

NO	81.2%
YES	17.1%
UNCERTAIN	1.7%

One year after U.S. entry into the war the Bureau asked: "Have you been convinced that the statements which our national leaders have made about freedom and equality for all peoples include the American Negro?" The answers, printed on December 19, 1942, were:

NO	82.2%
YES	17.7%
UNCERTAIN	1.1%

The progress-shouters seek, so to speak, to change the subject, to convince the Negroes that even though things aren't perfect, they are getting better day by day and will eventually work out all right. Their purpose is to persuade the masses not to conduct militant struggle against Jim Crow. If they are successful, the Negro people will miss the present opportunity to improve their status with the result that they might be condemned to second-class citizenship for decades to come.

It is not our intention here to argue that the Negro's conditions have not changed at all, nor to overlook whatever genuine progress has been made. No one can dispute, for example, the fact that Negro unemployment today is much lower than before the war, or that many Negroes have won genuine equality on their jobs as the result of trade union efforts. What we propose to do here is to look at the whole picture, to examine the true character of the gains that have been made since Pearl Harbor, to list the losses and the setbacks that have been encountered while these gains were being made, to show what was temporary and secondary and what was permanent about these gains and losses. It is necessary for militant Negroes to ponder these questions, for World War II will not last forever and they have lives to live after it comes to an end. They must understand the developments of the first eighteen months of American participation in the war, for the postwar pattern is foreshadowed in these developments.

First, the question of employment, which strikes so directly at the economic conditions of the Negro masses that there is quite often a tendency to subordinate all other questions to this one. There are many estimates of the number of Negro workers employed in war plants, the highest being a half million. This figure includes both those working on machines and janitors, porters, etc. All others listed as gainfully employed are either in nonwar industries and occupations, including domestic service, on the farms, or in the armed forces. The total in the armed forces is already over a half million and is expected to increase to a million by the end of 1943.

Meanwhile, in the face of the most severe manpower shortage in the nation's history and in the eighteenth month of the war, there is still a comparatively large body of able-bodied Negroes, estimated from 600,000 to 1,000,000, who remain unemployed. There are still hundreds of plants in the country that refuse to hire Negroes or that resort to token employment, and there are thousands of other plants—by no means all in the South—that will not permit Negroes to hold skilled or semiskilled jobs and that refuse to give Negroes equal pay for equal work. Even in New York, the State Committee on Discrimination reported recently, "discrimination because of color, race or creed still exists" and employers continue "the old practice of discriminating against Negroes not by barring them from employment, but by restricting them to such menial jobs as porters or other maintenance men" (*New York Times*, May 7, 1943). And in an industry as vital as the railroads, where Negroes have been employed for many decades, the Office of War Information admitted in April 1943 that "war or no war, unwillingness to employ Negroes in many types of railroad jobs persists."

Negroes hold more jobs than they did before Pearl Harbor, and in many cases better ones, and that is all to the good. But their jobs are not as secure as those of other workers. In plants where there are strong unions, the seniority of Negroes is generally protected. But even in such plants the probability is that when war production is ended or reduced after the war, they will be the first fired because they were the last hired. Thus it is clear that gains in Negro employment are by no means permanent and can disappear like last year's snow with the end of the war. This is not the least of the reasons why thoughtful Negroes are so concerned about the postwar world.

We have indicated why Negro employment increased—not

because of any widespread elimination of racial bias in employment but because of the manpower shortage. It is necessary to emphasize this point because there are many scoundrels pretending otherwise and trying to give the credit for the rise in Negro employment to the Roosevelt administration and its agencies—scoundrels like the Stalinist James W. Ford, who says:

The government has a well-established policy against discrimination of Negro citizens in war industries. That policy was established by President Roosevelt's Executive Order 8802, issued June 25, 1941. One cannot deny that much has been accomplished in the elimination of job discrimination, that many hundreds of thousands of Negro workers have been put to work in war industries. The Fair Employment Practices Committee (FEPC) was an effective instrument in exposing cases of discrimination and forcing employers to hire Negroes. . . . [*Daily Worker*, April 10, 1943]

To show how Ford lies we need only refer to the brief history of the FEPC.

Not even its own members ever claimed with Ford that the FEPC was "an effective instrument in . . . forcing employers to hire Negroes." They knew too well that Executive Order 8802, from which they drew their authority, gave them no powers to force anyone to do anything. The FEPC was set up by Roosevelt to ward off the projected march on Washington in the summer of 1941, and was a concession without any teeth in it. The FEPC helped a little by a few open hearings to publicize the scandalous situation in industry, and it prevailed on a few employers to hire some Negro workers. Its ineffectualness was amply demonstrated when it held a hearing in Birmingham in 1942, where it was more or less openly defied by the Jim Crow employers.

Despite its impotence, the FEPC was the object of much opposition, especially from the southern Democratic poll tax bloc in Washington, who hated it as a symbol of the government's right to "encroach" in any way on the right of the states to treat the Negroes as they please. This opposition resulted, in the summer of 1942, in Roosevelt's transfer of the FEPC from the jurisdiction of the White House to that of McNutt's War Manpower Commission, whose finances are controlled by congressional committees largely dominated by the poll taxers. Many labor and Negro organizations condemned this transfer as a move to make the FEPC even more powerless than it had been previously, and requested that it be restored to its previous status. Finally in December 1942, Roosevelt answered these protests with the statement that he saw no necessity for any changes in the situation because the FEPC is "still under direct control of the

Chief Executive." He also made reference to the announcement that the FEPC was planning soon to go ahead with a number of open hearings.

But the goose of the FEPC had already been cooked in spite of these typically Rooseveltian assurances. A month later Jim Crow scored another victory in Washington when McNutt, against the expressed wishes of the FEPC members, suddenly called off an already scheduled hearing on discriminatory employment policies of the railroads, a hearing which Negro leaders had described as a "key test" of McNutt's attitude toward the Negro. In the four months after this, the FEPC achieved absolutely nothing: some of its members resigned; Roosevelt promised, again after many protests had been made, that the railroad hearings would be held after all; McNutt and Attorney General Biddle called a number of organizations to a conference to suggest means of reconstituting and strengthening the FEPC; McNutt explained many times after that conference that the delay in further action was due to the difficulty in getting a new chairman for the agency. Finally a new chairman was secured, Msgr. Francis J. Haas, dean at Catholic University, which has barred Negro athletes from its track meets; and on May 27, 1943, Roosevelt issued a new executive order establishing a new FEPC, which like its predecessor has no power to abolish Jim Crow in industry. There isn't an informed person in Washington who honestly believes after these developments that the new FEPC will meet a happier end than the old one.

The fate of the FEPC is a sign of the things to come. To this it should be added, for the benefit of those looking ahead to the postwar period, that the FEPC had authority to investigate only war plants and was never intended to function after the war anyhow.

Roosevelt's own attitude can be gauged not only by what happened to the FEPC, which as he insisted was "under direct control of the Chief Executive," but also by a number of other events. It will be recalled that when Negroes were preparing for a march on Washington in June 1941, Roosevelt summoned A. Philip Randolph, Walter White, and other Negro leaders to the White House for a discussion. The following year Randolph declared on several occasions that the interests of the fight against Jim Crowism required that "free, independent and courageous Negro leaders have a frank, candid and plain talk with President Franklin Delano Roosevelt about the whole situation." Randolph even wired the White House an assurance that he wanted a discussion "in the interests of national unity, effective defense and victory for the United Nations and the cause of democracy." But on August 6, 1942, Roosevelt's secretary curtly replied: "Regret that owing to extreme pressure on the President's time impossible to make appointment requested." In 1943 Randolph apparently knows better than to ask again for such a talk.

Nor have Negroes forgotten Roosevelt's failure to intervene, as he had the power to do, to prevent the legal lynching of the sharecropper Odell Waller. And they see a deep significance in the contrast between his repeated condemnation of Axis atrocities and his continued failure to say a word against lynching in the United States. They are likewise bitterly aware of the contrast between his many declarations about the four freedoms and his cynical remarks last year while the fate of the anti-poll tax bill hung in the balance in the senate: "asked whether he thought the poll tax repeal bill should pass, he reiterated that he knew nothing about it, had talked to no one about it, and therefore could not express an opinion" (*New York Times*, November 21, 1942). And this is the man who will probably be at the head of the government when the present war is ended.

Of course the executive is not the only arm of the federal government. There is also Congress, and its present members may also be in office when the peace conference is held. But is there a single high school student in the nation who does not know that this Congress is at least as reactionary as the Roosevelt administration? This is the Congress which is admittedly more conservative than the previous Congress, which permitted anti-poll tax legislation to be filibustered to death. This is the Congress where the southern Democrats hold the undisputed balance of power and where both capitalist parties vie with each other in wooing the southern Democrats by appeasing them regularly on all issues affecting the Negro.

There is also the judicial division, the Supreme Court, now controlled by Roosevelt's appointees. Twice last year, while the sharecropper Odell Waller sat in death row for killing a man in self-defense, the court was asked to review the case, and twice it refused, not even explaining its refusal. Its attitude, however, was later made unmistakable by the liberal Justice Frankfurter, who stated: "As a federal judge I am unable to find any justification for summary interference with the *orderly* process of Virginia's courts of justice." That the poll tax bars Negroes and poor whites from service on Virginia's juries, that Waller was the victim of a lynch spirit and a viciously prejudiced judge—all this appears "orderly" to the gentlemen on the Supreme Court. And why not? It is in complete accord with the views expressed by this body when it upheld the poll tax laws; when it upheld the "white primary" rules, which bar Negroes from voting in the most important part of elections in the South; when it upheld the education, transportation, and other Jim Crow segregation laws of the South.

The law-enforcement agency of the administration is no better. The Department of Justice has been hinting lately that it deserves to be decorated with a few medals because it has followed up a handful of prosecutions for flagrant violations of the Thirteenth Amendment to the Constitution, which forbids slavery and involuntary servitude. But what has this or any other department of the government done to put an end to the bloody crime of lynching, which certainly violates that section of the Fourteenth Amendment to the Constitution requiring that no state shall "deny to any person within its jurisdiction the equal protection of the laws"? What has it done about the poll tax and other devices to disfranchise the Negroes in the South, all of which technically evade but plainly violate the first section of the Fifteenth Amendment, which reads: "The right of citizens of the United States to vote shall not be denied or abridged by the United States or by any state, on account of race, color or previous condition of servitude"?

What can be expected after the "war for democracy" of a government which refuses during that war to enforce its own laws for the democratic rights of the Negro people? Will such a government, after the "war for democracy" is won, be likely or willing to pass additional laws benefitting the Negro? And if it does, will such laws be worth the paper they are printed on?

But the capitalist plans for the Negro in the future are most glaringly highlighted by the government's treatment of the Negro in the armed forces today. It is not necessary to recount the whole story of that treatment in this place. Every Negro family is already too well acquainted with the details. But our discussion requires that we at least outline the pattern employed in the armed forces.

In 1940, the U.S. entry into the war growing imminent, leading Negro organizations appealed to Roosevelt to drop the Jim Crow bars that excluded Negroes from most branches of the armed forces and confined them to segregated regiments in the army and kitchen duty in the navy. Shortly before the presidential election that year, Roosevelt answered the protests by stating: "This policy [not to intermingle colored and white] has proved satisfactory over a long period of years, and to make changes would produce situations destructive to morale and detrimental to the preparations for national defense." And although this policy violates Section 4(a) of the 1940 draft act, which prohibits "discrimination against any person on account of race or color," it has been rigidly adhered to ever since, and applied to every Negro volunteer and draftee.

Protests and the needs of the armed forces compelled the military authorities to admit Negroes into many branches previously closed to them. But always, and under all circumstances, this was done on a strictly segregated basis. Negroes were permitted (a handful, anyhow) to enter the army air force, but only after an all-Negro squadron and a separate and, needless to say, inferior training center had been established. They were permitted to enter the navy in some capacities other than kitchen servant, but only after arrangements had been made to segregate them in small shore patrol ships and labor battalions in which they could not become commissioned officers. Similarly they were accepted into the coast guard and the marines in separate, all-Negro bodies. Negroes are permitted to take officer training—a grand total of twelve hundred during the first seventeen months of the war—but only with the understanding that they will not be allowed to command any white soldiers, although naturally with such a small number of Negro officers for such a large number of Negro soldiers, there will have to be and are many white officers in command of Negroes.

To change this "satisfactory" setup in the armed forces, says Roosevelt, "would produce situations destructive to morale." He does not say whose morale. But it is not hard to guess that he means primarily the morale of southern ruling-class opinion. To protect southern bias, therefore, the military authorities try to spread anti-Negro prejudices among hundreds of thousands of nonsouthern white youth in uniform, many of whom went to school with Negroes and were taught to regard them as equals. To prevent "situations destructive to morale," the military authorities export their prejudices to Great Britain, where the people greeted American Negro soldiers in the most friendly and comradely manner until they were ordered to desist in the interest of not hurting the feelings of bigoted U.S. Army officers and soldiers.

But the utter hypocrisy of Roosevelt's explanation for segregating Negroes in the armed forces has been bared most conclusively by his reaction to a very reasonable request made by several liberal and Negro organizations representing at least a million people. Very well, they said in effect, you don't want to end segregation in the armed forces and we won't press you on that; but why don't you at least permit the formation of a single mixed division, which would be made up of white and Negro soldiers volunteering to serve in it? It is hard to see how anyone could argue against creation of such a division on the ground that it would produce situations harmful to morale; being made up of volunteers who would want to show that it is possible for Negroes and whites to collaborate amicably and fruitfully, it would probably have the highest morale in the armed forces. Precisely for this reason Roosevelt not only refused to act on the mixed division petitions delivered to him—he even refused to comment on them.

This incident, and many others like it, indicate that what Roosevelt and the government are upholding is not morale but anti-Negro prejudice and the predominant southern technique for keeping the Negro "in his place." This is upheld in the armed forces because the southern rulers fear, in the words of a resolution of the Socialist Workers Party, "that no Negro trained to handle a gun would peacefully go back to the old life of discrimination, segregation, disfranchisement, and insult, after training in an army where he was treated as an equal with white soldiers." But the logic of segregation is such that once adopted as a policy for the armed forces there is nothing to stop it from being extended to all the major and minor organs and institutions of society. This is precisely what the enemies of the Negroes want and are striving for.

The issue of segregation is in many respects the most important one facing the Negro today. It is the last and strongest line of defense of those who want to keep the Negro down, the stronghold from which a thousand types of discrimination can be launched. Yet the only Negro member of Congress, William L. Dawson, who, like his colleagues Rankin and Bilbo, believes in the greater glory of the Democratic Party, and who claims to be a representative of the Negro people not only in Chicago but in the whole United States, recently declared that such issues as segregation "fade into insignificance in the light of the bigger questions raised by this war. America's enemies now are the foes of all minorities" (*PM,* April 23, 1943).

But flag waving won't solve the problems of the Negro people and it won't change the mind of a single one of their enemies. For on this one issue there is a remarkable unanimity among all leaders of southern ruling-class thought—both openly reactionary and liberal. The demagogues like Rankin, Talmadge, and Dixon rant and rave and threaten civil war at the very prospect of any breaches in the wall of segregation; they don't like it but they don't object too strenuously when Negroes in the South get jobs which were always closed to them before because this helps to win the war which they believe is being fought to save "the white man's civilization"; but they declare their readiness even to secede from the Democratic Party when there is talk of ending or altering the system of segregation. The southern liberals show their real colors when this problem is raised, as the publisher Mark Ethridge did when he warned that "There is no power in the world—not even in all the mechanized armies of the earth, Allied or Axis—which could force the Southern white people to the abandonment of the principle of social segregation" (July 1942). And in April 1943 when more than a hundred white southern liberals met in Atlanta to discuss a program for Negro-white relations, they expressed the same idea although much more hypocritically when they stated: "The only justification offered for those laws which have for their purpose the separation of the races is that they are intended to minister to the welfare and the integrity of both races." To minister to the welfare and the integrity of both races is truly a noble aim, and no doubt explains why every outspoken enemy of the Negro people is so determined to uphold the segregation laws and practices!

The truth is that all southern capitalists and their liberal agents stand so firmly on this issue because once segregation is ended, all else is lost for the oppressors of the Negro people. Once the wall separating them is removed, the Negroes and poor whites will see that their interests are the same and they will unite their forces to better their common conditions. And conversely, if the barrier of segregation can be maintained for the duration of the war, then the Negro-haters will be able to use it to extend and intensify their oppression and to take back whatever the Negroes have gained during the war. For the very basis of segregation is the myth of "white supremacy"—just as the basis of the persecution of the Jews in Europe is the myth of "Nordic superiority"—and so long as that myth can be preserved, the Negro will be unable to make permanent gains.

The government does more than its share to uphold this myth. Why should Negroes be segregated in the armed forces and not in federal housing projects? There is no logic in that, so—a little pressure from the southern congressmen, and Negroes are segregated in these projects even in northern communities. But why in housing projects and not in shipyards? The poison of segregation spreads further through the government apparatus and by way of that into all spheres of economic, political, and social life. Uncle Toms like F. D. Patterson of Tuskegee Institute hail the government when, for example, it opens the air force to Negroes on a segregated basis, declaring that this is "a definite improvement" in the conditions of the Negro people. These people fail to see, or at any rate to admit, that such "improvement" is comparable to the government striking off a few links in the chain binding the

Negroes only to surround him with another prison wall. But every thoughtful Negro sees in these developments the intention of their enemies, with the approval of the government, to establish a strongly enforced and far-reaching system of segregation which will freeze the Negro into a permanent position of second-class citizenship.

To fully estimate the Negro's status in postwar America, one must also understand the economic and political direction in which American capitalism is moving. In a recent pamphlet [*The Struggle for Negro Equality* by John Saunders and Albert Parker, Pioneer Publishers, June 1943] we summed up the process as follows:

The United States is the richest, most powerful capitalist country in the world. But no more than the others has it been able to escape the processes of decay which are inherent in capitalism and are developing ever more rapidly in this period. As in the other capitalist nations, here too greater and greater power and wealth are accumulated in the hands of the monopoly corporations and heavier restrictions are set on the rights of the masses.

In its youth capitalism was able to grant concessions: democratic liberties to certain sections of the masses, and slightly higher wages to the more skilled layers of the working class. Today, capitalism is in its death agony. To exist, it must snatch back the few concessions it was able to give in the past; it must depress the living standards of all the workers; it must destroy the democratic rights of all the masses. No capitalist nation in the epoch of imperialism is immune from this process, which is speeded up in wartime but was in operation before the war and will not be eliminated after the war if the capitalists remain in power. The United States capitalists follow in the footsteps of their German brothers, although at a different tempo.

Keeping in mind this background, Negroes will best be able to appreciate what capitalism in this country has to offer them. When the trend is toward the destruction of all democratic rights, when more regimentation is in store for the masses as a whole, Negroes have little to hope for from the capitalist system. When the employers are trying to take away the few democratic rights of the white workers, there is little chance that they will willingly extend new rights to the Negroes. The events of the last decade clearly indicate that under capitalism the prospect is not for Negroes to be raised to the status of the white workers but rather for the white workers to be driven down to the status of the Negroes. And once fascist reaction triumphs, the Negro's status may become even more intolerable than it is today. Negroes can learn from the fate of the Jews in Europe, who made some gains during the period of capitalism's rise only to be forcibly deprived of them when capitalism assumed the political form of fascism. Like the Jewish scapegoat in Germany, the Negro may face deportation, loss of whatever citizenship rights he now possesses, mass slaughter, and extermination.

251

Fortunately there is another perspective, the perspective of the socialist revolution and the establishment of a workers' and farmers' government, which will, as the Bolsheviks did in the Soviet Union under Lenin and Trotsky, not only destroy the economic cause of race discrimination but will also adopt and enforce legislation guaranteeing full equality to the Negro people and all other minorities.

It is in the light of this perspective that we can see that the Negro has made some genuine gains in recent years, gains which have a permanent character and cannot be erased at the mere command of the capitalists. These gains are in the trade union movement. More Negroes belong and there is a greater understanding of the need for Negro-white solidarity in the unions than ever before. What the white trade unionists have learned about the heroism and sacrifices of their black brothers in building the unions and what the Negro unionists have learned about the need for allying themselves with the labor movement will make possible the speedier entry of the unions into the political struggle against capitalism and for the creation of a workers' and farmers' government. In the unions and through the unions, in and through the revolutionary party, the Negro masses will be able to meet and defeat the challenge of their enemies in the postwar world.

THE NAACP EMERGENCY CONFERENCE

DETROIT, June 6—Climaxing its four-day emergency conference on the "Status of the Negro in the War for Freedom," an overflow crowd of more than 23,000 meeting here in the Olympia Stadium wildly cheered the statement of R. J. Thomas, president of the UAW, that his union would "continue to fight for equal rights for all workers regardless of color."

The conference opened on June 3, the same day that the Packard Motor Company was closed down by a strike which began when white production workers in the aircraft engine division walked off the job after three Negro workers had been promoted to machine jobs. Thomas pointed out that the UAW,

From *Militant*, June 12, 1943.

from the beginning, had defended the rights of its Negro members, and charged C. E. Weiss, company industrial relations officer, and other Packard Company officials with urging white employees to refuse to work with Negroes. Walter White, executive secretary of the NAACP, opened his keynote address to the conference on June 3 with the same charge against the Packard officials.

The crowd attending the Olympia mass meeting was electrified by Thomas's further declaration that he has "absolute evidence" that the Packard strike was promoted by agents of the Ku Klux Klan. The UAW was turning the evidence over to the FBI, he stated, and would demand a congressional investigation.

The firm stand taken in defense of the Negro UAW members at the Packard Company, not only by Thomas, but by other UAW officials who spoke to the delegates at earlier sessions of the conference, was one of the most effective demonstrations of solidarity between white and Negro workers that the majority of the NAACP delegates had ever seen.

Seven hundred and forty-three delegates from thirty-nine states attended the conference—the largest convention of the NAACP in many years.

The "Statement to the Nation," prepared by a committee elected on the floor of the conference, was far more representative of the desire of the delegates for militant action against Jim Crowism than were the cautious speeches of most speakers on the prepared program.

"The N.A.A.C.P. and its members are appalled at the wide discrepancy between our professed war aims of democracy and freedom and the treatment meted out to Negroes in nearly every part of our national life," the statement opens. "The issues with which we are concerned must be raised now. We refuse to listen to the weak-kneed of both races who tell us not to raise such controversies during the war."

Charging that the government itself sets the pattern of discrimination and segregation by the "continued ill-treatment of Negroes in uniform," the NAACP statement calls upon President Roosevelt as commander in chief of the armed forces to use his power to end the government's shameful treatment of Negro citizens. When this demand upon Roosevelt was read at today's closing session, it was applauded vociferously.

Among other demands is one that "representatives of the Negro press be given equal press privileges in attending and reporting Congressional hearings as well as Presidential and other official press conferences." The government is also asked to live up to the Constitution in its employment policies by guaranteeing equal opportunity for work for all regardless of race, creed, color, or national origin.

An attempt to insert a section in the NAACP "Statement to the Nation" praising the "no strike policy of the U.A.W.-CIO" and attacking strikes "inimical to the war efforts of our country and its allies" was defeated after a heated debate. Grace Carlson, delegate from the St. Paul branch of the NAACP made the motion to strike out this section. She pointed out that this might easily be interpreted as an attack on the United Mine Workers union, which was fighting in the interests of thousands of Negro miners.

Clarence Sharpe of Cleveland, James Anderson of Los Angeles, and several other delegates took the floor in opposition to the no-strike clause. Only one Stalinist delegate spoke in support of the inclusion of this section. By common consent, the committee which had prepared the statement agreed to its withdrawal after hearing the weighty arguments made against it.

Although the majority of the NAACP delegates attending the conference were not industrial workers, and therefore not closely aligned with the trade union movement, the statement calls upon Negro workers "to become full fledged members of organized labor on a basis of equality with all other workers."

'ZOOT SUIT RIOTS' IN LOS ANGELES

The latest outbreaks of violence and prejudiced action against Negroes and Mexicans have extended from coast to coast, menacing minority groups not only in the South, but in the North, the West, and the industrial Midwest. Taken together, they represent the most widespread and ominous attack on the victims of racial prejudice in any comparable period since the so-called race riots that followed World War I.*

In the Los Angeles area, which has been given the widest publicity, hundreds of Mexican and Negro youths and adults have been beaten senseless and stripped naked on the streets by

---

*More than seventy Blacks were lynched during the first year following that war, some of them returned soldiers still in uniform. From June to December 1919 approximately twenty-five "race riots" occurred in American cities; in many cases Blacks fought back, killing some of the white attackers.

By Philip Blake. From *Militant*, June 19, 1943.

sailors, soldiers, and civilians; hundreds of others have been arrested without warrant. The capitalist press helped to incite these attacks, and many police stood by laughing while they were carried out.

In and around Los Angeles a considerable minority of the population is Mexican or of Mexican descent. They are and for years have been the victims of discrimination in much the same way that Negroes are in the South. They are not wanted in many restaurants, etc.; they are segregated in housing, and consequently in the schools; they are barred from many jobs; they are the victims of police persecution and brutality. Many of the youth form together in gangs; some of them wear zoot suits as a form of self-expression, as many Negro and white youth do.

The capitalist press, largely anti-Mexican, has labored to create the impression that everyone wearing a zoot suit is a gangster, just as the New York press recently tried to smear every Negro as a mugger. As a result of their propaganda, lies, and half-truths they whipped up a certain hysteria against all dark-skinned people and helped to inflame the servicemen into vigilante action, praising them after the fighting had begun for doing a better job against the "gangsters" and "petty crooks" than the cops had done. The servicemen, joined by anti-Mexican elements, went after everyone with a dark skin. Carey McWilliams, author and president of the National Lawyers Guild in Los Angeles, reports that at least half of the people seriously injured were not wearing zoot suits and that the same proportion holds true for the hundreds arrested by the police.

The city council voted to make the wearing of zoot suits a misdemeanor; the police arrested a lot of Mexicans and Negroes; Los Angeles was declared out of bounds for the servicemen. For the time being the violence has subsided, and the press—seeing a decline in the city's business with the servicemen barred—is sanctimoniously calling for peace. But it is perfectly plain that no problems have been solved and that at the slightest provocation the whole thing may flare up again, if not through servicemen then through civilians.

What is necessary if the situation is really to be corrected, is an end to all discrimination and segregation practices against Mexicans and Negroes in industry, in social life, in housing, in the press, plus enforcement of their democratic rights, plus a widespread and deepgoing educational program on the meaning and effect of race discrimination; such a campaign can be launched most effectively under the leadership of the labor movement.

FEPC OK'S JOB SEGREGATION

The Fair Employment Practices Committee, set up by President Roosevelt with the proclaimed purpose of weeding out discrimination in war industry, has now become a government instrument for furthering segregation in the plants. This is the meaning of the approval given last week by the new FEPC Chairman Haas and high government officials, to the separation of white and Negro skilled workers in the Mobile shipyards of the Alabama Dry Dock and Shipbuilding Company. This is Roosevelt's method of upgrading skilled Negro workers. It smells of Jim Crow.

According to Lawrence Cramer, executive secretary of the FEPC, "The FEPC has in the past refused to decide hypothetically that segregation of Negro workers from white workers was discrimination referred to in the president's executive order. We always take the position that if in a situation any individual can show that by being segregated he is discriminated against, we will take action."

The implications of this statement of FEPC policy are staggering. This attitude is identical with the viewpoint held by the military authorities, who insist that segregation is not a form of discrimination and have, therefore, maintained a rigid pattern of Jim Crow in the armed forces.

This Mobile shipyard decision is a direct and serious blow at the Negro people at the precise moment when they are struggling for the right to skilled jobs. And now the government, under the pressure of the southern reactionaries, has arrived at the "Haas compromise," which is no compromise at all but a direct concession to racial prejudice.

The vile meaning of this decision is clearly expressed by the *Pittsburgh Courier* of June 12, which says,

---

By David Ransom, a pen name of Abe Stein (see Glossary). From *Militant*, June 19, 1943. In May, the Mobile shipyard owners had instigated an attack by thousands of white workers against Black welders hired under pressure of an FEPC ruling.

Opponents of the recent FEPC decision point out that if Negroes are segregated from whites on the job, it will be impossible to prevent discrimination against them; that in fact segregation is discrimination. They point out that the Alabama decision threatens to establish a Jim Crow job pattern throughout the country of frightening proportions. That every industry all over the country will seize on the formula of a segregated section or plant for Negro workers, and that after the war the Negro will be driven out of industry completely.

It would be fatal for the Negro people to take this blow lying down. This FEPC ruling threatens whatever progress they have made and whatever progress they may hope to make. Those who deluded themselves with the hope that the new FEPC would change things can now see that neither the wine nor the bottle has been altered. Roosevelt is still selling the same shoddy stuff. Now segregation is not only the avowed policy of the armed forces, it is well on the way to becoming the national government policy for war industry.

THE CASE OF DR. EDGAR KEEMER

Dr. Edgar B. Keemer is the latest colored citizen who, like Winfred Lynn of New York, has protested against the government's violation of its own Selective Service Act through its enforcement of segregation and discrimination in the armed forces.

Dr. Keemer, a Detroit physician, was turned down when he applied for a commission in the navy because the navy does not take Negro doctors even for the exclusive service of segregated colored personnel. He was then offered a commission in the army, but rejected it on the ground that the Procurement and Assignment Service permits a doctor to decide for himself what branch of service he will volunteer for.

From *Militant,* June 19, 1943. Dr. Keemer was aided in his case by the Socialist Workers Party and the American Civil Liberties Union. Under the pressure of mounting publicity and protest, the government dropped its case when it came to trial and Keemer never heard from the draft board or the military again.

His local draft board then tried to make an example of Dr. Keemer for daring to stand up for his legal rights. Although a father of three children, this practicing physician was called up for induction on May 18 as an ordinary private. Thereupon Dr. Keemer advised the board that he would not appear for induction as a private although he was ready and willing to serve as an officer in the navy. He has maintained this position since. The next move is up to the government authorities.

Dr. Keemer's request is indeed modest. He does not demand an end to the segregation policy. He simply wants the navy to accept colored officers on segregated ships and at training stations where colored sailors are stationed. But the brass hats in Washington will not make even this slight concession.

The Keemer case reflects the growing resistance by Negro intellectuals and workers to the Jim Crow system in the armed forces. In the interests of forging the bonds of Negro-white unity against the enemies of the exploited masses the trade union movement should rally to the defense of Keemer, Lynn, and other Negroes who are embarking on a similar course of protest and utilize these cases to launch a campaign against all forms of segregation and discrimination in the armed forces.

BLOOD IN STREETS OF DETROIT

Part of National Pattern

More violence against Negroes raged last week, taking a heavy toll of casualties in Detroit; Beaumont, Texas; Chester, Pennsylvania; and claiming a lynch victim in Marianna, Florida. The present crisis in race relations is already comparable to the one which developed on a national scale in 1919 and, if the recent

---

By Philip Blake. From *Militant,* June 26, 1943. The anti-Black pogrom in Detroit, June 19-20, carried out by white hoodlums including police and state troopers, resulted in 1,400 arrests (at least 1,000 Blacks), 600 injured (mostly Blacks), and 33 dead (26 Blacks). Sixteen of the Black victims were killed by police.

clashes in Los Angeles, Newark, Mobile, and southern army camps are taken into account, involves a greater number of participants.

DETROIT—A Negro and white motorist got into a fight at Belle Isle park on Sunday night, rumors sped around, and the fighting soon extended over a large part of the city. The original dispute was obviously accidental, but there is good reason for believing that Ku Klux Klan elements quickly intervened to aggravate the situation. Reports also make it clear that the city police did little to protect the Negro victims.

Two days later, when federal troops had been called in to end the fighting, at least twenty-eight people were dead, more than seven hundred were injured, some of them very severely, and approximately thirteen hundred people were under arrest. The great majority of the dead and wounded were Negroes, as were 85 percent of those arrested. Many homes and buildings were burned or looted; a number of cars and considerable property were wrecked; in these cases too, most of the damage was done to Negroes.

Local and federal agencies were said to be investigating fifth columnists charged with inciting the fighting. A UP dispatch on June 22, reporting that police were investigating why so many Negroes had gathered at Belle Isle on Sunday, indicates a possible attempt to pin the blame for the whole tragic affair on the Negro people. Apparently the fact that it was a blistering hot day had nothing to do with it.

Eyewitness Reports

By M. Williams

DETROIT, June 21—At 11:30 this morning I watched restless crowds milling about on Woodward Avenue and listened to the talk about the race riots. Groups of boys and young men aged between fifteen and twenty were hurrying up and down Woodward and into the side streets. These gangs were looking for Negroes, and when they found one, they would chase and stone him and try to capture and beat him.

From *Militant*, June 26 and July 3, 1943.

Some of the gangs were in cars, and they were ranging freely with absolutely no police interference in and around Watson Street, or a little along to the downtown area. On one side street, East Vernor Highway, I saw an overturned truck. A bystander told me that one of these gangs had stopped the truck, dragged out its Negro driver, and beaten him till he couldn't stand up.

At the city hall two Negro boys pursued by these gangs, appealed to two policemen for protection. A crowd quickly formed and the two boys were taken away in a patrol wagon. Nothing was done to the white hoodlums who had molested them.

One thing that I noticed particularly about these roving groups was that while they were mostly young poolroom kids in their twenties or even younger, there was almost always an older man who seemed to be their leader, who directed their activities, who encouraged them, and to whom they looked for orders.

Near Grand Circus Park a man about fifty years old came up to me and said in a low tone: "Tonight at eight. Up on Woodward." So I figure that the thing didn't lack organization once it was started.

The white people on the streets were as a rule quiet and took no part in the attacks on Negroes. Many attempted to warn Negroes getting off buses to go home and not come downtown until the trouble was over. Several times I saw pedestrians direct Negroes into department stores when they were being chased by the vigilante bands.

One white woman was so infuriated by the hoodlums that she attacked some of them with her fists. Other women showed their disapproval of the hoodlums by shouting at them to "leave the Negroes alone and go to work."

By a Negro

DETROIT—Regardless of published reports to the contrary, I know the "Paradise Valley" riot began as a defensive one. At 1:40 a.m. Monday I was standing among a group of orderly people at the corner of St. Antoine and Adams. There was no violence of any kind on that corner at that time although we heard rumors of brawls on Belle Isle.

Suddenly police in several squad cars drove up and without warning began throwing tear-gas bombs and shooting at men and women as they began to run.

At 8:30 a.m. I saw police drive up to the corner of Hastings and Farnsworth and fire indiscriminately in all directions.

At 8:30 p.m. I heard state troopers cursing colored women at Oakland and Owen. When the name-calling was returned by the crowd, the troopers fired repeatedly at point-blank range. Two were killed and many more lives endangered. These are not "rumors." They are facts.

By Two Whites

DETROIT—Woodward Avenue from Vernor to Watson was completely dominated by organized "white hundreds" mobs.* The white hoodlums were constantly rushing one block east toward John R, in attempts to penetrate the heavily populated Negro district beyond that street. When they penetrated the Negro district, the Negroes drove them back west of John R.

Then the police who had let the white mob through finished the job for the mob by machine-gunning the Negro defenders. In order to show their "impartiality," the cops gave the white mob the same dose—except with tear gas fired high like skyrockets and completely harmless. This "equality" treatment went on continuously.

After the retreat of the white crowd west of John R everybody laughed—and the cops joined in the exultant fraternization. When the hoodlums prepared for a new attack, many hurled bricks under the friendly, watchful eyes of the cops. Many openly carried knives—also under the eyes of the cops.

At around 9 p.m. the white mob surged forward and was again driven back. Then the city police and state troopers went to town. With machine guns, pistols, and rifles they fired hundreds of shots into the Negro ranks even while the hoodlums were still hurling bricks at the Negroes.

On the corner of John R and Montcalm the whites suddenly surrounded a Negro apartment house and began hurling bricks through the windows. From the house came a shot in an attempt to drive off the mob.

The police who were shooting at Negroes elsewhere, turned all their fire into the building. They shot to kill, and hundreds of bullets and rounds of tear gas were poured into the building. The

---

*This is an analogy to the Black Hundreds, an organization of reactionary, anti-Semitic groups in Russia formed during the 1905 revolution by landlords, rich peasants, government and police officials, and the Russian Orthodox clergy. They were most active in attacking revolutionary groups and carrying out pogroms against Jews from 1906 to 1911.

Negroes were finally driven out—that is, those who weren't killed or wounded—and lined up against the wall.

Later the cops hurried them away in cars while the crowd cheered its uniformed brothers.

Then of course the police drove the whites back—with tear gas fired high in the air.

Michigan CIO Condemns Anti-Negro Riots

DETROIT, June 28—A resolution on the anti-Negro riots in Detroit, presented to the eighteen hundred delegates at the Michigan State CIO convention today, was referred back to the resolutions committee amidst considerable confusion caused by the Stalinists and reactionaries.

The sentiment of the delegates was overwhelmingly in favor of placing the blame for the lynch terror on the employer-inspired Jim Crow setup in this country, and the resolutions committee expressed willingness to accept amendments from the ranks strengthening the resolution in condemnation of the Ku Klux Klan and in providing for a thoroughgoing investigation of the city authorities for the handling of the critical situation in Detroit. But the Stalinists insisted on placing the blame for the riots on Hitler and Mussolini. The reactionaries seized upon this opportunity to try to place responsibility for the Detroit clashes on the Japanese as well as on all aliens residing in this country.

These two forces combined and voted down the original resolution. When the delegates realized what had happened, they immediately asked the resolutions committee to bring back another resolution on this subject embodying the real wishes of the ranks. This resolution will undoubtedly be submitted at tomorrow's session.

The feelings of the delegates were clearly expressed in their thunderous ovation to the speech of Willard S. Townsend, member of the national executive board of the CIO and president

---

By John Saunders, a pen name of Arthur Burch. From *Militant*, July 3, 1943.

of the United Transport Service Employees union, who minced no words in exposing the real causes of the events of the last week:

Don't make the mistake of believing these racial outbreaks are isolated incidents in our national community or that they are all inspired from Berlin, Rome, and Tokyo. It's the very same forces that are fomenting racial strife that no more than three days ago pushed through Congress a slave-labor bill over the President's veto.* Not only are these forces fomenting racial strife but labor and nationality strife as well. They are the very same forces that are fighting against effective price control, anti-poll tax legislation, antilynch legislation, effective social security legislation, and everything that is decent and human in our American way of life.

While many were rioting in Detroit, the reactionary Congress was passing laws to enslave not only Negroes but all workers. The Smith-Connally Bill was passed not against Negroes but against the working people of this country. Prices are being pushed higher. Not only Negroes but all the people will suffer as a consequence. All must join to kill reaction in America.

Axis propaganda? Bosh! This combination of hate mongers is home-made. . . . This combination of hate mongers was doing a thriving business long before the cowardly Mussolini marched on Rome or before Schickelgruber [Hitler] planned his beer hall putsch.

Townsend's evaluation did not end here.

The basic causes for these racial incidents are found at the very roots of our social and economic system. A system which promotes discord among races, classes, and nationality groups as insurance against its own destruction. A system which by its very nature cannot effectively challenge slavery, insecurity, class and race antagonism. Divide the common people and rule has been the economic keystone of those who control the economic destiny of America. . . .

The Negro is a scapegoat in America because certain people can profit by his suppression. Race antipathy will die when nobody can profit by it.

DETROIT, June 29—The Michigan CIO Convention today passed a resolution blaming the anti-Negro riots in Detroit on intolerance fostered by the employers and their agents for the

---

*This refers to the Smith-Connally War Labor Disputes Bill, the first federal antistrike law in U.S. history. Roosevelt vetoed it because it did not go far enough (at this time he was threatening to conscript the coal miners to smash their strike). For provisions of the Smith-Connally Bill, see Glossary.

purpose of further exploiting the workers through the policy of divide and conquer.

Police, Politicians, and the Press

The official report of the Detroit Police Department admits that 15 of the 24 Negroes killed were shot by the police. None of the whites who died were killed by the police. The report listed 227 seriously injured. Of these 135 were whites, not counting the police and one soldier. Only 7 of these were injured by other whites or by unknown assailants; thus at most 7 whites were severely injured by the police. Here is how the police accounted for the 73 seriously injured Negroes: 36 beaten by whites; 11 shot by "unknowns"; one shot by another Negro; 4 wounded by stray bullets; 4 wounded by police "while looting stores"; 7 wounded by police "who were attempting to enforce order"; 6 "injured otherwise by police"; and one "accidentally wounded by police."

The mayor, the governor, and the commander of the armed forces in Detroit all joined in praising the press in the helpful and cooperative way in which they handled the rioting. The truth is that many of their stories were biased. The *Detroit News,* for example, dismissed the charges against the Ku Klux Klan by saying: "As to instigation by the Klan, we know that Negro hoodlums were aggressors just as often and quite as early in the proceedings as their white counterparts." That was the general line followed by most of the Detroit papers—to place equal responsibility on the white hoodlums and on the victims of the hoodlums. As for the murderous role played by the police, there was little comment of any kind on this question by the press.

No conflicts were reported in those neighborhoods inhabited by both Negroes and whites. The fighting took place only in areas from which Negro tenants are excluded or in which they are segregated. What a powerful argument against restrictive housing and all other forms of segregation!

There were also no outbreaks or conflicts within the factories of Detroit. The union officials and stewards took special steps to prevent any provocative acts on the part of their members. Many workers were heard to say that this was a terrible blow to the labor movement of Detroit. A number of others expressed the opinion that the union should have acted more positively to halt the rioting.

By Philip Blake. From *Militant,* July 3, 1943.

White members of the armed forces were also revolted by the lynch assaults. In some cases they sent letters and petitions to Detroit expressing their indignation. Sixty soldiers in Camp McCoy, Wisconsin, sent a letter to the mayor of Detroit asking: "Of what use is it if we defeat world fascism, only to find that while we paid with our lives for democracy, the fascist rule of the mob has been established at home?"

There were many evidences that the rioting against the Negroes did not lack organization. One physician watching from the Professional Building told the press: "These white hoodlums had a car loaded with bricks and iron bars, parked at the curb, where they were going for supplies. Their leaders could be seen directing them, pulling Negroes from cars and beating them mercilessly."

But federal, state, and city authorities don't appear to be much interested in determining what caused and who aggravated the Detroit tragedy. Despite the evidence contained in newspaper photographs and despite eyewitness accounts reporting organized leadership of the hoodlum bands, John S. Bugas, head of the FBI in Detroit, pooh-poohed the whole business—and, incidentally, showed how unconcerned he was about it—by saying: "Do you think that 200 kids, boys between the ages of 14 and 18, who stopped a street car, pulled off Negroes and pummeled them, were acting on orders? I don't."

Despite a lot of strong talk on the part of Governor H. F. Kelly and Mayor Jeffries at the beginning of the week, they had cooled down in a few days. Said Kelly on June 23: "Now our job is to see that those who took part in the rioting are punished and to find out what the causes were and who was responsible. Every effort will be made to bring them to the bar of justice so that such things will never again happen in Michigan." He then appointed a committee to report to him on these questions.

SWP on the Anti-Negro Terror

A series of assaults upon the Negro people throughout the country has reached a bloody climax in Detroit. This latest ferocious lynch attack murdered twenty-four Negroes, beat and

---

By the National Committee of the Socialist Workers Party. From *Militant,* July 3, 1943.

injured hundreds, and struck terror into the hearts of Detroit's community of almost 200,000 Negroes. This was not a "race riot" but an unprovoked attack by "white supremacy" mobs.

The hoodlums who constituted the lynch mobs in Detroit operated with comparative immunity. That is proven not only by the many eyewitness accounts testifying that the police either tolerated or directly aided the mobsters, but also by the official figures showing that 85 percent of those arrested were Negroes. Emboldened by their success, the hoodlums are undoubtedly ready for further lynch attacks against the Negro people.

It is unfortunately all too plain that the anti-Negro elements have made advances in their aim of keeping the Negro "in his place" and halting his struggle for equality and emancipation. Large numbers of Negroes have been terrorized and intimidated. Many others are becoming attracted toward "Negro nationalist" sentiments and feel hostility towards white people as a whole. There is great danger that these Negro workers will turn away in distrust and despair from the trade union movement.

The attacks on the Negroes threaten the unity of the working class. And this threat to labor unity comes at the very moment when the labor movement must mobilize its full fighting strength to beat back the union-busting offensive of big business and Washington.

Why has this epidemic of the lynch spirit broken out like a plague all over the nation?

The capitalist, liberal, and Stalinist press claim that Axis agents and Japanese "fifth columnists" provoked these outbursts. Although the Axis powers unquestionably exploit these acts of violence for their own reactionary ends, any informed person knows that such an explanation is absolutely worthless and nothing more than a fake alibi to cover up the real conditions and forces responsible for the crimes.

The real causes and culprits are here at home. Lynch assaults upon Negroes took place decades before the fascists came to power or the United States went to war with the Axis.

These attacks are an inevitable outgrowth of the Jim Crow system fostered by reactionary capitalist interests, protected by the Democratic and Republican parties, and buttressed by the government's policies of discrimination against Negroes in war industry and segregation in the armed forces. This vicious system breeds race hatred, officially sanctions and deliberately sharpens antagonisms between white and colored. The Jim Crow system provides the social basis for the poisonous propaganda and activities of the Ku Kluxers, Black Legions, Christian-Americans, and other native fascist cliques. The adherents, beneficiaries, and dupes of the Jim Crow system take advantage of every source of friction between white and Negro to stimulate ill feelings between them, inflame their prejudices, incite and hurl them against each other.

This carefully cultivated hostility has been aggravated by the consequences of war. Bad housing, poor transportation, dislocation of family life, juvenile delinquency, scarcity of food, frozen wages, and burdensome taxes in the face of soaring prices, afflict all sections of the working masses and create enormous discontent and rebelliousness. Because of their no-strike pledge and slavish subservience to Roosevelt's labor policies, the CIO and AFL leadership has completely failed to provide the workers with any program of resistance to the encroachments of the capitalists, to stop profiteering and the mounting cost of living. That is the reason why fascist demagogues and preachers of race hate and violence are able to receive a hearing from some workers.

For their own ends the ultrareactionary forces are trying to divert the justifiable indignation of the workers away from the real causes and authors of their misery. The actual instigators of these attacks come from the capitalist class and their conscious or unconscious tools. It has already been disclosed that agents of the employers planned and provoked the anti-Negro demonstrations in Mobile and elsewhere.

Every worker is aware that the capitalist interests are conducting today a furious campaign against the labor movement. The blows against the coal miners, the antilabor decisions of the War Labor Board, the passing of the Smith-Connally slave-labor act, Roosevelt's demand for the drafting of all strikers, have been high points of this offensive.

All workers must realize that the concerted attacks upon the colored people are an essential and integral part of this national union-busting drive. The employing class hopes by these murderous means to split the workers along race and color lines, to throw white workers against black, to undermine and demoralize the unions, and thus to turn the attention of the workers away from their real enemies.

Divide and rule: This policy, everywhere pursued by the possessing classes and their agents, has alone enabled them to hold down the exploited masses. Britain incited Moslems against Hindus. Hitler uses the Jews for scapegoats. All of them hurl the workers of one country against another in periodic world wars.

For generations here in the United States employers have grown fat and powerful by playing native workers against foreign-born, white against black, craft against craft. The American workers were able to build their powerful union movement in the last decade by sweeping aside, overcoming, and fighting against all these artificially fomented divisions. The Negro workers played a heroic role in the building of the industrial union movement. They fought side by side with their white brothers against the bosses. Race prejudice and discrimination cannot be permitted to penetrate again and regain a foothold within the trade unions.

The capitalist government bears a large share of responsibility for these attacks. The administration's recent decision for segregation of colored workers in the Mobile shipyards and the policy of segregation practiced in the armed forces provide official example and encouragement to the Jim Crow elements.

The government fails to enforce the Fourteenth Amendment or the federal statutes against discrimination, and even violates the provisions of the Selective Service Act against discrimination. This authorized lawlessness has encouraged similar lawlessness amongst the advocates of white supremacy. The failure of Roosevelt's administration to press for the passage of antilynching and anti-poll tax legislation has given aid and comfort to all enemies of the Negro people. Roosevelt has brought neither freedom from want nor freedom from fear to the Negro people. On the contrary they are today more terrorized and troubled than ever before.

What must be done to stop this lynch violence? Certainly no trust or reliance can be placed in the federal authorities, the army, state or municipal police, and the goodwill of the capitalist rulers, the action of Congress or the president. They have shown that they will not take the steps needed to protect Negro lives and rights.

The Negro people have both the right and the duty to protect themselves against lawless attacks of the lynch mobs. They have the right to demand that, in event of any future attacks, Negro troops be used and Negroes be deputized to defend them.

But the Negroes constitute only a small minority of the population. For their protection they require strong and reliable allies. These allies will come above all from organized labor, of which the colored workers form a significant section. The prejudices exhibited by some workers should not blind the Negroes to the necessity of uniting with the labor movement. Prejudices implanted in the minds of white workers by their enemies have been and can be overcome through action and education in joint struggle of black and white workers against their enemies and exploiters. The fundamental interests and aims of the white and colored workers in their fight for equality and emancipation are the same.

The chief responsibility for defending the Negro people rests today upon the trade unions. The CIO, most powerful organization of the working people in Michigan, was established and grew strong because of its policy of nondiscrimination against any worker, regardless of color, race, religion, or political affiliation. The labor leaders must do more than deplore these attacks upon the Negro people. They must do more than order their members to stay off the streets and appeal for grand jury investigations. They must summon their membership to take determined and organized action against the instigators and organizers of these lynch mobs. The unions of Detroit could have repulsed this threat to their very existence as they repulsed General Motors in 1937 and Ford in 1941. Detroit would be far different today and the native fascists would be cowering in their holes, demoralized instead of triumphant, had the union leaders called out the veteran flying squadrons to defend the Negro people.

These attacks are an alarm signal. They involve issues no less important to the unions than the fight waged against the auto barons in 1937. The hoodlums and hooligans who are today assailing the Negroes are training themselves for other acts of violence. Tomorrow or the day after they can be unleashed by the Fords, Wilsons, and Chryslers as storm troops and strikebreakers against the unions themselves. Workers, take warning! This is how fascist gangs were formed and fascism arose in Europe and crushed the labor movement. Do not permit them to take root here.

For their own self-protection the unions must use the same methods of struggle, the same fighting program that proved so effective against Harry Bennett's mobsters. Let the union officials call a great meeting of all the shop stewards in the Detroit area, acquaint them with the seriousness of the situation, and inform them of the union's campaign. The members of each local should be mobilized for action. Flying squadrons of union militants should stand ready to protect the rights of their Negro fellow workers menaced by the mobs. The various local unions should maintain order and clear their respective territories of anti-Negro, antilabor gangs.

Every local union should set up a vigorous antidiscrimination committee to combat employer-instituted discrimination in the shops and to ferret out the conscious Ku Klux Klan agents and provocateurs who try to stir up dissension between white and colored workers. The unions must carry on educational activities to explain to the backward workers the reactionary meaning of race prejudice and its menace to their own interests and organizations. The prejudices inculcated by capitalist institutions can and must be eradicated by union education. In addition, the Detroit labor movement should set up its own investigating committee and conduct its own public hearing, where the truth can be told about the causes, instigators, and beneficiaries of the anti-Negro terror, and where plans to prevent new attacks can be mapped out.

Such immediate steps in Detroit must be extended on a national scale. The unions can be content with nothing less than the leadership of the struggle to abolish Jim Crowism and to secure full economic, political, and social equality for the Negro people.

Such a program of action would help restore the shaken faith of the Negroes in the entire labor movement. It would create unbreakable bonds of unity between white and colored workers. By establishing the solidarity of the working class as a whole, it would clear the way to smash the capitalist antilabor offensive all along the line. Black and white, unite and fight your common enemies!

Roosevelt's Letter

The universal condemnation and the aroused sentiments of the Negro people to do something about anti-Negro violence have forced President Roosevelt to break his silence on this question. In a letter to Representative Marcantonio of New York last week Roosevelt stated, "The recent outbreaks of violence in widely scattered parts of the country endanger our national unity and comfort our enemies." Roosevelt also informed Marcantonio that he had asked the attorney general and other government agencies "to give special attention to the problem of race riots in this country."

This letter is nothing less than an insult to the intelligence of the Negro people. Ever since the war began, the Negro people

---

By David Ransom. From *Militant,* July 31, 1943.

have been telling Roosevelt that the government was preparing the way for anti-Negro explosions by its Jim Crow policies in the armed forces and government agencies as well as by its refusal to fight discrimination in the war industries.

As chief executive of a capitalist government which rests upon the pillars of private property and Jim Crow, Roosevelt can do nothing but make pretty speeches and set up super-agencies designed only to create the illusion that the government has the interests of the Negro people at heart. The Stalinists and many liberals are playing Roosevelt's game by trying to foster this same illusion. If Roosevelt and the government continue to give their kind of attention to the problem of anti-Negro violence, there are certainly going to be more of such outbursts, and on a larger scale.

R. J. Thomas on Flying Squads

The prolabor sentiment revealed in the *Pittsburgh Courier* poll of Negro opinion two weeks ago warrants the conclusion that the Negro people do not place any responsibility for the epidemic of anti-Negro outbursts on the labor movement, and that the unions have retained the good will of the Negro people.

But though the unions have not lost ground, they missed an opportunity to win added prestige among Negroes. Had the leaders of the United Auto Workers sent out flying squadrons to defend the Negroes from the assault of the white hoodlums, they would have given a demonstration of solidarity between white workers and the Negro people that means more than a library full of resolutions against Jim Crow.

The failure of the UAW to take such action rests not with the rank and file but with the leadership. This is proved to the hilt by the explanation which UAW President R. J. Thomas gave at a meeting of UAW educational directors in the Detroit area, held on July 11. Thomas declared that he had received many calls on the

By David Ransom. From *Militant,* August 7, 1943.

day of the pogrom urging that he call out the flying squadrons in defense of the Negroes in the affected areas.

He was opposed to this, said Thomas, not because it could not have accomplished the defense, but because the taking of the law in the hands of the flying squadrons would have been termed a "union revolution."

Surely one fact has penetrated even Thomas's skull. Whenever workers organize and act to defend their rights against the abuses of employers, the whole weight of public opinion, which is a fancy name for capitalist opinion, is arrayed against them. Has Thomas forgotten the sit-down strikes of 1937, which were also denounced by the whole capitalist press as a "union revolution"?

The Stalinist Complaint

It is no surprise to learn that the Stalinists have joined the chorus of those who place part of the blame for the anti-Negro violence upon the Negroes themselves. The Stalinists also blame the Negro people for the existence of Jim Crow conditions. Ben Davis, Jr., writing in the *Daily Worker* of July 18, makes the following statement in the course of an attack on the recent Chicago convention of the March on Washington movement:

". . . The resolution adopted on the anti-Negro outbreaks said, 'the blame must be put where it belongs, that is, at the door of the present government itself.' It is true that the Administration has not been sufficiently consistent in giving effect to the President's anti–Jim Crow orders, but labor in particular, and other patriotic Americans, including Negroes, have not rallied sufficiently to strengthen the President's hand."

It is needless to quote Roosevelt's statements that morale in the armed forces would be impaired if segregation of Negroes were ended. It is needless to cite Roosevelt's silence on important anti–Jim Crow legislation. For part of the support given by the Stalinists to Roosevelt consists in covering up Roosevelt's anti-labor and anti-Negro record. At first the Stalinists were blaming

---

By David Ransom. From *Militant,* August 7, 1943.

Hitler for the Detroit pogrom; now they blame as well—the Negroes.

Government Distortion and Slander

The agencies of "law and order," both state and federal, have opened up with all their light and heavy artillery against the victims of mob violence, which they are supposed to prevent and punish.

Prominent among these agencies is the Michigan governor's fact-finding committee, which was set up to investigate and report on the causes of the anti-Negro terror and which has sternly opposed all demands for a grand jury investigation.

The committee issued a very long report last week. It expressed many noble sentiments, advocating that the situation must be examined without bias or prejudice. It was filled with charts and graphs and statistics and maps and documents. It recommended that a study of the situation be made by "the proper social agencies" so that "there can be a frank, straightforward approach to this problem."

The committee's own approach to the problem has been well summarized by the August 13 Press Service of the National Association for the Advancement of Colored People:

Fully one-third of the digested text as reported in the Detroit dailies, August 11, concerns itself with minutely detailed descriptions of what the report described as "disconnected incidents provoked by a group of Negroes."

Violence of whites against Negroes is dismissed summarily in a short paragraph, despite the fact it is asserted this violence extended over a period of twenty hours, from 4 a.m., June 21 until 11 p.m. that same day. During this period 1,500 persons were arrested of whom 85% were Negroes. Seventeen of the 25 slain Negroes were killed by police.

Of the behavior by the police, who laughed when they saw

By Albert Parker. From *Militant,* August 21, 1943.

white hoodlums beating up Negroes and who shot to kill when they saw Negroes successfully resisting these attacks, the committee's report had nothing to find but praise.

The third part of the committee report is devoted to an attack on the Negro press, Negro leaders, and Negro organizations like the NAACP and the March on Washington movement for "inspiring" the riot. The governor's committee pretends that they are to blame because they urged the Negro people to seek equal rights. As the NAACP puts it, "Negroes have asked nothing but simple justice and the report to the governor calls them agitators."

Two members of the governor's committee were the county prosecuting attorney and the city police commissioner. The other two were the state district attorney and the state police commissioner. All of these men were heads of departments which were responsible in more ways than one for the heavy casualties in Detroit. So it would have been foolish to expect anything else of them.

But what about Francis B. Biddle? He refers to himself as a liberal and in recent months has even been posing as a friend of the Negro people. As attorney general he is the chief law enforcement officer in the country. Yet his contribution to the discussion last week was no less contemptible and reactionary than the report of the Michigan governor's committee.

Biddle sent an FBI agent to Detroit and when he got his findings wrote a confidential letter to Roosevelt, parts of which were made public last week. The chief emphasis in his letter was placed on the need for more police to handle future "race riots."

Then Biddle went on to pay lip-service to the need for better housing and recreational facilities, the lack of which he understands to be one of the causes of the anti-Negro attacks. But since he knows that the government is not going to do anything fundamental about housing, etc., he feels that the movement of Negroes to certain war production centers should be limited or stopped. Not the movement of white and Negro workers, but of Negro workers only.

Later in the week Biddle backtracked on this proposal, asserting that it was not a recommendation to Roosevelt but a suggestion, that careful study should be given to the matter and that he knew of "no present plan to prohibit migration."

All these slanders against the Negro people are committed in the name of preserving "law and order." Actually what they create is justified contempt and hostility for the officials trying to cover up their own criminal responsibility and to divert attention from the Jim Crow system which breeds anti-Negro violence. To the extent that they show Negro and white workers that they can rely only on themselves for the solution of their pressing problems, even these slanders perform a useful function.

THE MARCH ON WASHINGTON MOVEMENT'S NATIONAL CONVENTION

CHICAGO, July 4—The March on Washington movement today concluded its five-day constitutional convention, held here at the Metropolitan Community Church, after adopting a program calling for direct mass action methods to fight Jim Crowism and fixing a share of the responsibility for the recent murderous mob assaults on Negroes upon the administration.

About 110 delegates, representing local Negro groups from thirty-six communities, adopted a constitution and by-laws establishing the March on Washington movement as a permanent, all-Negro organization dedicated to securing full economic, political, and social equality for the 13 million American Negroes. A. Philip Randolph, president of the AFL Sleeping Car Porters union and founder of the MOWM, was elected national director.

As stated in the new constitution, the objectives of the organization will be to "awaken, teach, organize, mobilize, direct and lead the Negro masses to struggle and fight for their own liberation" and to "cooperate and collaborate with all progressive movements," including the labor movement, to achieve real democracy and full equality for the Negro people and all oppressed minorities.

The convention, by overwhelming majority, reaffirmed the original intent of the MOWM to organize an all-Negro march on Washington, although no date was set for the action. The National Executive Board was instructed, however, to fix a date for a feasible time. In the meantime, the resolution called for taking immediate steps to organize "local marches for specific objectives to organize and discipline groups in preparation for a national march."

The most debate centered on the first resolution introduced which called for a blanket support of the war.

The resolution, supported by Randolph, was vigorously opposed

By Art Preis. From *Militant,* July 10, 1943.

by Layle Lane, a member of the MOWM national committee. She pointed out that this resolution was in conflict with other resolutions which would be introduced, which correctly characterized the war as "imperialist on both sides" and "a struggle for the right to exploit the colored peoples in the colonies."

This contradiction was even more sharply shown in Randolph's address at the public mass meeting closing the convention this afternoon. He opened this address by emphatically declaring his support for the war and the United Nations.

Then he went on to declare, concerning the real objectives of the war and its character:

> But, be not deceived. This is not a war for freedom. It is not a war for democracy. It is not a war to usher in the Century of the Common Man. It is not a People's Revolution. It is a war to maintain the old imperialisms. It is a war to continue white supremacy and the subjugation, domination and exploitation of the peoples of color. It is a war between the imperialisms of fascism and the imperialism of monopoly capitalistic democracy. Under neither are the colored natives free.

In effect, despite his strongly critical attitude toward the conduct of the war and its objectives, Randolph was calling upon the Negro masses, in the name of democracy for themselves, to aid in an imperialist war to enslave further hundreds of millions of colored peoples of the colonies.

Following the adoption of the resolution on the war, the convention proceeded to enthusiastically endorse resolutions in support of the struggles of the peoples of India, China, Africa, the West Indies, etc., for immediate, unconditional independence.

The convention was held while Negro and progressive white sentiment was at its highest peak of fury and indignation against the recent anti-Negro terror in Detroit, Beaumont, Mobile, Los Angeles, etc.

The resolution adopted on these mass lynching bees declared

> that this meeting states definitely that it is unsound to place the blame for the cause of these race riots upon Hitler. The blame must be put where it belongs, that is, at the door of the present government itself. The cause of these riots is not Hitler but the policy of Jim Crow, segregation and discrimination, in and by the government and in education, housing, recreation, amusement, before the courts, in the armed forces and defense industry. Race riots and mob law, lynchings and racial terrorism obtained in America long before Hitler was ever heard of and will continue long after he is dead and forgotten unless Negroes receive the status of first-class citizenship in America.

However, the proposals of the resolution for stopping mob

attacks included merely a request that Roosevelt set up a national commission on race, composed equally of Negro and white members, to "study" the conditions leading to this expression of Jim Crowism and to bring in a report of findings and methods to stop these attacks; that Negro as well as white soldiers be sent into riot areas; and that a congressional investigation be made of the recent riots with the aim of enacting legislation to protect the Negroes and other minorities.

As in all the other resolutions dealing with specific aspects of Jim Crowism, there was no recognition of the fact that the organized labor movement is the most reliable ally of the Negro people. While stating the willingness of the MOWM to cooperate with other groups, including the unions, no direct appeal or concrete proposal for joint action was made, other than calling on other groups to demand that Roosevelt agree to meet with a committee of the MOWM.

The struggle of the Negro masses was emphasized largely as independent of the struggle of the working class as a whole for its rights and conditions, although it was pointed out on several occasions that the onslaught against the Negro people paralleled a tremendous drive against the working class and the unions.

Thus, while acknowledging the responsibility of the government and the administration for the attacks on the Negroes, no genuine proposal for the political emancipation of the Negro, along with the entire working class, was put forth. On the contrary, Randolph projected the idea of a "nonpartisan political bloc" of all the Negroes to use their organized strength within the framework of the existing capitalist parties. As Randolph stated it in his public address this afternoon:

"This bloc does not require that Negroes come out of either the Republican, Democratic, Socialist or Communist Parties. But it does require that when a crucial question of universal concern and importance to the Negroes arises, that Negroes will express their united political strength, regardless of party politics, on the issue. When this is done, it will strengthen the position of the Negro leaders in the Republican and Democratic parties. . . ."

In the same speech, however, Randolph sneered at the "black petty bourgeoisie and intelligentsia" who first "unloaded on the GOP on the grounds that it was the party of Father Abraham Lincoln" and "then when the political pickings got kind of slight . . . fled to the Democratic Jackass." He concluded: "Ere long they will learn that there is no fundamental difference between Democrats and Republicans either with respect to Negroes or labor, that they are like two peas in a pod, two souls with a single thought, tweedledee and tweedledum."

Here Randolph indicates the need for a great new independent party of the masses, Negro and white—a labor party—but all he continued to advise was the old policy of Negroes bargaining away their political power with one or another of the old-line capitalist Jim Crow parties.

While the convention went on record for a policy of direct mass action, a great emphasis was placed by some of the leaders on what was termed "nonviolent, goodwill direct action." This idea, as was made clear by several of the speakers, was literally Ghandism, passive resistance. The injection of this "goodwill" concept was a reflection of the influence on the convention of pacifist elements from such groups as the Fellowship of Reconciliation and the Norman Thomas Socialists.

In the course of the discussion on this proposal, it became clear that some of the delegates and leaders had in mind the discontinuance of mass action in favor of small, localized actions of a few individuals, such as going into restaurants which barred Negroes, etc.

One delegate, who identified himself as an active unionist in the steel industry, declared:

"We didn't build our unions that way. When the strikebreakers and cops attacked our picket lines, when their bullets began ripping and their clubs to hitting, then we had to fight to defend ourselves and prevent them from smashing our lines. If we didn't do that, there wouldn't be any unions today."

Although there was obvious confusion as to the exact meaning of "nonviolent, goodwill direct action," a resolution endorsing it was passed.

A disappointing feature of the convention was the little time set aside for the delegates to discuss and legislate.

A good deal of time was taken up with too many "prominent" speakers whose contradictory ideas only served to confuse and disorient the convention. It seemed as if an effort was being made to give the MOWM a "respectable front," even to the detriment of the convention and its actions.

PROLABOR SENTIMENT POLLED

Each week the *Pittsburgh Courier*'s Bureau of Public Sentiment asks more than ten thousand Negroes—workers and middle-class elements, southerners and nonsoutherners—to express their views on various current issues. The results of this survey are widely recognized as the nation's most authoritative and representative poll of Negro opinion.

Last week the *Courier* printed the results of answers to the question: "Should Negro workers seek closer co-operation with organized labor?" 96.4 percent of those questioned said yes, 2.4 percent said no, and 1.2 percent were uncertain.

Such an expression of overwhelmingly prolabor sentiment among the Negro people would be significant at any time. But it is doubly significant—and heartening—at the present time. For it comes more than a month after the tragic anti-Negro terror in Detroit and other cities. And it comes at the height of the worst barrage of antiunion propaganda and labor-baiting in recent years.

It shows the Negro people have learned the lesson that their fate is inseparably connected with that of the white workers and that the labor movement, although some backward sections of it continue to practice race discrimination, is their most dependable ally in the fight against Jim Crowism. It shows they have learned this lesson so well that they remain unshaken by the anti-Negro riots, whose purpose is to divide Negro from white, and that they have not fallen into the trap of blaming all white people for such anti-Negro attacks. It shows also that they have not been greatly impressed or affected by the antilabor editorials, speeches, and radio addresses, which are designed to discredit the unions and lessen their prestige and attractive power.

The prolabor sentiment of the Negro people is a cause for rejoicing in the labor movement. It must also be the occasion for labor to recognize its own responsibility toward the Negro people. The labor movement owes a debt to the Negroes for their loyalty

An editorial, *Militant*, July 31, 1943.

and solidarity and support. It can repay that debt, and strengthen its own power at the same time, only by making ever greater efforts to integrate the Negro workers in the leadership and ranks of the labor movement and to help destroy Jim Crowism wherever it exists.

THE HARLEM OUTBREAK

A Protest Against Intolerable Conditions

Five killed, more than five hundred injured, more than five hundred arrested, property damages exceeding $5 million—these were the immediate results of the outburst in Harlem last Sunday and Monday.

It began Sunday night when a white policeman shot and wounded a young Negro soldier who had objected to the policeman's maltreatment of a Negro woman he was arresting. The rumor spread that the soldier had been killed, and resentment rose high. Groups began roaming the streets, fighting with police, breaking store windows, carrying off merchandise. With the exception of forty police injured, all of the casualties were Negroes.

What set these thousands of people into motion in this way? The shooting of the soldier was only a chance incident; it could have been precipitated by some other accidental event. The real cause must be sought in the social, economic, and political conditions of the Negro people.

On several occasions in the past year Negro leaders have been compelled to complain publicly about the brutality of the New York police toward Negro citizens. More than one outbreak provoked by police brutality has been narrowly averted in Harlem in recent months. The Negro people are sick and tired of being beaten, maimed, and thrown into jail on the slightest pretext. They are revolting against victimization by the police who have been taught by the press that all Negroes are muggers and must be dealt with viciously.

Another and equally important factor in the Harlem conflict was the fact that a Negro soldier was involved in the initial

From *Militant*, August 7, 1943.

incident. Nothing rankles in the Negro people so much as the true stories they hear and read about the treatment of the Negro soldiers, especially in southern camps. Many Harlemites have sons and brothers in Camp Stewart, Georgia, and other "hell-holes," as the soldiers describe them, and they know that their relatives, being trained to fight in a "war for democracy," are themselves Jim Crowed and insulted in a manner to make Hitler green with envy. Every Negro leader in Harlem recognizes this to be one of the basic causes of last Sunday's outbreak.

On top of these are the economic conditions in Harlem, aggravated in the extreme by the war. Rents are uncontrolled. Prices are higher, the quality of food is generally lower, and food is scarcer than in other parts of the city. Negroes have the worst-paying jobs, despite the manpower shortage. The Negro people suffered from the lowest standard of living in the city before the war; today they are even worse off.

On Sunday and Monday the Negro people carried on a spontaneous protest. Their protest took on a distorted, elemental, and chaotic form, as protests usually do in the absence of a clear program and a trained leadership; under these conditions the protest could not possibly win what the demonstrators wanted. But it is perfectly clear that they were trying to show in some way that they were fed up with present conditions and ready to fight against them.

The Communist Party, which has considerable influence in Harlem, was among the first to denounce the protesting Negroes. Acting in the interests of the Stalinist bureaucracy in the Soviet Union, these Stalinist finks have betrayed the Negro struggle as well as the labor movement at home.

For La Guardia—who knew long ago what was coming and failed to do a thing about it but make speeches on the need for keeping calm in times like these—the Stalinists have nothing but praise. For the Negro masses they reserve their vilest slanders and attacks.

In the same language the capitalist press uses in denouncing "hoodlums and vandals," and with the same spirit of hatred and contempt, a front page editorial in the August 3 *Daily Worker* says:

". . . groups of irresponsible elements began a wholesale looting of stores owned by white storekeepers.

"This looting of stores was a shameful act at this moment in our nation's history. . . ."

Like the capitalist press the Stalinists neglect to mention the fact that people are hungry in Harlem. Yes, mothers accompanied by six-year-old children took food from the window-broken grocery shops. The Stalinists attack them as "irresponsible." That is the voice of well-fed bureaucrats, not of a party genuinely concerned with the suffering of the masses.

"A shameful act," they say. But not half so shameful as the cynicism, baseness, and treachery of the Communist Party, and not a hundredth as shameful as the Jim Crow system that produces such acts—a system which the *Daily Worker* editorial does not mention, let alone blame.

'Not Another Detroit'

"This is not another Detroit! This is not a 'race riot'." Thus Mayor La Guardia, the liberals, Stalinists, and "respectable" Negro leaders hastened to assure the world that the August 1-2 outbreak in Harlem, deplorable as it was, could have been much worse.

It is true that there were marked differences between the events in Harlem this week and the tragedy in Detroit last June. In Detroit organized bands of hoodlums and advocates of white supremacy intervened in a minor clash to aggravate the situation and terrorize the whole Negro population; such bands were absent from the Harlem outbreak. In Harlem a large section of the Negro people gave a demonstration of their dissatisfaction with the conditions under which they live; the only whites to molest the Negroes were the police, with the result that whites were able to walk freely through the streets at the height of the demonstration, and the affair never took on a Negro-versus-white complexion.

Nevertheless, the underlying cause of the Harlem events was the same as the underlying cause of the Detroit events—the maintenance of the Jim Crow system, which assumes the most oppressive form in times of social crisis such as we are now passing through.

The capitalist, Stalinist, and liberal press congratulate La Guardia on restoring "order" and on handling the situation so that greater harm did not result. But what now? Does anyone seriously believe that this has solved the situation? The underlying causes of the outbreak remain; the authorities have not proposed and will not propose any measures to eliminate these

---

An editorial, *Militant,* August 7, 1943.

causes. This week Jim Crowism took five lives and inflicted injuries on hundreds. What is to prevent it from taking a toll ten times greater next week? What is to prevent it from developing into the form and on the scope of the Detroit anti-Negro terror?

The *Militant* does not denounce the masses of Harlem, who felt constrained in their desperation to demonstrate against Jim Crow in the manner which they did. We recognize it to be an expression of their discontent, of their desire to conduct a militant struggle against their Jim Crow conditions. We understand that it happened the way it did because they are lacking the program and leadership able to direct their struggle into fruitful channels and against the real enemy—the capitalist system which promotes and upholds Jim Crow.

Until the Negro people forge a fighting program and leadership—which they will find only through an alliance with the militant labor movement—there will always remain the social conditions breeding Harlems and Detroits.

Who Was to Blame?

There was remarkable unanimity of opinion among the well-known Negro leaders and in the Negro press during and after the August 1-2 outbreak in Harlem. Practically every one of them—whether conservative, liberal, Stalinist, or "radical"—joined in calling for the restoration of "law and order" as the most important need of the Negro masses and in denouncing thousands of Harlemites as hoodlums, vandals, irresponsible elements, etc.

The *Pittsburgh Courier* headlines screamed: "Disgraceful Scenes Enacted As Hoodlum Elements Loot Stores." The *Chicago Defender* expressed its disapproval by refusing to print a single picture relating to the affair. The *Daily Worker* echoed the capitalist press by calling it a "shameful act." A. Philip Randolph, who delights in referring to himself as a militant and dynamic leader, voiced "great sorrow and distress" and delivered a short lecture to the masses on the need for observing the law.

Virtually all the Negro papers hailed the behavior of the New York police—the same police whose brutality to Negroes was one of the chief causes of the outbreak. They seem highly elated and

By Albert Parker. From *Militant,* August 14, 1943.

relieved that "only" six died, most of them at the hands of the police.*

These Negro leaders and editorial writers knew, as most of them have since half admitted, that the Harlem outbreak was fundamentally a protest and demonstration against the oppressive Jim Crow conditions to which the Negro people are subjected in even the "most liberal city in the country." It was not a planned and organized protest; its participants did not understand the program for abolishing Jim Crow; under such conditions the demonstrators could not do more than show their deep dissatisfaction and their strong impulse to resist Jim Crow attacks on their rights and conditions.

These Negro leaders and writers know as well as the *Militant* does that the responsibility for what happened in Harlem lies not on the Negro masses, but on the capitalist system which breeds discrimination and segregation; on the White House and Congress and the bureaucracy of the armed forces, which inspire and set a reactionary example for the most backward elements of the white population; and on the propaganda and educational machinery of the nation, which upholds and spreads the ideas of white supremacy.

But none of these leaders used the same vituperative language against the real culprits that they used against the desperate and harried victims of the Jim Crow system.

How have these leaders reacted to the present crisis in the struggle for equality? At best, they offer a program for fighting defensive, rearguard actions. At worst, they counsel patience, "tolerance," the subordination of the Negro people's interests to the needs of "national unity," and the postponement of the anti–Jim Crow fight to some future date after the end of the war. In no case do these leaders present a bold, realizable program; all they can inspire is defeatism and despair.

As a result the masses do not have a program. They see no way out of the crisis. Their conditions, the increase of reaction, the growing gap between the democratic slogans of the war and freezing of the second-class citizenship status of the Negro—all these convince the Negro masses that now is the time for struggle. They see the need to fight, they *want* to fight—but they don't see how.

What can result from such a situation but blind, chaotic, bitter, misdirected, and hopelessly futile outbursts of the kind witnessed in Harlem? Only the most naïve optimist will believe that the

*One of the injured had died since the initial reports, raising the death toll from five to six.

same thing won't happen again, on an even greater scale, in Harlem and elsewhere.

And the blame for it rests in part on those people who present themselves as the leaders of the Negro masses but who have led them only into a blind alley. No wonder these people, recognizing their own responsibility, were so violent and unrestrained in their denunciations of the masses.

As for us, who recognize the real causes of the Harlem outbreak and the real forces to be censured for it, we see in these developments the need to intensify our efforts to win the Negro people over to the program of revolutionary socialism.

Some Faulty Evaluations

This whole discussion reminds us of many of the slave rebellions that took place a century or so ago. We all know how cruelly the slaves were oppressed and exploited—and that the arguments raised on behalf of the maintenance of slavery sounded monotonously like the arguments raised on behalf of the maintenance of Jim Crow today. Many of the slaves were ignorant and superstitious, they had no understanding of the forces at work in society, they rarely had leaders who knew how to give them the proper guidance.

But when they saw no other way out, when their patience came to an end and their resentment reached a boiling point, they revolted—in most cases blindly, often realizing that they had little chance of success. In many instances they resorted to arson and robbery, often innocent bystanders (like the small storekeepers in Harlem) were killed and beaten.

Now the question arises: who and what were to blame for the "excesses" committed during these revolts? If you leave aside the sociological, economic, and political explanations, then you could come to the conclusion, as some well-meaning abolitionists did in that period, that the slaves were to blame. But the verdict of history is that the slave system and the slaveholders were responsible. And today the Negro people and the labor militants pay honor and tribute to the memories of those brave, unlettered slaves who didn't have a full and correct program but who had the courage to fight against oppression in the best way they could see.

By Albert Parker. From *Militant,* September 4, 1943.

We don't pretend that the Harlem outbreak was completely identical with the slave revolts, but we do maintain that the same spirit was evidenced. Those who look only at the effects and shut their eyes to the causes will learn nothing from the Harlem events. Those who see the indissoluble connection between the two will be able to learn at least one thing useful for the struggle against Jim Crow—namely, that the masses today are ready to fight and are desperately seeking the correct program.

FOUR FREEDOMS AT HOME

Following are a few items picked from last week's press as evidence that Jim Crow is as hale and hearty as ever, apparently working on the job twenty-four hours a day.

Henry Ford, who posed as a "friend of the Negro people" during the period when he still hoped to be able to use Negro workers to prevent the unionization of his industrial empire, stands charged with "violating the letter and the spirit of the executive order on Fair Employment Practices."

According to Ford Local 600 of the CIO United Auto Workers, the Ford Motor Company has consistently refused to hire Negro applicants through regular employment channels; has subjected all Negro applicants to investigation by its notorious Sociological Department; has repeatedly refused to honor an agreement with the union providing for job preference for the wives, sisters, and daughters of Ford workers called to military service when those women have been relatives of Negroes, etc.

B. F. MacLaurin, international representative of the AFL Sleeping Car Porters union, reports that "in many areas of the South Negro locomotive firemen and train porters, whose occupations have been declared deferrable, have been drafted while white locomotive firemen have been exempted. . . . Two cities in which this procedure has been common are Augusta and Macon, Georgia."

MacLaurin also charges that the southeastern railroads "are hiring relatively large numbers of white firemen—more than are

---

By Albert Parker. From *Militant,* August 28 and September 18, 1943.

needed for their present needs—and hoarding this potential reservoir of manpower while they await the drafting and eventual elimination of Negro firemen."

Barnesville, Georgia, has its own brand of work-or-fight order, issued by the mayor of the town in a circular addressed to all domestic servants. (All domestic servants in Barnesville, according to the NAACP Atlanta branch, are Negroes.) The order reads as follows:

"Those living in the city of Barnesville, whether men or women, who have been employed as cooks and nurses, and who are not now employed, will be arrested and prosecuted and no excuse except a certificate from a physician will be accepted.

"Those who do not like the terms of this warning must realize that we all, regardless of financial means, must either work, fight or leave this city. This is the final warning. The police force of the city has been instructed to enforce this warning."

The *Chicago Defender* has unearthed a very illuminating document issued by the commanding general as "educational" material for Camp Stewart, Georgia, scene of a number of armed clashes involving Negro soldiers.

One part of the document amazingly enough asserts: "Most slave-owners were good-hearted Christian people who liked for everyone around them to be happy. They were, as a rule, good to their slaves."

Another part of the document, addressed to the officers, advises them to "use your S-2 Section and organize a counter-subversive system. Select as secret agents qualified and patriotic men in each barracks. Instruct these men carefully and secretly. Give them code names and have them mail their reports to you except in emergency."

Thus the army bureaucrats expect to curb the dissatisfaction of the soldiers, which arises from the segregation system and the Jim Crow treatment of the army, by spying on them.

In fascist Germany the Jewish oppressed minority was made to wear a yellow star so they could more effectively be singled out for discrimination. It used to be said that Negroes were able to escape this degradation in the United States because most of them were recognizable by their darker color as Negroes.

But now in Sandersville, Georgia, the chief of police has announced that all Negro men and women over the age of sixteen must carry identification badges indicating the name of their employer and their work schedule—or else face arrest and prosecution. The order does not apply to whites.

The mayor of Waltersboro, South Carolina, denied last week that the sale of Negro papers had been banned in the city and at the army air base two miles away. But a representative of one of the Negro papers insists that the town's police chief took him before the mayor, who said:

"You know better than to try to sell such a damn newspaper as this around here. I've been trying to keep these white folks off you n-----s' necks but the first thing you know they're gonna have you strung up on one of these trees. Since these damn Yankee soldiers have been coming down here, they've been putting hell in you. I don't want another one of these damn n----- papers sold around here. I mean that too" (*Afro-American*, September 11).

Whatever the situation is in Waltersboro, it is a fact that many army camps in the South have discouraged if not prohibited the sale of militant Negro papers.

Hitler is retreating on the eastern front and Mussolini is an ex-dictator. But Jim Crow is as brazen and aggressive and powerful as he ever has been during the twentieth century. If the Negro people want to overthrow *this* dictator, then they dare not wait until the end of the war before they start to deliver their first blows.

TWO KINDS OF JUSTICE

Last week's issue of the *Militant* contained two short items which reveal as much as a volume could about the position of the Negro in the U.S. Army.

One item was about a colonel who was telling the faculty of the University of Maryland about a university course to be attended by army students. When asked if Negro soldiers would be permitted to attend, the colonel answered with a laugh: "No. We don't have enough trees around here to hang 'em from."

The second item dealt with the court-martial, demotion, and imprisonment of a former unionist, S. Sgt. Alton Levy, stationed at the Lincoln Air Base in Nebraska. His crime? That he had dared to speak against the brutal Jim Crow treatment of Negro soldiers.

By Albert Parker. From *Militant*, September 25, 1943.

Note the contrast. One man speaks with the voice of the slave-holder and the lynch mob; nothing happens to him. The other speaks on behalf of democratic rights and equality; he feels the heavy hand of the brass hats, is put at hard labor for four months, and is in effect warned never to open his mouth on this question again.

Since then we have been provided with two more examples, offering an equally vivid contrast. Both of them centered around courts-martial in Michigan.

The first was the case of another colonel, William T. Colman, former commanding officer of the big air base at Selfridge Field, tried by an army court on twenty-eight charges, the most important of which was the shooting of a Negro soldier, Pvt. William McRae. Colman was quoted later as saying: "I have given orders repeatedly that a Negro chauffeur should never be sent to drive my car." Because someone violated these orders, Colman shot McRae on May 5 of this year. Other charges against him included drunkenness, fraudulent transfer of enlisted men, acceptance of a vacation lodge for personal use from a private contractor, misappropriation of government property, etc.

The military court dismissed twenty-three of the charges and found Colman guilty on four of the drunkenness charges. He was also pronounced guilty of shooting McRae—but the charge on this count was changed to read "careless use of firearms"!

The penalty? Colman was reduced to the rank of captain and made ineligible for promotion for the next year. And that was all. No imprisonment at hard labor for Colman. He is still in command of a considerable number of soldiers—some of whom may again be the victims of his "careless use of firearms" merely because he doesn't like their color.

The other case concerns four Negro soldiers at Fort Custer, Michigan. On June 21 these men heard about the outbreak of anti-Negro violence in nearby Detroit, where two of them had families. They tried to secure arms and trucks in order to ride to Detroit and defend their friends and brothers, but were arrested and held "for investigation." As the *Militant* said at that time: "An honest investigation should disclose only that these soldiers wanted to fight for democracy."

On September 14, the same day that Colman's "punishment" was announced, the AP carried a dispatch revealing for the first time that these men had been court-martialed and found guilty of violating four articles of war. One had been sentenced to twenty years at hard labor, another to eighteen years, and the remaining two to fifteen years. The AP dispatch announced that the commandant of the Sixth Service Command had reviewed the sentences and reduced them. The final result was: the soldier sentenced to twenty years will now serve ten; two others will serve eight years; the fourth was cleared of the charges.

The contrast in these cases is so striking as to make extended comment unnecessary. In one an officer breaks half the rules of the army, shoots a man because he doesn't like his color and gets off with a slap on the wrist. In the other, soldiers are guilty of trying to combat lynch attacks on their people and are thrown into prison as though they were criminals.

In the armed forces, where the will of the authorities is not to be questioned and where there is no pretense of democratic rights, it is impossible not to recognize that there are two kinds of justice— one for those who defend reactionary institutions and practices, another for those who want to change or abolish them. The same situation prevails in civilian society.

The existence of two kinds of justice arises from the conflict between the ruling capitalist class and the exploited working class. As long as this conflict lasts—and it will endure as long as there is private ownership of the means of production—class justice will continue.

The militant white and Negro workers must unite in protesting the harsh treatment meted out to Alton Levy and the Negro soldiers at Fort Custer, and they must demand their unconditional release.

FOUR FREEDOMS ABROAD

The Stalinists and other misleaders of the Negro people may talk a lot about the "four freedoms," the Atlantic Charter, and other paper promises of democracy. One fact, however, sticks out like a sore thumb. The United States sides with its "democratic" allies against the oppressed peoples who strive for freedom. Though they all may quarrel over the exact division of the colonies, they all agree on one point—these colonial peoples are to remain enslaved.

Take the fate of Ethiopia, Eritrea, Somaliland, and Libya. Mussolini boasted these African colonies were to be the foundation of Italy's fascist empire. Though Mussolini has been replaced by Marshal Badoglio, and the Italian ruling class has switched

By David Ransom. From *Militant*, November 27, 1943.

from the Axis to the side of the "United Nations," there has been no change in the imperialist plans of the Italian ruling class.

They are still fighting a war for profits and colonies. And as a reward for deserting Hitler they hope to regain their African colonies now under Allied military control.

About a month ago, George Padmore, London correspondent for two leading Negro papers, reported that Badoglio was pressing Italy's colonial claims on American and British government representatives. This week, Count Sforza, so-called antifascist and liberal, who had previously endorsed Badoglio's colonial demands, again urged that Eritrea, Somaliland, and Libya be returned to Italy in order to "avoid a rebirth of fascism." Another leading Italian figure, Dr. Adolfo Omedeo, rector of Naples University, said that Italy should be given a mandate over Ethiopia.

Through the mouths of their spokesmen, Badoglio and Count Sforza, the Italian ruling class voices its demand for these colonies. It remains to be seen whether or not the Americans and British will return these colonies to the Italians. But one thing is sure. Not one of the statesmen of the United Nations will see to it that these colonial peoples are given the right to rule themselves.

Another of America's allies, the French Committee of National Liberation, made its war aims clear to the people of Lebanon this week. The so-called Free French answered the demand of the Lebanese people for independence with the usual reply of colonial despots—armed force.

Tired of broken promises, the Lebanese voted several weeks ago to establish complete sovereignty now. Their newly elected government asked the French in effect to leave the country. The delegate-general of the Free French proceeded "democratically" to proclaim martial law, dissolve the Lebanese government, and arrest as many members of the government as he could lay his hands on.

When the Lebanese people protested the arrest of their leaders, and called for the restoration of their civil liberties, the French called out the troops to machine-gun the demonstrators. Although the French have imposed a strict censorship, the casualties are known to run into hundreds.

A GOVERNMENT STUDY ON HIRING

The government spends millions of dollars on propaganda, but when it comes to telling just how Negroes benefit from this so-called war for democracy it shuts up like a clam. It's easy to see why. Despite all of Roosevelt's promises, despite his executive orders 8802 and 9346 and the FEPC, the Negro still remains a second-class citizen.

Nothing proves this better than the War Manpower Commission's recent study on the status of Negroes in industry, a study which the Office of War Information has tried to bury.

This study reveals that employment of Negroes in war industry rose from 5.8 percent in July 1942 to 7.3 percent in July 1943. This tiny increase of 1.5 percent comes in the face of the most severe labor shortage in the history of the country. It comes at a time when a reactionary Congress talks about labor conscription because of a lack of manpower.

The commission further finds that in the South, Negroes are concentrated in those establishments and occupations where heavy unskilled work is performed. There is no "hiring of Negroes to meet the demand of establishments seeking workers for skilled jobs."

Nor are conditions much better outside the South. Though Negroes, in cooperation with the unions, particularly the CIO, have won some skilled jobs, there is no "significant use of skilled Negro workers in war industry as a whole."

The opportunity for varied employment with a chance for advancement remains limited, the report states. Negroes as a whole have been employed "in a few concentrated industries as unskilled workers in large numbers with little or no chance to upgrade themselves."

After reviewing the information contained in this report, Negroes can easily understand why the government is unwilling to have this study given too much publicity. It shows that though employers will hire Negroes for unskilled jobs when no one else is

---

By David Ransom. From *Militant*, December 18, 1943.

available, they refuse to let down the barriers of discrimination and hire Negroes for semiskilled and skilled jobs.

That isn't all the study shows. It proves conclusively that the government has done nothing to force employers to hire Negroes. Two years have gone by since the United States entered the war; the government has made a lot of promises, but the Negro is still on the outside looking in, so far as equal treatment in industry goes.

If the Negroes find the same vicious practices of discrimination continued under the conditions of an acute labor shortage in wartime, what then will their plight be when lines of unemployed begin to form again at factory gates?

If Negroes remain concentrated in a few industries as unskilled workers, and the study shows this to be the case, then they will be the first ones squeezed out of industry when the war factories begin to slow down.

That is why the progress-shouters who point to the number of jobs Negroes now have and praise the Roosevelt administration for breaking down Jim Crow in industry are misleading the Negro people.

THE CASE OF WINFRED LYNN

On December 8, the United States Circuit Court of Appeals sitting in New York City will hear the Winfred Lynn case.

The Lynn case originated in June 1942 when Winfred Lynn, a Negro worker of Jamaica, Long Island, notified his draft board that "I am ready to serve in any unit of the armed forces of my country which is not segregated by race. Unless I am assured that I can serve in a mixed regiment and that I will not be compelled to serve in a unit undemocratically selected as a Negro group, I will refuse to report for induction."

The Lynn case is thus a part of the struggle of the Negro people against the whole Jim Crow system. To date it is the only court test of the legality of the U.S. Army's discriminatory treatment of Negro soldiers. The legal basis of the Lynn case rests on the 1940 draft act, section 4(a) of which specifically states that "in the

From *Militant*, December 11, 1943, and February 12, 1944. Lynn's appeal eventually reached the Supreme Court, where it was turned down on a technicality.

selection and training of men under this Act, and in the interpretation and execution of the provisions of this Act, there shall be no discrimination against any person on account of race or color."

In practice, of course, Winfred Lynn, like all Negro draftees, was selected from a separate Jim Crow quota, in clear violation of the 1940 draft act itself. Lynn accepted induction in order to make the test case. He is suing the army authorities to be allowed to return to civilian life on the grounds that the Jim Crow method of his selection violates the draft act.

The National Association for the Advancement of Colored People has described the vicious Jim Crow system of the army and navy brass hats: "The treatment of Negroes in the armed services is marked by daily subjection to the indignities of segregation and discrimination with the constant recurrence of brutalities and murders by civilian and military police."

The American Civil Liberties Union, the March on Washington movement, the National Association for the Advancement of Colored People, the National Council for a Permanent FEPC, the Workers Defense League, and other liberal and labor organizations have endorsed the Lynn case.

The National Citizens Committee for Winfred Lynn was recently formed to publicize the case and win labor and liberal support.

NEW YORK, February 4—The U.S. Circuit Court by a 2-1 decision today upheld the army's Jim Crow segregation policy in filling draft quotas.

Arthur Garfield Hays of the American Civil Liberties Union defended Lynn. The defendant's brother, Conrad Lynn, the Jamaica attorney who first pressed the case and undertook the defense, was inducted a few months later.

By appeals to the defendant, to the NAACP, and to Conrad Lynn, federal authorities have consistently attempted to quash the case, which has attracted much national attention and support. Forced to an open decision by the determination of the Lynn brothers to make this a thorough test of the statutes, the higher court has given sanction to the clearly illegal discriminatory draft practices of the armed forces.

THE CASE OF MILTON HENRY

For some time, now, the army has been making a practice of expelling those men who object to the undemocratic and insulting system of maintaining separate, Jim Crow units for Negro soldiers. It is obvious the brass hats do not intend to stand for any criticism of their discrimination policies.

These expulsions have taken different forms. The men may be judged physically unfit, mentally deficient or morally lacking in the qualifications for making a "good" soldier. In known cases in the army as well as the WACs, Negroes who refused to abide by the Jim Crow regulations were judged by the army psychiatrist as—plain crazy.

Although news of these cases is usually carefully censored, the military does not hesitate to blast forth publicly whenever they think they can angle the case to imply that the rebellious Negro is a menace to the American people.

Take the case of Milton R. Henry, who was dismissed April 25 after a court-martial at Selfridge Field, Michigan. He had enlisted as a private in April 1941 and worked up to second lieutenant in the 553rd air corps squadron. The charges filed and "proved" were "AWOL nine times and disrespect to two superior officers."

It developed that Lieutenant Henry had been ill for some time with a chest disease which, according to medical testimony, may cause great fatigue. Twice he had been examined and x-rayed by a medical board, and a transfer to limited service had been advised. This advice was ignored. The basis for the AWOL charges was Henry's inability to awaken in time to report for duty.

As reported in the capitalist press, Lt. Col. A. R. De Bolt and Lt. Col. Charles A. Gayle charged the defendant with being disrespectful. These members of the reactionary officers' caste quoted Henry as saying: "I got my promotion by initiative and integrity;

By Charles Jackson, a pen name of Dr. Edgar Keemer (see Glossary). From *Militant,* May 6, 1944.

you officers can't say that. All revolutions have been initiated by minorities. Remember the French revolution and the Russian revolution. In each case it was a minority who ruled, and some day I, too, will be in a position to dictate." What the officers had said to Henry before this and whether he affirmed the statement, denied it or claimed to have been misquoted was not recorded in the press.

What puzzles us is the lightness of the sentence after such a defiant statement. No dishonorable discharge, no fine, no time in the jug; just dismissal from the service. Remember that in an army orientation handbook, the new soldier is pointedly told that in case of a "revolutionary" uprising, even in his home town, he must remain loyal to the army. Violations are punishable up to death.

All indications point to the fact that Milton Henry had been an efficient, conscientious young man with the courage of his convictions. He had enlisted in the army under the common, false impression that by fighting for "democracy" over there, he would receive his rightful portion of it over here. Obviously disillusioned after three years of Jim Crow treatment, he got to the point where he could keep quiet no longer.

As an example of what he had to put up with, look at Selfridge Field, the beautiful base for the advanced training of American fighter pilots—pardon me, my error. I meant Negro fighter pilots. Anyway, at Selfridge Field, Negro lieutenants are barred from entering the regular officers' club. Barred in spite of the fact that the majority of the men there are Negroes; barred in spite of the fact that such a policy openly violates the State of Michigan's civil rights law. Furthermore, under the familiar army caste system, Lieutenant Henry was prohibited from fraternizing with the noncommissioned men. Consequently, he had to travel twenty-eight miles to Detroit at his own expense for any type of recreation. This is just one of the many inconveniences confronting a soldier at this base if he happens to be a Negro. A Negro soldier was recently shot there by the drunken commanding officer. Several recent exposés have shown Selfridge Field to be rotten with Jim Crow discrimination.

These militant elements which the army is finding necessary to purge serve to reflect the seething, simmering, potentially explosive feeling that is present in the masses of Negro soldiers. The segregated, second-class, Jim Crow army "for Negroes" is a dead giveaway to the hypocritical character of the high-sounding phrases such as "liberation of oppressed people," "four freedoms," etc., which are being applied to this worldwide slaughter.

The Henry case merely represents another ugly bump on the army's angelic face. It is an external symptom of the inner, rotten poison of Jim Crowism. Dr. Brass Hat prefers to cut off the pimple instead of cleaning out the patient with the castor oil of democracy.

ARMY SUPPRESSES PAMPHLET

The House military affairs subcommittee, headed by Representative Carl T. Durtree, North Carolina Democrat, makes the accusation that the pamphlet *Races of Mankind* is spreading "communist propaganda." The committee bases its charge on the fact that the pamphlet explodes the myth that one group of people is automatically superior in ability over another group simply because of skin color or other racial characteristics. The pamphlet proves that the opportunities for development of the mind, the condition of health and home surroundings, etc., are, in reality, the important factors that mold a "superior" person. These factors, of course, are all manifestations of the person's economic status. For example, the pamphlet shows that a poor southern rural white may prove "inferior" in intelligence tests to a northern Negro raised in a large city under better economic conditions.

Fifty-five thousand copies of this pamphlet were purchased for an army orientation course. The distribution of the pamphlet, however, was abruptly stopped by the reactionary officers' caste on the ground that the pamphlet was "too controversial."

In this instance, the destiny of capitalism and racial hatreds are exposed to be solidly bound to each other. First, it is interesting to observe that this pamphlet, written by scientists, after demonstrating the foolishness of the "white supremacy" fable, comes to the conclusion that the way to defeat the forces that foster such a policy is to tone down any active fight on American capitalism (with its policy of segregation in the army, navy, and industry) and to unite with the same capitalists to beat Hitler, the advocate of Aryan superiority.

If the authors of this pamphlet knew as much about social forces as they do about anthropology, they would realize that when the German workers overthrow Hitler, they will also throw

By Charles Jackson. From *Militant*, May 13, 1944. *The Races of Mankind*, by Ruth Benedict and Gene Weltfish, was published in 1943.

out the window his "master race" ideology, which represents in their minds an integral part of the rotten fascist regime which has brought them nothing but slavery, suffering, and death.

The significant point, however, is this: the military affairs subcommittee, representing American capitalism (which is surely interested in winning this war in order to exploit a larger slice of the world's resources and labor), lashes out with familiar red-baiting tactics at a pamphlet that teaches racial equality, despite the fact that this pamphlet urges support of the war.

This can mean only one thing—that American capitalism is making known to all liberals, pussy-footers, and other people of "goodwill" the fact that it does not want the myth of white supremacy exploded by scientific truths.

The red-baiting tactics of the committee plainly imply that all who preach racial equality are automatically "communists" in the sense that they are opposed to "our form of government." In effect, the congressional lackeys of big business declare that they do not intend to tolerate any dulling of the edge of the vicious weapon of race prejudice even though American capitalism is engaged at the present time in a life-and-death struggle with another imperialist power.

This case is but one example of a well-defined policy of the U.S. government in regard to treatment of the Negro people. They do not intend to give us our equality because they want to keep the workers divided. No one freely gives up a method that has repeatedly proved profitable to him.

It all boils down to this: If you are for capitalism you are supporting a system that breeds racial bigotry and oppression; if you are for racial equality you can realize your aim only by allying yourself with capitalism's only genuine enemy, revolutionary socialism. Which side are you on and what are you doing about it?

JIM CROW TERROR IN LOUISIANA

In the town of New Iberia, Louisiana, leaders of the Negro community had the "effrontery" to demand and secure a government school to train Negro welders for war work. On the evening of the day the school opened, May 15, four of the local Negro leaders—two physicians, a teacher, and the president of the local

From *Militant*, June 24, 1944.

NAACP—were waylaid by agents of the sheriff's office and the superintendent of schools, subdued at gunpoint, severely clubbed, and driven from town. Four other Negro citizens—two physicians, an insurance salesman, and a woman school teacher—were threatened and compelled to flee the town.

These brutal actions of the "white supremacy" scum were carried out by the official guardians of "law and order." The whole upper crust of the white ruling class combined to conceal the crime and the criminals, and the Negro community was terrorized to prevent exposure. Only weeks after the attacks, when the victims issued affidavits and the National Association for the Advancement of Colored People disclosed the events, did the facts become public.

As a consequence of these terrorist acts, the entire Negro community has been left without proper medical aid, and two patients in the Negro hospital, maintained by one of the expelled physicians, are reported to have died as a result of lack of care.

The outstanding victim of the assault was J. Leo Hardy, a retired businessman, who was president of the local branch of the NAACP, and who had led the committee that secured the welders' school against the open opposition of the town officials.

All the beaten victims were taken from their homes or places of work at night, driven in the sheriff's or deputies' cars to the town outskirts, abused, kicked, and clubbed, and forced to walk miles on foot to refuge in neighboring towns.

The federal government agencies, the War Manpower Commission and U.S. Bureau of Education, helped to bolster anti-Negro prejudices by first establishing an all-white school for war workers and then refusing to establish a similar school for Negro workers. Only after an appeal to the FEPC office in Dallas, Texas, was a segregated school for Negroes set up.

To date, the federal government has taken no action against the "white supremacy" gangsters, and the victims are unable to return safely to their homes, families, and possessions.

THE SOUTHERN ATMOSPHERE

Editor:

The atmosphere here in the Deep South fairly crackles with the leashed fury of the Negro people at generations of degrading repressions. And more Negro blood has flowed in the South since Pearl Harbor than you would know about from reading the papers. The following "incidents" reported to me never saw print:

Louisiana, white woman: "Why, them niggers are trying to take over the South. One hundred fifty of them marched on our town a while back, were going to take it over. We got word they was coming, and a crowd of white MPs and the town's strong men went out to meet them. They got as far as the depot there. Our men stopped them with bullets." I asked were the Negroes armed. She said sure, "but we shot first." I remarked that I hadn't read that in the papers. "Sure not," she said. "A lot of other things like that aren't in the papers, either. Them niggers'll learn that this ain't the North!"

Mississippi, farmer: "Why the other day, one of them niggers got on the bus and set right down by a white woman. The bus driver told him to git up and he refused to do it. The bus driver called ahead to have the sheriff meet the bus at the next stop and a squad of armed men met the bus and ordered the nigger to git off and he jist set there. They had to drag him off the bus and they filled him full of lead on the spot. But that won't cure them. We got to do more than kill one nigger to cure them."

All bus drivers, I was told, carry guns now. "They have to, the niggers has got so bad."

I got on the bus at Alexandria, Louisiana, and there were no empty seats. As I was standing in the aisle, perfectly willing to take my turn at standing, the driver came back and ordered a Negro sailor to get up and give me his seat. I protested that I didn't want to take another's seat, but the driver again rudely ordered the sailor to get up and move back. I had to take the seat;

A letter to the editor, *Militant*, August 5, 1944.

I knew that if I protested again it might make trouble for the Negro.

It is practically worth a Negro man's life to be seen talking to a white woman, so I couldn't even apologize to him. It was a very uncomfortable ride for me; but I noted that the Negroes didn't take it uncomplainingly. They muttered among themselves quite audibly, and I heard one man say distinctly that "in some parts of the country, service men of all colors get the choice of seats," and there was a general murmur of approbation from the Negroes. It is a new thing in the South for Negroes to dare to publicly state their discontent.

One significant thing I have noticed. There is more friendly, easy talk between whites and Negroes, in spite of the terrorism, than there ever was in the days before the war. I have seen white boys and men talking to Negroes on the buses many times, talking as men talk to each other. In Baton Rouge I spoke to a friend about the "Negro menace." This friend, certainly no radical, replied that the situation is due almost solely to the fear that has taken hold of the white people, and their reaction to it. They are treating the Negroes so badly that they are making inevitable the explosion that seems imminent.

D.S.
Baton Rouge, Louisiana

ANTI-NEGRO STRIKE IN PHILADELPHIA

Company Agents Hope to Smash CIO Union

PHILADELPHIA, August 7—In a desperate move to smash the CIO Transport Workers Union, the Philadelphia Transportation Company, acting in collusion with leaders of the former company union, last week inspired a six-day municipal transportation stoppage against the training of eight Negro workers for operating jobs on streetcars and buses.

Using the timeworn device of divide and rule, the company and its agents provoked this antilabor race-hate action with the aim of splitting the ranks of the CIO union, which a few months ago

---

By Art Preis. From *Militant*, August 12, 1944. The strike began on August 1.

won a collective-bargaining election against the company-sponsored PRT (Philadelphia Rapid Transit) Employees Union. This company outfit for years had upheld the PTC's flagrant Jim Crow policies and had campaigned against the TWU with the slogan, "A vote for the CIO is a vote for niggers on the job."

Following the election victory of the CIO, the former company-union leaders intensified their open Jim Crow agitation. This agitation was conducted on company property with the tacit consent of the union-hating bosses. The pretext for the action was provided when the company, after months of protest, was compelled to abide by an FEPC order to hire and train Negroes for operators' jobs. The CIO supported the FEPC order.

The stoppage was precipitated early last Tuesday morning, when an organized minority of backward workers, incited and led by the company-union officials, forced a discontinuance of work by close to six thousand PTC employees, most of whom knew nothing of the walkout in advance, had not voted for it, and did not even know the issue involved. Squads of goons roamed the city and invaded the carbarns, halting public conveyances, warning the operators they were "sick" and had better stop work. The CIO officials, taken by surprise, were unable to prevent the walkout.

The hand of the company was almost immediately revealed when, at the first meeting of the workers, held on the company's property at the Tenth and Luzerne streets carbarn, the last two heads of the PRT Employees Union assumed open leadership of the Jim Crow action.

James McMenamin, known to be a frequent visitor to the company's executive offices, pushed himself forward as the self-styled strike leader. His chief lieutenant was Frank Carney, head of the defeated company union. They and their henchmen played on the prejudices of the workers, exhorting them with vicious race-hate speeches against "niggers taking white men's jobs." While raising a completely false issue of seniority rights to excite the workers' justifiable fears of job insecurity, McMenamin emphasized that it was "a strict black and white issue" and "no labor union is involved in this."

The complicity of the company is shown both by its actions just preceding and during the walkout and by its whole history of antiunion, anti-Negro policies. It had always let it be known that its jobs were "white men's jobs." Negroes were hired only for sweeping carbarns, washing equipment, cleaning switches, and repairing tracks. The company union had a contract including a clause barring Negroes from operators' jobs.

Last November, local Negro organizations, after persistent

pressure and agitation supported by nearly 400,000 Negroes in Philadelphia, were able to wring an order from the FEPC requiring the traction company to hire and upgrade workers without racial discrimination. The company opposed the FEPC ruling, hiding behind its Jim Crow company union contract.

After the CIO won sole collective bargaining rights, the company suddenly "agreed" to comply with the FEPC directive and announced it was going to train eight Negroes for operators' jobs. This was the signal for anti-Negro placards to be posted on company walls—which the management permitted. Open agitation against Negro hiring and upgrading became rife—on company property and with the knowledge of the company. Company officials were "warned" in advance that a group of two hundred white workers intended to "quit" if it complied with the FEPC order.

CIO officials point out that the company never issued an appeal for a return to work; urged "settlement" of the "strike" by rescinding the FEPC order; admitted knowing about anti-Negro placards and literature on its property; and turned off the power on a subway line when a group of union men agreed to return to work. McMenamin replied to a reporter's question on the source of his finances: "We don't have to worry about money. We're getting plenty from higher up."

The capitalist press conspired to conceal or minimize the complicity of the company. The big-business press seized on this company-inspired action to launch an antilabor campaign against all genuine progressive struggles in the workers' interests. At the same time, the press fed fuel to the anti-Negro flames, which threatened to burst into violent hoodlum assaults against the Negroes, with scare-head stories about "Negro terror gangs roaming city," and playing up every incident of Negro-white physical conflict.

Almost from the first, city officials declared they were "helpless," while company-union agents were being driven to meetings in police cars. The walkout was halted only after the army, under orders from President Roosevelt, took over the transportation system, threatened to revoke draft deferments of all strikers and bar them from jobs for "the duration," and manned the public conveyances with armed troops. Four leaders, including Mc-Menamin and Carney, were arrested on charges of violating the Smith-Connally Law and released on $2,500 bail.

The workers stayed out for three days after the army moved in. They did not believe that Roosevelt's government, which upholds Jim Crow discrimination and segregation throughout the armed forces, really meant business. Thus, McMenamin, on Friday morning, told workers at a mass meeting to return to work with the statement: "As we are going under Government operation, there will be no colored operators."

At the noon meeting previously, strikers had defied the army back-to-work order with shouts of "Put us in the army where we can fight beside white men!"—a clear reference to the government's own Jim Crow in the armed forces. One worker declared: "Why doesn't the President put them [Negroes] on the streetcars right under his nose in Washington?"

The CIO leadership failed to influence the workers because it had no fighting program to better their conditions and unite them in common struggle against their real enemies, the bosses. Underneath their misdirected attack against the Negro workers lie real grievances against the company, a real fear of unemployment, which company demagogues were able to direct against Negroes "wanting to take your jobs."

Although the transit workers have gone back to work, there can be no denying that the labor movement has been dealt a terrible blow. The ranks of the union have been split. The poison of race hatred still infects the workers. They can be united once more only when the union proves to them in action that it is defending their real interests and offering them some security against prospective unemployment. Only in common struggle for their own needs against the offensive of the employers and government will the workers, Negro and white, forge unbreakable unity.

Where Is Your Liberty?

When the army took over [the Philadelphia Transportation Company], one southern soldier started separating the passengers Jim Crow fashion. This is in line with civilian policy in the South and, of course, with military policy in all American army camps, on transport ships, and on every beachhead where fly the Stars and Stripes. Soon after the introduction of this repulsive color quarantine, four hundred angry Negroes gathered to teach this soldier some democracy. Dr. J. P. Turner, civic leader, managed, however, to disperse the crowd. When a southern soldier is spreading color quarantine, he must get "military respect." If the

---

By Charles Jackson. From *Militant*, August 19, 1944.

black masses try to reestablish a little democracy, they are "rioting." At the height of the strike, a colored worker rang the famous Liberty Bell and shouted, "Oh Liberty Bell, where is your liberty?" The capitalist court sent him to a mental institution for asking such a question.

Springboard for Repression

Editor:

The anti-Negro walkout in Philadelphia engineered by company agents of the Philadelphia Transportation Company is being used as a springboard for new repressive moves against the American labor movement. The Philadelphia press is unanimous in calling for new and more "effective" legislation to end all strikes for good.

The *Philadelphia Record,* so-called liberal, prolabor, and pro–New Deal newspaper, in an editorial entitled "Tell 80,000 Other Strikers the Philadelphia Story," praises the government's "handling of the Philadelphia transit strike crisis" and asks, "why can't this method be a model for the nation?"

"Now that the handling of the PTC strike has established a successful precedent," says the *Record,* such measures should be promptly applied to all strikes, and then proceeds to urge that the precedent be applied to the current truck drivers' strike in the following manner:

"We would like to see Uncle Sam move in on the truck strike as he did on our trolley strike. We would like to see him: (*a*) arrest the strike leaders, (*b*) take over the fleets of idle trucks, (*c*) give the strikers an ultimatum to return, (*d*) put soldiers on the trucks, to protect the men who go back to work and to run the trucks of those who don't, (*e*) cancel draft deferment, supplementary rations and job eligibility of men who refuse to resume their jobs."

The strike of the truck drivers was caused by the refusal of the owners to abide by a War Labor Board decision granting the workers an increase in wages. Roosevelt has ordered the army to seize the trucks to enforce the WLB order.

"It's our opinion," says the *Record*, "that Uncle Sam will have to

A letter to the editor, *Militant,* August 19, 1944.

apply the 'Philadelphia Method' only a few more times before the whole country understands that from now on the government's patience is exhausted; *that from now on the no-strike pledge is going to be kept—or else!"*

The *Philadelphia Record* is a spokesman for the New Deal and its government. Using the reactionary company-union action of the Philadelphia Transportation Company as a springboard, they mean to open a general offensive against the bonafide trade union movement. Labor can meet this challenge by closing ranks; by uniting all workers regardless of race, color, or creed against the common enemy, the exploiters and their government. Race prejudice is a weapon of reaction that strikes at the heart of the labor movement. That is the lesson of the PTC walkout and its aftermath.

Jerry Miller
Philadelphia, Pennsylvania

Transport Union Elections

Philadelphia Local 234, CIO Transport Workers Union, collective-bargaining agency for the municipal transit employees, last week elected a Negro worker, Maxwell Windham, as vice-president. Four other Negro members were elected to the local's executive board. Over 2,200 votes were cast.

This was the loyal union workers' demonstrative answer to Jim Crowism. A few weeks ago the Philadelphia Transportation Company, in collusion with its company-union agents, incited an anti-Negro walkout with the intention of smashing the TWU through racial conflict.

A handpicked grand jury just two weeks ago concluded its "investigation" of the "strike" by whitewashing the company, defending its Jim Crow policies, upholding company unionism, and attacking the CIO, which had opposed the Jim Crow walkout.

From *Militant,* October 21, 1944.

NO MIDDLE GROUND

Almost every day, some incident occurs that indicates that "middle class" Negroes will inevitably be swept up and carried in the wake of anti-Negroism just the same as those who work for wages. Racial prejudice knows no economic distinctions, and a brown man is brown for life. Strange as it may seem, the skin color does not change in accordance with the bank balance. In their attempts to maintain economic oppression over all the working people, the ruling class will resort to igniting on a nationwide scale the well-laid tinders of anti-Negroism. There will be no compassion on "better class" Negroes; there will be no escape for the "talented tenth"; there will be no middle ground.

By far the best (or rather, worst) example of the nonimmunity of "better class" Negroes to the vicious poisons of anti-Negroism was revealed in the recent exposure of the barbaric lynching of the prominent Rev. Isaac Simmons of Amite County, Mississippi. This sixty-six-year-old farmer-minister was the owner of a 220-acre tract of land, completely debt free (which is extremely uncommon in those parts) and rich in timber. Furthermore, the land had recently shown evidence of containing heavy oil deposits.

Apparently the whites in this area decided that not this Negro, but they, should reap the harvest of the oil riches. The owner of the adjoining property began provocations against Simmons by directing him not to cut any more timber from his (Simmons's) land. Realizing the obvious fact that they simply intended to take his land from him, Reverend Simmons consulted lawyers in two of the nearby towns in order to protect his interests. Seeing that this was a "smart nigger," the whites evidently decided to make an example of him.

Six of them beat him up and his forty-six-year-old son, Eldridge Simmons, cursed them, and told Reverend Simmons he shouldn't have been so "smart" as to seek legal aid. Driving to a secluded

---

By Charles Jackson. From *Militant,* September 2, 1944.

spot, they put three shotgun blasts in the sixty-six-year-old man's back and then mutilated him, including cutting out his tongue. After beating and threatening the son if he told on them, they finally let him go. The son made the news known and directed the sheriff to the body, and also named the five men who were known to him. The sheriff and the constable then arrested young Simmons "for his own safety" and kept him in the cooler for a month. They finally let him go and advised that he leave town. The official verdict stated that Reverend Simmons died at the hands "of unknown parties."

It may well be, then, that the anger of a misdirected mob of whites might vent itself first—instead of last—on the "better class" Negroes. These are the ones who think they can ignore the class struggle because they have confidence in finding some haven, by virtue of their money, where they will be protected from the interracial chaos that is sure to be instigated by the desperate capitalists in their attempts to keep their decrepit system of war and depression. In several nationwide polls that have recently been conducted among whites as to their impression of the Negro struggle, this trend has been noticed. In many of the remarks we have seen this thought: The Negro is getting too many concessions already. He is making too much money out of this war— more than he ever made and more than he is entitled to.

Could such clues as these be an indication as to the future twisted reasoning of the prejudiced and misdirected white? If so, it means that the Negro intellectual as well as the Negro worker should apply himself now to the task of making firmer and firmer our alliance with the progressive labor movement, for that is the only ally that will want to, will need to, and will be strong enough to protect us as a color minority in the trying days that are sure to come.

EQUALITY DECREED—IN GERMANY

Coincident with the entry of Allied troops into Germany the London headquarters of the Allied Military Government announced, with great fanfare, that, in occupied Germany, there would be no toleration of "discrimination because of race, color or creed."

About the same time plans were made public for the establishment of several Jim Crow army rehabilitation centers here in the United States for the physical and mental building up of combat-fatigued soldiers who have seen particularly strenuous action overseas. The official statement revealed that the beautiful relaxation centers—forty-nine of them, at Hot Springs, Arkansas; Santa Barbara, California; Asheville, North Carolina; Miami, Florida; and Lake Placid, New York—are to be restricted to white veterans only. The army summarily took over Hotel Pershing, in Chicago's overcrowded South Side ghetto, and announced that it would be made available as a Jim Crow rest center for the returning, combat-shocked Negro veterans.

The AMG announcement on German policy, hopefully played up by the Negro press, was never intended to apply to Negroes. This needs no further proof than the fact that brown soldiers are working in service units today on German soil although many of them are qualified for different duty, from which they are barred because of their color. Not a democratic army, but an army composed of separate lily-white and separate Jim Crow units is slaughtering and being slaughtered, in order that the AMG "racial equality" decree may be posted in each succeeding town.

The Jim Crow rest centers for Negroes in America shocked many of the liberals who have drawn no lesson from the events in Europe. "Why," they exclaim, "in New York, New Jersey, and California, where three of the lily-white army centers are located, even a Negro civilian is not usually barred from the hotels. Furthermore it seems that one who has proven his loyalty by risking his life should surely be given equal consideration. And

By Charles Jackson. From *Militant*, September 23, 1944.

didn't we just read about the army abolishing Jim Crow in the 'liberated' areas of Germany? . . . Wonder if President Roosevelt knows about this terrible wrong?"

A nation's army is its official mouthpiece when it is at war. By its example the U.S. Army is again telling you: Wake up, Black worker; read the signs of the times. You can't expect to gain your equality as a result of the war. The ruling-class exploiters plan to use you exactly as the Nazis used the Jews. They will try to set the white worker upon you and you upon him. They hope, thereby, to crush the labor movement and destroy the power of the American working class. Through racial strife they hope to set brother against brother. While defeating a competitor—German imperialism—under the guise of racial liberation, they are laying the groundwork for anti-Negro terror by fostering Jim Crow here at home. Working-class solidarity and independent political action are the only powerful protectors against American fascism. You should spare no effort to forge them now, for the warning is clear: "It's not my brother, nor my cousin . . . but me, Oh Lord."

BRITONS REJECT RACIST INDOCTRINATION

White brass hats and backward American soldiers are attempting to introduce Jim Crow practices against American Negro troops in England. The British people, however, are demonstratively opposing the effort, according to the illuminating account of Roi Ottley, noted American Negro author, in the New York daily *PM*.

Ottley, who gives a wealth of factual detail, describes the "noose of prejudice . . . slowly tightening around the necks of the American Negro soldiers . . . tending to cut off their recreation and association with the British people."

Contrary to the treatment accorded Negroes in America, the British people received the Negroes with genuine hospitality. "To put it in the language of a Negro soldier, 'I'm treated so, a man don't know he's colored until he looks in the mirror.'

"Negroes were invited to British homes, churches, and trade

From *Militant,* September 30, 1944.

union meetings. Easy and friendly associations developed between the races."

But backward white American troops, inspired by their officers, are "attempting to discipline the British people." Strong-arm methods have been introduced; Negro passes are restricted and proprietors of bars, restaurants, and other public places are told to exclude Negroes or be boycotted.

Bitter fights have broken out between Negro and white troops in many billet areas. "This distressing racial situation must be laid squarely on the doorstep of white officers." Although there are formal regulations against discriminatory practices, "some of them [officers] never bother to read the instructions." An RAF flier told Ottley that at an indoctrination course addressed by an American lieutenant, the lecture consisted of an "explanation" of why British white troops should not associate with Negro Americans.

The British, particularly the workers, are resisting this Jim Crow indoctrination. After an armed clash at Leicester between white and Negro soldiers, signs appeared on bars and restaurants, "For British Civilians and U.S.A. Negro Forces Only."

When two Negro soldiers were court-martialed and sentenced to death for alleged rape in Gloucestershire, 33,000 workers protested to the American authorities, charging the Negroes were sentenced because of their color. Workers in a large local factory went on a protest strike.

NEWS FROM THE SOUTHERN FRONT

That the brown boys in uniform are getting fed up with treatment as official "racial inferiors" is being reflected even in the heart of the reactionary South. According to a *Washington Times Herald* story which Secretary of War Stimson is busy trying to water down, sixteen thousand Negroes in ill-famed Camp Claiborne, Louisiana, mutinied, beat their officers, confiscated ammunition, and attempted to settle some scores. After one officer and two enlisted men were injured, MPs regained control with the use of gas.

In Mobile, Alabama, the brutal treatment by MPs at Brookley Field provoked a soldiers' uprising, as a result of which nine

By Charles Jackson. From *Militant,* September 30, 1944.

Negroes were court-martialed for mutiny. Their long prison sentences and dishonorable discharges were recently upheld by a board of review in Washington.

At Camp Gordon, in Tallahassee, Florida, Lieutenants Belle, McCormick, and Maddox, after hearing of the so-called antidiscrimination order, refused to move to the rear of an army-owned bus when so ordered by the driver. When an MP found he could not arrest them because of their superior rank, civilian officers were summoned. With shotguns and pistols trained on them, the three lieutenants were taken to jail and booked for "inciting a riot." In the meantime, the Dixie bus driver who recently shot dead a Negro soldier in Durham, North Carolina, for refusing to get up and move to the Jim Crow section, was pronounced innocent and freed by a jury which found it necessary to deliberate only twenty-seven minutes.

It is plain to see that things are getting no better—they are getting worse. The Negroes in uniform are under military discipline. But how about our comfortably situated spokesmen here at home? They are militant in words only. They continue to restrict their protests to the verbal sphere. And even these harmless yappings are sandwiched in between patriotic bootlicking.

Negro soldiers and sailors are very bitter about Jim Crow. Are we willing to organize militant action to protest this discrimination? That is our only worthwhile weapon of protection. It is better to march now than have to run later.

SOLDIERS STRIKE IN ARIZONA

Editor:

Fifty-seven Negro soldiers won a substantial victory at Marana Army Air Field, as the result of a strike on September 11. Their demand for extra pay for working in the aviation cadet mess hall was granted, the brass hats awarding the men twenty-five dollars per month additional pay. At the same time, however, the brass hats simultaneously increased the workweek from fifty-six to eighty-four hours! This inhuman schedule is now being protested.

More important than the added hours is the significance of a real victory won by the solidarity of the Negro soldiers. At four o'clock in the morning on September 11, the first shift of sixteen

A letter to the editor, *Militant,* October 7, 1944.

men reported to the mess hall and announced that they would not work unless they got the extra bonus, 50 percent of their base pay, to which army regulations entitled them for such work. They were immediately imprisoned, and a "talk" was given to the second shift by the executive officer of the field, Major Tilden, and the white commanding officer of the Negro squadron, Lieutenant Shoupe. The second shift also refused to go to work, and were sent to the guardhouse.

The two remaining shifts likewise failed to report for work, but no disciplinary action was taken against them. Undoubtedly the officers felt the situation was getting "too hot to handle"; the largest concentration of Negro troops in the country is in this area, near Tucson.

Most of the fifty-seven soldiers had been on KP duty for nineteen months or more, doing the most menial work in the army air forces, under constant abuse and subjected to notorious speedups. For the last nine months, they have been serving the cadets without receiving the bonus. In addition, for over eighteen months they were punished for minor infractions by extra details of mess duty!

B.R.
Tucson, Arizona

THREE ELECTROCUTED IN FLORIDA

The capitalist ruling class of the State of Florida last week pulled the Raiford State Prison electrocution switch to murder three Negro youths—James Davis, sixteen; Freddy Lee Lane, nineteen; and James Williams, twenty-six. It was a streamlined job of legal lynching.

First, there was the hue and cry that a white woman had been "raped." Then, there was the quick seizure of three Negroes—the first three who came along. A little "encouragement" with fists, boots, rubber hose, and clubs extorted the usual "confessions."

"Strictly legal" was the motto. On August 31 there was a "trial." No other Negroes were present. No jury. It was held in secret session before a judge and twenty selected white spectators. Florida law says that's legal, when you have a "confession."

Outside the courthouse a mob gathered. "Order" was preserved

An editorial, *Militant,* October 21, 1944.

by the militia, whose commander reassured the "defenders of southern white womanhood" that "justice" would be done. He pronounced the verdict in advance: "They will be electrocuted." The "trial," from the entrance of the judge to pronouncement of the death sentence, took less than eighty minutes.

Some liberals, learning of the case, finally secured a defense lawyer on September 14. An appeal was filed. The state's attorney duly filed a counter-motion before the Florida Supreme Court to dismiss the appeal because it was "frivolous." No defense lawyer was present at the "hearing." The Ku Klux Klan had been holding meetings. Word had been spread it wouldn't be "healthy" for any lawyer to defend the convicted Negroes. The state supreme court speedily dismissed the appeal.

Thus these three Negro youths were rushed to their execution amid conspiratorial silence from the big-business press, the Roosevelt administration, and the Republican candidate. All these false "friends of the Negro people" keep quiet about this crime because it belies their blabber about "democracy" and "equality," because it is an integral element in the Jim Crow system they uphold together.

This latest legal lynching once more demonstrates that the working class can place no reliance whatsoever upon the capitalist government or its supporters to halt murder and oppression of the Negro people in the South—or in the North. Only the mass pressure and action of the organized workers, white and Negro, can effectively oppose the vile Jim Crow system and its murderous consequences.

SIU ENDANGERS HIRING HALL

Roosevelt's Fair Employment Practices Committee, after six months of investigating charges of discrimination by the Seafarers International Union, AFL, against Negro seamen, recently held open hearings on this question in New York City. These hearings are not the first of this kind. An investigation of the union's shipping practices was conducted by a similar New York State committee last year.

All the investigations and hearings to date—and the probe is hardly more than begun—have leveled an attack against the union which cannot be answered so long as it continues to discriminate against Negro seamen. The FEPC has accused the SIU of "discriminating against both white and Negro seamen" because it ships Negroes only in the steward and engine departments and refuses to ship white workers to jobs aboard ships assigned to the Negroes. According to Emanuel Block, FEPC attorney, "This disrupts the orderly and efficient use of the already short supply of manpower in the industry."

Unable to answer these charges of discrimination, John Hawk,

By F. J. Lang, a pen name of Frank Lovell. From *Militant,* October 28, 1944. The maritime industry was organized by two unions: the Seafarers International Union, AFL, led by Harry Lundeberg, on the West Coast; and the Stalinist-dominated National Maritime Union, CIO, led by Joseph Curran, on the East Coast. One of the central issues for workers in maritime, because of the casual nature of the work, was control of hiring: whether by the government, the bosses, or the union. The SIU had won the union hiring hall while the NMU had not. The Merchant Marine Act of 1936 had attempted to shackle sailors with the Continuous Discharge Book, known as the fink book, under which each worker would be required to carry a book listing his employment record—providing an easy method to blacklist militants. Lundeberg supported the war but remained critical of government intervention into the unions. Curran worked with the CP throughout the war, broke from the Stalinists in 1946, and drove the CP out of the NMU in 1949, using the anticommunist witch-hunt.

first vice-president and secretary-treasurer of the SIU, refused to participate in the FEPC hearings and issued a statement that the charges are "absurd on their face, because they allege discrimination against both races. The most casual inquiry would have satisfied this committee that in none of the instances set forth as charged has the war effort been affected."

Thus an attempt has been made by both the FEPC and the SIU leadership to shift the argument to a question of whether discrimination against Negro seamen impedes the war effort. Again the "war effort" serves to screen an attack against unionism. The whole question boils down to the fact that discrimination against Negro seamen by the SIU endangers the union hiring hall. These discriminatory practices by maritime unions invite intervention by government agencies and provide an excuse for government control of merchant shipping.

Merchant seamen in this country have waged a defensive struggle against the persistent government drive to abolish their union hiring halls since passage of the Merchant Marine Act in 1936. The government, through the various wartime agencies established under the powers of the U.S. Maritime Commission, is now preparing a showdown on this question: Will seamen ship through their union halls or will they be regimented in a government shipping pool?

The SIU leadership after refusing to participate in the FEPC hearings gave a seemingly progressive reason for this stand: unions cannot permit government agencies to poke into their internal affairs. But this is only a half-truth and a dodge to continue the practice of discrimination. And this practice is an open invitation to government intervention.

The government is no more interested in Negro equality than is the SIU leadership, as is attested to by discrimination against Negroes in the army and navy. The government utilizes this issue in the maritime industry as part of its attack upon the union hiring hall. The government will be able to employ this weapon against the union hiring hall so long as every union man does not enjoy equal shipping rights.

The Stalinist leaders in the NMU are now concerned with the question of Negro rights primarily in connection with their drive to discredit and smash the other unions in the industry. The leaders of these unions, imbued with race prejudice, make it possible for the Stalinists to conduct their campaign in part around a progressive issue and thus appear as the champions of "equal shipping rights."

The only place where seamen have ever had equal shipping

rights is in their own union hiring halls under a system of rotary shipping, never in the government pool.

A successful fight against government regimentation through the pool requires the solidarity of all seamen. No union can stand up against the pressure of the boss if it does not organize and protect every worker in the industry.

Seamen today must win the wholehearted support of the entire labor movement in their struggle to defend the union hiring hall. Workers in other industries are facing a similar problem. They feel the pressure of government regimentation. In the maritime industry the problem is more immediate and acute than elsewhere. The shoreside workers understand the importance of protecting the union hiring hall against government intervention. But they will not tolerate union Jim Crow practices and they will not rally to the defense of a union that lays itself open to government intervention by discriminating against Negroes.

CIO COMMITTEE FIGHTS JIM CROW

Just because the Negro worker today is a hundred times as trade union conscious as he was fifteen years ago, and just because there is a concerted effort on the part of the progressive labor movement to fight for industrial equality regardless of race, is not enough to warrant a shout of victory. These tendencies have forced the ruling class to imprint more firmly the pattern of segregation and thereby more forcibly crystallize the well-indoctrinated interracial prejudices. The attacks upon the color line have not caused the owning class to discard it as an antilabor weapon but, rather, to draw it all the more tightly.

The CIO, which contains more progressive elements than any other union organization in the country, has recently embarked on a counterattack which, if carried on with increasing militancy, will bode no good for the vile plans of those who want to continue their exploitation by pitting the Negro and the white workers against each other. A significant unit in this counterattack is the CIO Committee to Abolish Racial Discrimination. This committee has been setting up new branches all over the country and on

---

By Charles Jackson. From *Militant*, November 4, 1944.

more than one occasion has been the instrumental factor that meant success instead of defeat in various fights against racial discrimination.

According to Director George Weaver's most recent report, the number of state, county, and municipal committees has increased from fifty as of March 15, 1944, to eighty-five as of August 15, 1944. Most significant is the fact that committees have been organized for the first time in Georgia, North Carolina, West Virginia, Kentucky, Texas, Kansas, and Alabama. Any movement capable of organizing effective branches committed to abolish racial discrimination in those states really means business. Furthermore, it bids fair to become the medium through which will come the final victorious assault on all the forces of reaction that are so firmly entrenched in the "deah old South."

In a series of conferences held by the Ohio state committee, the importance of upgrading and seniority rights without regard to race was stressed. One of the discussions centered upon the responsibility of the union in the postwar period in relation to the minority question. The importance of maintaining full employment was considered the key to the racial question. It was admitted that without full employment, the scramble of returning soldiers and war workers to compete for too few jobs will pit majority groups against minority groups and vice versa. On this point, of course, we know and we warn again that it will be impossible to maintain full employment until we have socialism.

The Michigan state committee initiated the prosecution of the Cody Hotel in Grand Rapids, involving discrimination on July 11 during the Michigan CIO convention. The delegation from Local 208, UAW-CIO, had arranged to house their delegates at this hotel. The local had received written confirmation from the manager agreeing to house the entire delegation. The white delegates arrived first and were housed. Later, when the Negro members of the delegation arrived, they were refused accommodations. The following resolution was submitted to the convention and unanimously endorsed: "That the hotel be criminally prosecuted and that until these issues are resolved in favor of CIO policy, the Hotel Cody be placed on the unfair list." Similar action was initiated last week by the UAW-CIO against the Webster Hall Hotel in Detroit.

The Philadelphia committee, the Industrial Union Council, which was only appointed in April, reports successful cases involving discrimination in upgrading Negro workers in the steel industry in the Philadelphia area. One was a job as narrow-gauge engineer, a job never yet held by a Negro. In the industrial cases, the Committee to Abolish Racial Discrimination has been working in close collaboration with the FEPC.

The CIO has come out flatly for integrated housing in the federal projects and has put up many successful fights against the housing authorities for increased facilities for minority groups. Its continual efforts, which reflected the politically advanced workers of industrial Detroit, finally broke down the reactionary government policy of denying Negro workers admittance to the many vacant units in the Willow Run project. As of August 1944 some seventy-five Negro families had moved into this project without any incidents whatsoever.

In areas where there was already friction, this committee has made efforts to educate the backward, prejudiced workers so that working-class solidarity could be maintained.

An outstanding example was in Marion, Ohio, where a group of Mexican workers had been imported. Feeling the job insecurity that is normal under capitalism, with its ever-increasing catastrophic depressions, many of the workers showed resentment against the Mexican workers. Largely through the efforts of the county antidiscrimination committee the white workers were educated, the Mexican workers were unionized, and a dangerous struggle between workers was averted.

These are only a few examples of what the CIO is doing. It deserves and has the allegiance of the Negro people. With the more crushing oppressions that are planned by the ruling class, the labor movement will have to adopt more militant means to defend the brown workers against race discrimination. In defense of the trade union movement itself, it is of utmost importance that every militant worker, black or white, rally support within his union to fight discrimination and Jim Crowism wherever it rears its ugly head.

FIFTY FOUND GUILTY
OF NAVY 'MUTINY'

SAN FRANCISCO, October 26—In a drastic move to maintain its vicious Jim Crow segregation policy, a seven-man, gold-braid, navy court-martial has found fifty Negro sailors guilty of "mutiny." Penalties may range from extended prison sentences to the maximum, death. The verdict was brought in *after only forty-five minutes of deliberation* upon the conclusion of thirty-three days of contradictory testimony and summation arguments.

The case goes back to the Port Chicago disaster, when a ship being loaded with ammunition blew up, causing the death of 327 men and tremendous damage. The great majority of the men were Negro sailors in "labor battalions" doing longshore work. All the men brought to trial were involved in the tragedy, being either survivors or among the squads that cleaned up the wreckage and remnants of bodies dismembered by the explosion.

This disaster caused a profound reaction in the men and appears to have brought to the surface their resentment against navy Jim Crow policy. Up to the outbreak of hostilities, Negroes were accepted in the navy only in the capacity of messmen. "Only after things got *hot*," stated Thurgood Marshall, chief counsel for the NAACP, "did the navy open up other opportunities to Negroes in other capacities." Even then they were Jim Crowed into segregated units. "Somehow or other," Marshall pointed out, "these units *happen* to get assigned to the dirtiest, hardest, and most dangerous jobs."

The navy uses Negro labor gangs extensively in the San Francisco area to load ships. They usually work under the direction of white officers. Training for skilled types of work is often insufficient. It has been pointed out that the longshore-

---

By Robert Chester. From *Militant*, November 11, 1944. The fifty sailors were part of a larger group that refused to load ammunition after an explosion killed 327 men on July 17. Hundreds of the protesters were shipped to the South Pacific, 256 were arrested, and 50 were court-martialed and sentenced to terms ranging from eight to fifteen years.

men's union does not permit men to work ammunition until they have had five years' experience. Yet some of the men at Port Chicago were put in ammunition after two or three months' training. On top of that, navy officers often use speedup methods, pitting one crew against another. It has been reported that officers in charge would make side bets with each other on the comparative outputs of their gangs.

The trial testimony showed that the men feared to continue loading ammunition after Port Chicago. Petitions had been circulated asking for transfers to other types of work, stating that they feared to work ammunition after seeing the effects of the blast. These petitions were used as the basis for the charge of "conspiracy to mutiny." Although much reference was made during the trial to "refusal to work" lists, no clear-cut evidence was presented that the men had refused to obey direct orders from their officers.

One important point stands out from the testimony. Any exhibition of resentment by the men against their lot was immediately translated by the officers into a threat against their authority and discipline. The whole navy system of intimidation was brought into play.

When the news that the men did not wish to handle ammunition reached the officers, a series of questionings and musterings were held. Men were questioned individually and statements drawn up by the officers were given to them for signature. Groups were lectured and the navy manual on mutiny read. Many of the statements were not taken verbatim.

One ensign testified that he asked the men to tell him "all about it" and then selected that which he thought was "important." Another officer testified that he took down notes in longhand and then dictated statements that he considered were "the substance of what the men said . . . excluding irrelevancies." Many of the men testified that they were told to sign the statements, and did so because "they thought they had to."

The army and navy have made a whole system of allowances for battle fatigue, shell shock, and psychological reactions to the horrors of war. Yet in this case, where the men went through one of the severest munition disasters of the war, no consideration for its effect was made.

In his final statement Prosecutor Lt. Cmdr. James F. Coakley, who has been accused by Thurgood Marshall of prejudice, said: "Any man so depraved as to be afraid to load ammunition deserves no leniency."

The case has held the interest of Negroes all over the country. They see in it a representation of the whole system of discrimination as practiced by the U.S. armed forces. They see in it a repetition of the discrimination they have experienced all their lives. Many young Negroes, believing this a "war for democracy," hoped that by joining the armed forces they could win some for themselves. Their experience has proved otherwise. All the conflicts in society are reproduced in the army and navy with intensified force.

This trial, the largest mass trial in navy history, bids fair to become the Negro cause célèbre of the war. Resentment is piling up. The imposition of sentences will touch off movements of protest by colored workers all over the country. Their demand will be "Free the fifty sailors."

SGT. BROWN'S LETTER

Dear Yank:

I am an American Negro with three years in the Army; and, if it makes me any more a soldier there is not a blemish on my service record. Griping is not my job, but right now I am really angry.

. . . I have written letters back home in which I have told about the lack of racial segregation in England and the freedom which the colored soldier enjoys here. For this, I was called up to battalion headquarters, taken out to a mess tent where none of the colored battalion personnel could hear and asked by the battalion executive and my battery commander why I insisted on flaunting in the officers' faces (through mail) the fact that the colored man enjoys much more equality in England than he does in the Southern States.

My answer was that there was no intent to flaunt anything in anyone's face. I write to tell my people back home things of interest, and so far as I am concerned (and I understand postal regulations will bear me out) the censor is an impersonal machine whose only function it is to pick out information of value to the enemy. The officers agreed that what was contained in my letters was of no harm militarily. . . .

Since then I have received letters from my parents (who have five other sons in service) and my friends stating that not one of

---

A letter to the army's weekly, *Yank*, September 8, reprinted from *Militant*, November 11, 1944.

my letters has arrived without something cut out and asking why I don't tell them about the English people. . . .

Mail is supposed to be morale building, but this sort of nonsense only makes the people back home more miserable and the men here prone to feel disrespect for their superior officers.

Sgt. James R. Brown

JUST A NEGRO SOLDIER

I'm just a Negro soldier
  Fighting for "Democracy,"
A thing I've often heard of
  But very seldom see.

In the South I was just a "nigger"
  On whom the boss man kept close track
To see that I grew no bigger
  Than the clothes upon my back.

In the North, of course, it's different,
  That is, they had a different name
For Jim Crow it was segregation
  But it amounts to just the same.

Yet I must be patriotic
  Must not grumble or complain
But must fight for some "four freedoms"
  On which I'll have no claim.

I must fight under every condition
  Face bayonet, shot, and shell
But with Jim Crow "recognition"
  Tho' I crash the gates of hell.

They expect me to be loyal?
  But in my heart I'm not
For how can a second-class citizen
  Be a first-class patriot?

To hell with a war impelled by greed
  While the hungry masses cry
But to win complete equality
  I'd fight and gladly die.

By Bill Horton. From *Militant*, November 11, 1944.

HOW TO WIN THE STRUGGLE

In order to carry on an effective struggle for Negro equality we must first trace back the stream of inequality until we have found and marked the source from whence it flows.

Just what comprises Negro inequality? If not the whites, certainly every Negro here knows the answer to that one. In the South the Negro knows what it is to be denied, either through legal maneuvers or intimidation, the right to vote. He knows what it is to be contemptuously referred to as "boy," "George," "Uncle," or just plain "nigger." He knows what it is to enter a streetcar and meet the signs: "This end of car for white people; this end of car for the colored race." He may know what it is to see an innocent man beaten, dismembered, hanged, shot, and burned to a crisp on some trivial accusation and without a trial.

In this nation's capital, a woman recently reported that she was raped by a Negro. Police rounded up eleven Negroes in twenty-four hours. The woman then admitted that she had fabricated the story. In the Deep South usually the first Negro would have been lynched, without a wait of twenty-four hours.

Even in some northern states the Negro knows what it is to be turned down at a theater box office or else directed around the alley to the balcony entrance. He may know what it is to insist that a waiter serve him a drink in states where there is a civil rights law and then have the waiter break the glass in his face. Negro women in Indiana who were delegates to a convention of the Mothers of World War II were recently refused rooms in an Elkhart hotel. They had to return home. In Washington, D.C., in the Church of the Immaculate Conception, a Negro woman was asked to get off her knees and go behind the ropes to the Negro section to pray. Even in death the Negro cannot rest. In a Catholic cemetery in Chicago, plans were recently made to dig up the grave of a colored woman buried accidentally among the whites.

A speech by Charles Jackson, November 12, 1944, at a public forum of the New York School of Social Science. From *Militant*, November 25, 1944.

In the South or the North, the Negro knows what it means to be segregated into a ghetto of shacks near the railroad tracks. He knows what it means to be discriminated against in industry: to get the dirtiest jobs at the lowest pay, to be the last hired and the first fired.

The unkindest cut of all, however, has come since this "land of the free" has been engaged in the present colossal slaughter, which, they would have us believe, is being waged for the most lofty and humanitarian ideals. In a war for "democracy" the Negro has been officially labeled a second-class citizen by his own government. In the army, the navy, and the marine corps, Negroes are set aside in separate regiments, quarantined from English-Americans, Italian-Americans, German-Americans, Japanese-Americans, and Jewish-Americans. Any soldier with a "drop of Negro blood" in his veins must, on orders of President Roosevelt and his War Department, and in violation of the Selective Service Act, train and fight not in the regular army, but in the Jim Crow army. There he is sure to get the dirtiest and most hazardous work and the added scorn and persecution of white civilians and soldiers alike.

The anticipated results of this policy are occurring every day. In Petersburg, Virginia, last week, a local policeman arrested a Negro soldier for some undetermined reason and took him to the firehouse. Another soldier asked the policeman what the trouble was, and he was also arrested. Sgt. Abraham Jackson made similar inquiries and was ignored. Thereupon he started for the firehouse to rescue his men. He was promptly shot down by the local police. At last reports he was not expected to recover. But let us not be too hard on the police system of the capitalist government. In Miami, Florida, five Negro policemen were hired—but with a reservation: they cannot arrest any white person, no matter what crime he may be in the act of committing.

Reported by the *New York Times* and the *Pittsburgh Courier* of November 11, and incidentally by the *Militant* some three weeks earlier, was the reactionary policy established in regard to the all-Negro Ninety-second Division now in combat on the Italian front. The policy is this: As Negro officers are killed, they are replaced by whites, instead of the customary replacement by advancing lower officers. Also there must not be, under any circumstances, a Negro officer who is superior in rank to a white officer in that sector.

We understand what Negro inequality is. Now just what is the Negro's conception of equality? What does the Negro want? The Negro wants what everyone else wants—no more, no less. He wants a dependable annual wage capable of bringing him all the necessities of a healthy and happy life. In short, economic security. He wants political freedom, a voice in the way things are done, a vote, and a representative who understands his problems. In addition to this he wants complete social equality. Let us get this straight—the mind, the body, and emotions of the Negro are inherently the same as those of any other race. Therefore, just as the white man would resent the stigma of social inferiority, so does the Negro resent it. To stamp an entire group of individuals as inferior simply because they have more melanin or less carotine in their skins—absolutely inert pigments—to do this is contrary to scientific truth.

Now what is the direct instrument of repression that condemns the Negro to second-class citizenship? It is the state, that is, all the various agencies of government from top to bottom. Through their actions and their failures to act, they condone, teach, foster, and enforce the oppression of the Negro people. Who protected Noble Ryder, the recently freed murderer who lynched an aged Negro preacher in Liberty, Mississippi? The sheriff. Who upholds white supremacy in the South? The courts. Who holds Negroes in Georgia in the chain gangs for stealing a loaf of bread? The state. Who leads the pack in race-baiting? Your government officials such as Chauncy Sparks and the poll tax senators. Who tenaciously insists upon a Jim Crow army? Roosevelt and his War Department. Who carries out this policy? The brass hats in the army and navy.

The Federal Housing Authority recommends discrimination in its official manual. The Office of War Information has a standing order that a messenger shall watch the news ticker and bring all copy on race or color to the "Negro Censoring Division." At the Arlington Hotel in Hot Springs, Arkansas, the army set up a rehabilitation center for soldiers and their wives. The management of this hotel happens to house, without discrimination, Indians and all other races and nationalities. A Negro lieutenant and his wife registered at the hotel and were given rooms. But as soon as this was discovered by a white army captain, he ordered their removal. They were removed.

But how about individual prejudices? Remember, these are not inherited, they are acquired. H. Scudder Mekeel, associate professor of anthropology at the University of Wisconsin, told the National Committee for Mental Hygiene last week: "With Brazil and Russia as examples, we can say that racial prejudice is not inherent in the human animal. . . . What we need to do is to deflect, modify, or transform the processes at work in our society so that children will no longer learn prejudice and discrimination. . . . The cradle is the best place to start."

Well, that's not news to the American educators. Not for nothing are the "nigger" dolls used in the nurseries and the tale of "Little Black Sambo" taught in the kindergartens. The history books, the comic strips, the radio, and the cinema all contribute to the formation of the Negro stereotype—a petty thief, a clown, an ignoramus. Whoever attempts to teach equality is usually stymied. Last month, the subway lines right here in New York barred a poster showing babies of all races side by side. You remember the revealing pamphlet *Races of Mankind*, which torpedoed the myth of racial inferiority, giving statistical proof from the records of drafted soldiers? That was too much truth for the army brass hats, and they recalled fifty thousand copies that had been distributed for soldiers' libraries. Directly or indirectly, the agencies of government are responsible for individual prejudices.

Why would the government officials want to foster such a policy? President Roosevelt is well known as a humanitarian. Mrs. Roosevelt has even been photographed with Mrs. Bethune, Negro soldiers, and Negro children. Many government officials welcome Negro leaders to their offices to confer with them on race problems. Some of the most reactionary southern governors have sponsored drives to obtain funds for Negro colleges. Now, I don't think we are fooled by these patronizing gestures. It is plain that the state in America is invariably anti-Negro. But back to the question. Where there is an effect there must be a cause. Maybe with the following facts we can better follow the trail.

In 1848 Karl Marx, after making a scientific analysis of the history of society, arrived at the conclusion that the state was supported and kept in power by and for the ruling class in society. Whoever owns the means of production makes up the ruling class. The state serves to protect the interests of the exploiting minority over the exploited majority. In slavery days the judges, law officers, and governors, that is, the state apparatus, unfailingly upheld the interests of the slaveholder over the slave. In feudal days the state was always on the side of the noble and against the serf.

We have reached the point in America today where it is the monopoly capitalists who own and control the means of production. The industrial workers, on the other hand, comprise the exploited majority. True to the Marxist analysis, every agent of the state from top to bottom must do the bidding of the monied interests. If he defies the capitalists he is soon kicked out in one way or another. Now what has that got to do with the Negro? Marx said that no ruling class has been able to long exploit the vast majority unless that majority was split within itself. The capitalists know this and they make the most of it. Whether based on race, religion, nationality, language, or custom, the axiom "divide and rule" is never forgotten and never neglected by those who are in power.

They take the most convenient minority within the group of exploited people and set them up as a scapegoat. The other oppressed people are permitted—even trained—to kick around this minority at their leisure, thus unconsciously venting the perfectly natural resentment which arises from their economic insecurity. The ruling class, through control of the educational system and the state apparatus, deliberately fosters prejudice among the masses against the designated minority. They inoculate this venom in such large doses that it is practically impossible for even the most mentally alert individual to escape from its degrading effects.

In America, of course, the Negro is a natural for the capitalists. His dark color makes him easy to recognize. His background of slavery is also played up to give the impression that he is inferior and as docile as a dumb animal. The history books put out by the capitalists, by a crime of omission, imply the lie that the darker races have never been "civilized." They tell us of the pyramids and other wonders of the world, but they fail to say that they were built by black Egyptians centuries ago. The features of the Sphinx betray by their Negroid characteristics, the existence in the valley of the Nile of a highly civilized Negro race. The books of the capitalist class don't tell us that, and no white scientist has been able to even explain how those engineers accomplished these feats. Their propaganda depicts the black man in the very worst light simply because he is a useful minority to turn to their ends. As a result of the tremendous pressure of their gigantic propaganda machine, millions of Americans are color conscious. "What's white is right: what's black, stay back."

Although in the Dick Tracy comic series crime never pays, we find the opposite is true in real life America. The crime of Jim Crowism, the crime of indoctrinating prejudice into the workers, and the crime of denying the Negro people equality, are very good-paying crimes for the American capitalist. For it is largely as a result of racial divergence in the working class that the capitalist is able to remain in power. He knows full well the day of working-class solidarity will be his day of reckoning.

Now, let's look down the trail. Negroes are denied equality either through official government action or official government lack of action. The government is under control of the ruling class. That class is the capitalist class, which comprises only a small minority of the population. These capitalists, through their government agencies and through their control of the means of information, indoctrinate the people with the lie that a man is inferior if the color of his skin is dark. They do this so that they can keep their economic slaves, the workers, white and black, split and fighting among themselves. Thereby they are able to spend their winters in Florida clipping stock coupons while the workers toil in the shops for a mere existence. These leeches suck the lifeblood of the American working class by setting up the Negro as a straw man and then shouting: "Don't give a Black a break: give the Black the boot." By this system of capitalism, race prejudice is made profitable.

Therefore we say that this system—capitalism—is the basic and fundamental enemy of the Negro people. Here is the spring from which flows the vile potion that cascades down to form the final stream of Negro inequality. We have found the source—let us mark it well. This is the reason why the fight against Jim Crow without a fight against capitalism, well intentioned though it may be, is an endless and fruitless fight. To establish Negro equality, we must abolish capitalism.

Furthermore, the capitalist methods of exchange are outmoded. The assembly lines and mass production, along with thousands of chemical and engineering discoveries, have so improved the means of production that the potential output is gigantic. But the policy of exchange for profit is holding back the productive forces. When the masses cannot pay enough for the capitalists to make a substantial profit, the capitalists simply close down the factories and let the workers shift as best they can, even though the people may be in need. It is only when they are warring with a rival imperialist power for foreign markets, that the factories run full blast, and then the workers and their sons are sent to die on bloody battlefields. History is bearing out Marx's prediction that increasingly savage wars and depressions are inevitable under the decaying capitalist economic anarchy.

Again, how does this affect the Negro? Well, we all know that the Negro is the last to go on a job when things are getting better, and the first to be pulled off when things are getting worse. That is why—and remember this—you have Negro employment only when you have full employment. Therefore, under capitalist production, the average Negro can look forward to a good-paying job only during war, whereas during the long years of depression he has to depend either on the breadline or the relief roll.

Now what would bring the Negro full equality? What would bring him full employment? We say not capitalism, but socialism. Socialism with its nationalized property and its planned economy. Now factories hum only with the production of instruments of death and destruction, manufactured solely for the profit of the few. Under socialism factories would hum with the production of instruments of life and construction, manufactured to supply the needs of the many. World socialism, without a doubt, would bring with its classless society full equality, full employment, job security, peace, and plenty to not only the Negro people but to all mankind.

Will we get socialism by talking about it, hoping for it, or praying for it? Hardly. We've got to fight for it in an organized fashion. Like every ruling class in the past, the capitalists will not relinquish their stranglehold on the workers of their own free will. The industrial workers, for the very good reason that they are the most oppressed and at the same time the most highly organized group, will lead the socialist revolution. They will take over the means of production and thereby lead the way for the liberation of the farmers and the white-collar workers. The capitalists during this period will try desperately to retain or regain their exploitive power on a world scale. They will try, in vain, to hold back the wheel of human progress. Their main weapon in America will be to set the white against the black and to bring on a racial war within the working class. The capitalists will be willing to exterminate the Negro minority if their preservation makes it necessary. The new workers' and farmers' government, on the other hand, for the very basic reason of self-preservation, will immediately have to grant and enforce full equality for the Negro people. It will have to do this to counteract the capitalists and to demonstrate that its program is reliable.

When such a government gets control of the means of communication, it will have to embark immediately upon an educational program to enlighten backward white workers and thereby destroy the false ideas of white supremacy which have been indoctrinated in their minds by bourgeois society. Thus the very first step in the direction of socialism will also give birth to Negro equality.

This is no pipe dream. The socialist revolution was scientifically outlined a century ago and has been demonstrated in real life in that greatest of all spectacles in human history, the Bolshevik revolution of 1917. This fact is obvious: nothing short of a proletarian revolution will bring the Negro full equality in America.

The Negro struggle, therefore, is inseparably intertwined with the struggle of the world working class. Our fight is not hopeless if we realize its breadth. We Negroes are outnumbered ten to one from a racial point of view. That is true. But as workers we are part of the vast majority. The white worker of this country is our ally, not our enemy. His prejudices have been artificially learned and may be just as easily unlearned when he sees the necessity of working-class solidarity. He needs us and we need him. Necessity will force us to get together. Our allies also include all the workers and peasants of imprisoned Europe, who are now pitted against each other by the German and Anglo-American imperialists but who tomorrow will rise and take their destiny into their own hands. The toiling masses of India, China, and Africa are also on our side. When they are free, we will be free.

A word of warning about our false friends. A false friend is one who aids us in the struggle but at the same time leads us to believe that we can win full equality within the confines of the present capitalist system. What shall we do about these false friends? If such a friend still clings to the old order because he knows nothing of the dynamics of the world class struggle, we must educate him by patient explanation. Into this category fall some of our preachers, our "race leaders," and some opportunistic labor leaders. In this bed also rest our antiwhite militants as well as the weak-kneed pacifists, who think that the problem will be solved by people of good will getting together on the basis of brotherly love. It should be obvious that it is too late in history to go back and call the roll and count in the Negro as a paid-up brother in good standing. Look how the Negro has fared during the war. Judge Hastie, reporting for the NAACP this past June, said that all forms of Negro brutalizing increased in 1943. If they stopped to draw blood from us even while engaged in an outside brawl with German imperialism, then what can we expect when Germany is defeated and they are free to turn their entire strength against the Negro and the American labor movement? We should try to awaken these reformist leaders, and if they don't see the light we should fight relentlessly against them.

If we find, however, a false friend who supports capitalism even after he has become familiar with and participated in the class struggle—beware of him, for he is a hired quisling for the ruling class. Into this category fall the Stalinists, who, because they parade under the banner of Communism, are still quite a factor in the Negro struggle and in the labor movement. They live primarily on the world prestige of the Russian revolution. Since the degeneration of the Soviet state, however, and the rise of the counterrevolutionary Stalinist bureaucracy, the Communist parties throughout the world remain only as agencies of the reactionary clique in the Kremlin. These servile lackeys, for example, are now crawling on their bellies before President Roosevelt and American capitalism. Now many workers contend that Roosevelt was the lesser of the two evils in the past election. We won't go into that now, since it was covered in the *Militant,* but I want to tell the Negroes again that the idea that Roosevelt, the "leftist" henchman of big business, intends to give or would be permitted to give the Negro the equality he demands, is a brazen lie. The only substantial advancement of the Negro's cause in the political arena will come with an independent labor party.

Now what does American capitalism plan in the period ahead? It plans further oppression of the Negroes in the form of extended restrictions; Negro-baiting by government spokesmen; company-inspired anti-Negroism in the labor movement such as we saw in Philadelphia this summer, and again in Detroit last week. After the defeat of Germany there will be further brutalizings, lynchings, and mass pogroms. All this will be deliberately instigated to further divide and crush the labor movement. If labor does not put up a strong fight to protect the Negro, and if it fails to rescue society by setting up a workers' and farmers' government, then we are sure to see fascism or some similarly barbaric political monster stalking the United States.

Even now the capitalists are priming Gerald L. K. Smith, the Jew-baiting and Negro-baiting rabble rouser, for this very job. Harry Bennett, vice-president of the Ford Motor Company, admitted in October before a House committee that he gave Smith $2,000 to fight the unions. Government records show that New York and Detroit industrialists have contributed much larger amounts to Smith's campaign as the presidential candidate of the America First Party. Under fascism, the Negro people would be even worse off than the Jews in Nazi Germany. They would be tracked down, deported, or exterminated. This would apply to rich and poor Negroes alike.

What can be done at present to further the Negro struggle for equality? The Negro organizations should adopt the strategy of militant mass action in their demand for democratic rights. This should be done with the support of the progressive labor unions such as the CIO. Realizing that to be anti-Negro is in essence to be anti–working class, politically advanced white workers should carry on now a relentless fight against all forms of industrial discrimination and segregation. When a crisis comes they should call for workers' defense guards to protect the Negro workers from fascist attacks. Finally, the keeping alive of the class struggle in the shops is all-important to the Negro, because more interracial education can be obtained on a picket line during a strike where white and black workers are in common struggle for basic needs, than can be gleaned in a dozen pink tea liberal discussion groups.

The fighters for socialism today are found in the Socialist

Workers Party and among the Trotskyists of the Fourth International. Our Marxist analysis brings us to the conclusion that the Negro struggle in the coming period will be largely a defensive one. It will mount in intensity with rising world class struggle and will be resolved only when the workers come to power. That is why we say:

The only way to win full Negro equality is through a simultaneous struggle for the liberation of all the toiling human brothers—be they black, brown, yellow, or white. Negro workers, to avert a losing race war, prepare now for a victorious class war!

WHAT GREEK CIVIL WAR TEACHES US

The Greek masses have been engaged in a bloody war against British imperialism. The Negro people in America are engaged in a social struggle for full citizenship and complete equality. Far removed tactically and geographically as are these two struggles from each other, yet they have a political interconnection that deserves close scrutiny.

We have all seen how the brave Greeks under the ELAS have carried on their civil war in such a resolute fashion. Invaded by the Italian fascists and then by the Nazis, oppressed, famished, enslaved, and diseased, still they are struggling courageously against the attempts of Churchill under the guise of "liberation" to enforce upon them a government composed of the same exploiting traitors who helped oppress their own countrymen at the time when the Nazis were overrunning the country.

In this most recent war between the British military arm and the Greek people, it is well for us to remember that the British and their Greek puppets have mercilessly fired on and murdered men, women, and children. They have used machine guns, tanks,

---

By Charles Jackson. From *Militant,* January 6, 1945. The Nazi occupation forces withdrew from Greece in September 1944, partially as a result of the efforts of the Greek partisan movement, the ELAS (National Popular Liberation Army), which was led by the Communist Party. Following Stalin's orders, the ELAS welcomed British troops into the country, who then, along with Greek monarchist forces, turned around and began armed attacks against the ELAS in December 1944. A truce was reached in February 1945; however, civil war broke out again, lasting from 1946 until 1949, when the left-wing forces were defeated.

planes, and heavy artillery against the "liberated" Greeks—the same instruments of death that are ostensibly so badly needed on the German front.

The American government has tried to give the impression that it is blameless for this British policy in Greece. Like Pontius Pilate, it has tried to wash its hands of the whole affair. Each and every gangster in a murder mob, however, is equally guilty of the crimes committed by his cohorts. Let us not forget that many of the weapons that were used against the Greek workers had been manufactured here for the profit of American capitalists.

What bearing do these facts have on the Negro struggle? Simply this. We should thereby be forewarned of the methods that will be adopted by the ruling class in dealing with all those who oppose its vile interests.

Even a "leftist" Greek government—let alone a real revolutionary workers' state—threatens the interests of British imperialism and is consequently attacked. In the same way, complete racial equality, which would lead to closer working-class solidarity, is contrary to the interests of American big business. The forces which strive for such equality, mainly the Negro masses, will also, if it becomes necessary, be ruthlessly attacked.

In view of these recent events, on what sort of reasoning do some of the Negro leaders base their contention that this war will advance the Negro's cause? Isn't it obvious to them that the military might of Britain is directed by *white* men? Don't they realize that these valiant Greek forces of liberation were composed of *white* workers? If the reactionary stench given off by decaying capitalism will include white men giving orders to shoot down white women and children, then what can we expect to be the fate of the blacks and browns?

Let us not fail to learn from these tragic events. The Greek people, who have fought off the fascists, the Nazis, and now the British imperialists, will soon realize that their only hope lies in the overthrow of the capitalist system itself.

In America we have seen Negroes denied full citizenship, oppressed, and lynched. We have also seen white workers and farmers condemned to lives of poverty, prejudice, and ignorance. Let the people themselves, be they here or in strife-torn Europe, get together as the working class and remove the system of exploitation and inequality which is the cause of all this domestic and foreign oppression. Only with socialism will either of these struggles for liberation be brought to a victorious end.

LABOR SHORTAGE AND THE BROOM

SAN FRANCISCO, January 3—The San Francisco Bay Area has, according to various government officials, a severe manpower shortage. Periodic statements in the daily press stress the constant need for more men. Yet, in practice, this need takes second place to the practice of discrimination against Negroes. This practice is general. Here are a few experiences suffered by men working in a prominent, government-built shipyard, devoted exclusively to navy work.

"Discrimination begins from the time we hit the yard. I always watch what happens to a group of recruits," said Joe Green as he illustrated the scene with sardonic pantomime.

They come up to the foreman's desk and he sizes them up. He takes the white men first. "OK you," he says pointing to the first man (white), "you start working here—this man will show you what to do—and you" (white man, too), "you come over here—you work on this machine, this man will show you how"—and so on.

And then he comes to the colored man. He picks up the paper, looks at the man quick, scratches his cheek and walks around a little. Then he comes back and looks at the man again and says: "Well, I ain't got any openings just yet—I expect to have some soon—we have to keep you busy—suppose you take this broom for a while and sweep this aisle. As soon as I get something for you I'll put you on a machine." That job never comes up.

It's a funny thing about that broom, it's like a cancer on the nose. Once you got it, it sticks, you just can't get rid of it.

Men take it as long as they can. They are hired as machinist's helpers and they are interested in learning the work. They want to improve themselves. But they don't get the chance. So they quit. Colored men keep coming and going. I've seen over eighteen men go through my department in the last year.

Suppose you put up a squawk, as my friend here tried. He's been fighting to keep on the work he was hired to do, but he's still on the broom.

By Robert Chester. From *Militant,* January 13, 1945.

"I was hired in a midwest state," his friend picked up the story.

I signed a six-month contract as a machinist's helper. They paid my fare
out here and gave me a room in the dormitory. The first week I got a
break and worked on the machine as a helper. Then I was shifted to
nights because, they said, the job I was on was finishing. On nights the
first thing they did was give me the broom. There's where my trouble
started.

I refused to take the broom. Pushing a broom is laborer's work and my
contract said machinist's helper. I told them so. They sent me to the
personnel department. After hearing my story, the personnel manager
said: "OK, I'll put you back on days and see that you get machinist's
helper's work. But don't tell anyone what happened on nights."

The foreman took me to the quarterman and told him I was being
transferred back to days. The quarterman said: "I don't have any work
for him—put him back on nights." So back I went to personnel. Personnel
then told me to stay on my other job until they find something. So I
stayed. A week later they put me on polishing brass. Meanwhile I found
out that a white man had been put on the job I originally had.

About that time we got a new foreman. He assigned me to picking up
sticks and scraps. I refused. He sent me to personnel and we went over the
whole business again. Finally, personnel said: "Do as you are told or get
your release." I was pretty sore and said the release is OK with me.

But I had to change my mind. I didn't have any money. The checks
come through the week after you work, and they take out your rent, war-
bond money, and other things in advance. I had been borrowing money
from my friends. I did not have the price of a fare home. The release they
would give me would prevent me from taking a job on any other war
work.

I went back to personnel and said that I would stay on and take
anything that they gave me. He got nicer then and sent me back to the
quarterman. The quarterman acted big. "As long as you take orders, OK,"
he said, "but if you come here to tell me how to run the shop, I get sore."
And I stood there and took it. I've been on the broom ever since.

The first man took up the story again.

My trouble was getting a raise. I have been here sixteen months. I was
an experienced machinist before I came here and I started before most of
the colored men were hired. That is how I missed the broom. I got a
reputation for doing good work.

My kick was that I worked at machine operator's wages. White men
were doing the same work at machinist's wages. I went to the quartermaster for a raise. He said he could not recommend it—I would have to
see the shopmaster. I knew that was not right, so after a week I went to
personnel. They send me back to the quartermaster. I went back and kind
of put him on the spot.

I saw some kind of conference between him and personnel. Then they
came over to me and told me that the only way to get a raise was to

transfer into a different department. If I wanted a transfer they would work something out.

What they worked out was this: I had to take a test on a complicated boring mill that they knew I could not handle. Then if I failed, I would be dropped to a helper at a lower rate than I was getting. That way they forced me to stay on my old job.

I always get the heavy or the tedious or the complicated jobs. The others get the gravy. One time they gave me a heavy plate job to do. I struggled with it for two weeks. Usually jobs are kept working on night and day shifts. Yet for over a week I would come back to the machine and find everything just as I left it.

I finally got my raise. It happened this way. I had a colored helper working alongside me who I was teaching the ropes. One day they shifted him. A couple days later they put a white man in his place. I could see that he was raw—I had to keep showing him what to do. Then one day at the time clock I noticed that his card was on a different rack. As soon as I got the chance I looked at his card. *He was getting machinist's wages.*

I got sore. I went to the second steward and said "I'm quitting. I'm tired of having to work at lower wages because of the color of my skin." We went to boss and beefed. That week I got my raise.

White men advance fast in the yard. They get the opportunities for better jobs and more pay. When firings come the colored men on the broom and the lower ratings are going to be fired first. The yard has over ten thousand men but I don't know of one colored man getting higher than machinist, second class wages, or having the job of leaderman.

They keep talking about the four freedoms over there. They ought to try to save a few for us here at home.

THE DEMAND FOR LABOR
CONSCRIPTION

The reactionary drive for a national service law conscripting labor for work in private industry is being conducted under cover of an alleged manpower shortage. The top estimate of the "shortage" quoted by the slave-labor advocates is 300,000. The total labor force is approximately 55 million with 1 million

---

From *Militant,* January 20, 1945. In January 1944, the Roosevelt administration had proposed a labor conscription law which would have given the government and employers the power to compel workers to work anywhere, move anywhere, and accept any hours and wages the employers dictated. The response within the labor movement was almost unanimous opposition. Only the Communist Party endorsed the plan. Roosevelt soft-pedaled the plan as the 1944 elections neared; he raised it again after the votes were counted, but it was never enacted.

unemployed. Proponents of a labor draft do not even pretend that a national service law will increase the total manpower available for employment.

The argument is advanced that nothing less than total regimentation of the whole working population is required to accomplish a shift of workers from nonessential to essential industry. The flagrant disproportion between means and end—total labor conscription to effect a relatively minor shift in the labor force—exposes this manpower "shortage" ballyhoo as a patent fraud. What are the facts?

The author of a study on the manpower question published in *PM,* January 5, discloses that a huge reservoir of manpower "is not being fully tapped for war production because of racial or religious prejudice." There are over 13 million Negroes in this country, the overwhelming majority of whom are laboring people. But the dollar patriots consider it more important to perpetuate the myth of white supremacy than to utilize Negro workers in war production. The following are a few examples cited by the author to illustrate this attitude.

In the huge cotton textile industry in the South, almost no Negroes are being used except in custodial jobs—and a lot of GI's are sleeping beneath tin tents because there is not enough canvas being produced in this country.

In war plants of St. Louis and Cincinnati, practically no Negroes are employed in production jobs.

The Western Cartridge Co., of Alton, Ill., across from St. Louis, has not one Negro among its 10,000 employees.

The Houston Shipbuilding Corp., of Houston Tex., imports white welders from other parts of the country, while Negro graduates of a Houston welding school must go to the East or West Coast to find jobs.

The railroads, which are crying for manpower continually, are railroading Negro firemen out of jobs—jobs which must be taken by whites who could be doing other jobs.

These examples could be multiplied a hundredfold. Many lily-white corporations erect a color bar, not only against Negroes, but against Mexicans, Filipinos, Chinese, etc. Others discriminate against Jews and Catholics. Those who scream the loudest about the manpower "shortage" are the most diligent in fostering race discrimination and religious prejudice. James F. Byrnes, the manpower czar, is a leading exponent of white supremacy. As a poll tax senator from South Carolina he led the Jim Crow contingent in Congress, at one time conducting a filibuster against an antilynch bill, which he threatened to carry on for one hundred years. This is the man whom Roosevelt and Congress have endowed with almost supreme power over the lives and welfare of the people. Naturally, "Simon Legree" Byrnes favors a slave-labor law.

When Roosevelt demanded a national service law in his recent message to Congress, he gave as his main argument the necessity of having "the right numbers of workers in the right places at the right times." He neglected to add, "with the right color and religion."

If, for the sake of argument, we should admit that there actually is a manpower shortage of 300,000 workers, the only kind of legislation required to relieve it would be a law making it a crime to discriminate against workers for race, color, or creed. But the ruling capitalist class, which constitutes a tiny minority of the population, maintains its power by applying the axiom "divide and rule." The rotting capitalist system is a stinking cesspool of race discrimination, prejudice, exploitation, and oppression. War or no war, manpower shortage or mass unemployment, discrimination and prejudice, which divide the workers for the benefit of the exploiters, are an integral part of this social system.

73 COURT-MARTIALED FOR PROTEST

The army has just revealed that seventy-three members of a Negro labor battalion who had been put to work on Oahu in the Hawaiian Islands have been convicted of "mutiny" by an army court-martial, sentenced to from fifteen to twenty-five years at hard labor, and given dishonorable discharges.

According to Walter White, executive secretary of the NAACP, the court-martial resulted from a no-work protest lodged by the soldiers when it was made known that their colored officers were all to be replaced with prejudiced southern white officers.

It seems that there existed in this battalion the same reactionary policy that holds true for the Ninety-second in Italy. That is, as soon as any Negro officer is transferred or otherwise made absent, a white officer replaces him. If there happens to be any Negro officer who has a higher rating than the transferred officer, then the white officer is advanced to such a rating that he is above this or any other Negro in this section. This policy is

By Charles Jackson. From *Militant,* February 24, 1945.

carried out regardless of the white officer's lack of qualifications or lack of years in service.

The Negro officers drew up a perfectly legitimate protest and delivered it to the War Department through perfectly legitimate means as provided for in the rules and regulations. They were careful to make their objections known through nothing but the regular channels.

And what did such polite comment on the policy of the big shots get for them? To the brass hats such impudence deserved—and received—a slap in the face. They were immediately removed from the post and replaced by all white officers. Thus did Roosevelt's War Department make it known again that it does not intend to recognize the suggestions or objections of even Negro officers as to the official anti-Negro policy.

The Negro soldiers in the battalion, already resentful of the fact that they were designated to pick-and-shovel duty regardless of their qualifications, quite naturally did not relish the idea of being bossed around by the prejudiced white officers. Furthermore, they naturally felt like showing some loyalty to their former Negro officers, who had just received such a dirty deal. They refused to leave their barracks to work.

The colonel was forced to ask one of the transferred Negro officers to order them out. They complied. The men were read the Sixty-sixth Article of War and given ten minutes to get their mess gear and go to work, which they finally did. They even complied with the demand that they make up the lost time.

On the basis of these events they were held on mutiny charges a few days later and were subsequently sentenced to from fifteen to twenty-five years.

Although these facts were allowed to come through, there must have been other contributing conditions that made the War Department's sentences seem all the more vicious, because additional parts of White's report were censored by the army authorities.

This is another Port Chicago case or even worse. It is time the Negro organizations made some mass protest against such high-handed methods, which are being used to keep the Negro "in his place" in this so-called war for four freedoms.

As after the case of the fifty sailors, we say again: the Negro masses must make themselves heard and seen in protest against this case or else there will be many more.

PLIGHT OF JAPANESE-AMERICANS

Several incidents have recently been reported on the West Coast which indicate an impending campaign of intimidation, terrorization, and violence against a different—but similarly persecuted—racial minority, the Japanese-Americans. The Negro people, even if only in the interest of their own defense, cannot afford to overlook or condone this familiar type of left-handed blow at a group of American citizens whose only offense resides in the fact that they happened to be derived from the "wrong" racial origin.

Soon after the shooting stage of the war with Japan began, these citizens, in flagrant violation of their civil rights, were yanked from their farms and homes and were herded into virtual concentration camps, known officially by the polite name of relocation centers. This illegal repression was carried out by the law-enforcement agencies after a campaign by the capitalist press to whip up racial prejudice under the guise of national patriotism.

The real motivators, however, were a big-business outfit called the Associated Farmers, along with other reactionary interests which stand to profit—war or no war—by the elimination of competitors and by the persecution of a minority within the working class.

Now that these citizens are beginning to trickle back to their homes, these same profit-hungry exploiters have declared another open season on Japanese-Americans and have signified that they intend to employ every weapon at their command.

The American Legion is circulating inflammatory, fascist-type leaflets, and the district attorney of Los Angeles is whooping it up with the claim that he knows (but evidently can't catch to arrest) people who threaten to "shoot on sight" any returning Japanese-American.

What is worse, a mob of thugs schooled in KKK tactics has evidently been hired and has begun its evil, cowardly work. The

By Charles Jackson. From *Militant,* March 10, 1945.

home of Bob Morishege, of Selma, California, was set afire and burned, and shotgun barrages were fired at the homes of two other Japanese-Americans of Fresno County: S. J. Kakutani and Frank Osaki. At the last report, none of those responsible for the outrages against these peaceful citizens had been arrested.

The sinister methods to which these mobsters resort was brought out by Mrs. Joseph Holzman's report to the Los Angeles police that twice she was threatened by anonymous telephone calls in connection with her employment of two Japanese servants. "Better get rid of them," said the voice, "or we'll get rid of you and take care of them."

Stating that an injury to one is an injury to all, Myra Tanner Weiss, Socialist Workers Party candidate for mayor of Los Angeles, has issued a call to organized labor to condemn this campaign of intimidation and violence against the Japanese-American minority.

Showing that the entire working class, regardless of race or national origin, could ignore this threat only at its own peril, she said: "If today the Japanese-Americans can be attacked with impunity, tomorrow it may well be the Negroes, the Mexicans, the Filipinos, the Jews—leading to violent attacks upon the labor movement, which is always a target of reaction."

In her letters to the CIO and the AFL, Weiss stated that she had made the fight against race hatred and race discrimination a prominent part of her platform and that she believed the same should be done in the whole organized labor movement. When we wake up to the uselessness of "shifting our weight around" from one capitalist party to another and line up solid behind this type of fighting program, then we will be getting somewhere in our struggle for Negro equality.

In addition to that, through our Negro organizations we must go to bat for a Japanese-American just as quickly as we would for another Negro. These people are obviously being denied their full citizenship rights just as we are. They are pictured in the capitalist press as toothsome, "brown-bellied bastards" and are described by the capitalist commentators as "half-man and half-beast." This vicious type of prejudice indoctrination is familiar to every Negro.

The Japanese people are intelligent and alert, and beneath their external racial characteristics they are indistinguishable from any other human, be he white or black. The working class in Japan is economically enslaved and driven to war by Japan's four ruling industrial families, whose lust for profits and power is the same as that of America's sixty and Britain's thirteen richest families.

The Japanese-American workers are not only our comrades in the world class struggle for socialist liberation, but they are also our brothers through oppression in this capitalist "democracy."

Let us not fail to rally to their side and fight back against the attacks of the common enemy!

THE STALINIST 'SILENCE' POLICY

Earl Browder has publicly stated in the March 4 issue of the *Sunday Worker* that "It has been the studied policy of American Communists to refrain from public discussion" of the issue of Jim Crowism in the army.

In his article discussing the new policy of the army to commission "Communists," he deals with the Negro question and makes it clear that the "Communists" intend to ignore the reactionary army policy of Jim Crowing the Negro soldiers.

He states (believe it or not) that they are convinced that the army leadership is "soundly democratic" and that "it would move to modify and finally abolish" Jim Crowism without any "organized pressure." He further says that the Stalinists "are today happy indeed" that "progress is being recorded." According to Browder, his "judgement [on the value of the silent policy] has been confirmed." In other words, by not fighting back against the reactionary policy of the army brass hats—wonder of wonders—a great victory has been gained.

The facts are against Browder's perfidious claim that a "policy of silence" will gain concessions from the army brass hats.

Their anti-Negro acts must be fought against *now* by the Negro people as well as by the trade union movement, which is the basic target of these armed bodyguards of the American capitalist class.

Alert Negro militants who want to fight for Negro rights with a real fighting outfit are getting "hep" to the bureaucratic maneuvers of Browder and his gang. They are lining up in ever increasing numbers behind the banner of Trotskyism and the program of the Socialist Workers Party.

By Charles Jackson. From *Militant,* March 24, 1945.

CONGRESSMAN POWELL, CONTORTIONIST

The feeble capacity of those political leaders who attempt to straddle the fence of reality by calling for racial equality and, at the same time, giving full support to the very system of capitalism which makes Negro oppression profitable, is further exemplified by the antics of Harlem's fair-haired faker, Congressman Adam Clayton Powell, Jr.

This formerly outspoken champion of Negro rights, whom the voters of Harlem sent to Congress with confidence in his integrity, is now playing the role of a slick betrayer of the Negro masses. In his corrupt attempt to make further personal, opportunistic gains he is whitewashing the role of American imperialism and its present political agent, the Roosevelt administration.

In a recent debate on the slave-labor bill, Powell was so anxious to honey up to the Roosevelt administration that he, the ostensible Negro spokesman, spoke against the incorporation into that reactionary measure of a nondiscrimination amendment. Here is his excuse: "I opposed it because there was an order by our commander in chief, Executive Order No. 8802, which assured that in war industries there would be no discrimination." He claims that he is opposed to "too much protection" against anti-Negroism—as if such could be possible in present-day America! Such is the flimsy excuse offered by this faker for lining up with Rankin, the Negroes' most open and outspoken enemy.

Powell further stated in the House of Representatives on March 6 that order 8802 (FEPC), "has been obeyed [now watch the wording] more or less in increasing numbers in our war plants." By such weasel-worded phraseology he tries to substantiate the lie that the FEPC has brought Negroes equality in hiring and in upgrading in industry. A claim as obviously false as this one needs no rebuttal as far as Negro factory workers are concerned.

The fact that this political contortionist is no longer interested in liberating the Negro masses but only in advancing his own

By Charles Jackson. From *Militant*, March 31, 1945.

prestige among the ruling class is further borne out by the type of "fight" he is advocating in his public speeches.

The March 17 issue of his own paper, *People's Voice,* carries a report of his recent address in Detroit where he condemned Negro "nationalism." "The National Association for the Advancement of Colored People," said Powell, "should now change its name to the National Association for the Advancement of Common People."

We certainly have nothing against the common people— whoever they are. If, by using the scathing term *common people* the congressman means the working class—(and if so, why is he afraid to say so?)—then we agree that they need advancement even to the position of absolute rule in order to displace the present handful of exploiters. In fact, we are always telling the Negro people that only by militant struggle alongside the white workers will they successfully attain equal citizenship rights.

Only the simplest fool or the most deceptive liar, however, will today contend that there is no further need to struggle for Negro equality as such. The most naïve country bumpkin knows that throughout the greater part of America a black man cannot go to the same places, engage in the same political activity, or hold the same jobs as a white man.

We cannot ignore the fact that the Negro is doubly oppressed— as a worker and as a Negro—and therefore he must put up a special struggle for basic democratic rights which is not necessary for the white worker. Down with the government and civilian Jim Crow that unjustly condemns us to second-class citizenship!

Instead of diluting or disbanding the NAACP, Mr. Powell, we need to build it bigger and stronger. We also need to transfer its strategy into the stream of militant mass action along with the progressive labor movement so that we can force the big-business government to grant our democratic demands.

HUNGER STRIKE BY SEABEES

In a dramatic protest against racial discrimination in the granting of advanced ratings, over one thousand Negro Seabees at the Port Hueneme base, near Oxnard, California, went on a hunger strike on Friday, March 2.

The protesting Negro Seabees are members of the Thirty-fourth Construction Battalion who were returned to this country last November after serving twenty-one months at Tulagi and Guadalcanal, in the South Pacific.

This action of the Negro veterans was taken after they had been denied for three years the opportunity to advance in ratings. Their spokesmen, according to Norman O. Houston, a representative of the National Association for the Advancement of Colored People, charged that their southern white commanding officer, Comdr. P. J. McBean, of Meridian, Mississippi, refused to grant promotions to Negroes but brought in white men to fill higher posts.

Naval officials acknowledged the fact of the hunger strike when they issued a statement claiming that the demonstrators had appeared for all meals last Sunday after a two-day fast. Houston, the NAACP investigator, declared, however, that the strike was continuing, according to information of men from other battalions leaving the base.

Several of the alleged leaders of the hunger strike were reported held in the brig on a "safekeeping" charge, although public relations officials of the navy stated that no disciplinary action was contemplated and that the incident was "closed."

Despite the fact that the Negroes are in segregated battalions assigned to hard labor and that numerous complaints have previously been made about discrimination, Commodore Quigley, advance base depot commander, sought to dismiss the complaints with the claim that there is "no color line or discrimination against members of the battalion."

By Henry Jordan. From *Militant*, March 10, 1945. *Seabees* is a word derived from the initials of the words *construction battalions*.

It is a notorious fact that Negroes are discriminated against and segregated as a matter of official policy throughout the armed forces. This protest of one thousand veteran Seabees, in the face of possible severe retaliation, was a desperate measure. It was undoubtedly undertaken as the result of discriminatory acts which they viewed as intolerable.

The Negro people are extremely skeptical about this "war for democracy" in which Negro boys who are asked to fight and die are Jim Crowed in the military forces.

WACS, SEABEES WIN CASES

The fight against Jim Crow policies of the U.S. Army and Navy recently registered two victories when higher military bodies were forced to withdraw harsh and discriminatory penalties inflicted upon four Negro WACs and fifteen Seabees.

The reversals in these cases were not brought about by any burst of generosity or love of fair play on the part of the military authorities, but through the militant stand taken by the nineteen Negro servicemen and -women involved. These courageous Negro men and women used the method of militant protest, the only avenue left open to anyone who wants to fight the oppressive Jim Crow setup of the armed forces.

The Seabees were part of a much larger group of Negroes who were dishonorably discharged for a sitdown strike in 1943 against navy Jim Crow policies. Fifteen petitioned for a review of their discharges. Legal representatives of the National Association for the Advancement of Colored People, the American Civil Liberties Union, and the CIO War Relief Committee aided the Seabees in their hearing before the Naval Review Board. As a result the "dishonorable" discharges were changed to discharges "under honorable conditions" for fourteen of the fifteen petitioners.

The protest of the four Negro WACs took the form of a refusal to return to work under discriminatory conditions at Lovell General Hospital in Massachusetts. Earlier attempts by these and scores of other Negro WACs to get an adjustment of their grievances against the army officials, who were assigning all the

An editorial, *Militant*, April 14, 1945.

dirty work to the colored WACs, had been unsuccessful. Their refusal to work brought down upon them court-martial sentences of a year. This verdict has now been overruled by a higher military court, the prison sentences voided, and the four WACs ordered restored to duty.

Credit for this latest setback to Jim Crow must go not only to these nineteen brave servicemen and -women, but to millions of fighting members of Negro, labor, and liberal organizations, who supported their cases. Not a hat-in-hand policy of begging favors, but militant, uncompromising struggle gets results in the fight against Jim Crow! Although Jim Crow in the U.S. Army and Navy has yet to be defeated, these two victories point the way. We salute the four Negro WACs and fifteen Negro Seabees, who at great personal risk carried through this frontline fight against Jim Crow—a genuine fight for democracy.

162 OFFICERS ARRESTED, RELEASED

The 162 Negro flying officers arrested at Freeman Field, Indiana, early in April for protesting against army segregation policies were freed on April 26, according to Leslie Perry, Washington representative of the National Association for the Advancement of Colored People. Mass arrests of Negro officers of the 477th Bombardment Group followed upon their refusals to sign an endorsement of the Jim Crow plan for separate clubs for white and colored officers at Freeman Field.

Demands that charges be dropped against three Negro officers who were arrested at this same field for "jostling" a provost marshal are also being pressed by the NAACP. The charges were made after the Negro officers attempted to enter an officers' club which had been reserved for white officers.

Further demands of the NAACP are that the War Department remove Maj. Gen. Frank Hunter and Col. Robert Selway from their posts and that a thorough investigation—"not a white-wash"—be made of the Jim Crow setup at Freeman Field.

According to the April 28 *Pittsburgh Courier,* Major General

From *Militant,* May 5, 1945.

Hunter was expected this week to reveal the status of the War Department's investigations into the arrests of the Negro flying officers. Because of the vigorous nationwide protests against this Jim Crow outrage, "it was generally felt that Colonel Selway would be relieved entirely of command of the 477th."

ROOSEVELT DEAD, TRUMAN IN

Roosevelt, regardless of the lofty phrases that flowed from his silvery tongue, proved by his actions that he was 100 percent Jim Crow.

In mobilizing the armed forces for a purported war of "democracies against fascism" he refused to allow Negro and white Americans to be integrated into the same regiments. Jim Crow was thus togged out in official army uniform. That was Roosevelt.

He often condemned the Nazi racist ideology, but could never find time to say one word against the widespread brutalities against and murders of darkskinned American troops in the southern states of his own country. He spoke out against the lynching of a fascist by the irate Italian workers, but during his entire twelve years in office he completely ignored the dozens of lynchings of Negroes.

Almost every concession he made (such as Negro WAVES, WACs, a handful of naval officers, elevation of Davis to rank of general, etc.), was a token concession made—by strange coincidence—just before election time. The basic grievance of Jim Crow in the army was consistently ignored in his official utterances and in his Democratic Party platforms. The only major advance of the Negro masses under his regime was the FEPC—and that was granted only in a frantic move to avert a march of a hundred thousand Negroes on Washington. That was "our friend" Roosevelt.

According to all indications the forces of Jim Crowism, white supremacy, and second-class citizenship for the Negro will be greatly strengthened under "liberal" President Truman. His home is the state of Missouri, where colored farmers were recently driven off their land. Both his parents were proslavery. His close

---

By Charles Jackson. From *Militant,* May 12 and 19, 1945. Roosevelt died on April 12, 1945, and was succeeded by Harry S Truman.

associates in the Senate and now in the presidency are anti-Negro and antilabor reactionaries such as the South Carolinian, James F. Byrnes, who threatened to filibuster the antilynching bill "until the year 2,000 if necessary."

Although Truman has denied membership in the Ku Klux Klan, Michael Carter, who interviewed him for the April 21 *Afro-American,* states that he would be "at home on a cotton planter's veranda where the colored people . . . bow and scrape." When queried about the lack of a forceful plank on racial equality in the party platform he retorted, "Why shouldn't we conciliate the South?"

The *Nation* of April 21, 1945, quotes a 1940 speech before the National Colored Democratic Association. "Before I go farther," said Truman, "I wish to make it clear that I am not appealing for social equality for the Negro. The Negro himself knows better than that, and the highest types of Negro leaders say frankly they prefer the society of their own people."

The plainest handwriting on the wall, however, is the fact that the Hearst press and other organs of the most rabid antilabor and anti-Negro forces in America have taken Mr. Truman to their breast and acclaimed him as one of their own.

Lest we forget, Harry Truman, the new chief executive, is the same Truman who supports segregated schools in Missouri, who believes that Negroes should be physically thrown out of restaurants in his home town of Independence, and who stated that he has never invited a Negro to his home for dinner and never will.

He is even now laying the groundwork for anti-Negro attacks in which the fascist agents of big business will be whitewashed and the Negroes themselves blamed. This is proved by his statement quoted in the *Call* of April 23, 1945. "Negroes," said Truman, "are going too far in St. Louis. There Negroes have started a 'push day' once a week, when they shove white people out of bars. Why, St. Louis is sitting on a keg of dynamite. And they've got a 'push day' in Washington, too! I won't let my daughter go downtown on the streetcars on Thursday any more. It's not safe. They push white people off the street cars."

DEATH KNELL OF FEPC

FEPC has been dealt a crushing blow by Congress. The original request for an appropriation of $599,000 was slashed to $250,000. This is little more than one-half of last year's woefully inadequate appropriation. It sounds the death knell of FEPC.

Total salaries alone for committee members and employees last year amounted to not less than $352,000. Since FEPC must prorate its appropriation in twelve equal portions for the coming fiscal year, its personnel must be greatly reduced. If the war with Japan ends in the meantime, FEPC will be immediately dissolved. Thus the committee may not even receive the full $250,000.

Yet last year alone five thousand job discrimination cases were docketed. With the evil of Jim Crow growing more deadly every day, FEPC obviously will not be able to so much as adequately survey the situation, much less do anything about it.

Both Republicans and Democrats formed a united front on this question. They agreed to kill FEPC by reducing its appropriation. They even agreed to put in an amendment specifying that the committee should be liquidated. This amendment gives the green light to every employer who believes in the race theories of Hitler and the Southern Bourbons.

The 13 million colored people affected by this united front of reaction should particularly note the role played by Representative Vito Marcantonio of the American Labor Party, and that of the Stalinists. Marcantonio considered the $250,000 appropriation "satisfactory." The Stalinists hailed it as a great victory.

The lesson for the colored people is clear. If they hope to defend their democratic rights they must organize on the political field. They must put militant representatives in office who will really fight for genuine democracy. They must join with the labor movement to organize an independent labor party.

By Louise Simpson, SWP candidate for city council from Harlem in the 1945 municipal elections. From *Militant,* July 21, 1945.

LIAR EASTLAND AND THE PRESS

On June 29 Senator Eastland of Mississippi filibustered in the Senate against continuance of the Fair Employment Practices Committee. He flung two foul accusations against the Negro people. He said that "high-ranking generals" had characterized the Negro soldier as an "utter and abysmal failure." He said that French Negro Senegalese troops dressed in American uniforms had locked five thousand Christian German girls of good family in a subway at Stuttgart for five days, "kept them there and criminally assaulted them."

The capitalist press gave great prominence to these accusations of the southern gentleman. The capitalist press did not say whether the chivalrous senator was lying or telling the truth. The *Militant* on the contrary, flatly accused Eastland of lying.

Now this accusation of the Southern Bourbon senator has been publicly exploded as a gross fabrication. In a speech before the Senate on July 12, Senator Wagner revealed that all the high-ranking generals had denied point-blank the truth of Eastland's accusations. The fact that most of these generals are themselves steeped in race prejudice gives their denial all the more weight.

As for the Stuttgart atrocity tale, inquiry made at the French Embassy and checked by them with French High Command, according to Wagner, "has brought a categorical denial of this story. Thus the charge is not only irrelevant, but also untrue." Allied Supreme Headquarters likewise denied the truth of the story.

One single fact alone—aside from these official denials—blows up the senator's fabrication about the subway rape: *there is no subway in Stuttgart!*

Yet in the face of these facts the capitalist press did not give equal prominence to the exposure of Eastland's lies. In fact most of the capitalist press did not even mention the exposure! So far as their record is concerned, Eastland's declarations still stand.

An editorial, *Militant*, July 21, 1945.

Bigots who drink up such filthy propaganda will continue to circulate the story as genuine.

Could a more revealing light be thrown on the role of the capitalist press in besmirching the Negro people?

TRUMAN AT POTSDAM

Throughout the war the Negro people have had to endure racial discrimination in almost every phase of their daily lives, in travel, in employment, in the military, and in a thousand other ways. Still worse, they had to stand by and swallow the crap of the capitalist war propagandists. This was a war of the "democracies against the fascist oppressors," we were told.

But what capped the climax in this hypocritical farce was when Harry Truman, president of capitalist America, where Jim Crow is not only accepted but is enforced, signed the Potsdam declaration, which states that discrimination in Germany shall not be tolerated.

If the big-business government of America is so concerned about bringing "democracy" and "justice" to the rest of the world, why doesn't it clean up its own backyard by correcting some of the injustices which is fosters against Negroes here at home?

While Truman was in Potsdam preaching American democracy, two hundred Negro citizens in Tuskegee, Alabama, were refused the vote by the legal authorities. In Macon County, with a population of around thirty thousand, of which 80 percent are Negroes, only about ten colored citizens have been certified to vote.

While Truman stirs the stew of "justice" in Potsdam, three Negro WACs sit down in the "white only" section of a waiting

---

By Charles Jackson. From *Militant,* August 18, 1945. The Potsdam conference, held July 17 to August 2 in Potsdam, Germany, was a summit conference of the United States, Great Britain, and the Soviet Union. They agreed to disarm Germany and divide it into American, British, French, and Russian zones of influence; Nazi ideology was to be replaced with "democratic" ideas. The conference also issued an ultimatum to Japan, which Truman used as political support for the atomic bombings of Hiroshima and Nagasaki, August 6 and 9, which incinerated hundreds of thousands of people.

room in Louisville, Kentucky. They are called abusive names, beaten over the head and dragged across the floor by the civilian representatives of "law and order," and then court-martialed by the military for violation of the Ninety-third Article of War.

While Truman talks of educating the Germans in democratic ideals, the schools, the church, the movies, the radio, and the newspapers in America all unite to brand the Negro as a lazy, ignorant, criminal half-man, and in this way to perpetuate the myth of white supremacy.

While Truman spouts that discrimination in any form will "not be tolerated" in Germany, the very army brass hats that got him there continue their rigid practice of separating the Negro soldiers into Jim Crow units, where they can be given the lowest and dirtiest duties. In the case of an exception that was made to build up the illusion that Negroes were making gains from this war, this is "corrected" and the Negroes who had been allowed to volunteer for combat are again reduced to the status of "service" units. I refer to Seventh U.S. Army Provisional Company No. 2, which served in the European campaign with the Twelfth Armored Division with much courage and honor but which has now been again condemned to unskilled labor duty by Mr. Truman's War Department.

While Mr. Truman affixes his signature to a document which demands "equality under the law . . . without distinction as to race . . ." a federal judge representing all the authority of the ruling-class government decrees that a federal housing project in Hamtramck, Michigan, which was built with the funds of black and white alike, shall only be occupied by members of the white race.

We could go on endlessly to expose the lies of the American capitalist spokesmen when they claim to be for equality and justice, but the important point is to understand why they do this. As Mr. Truman himself admitted in his radio address of August 9, the conditions of economic chaos and human misery in Allied-controlled Germany are terrific. The imperialists, in order to cover up their real aims to enslave the German workers and to exploit that country, have donned the robes of guardian angels who are there to see that democracy, justice, and equality are carried out in that unhappy land.

Their actions, however, expose them as both national and international liars. They worship greed, not justice; profits, not democracy; hatred, not equality. The capitalist government not only "tolerates" but enforces discrimination here while granting a fake "political freedom" to starving Europe, over whose carcass it is snarling like a hungry wolf.

GLOSSARY

American Civil Liberties Union—founded 1920, growing out of defense of conscientious objectors in World War I; participated in Scopes monkey trial, Sacco-Vanzetti case, 1954 school desegregation case.

American Federation of Labor (AFL)—founded 1881 as a federation of skilled-craft unions; split in 1935 (leading to formation of CIO); unified with CIO, 1955.

American Youth Congress—founded by liberals in 1934 but became a Communist Party front; fought for passage of American Youth Act (a WPA for youth), which never passed; claimed 4,600,000 members in 1939; supported by Eleanor Roosevelt; leaders brought to White House in June 1940 where they quarreled with Franklin Roosevelt; became a shell during Stalin-Hitler pact and died in 1942.

Atlantic Charter—declaration issued by Roosevelt and Churchill, August 1941, stating the U.S. and Britain sought no territory or other "aggrandizement," respected the right of peoples to self-determination, and wanted international disputes settled peacefully.

Attlee, Clement R. (1883-1967)—British Labour Party leader; objected to nonintervention in Spanish civil war; served in Churchill's coalition cabinet during war; prime minister, 1945-51.

Attucks, Crispus (1723-1770)—born a slave; escaped 1750; led Boston crowd in 1770, protesting violence by British troops against an apprentice; troops attacked crowd and Attucks became first martyr of American Revolution; this is known as Boston Massacre.

Badoglio, Pietro (1871-1956)—commander in chief of Italian forces in Ethiopian campaign; premier of Italy, 1943-44.

Baldwin, Roger (1884-   )—a founder of American Civil Liberties Union; supported Minneapolis defendants; ACLU executive director until retiring in 1950.

Bethune, Mary McLeod (1875-1955)—founder and president of National Council of Negro Women; advisor on minority affairs in Roosevelt administration, 1936-44; vice-president of NAACP.

Bevin, Ernest (1881-1951)—British class-collaborationist labor leader; minister of labor and national service in Churchill wartime cabinet; foreign minister of Labour government, 1945-51; helped lay groundwork for NATO alliance.

Biddle, Francis B. (1886-1968)—Democrat, NLRB chairman, 1934-35; U.S. attorney general, 1941-45; U.S. member of Nuremberg war crimes tribunal, 1945-46.

Bilbo, Theodore G. (1877-1947)—ultraconservative southern Democrat; governor of Mississippi, 1916-20, 1928-32; senator, 1935-47; died while being investigated for intimidating Black voters in Mississippi and taking bribes.

Black Legion—white racist and antiunion organization formed in mid-1930s with close ties to Ku Klux Klan; centered in Detroit.

Blum, Leon (1872-1950)—French Socialist Party leader; headed Popular Front government, 1936-37; also premier briefly in 1938 and 1946-47.

Breitman, George (1916-   )—joined American Trotskyists in 1935; editor of *Militant,* 1941-43 (until he was drafted) and after the war; editor of books by Malcolm X and Leon Trotsky.

Browder, Earl (1891-1973)—head of American CP, 1930-44, and of Communist Political Association, 1944-45; led CP through zigzags in policy; became scapegoat for previous policies during postwar reorganization and was expelled in 1946.

Byrnes, James F. (1879-1972)—South Carolina Democratic congressman, 1911-25; senator, 1931-41; Supreme Court justice, 1941-42; director of economic stabilization, 1942; director of war mobilization, 1943; secretary of state, 1945-47; governor of South Carolina, 1951-55.

Carlson, Grace (1906-   )—joined Trotskyist movement in 1936; on National Committee of SWP from 1941; imprisoned in Minneapolis case; candidate for vice-president of U.S., 1948; left SWP in 1952 to return to Catholic Church.

Chamberlain, Neville (1869-1940)—Conservative prime minister of Britain, 1937-40; known for appeasement of Hitler in Munich pact.

Citrine, Walter (1887-   )—British labor leader, general secretary of Trades Union Congress, 1926-46; was knighted in 1935 for his services to capitalism; played a leading role in Attlee government after war.

Civilian Conservation Corps (CCC)—established in 1933 to provide work and training for unemployed single men; at peak in 1935 had over 500,000 members in over 2,600 camps; abolished in 1942.

Congress of Industrial Organizations (CIO)—initiated in 1935 as a committee inside the AFL, the CIO was a federation of unions organizing on an industry-wide basis rather than by craft; the CIO unions were expelled from AFL in 1938, and the two federations merged in 1955.

Cox, Edward E. (1880-1952)—Democratic congressman from Georgia, 1925-52.

Crosswaith, Frank R. (1892-1965)—Social Democratic labor leader; helped found Sleeping Car Porters Union; was SP candidate for several offices; a leader of American Labor Party in New York; chairman of Negro Labor Committee; general organizer of International Ladies Garment Workers Union.

Darden, Colgate W., Jr. (1897-   )—Democratic governor of Virginia, 1942-46; then became a college president and director of Du Pont.

Davis, Benjamin J., Jr. (1903-1970)—Black lawyer and CP leader; elected to New York City Council on CP ticket, 1943; reelected in 1945 as a Democrat; voted with Democrats to impose sales tax and abandon effort to desegregate Stuyvesant Town housing project; sentenced to five-year prison term under Smith Act in 1949.

Davis, Benjamin O., Sr. (1877-1970)—first Black brigadier general; worked his way up from ranks beginning in 1898, became full colonel in 1930, general in 1940.

Dawson, William L. (1886-1970)—Black Democratic congressman from Illinois, 1942-70.

Dewey, Thomas E. (1902-1971)—Republican politician; New York County district attorney, 1937; governor of New York, 1943-55; unsuccessful presidential candidate, 1944 and 1948.

Dixon, Frank M. (1892-1965)—Democratic governor of Alabama, 1939-43.

Douglass, Frederick (c. 1817-1895)—abolitionist leader; escaped from slavery in 1838; edited *North Star* for seventeen years; in Civil War helped organize two regiments of Black troops.

Drake, John G. St. Clair (1911-   )—social anthropologist and professor of African studies; coauthored *Black Metropolis: A Study of Negro Life in a Northern City* (1945).

Fair Employment Practices Committee (FEPC)—concession by Roosevelt in June 1941 to prevent march on Washington; held hearings that publicized employment bias but had no enforcement power. Roosevelt terminated its independent status in July 1942 under pressure from congressional Dixiecrats who wanted to control its financing and kill it; he was forced to restore independent status in May 1943. When Roosevelt's emergency powers ended near close of war, Congress assumed jurisdiction and cut off funds. Ended in 1946.

Ford, Henry (1863-1947)—founded Ford Motor Company in 1903 and headed it until 1945; apostle of mass production methods; stringent opponent of unions.

Ford, James W. (1893-1957)—Black American Communist Party leader; CP vice-presidential candidate, 1932, 1936, 1940; organizer of Negro Labor Victory Committee; harsh critic of March on Washington movement.

Fourth International—founded in 1938 as revolutionary successor to Second (Social Democratic) and Third (Communist) Internationals; led by Leon Trotsky until his death in 1940.

Franco, Francisco (1892-1975)—leader of fascist forces in Spanish Civil War (1936-39); dictator of Spain from 1939 until his death.

Future Outlook League—Ohio civil rights organization founded in 1935; fought job and housing discrimination with boycott and picketing tactics; had slogan of "Don't buy where you can't work."

Garner, John N. (1868-1967)—southern Democrat and segregationist; Texas congressman, 1903-33; vice-president under Franklin Roosevelt, 1933-41; referred to as "Cactus Jack."

Garvey, Marcus M. (1887-1940)—Black nationalist leader; founded

Universal Negro Improvement Association in 1914 in his native Jamaica; moved to New York in 1916 and established UNIA in nearly every urban area of the U.S.; advocated "back to Africa" movement, projecting plans for Blacks to resettle in Liberia; imprisoned in 1925 and deported in 1927; died in London obscure and impoverished.

Goering, Hermann (1893-1946)—leading Nazi; head of German air force; held important posts in Hitler's government.

Green, William (1973-1952)—president of American Federation of Labor from 1924 until his death; conservative craft unionist.

Haas, Francis J. (1889-1953)—Catholic priest; federal mediator in 1934 Minneapolis teamster strikes; became chairman of FEPC at its reorganization in May 1943; resigned in October to become a bishop.

Haile Selassie (1891-1975)—Negus (emperor) of Ethiopia; driven from the country by Italian conquest, 1936; returned in 1941; deposed in 1974 by the military during revolutionary upsurge.

Hastie, William H. (1904-1976)—Democrat, first Black appointed to federal bench; U.S. district judge of Virgin Islands, 1937-39; civilian aide to secretary of war, 1940-43; governor of Virgin Islands, 1946-49; judge of 3d U.S. Circuit Court of Appeals, 1949-71

Henry, Milton—became outstanding attorney in Michigan and leader of Freedom Now Party; associate and defender of Malcolm X in 1964-65.

Hillman, Sidney (1887-1946)—president of Amalgamated Clothing Workers and number two figure in CIO; helped organize Labor's Non-Partisan League and its New York affiliate, the American Labor Party, in 1936, as well as CIO Political Action Committee in 1943, to corral labor vote for Roosevelt; chief labor backer of Roosevelt administration during war.

Hitler, Adolf (1889-1945)—head of German National Socialist Workers Party (Nazis); established fascist regime 1933; committed suicide with defeat in World War II.

Hoover, Herbert (1874-1964)—Republican president of U.S., 1929-33; organized civilian relief in Europe after World Wars I and II; toured Europe in 1938, met with Hitler, launched campaign against U.S. intervention in European war; said main source of dictatorship was planned economy. Raised funds to aid Finland against USSR.

Hull, Cordell (1871-1955)—southern Democrat and poll taxer; congressman from Tennessee, 1907-21, 1923-31; in U.S. Senate, 1931-33; secretary of state under Roosevelt, 1933-44.

International Federation of Trade Unions—sometimes called the Amsterdam or "yellow" International; major international trade union body before World War II; controlled by reformists.

International Labor Defense (ILD)—organized by Communist Party in 1925 to defend class-struggle prisoners; as CP degenerated, became factional tool of Stalinism; played prominent role in defense of Scottsboro Boys; merged into Civil Rights Congress in 1946.

James, C. L. R. (1901-   )—West Indian active in British and American Trotskyist movements; split from SWP in 1940, rejoined in 1947, and quit again in 1951; author of *Black Jacobins, World Revolution*, and other books.

Jouhaux, Leon (1879-1954)—general secretary of the General Confederation of Labor (CGT), the main union federation in France; was social patriot and class collaborationist.

Keemer, Edgar B. (1913-1980)—Black doctor indicted as draft dodger in Detroit in 1943 because he opposed discrimination in the navy; case was dropped when he fought charges with aid of ACLU and SWP; active in SWP, 1943-47; wrote column for *Militant*; imprisoned fourteen months as an abortionist, 1959-60; wrote autobiography, *Confessions of a Pro-Life Abortionist* (Vinco Press, 1980).

Kelly, Harry F. (1895-1971)—Republican governor of Michigan, 1943-47.

Knights of Labor—Nineteenth-century American labor body; founded 1869; admitted Blacks after 1883; fought for eight-hour day, abolition of child labor, equal pay for equal work; had 700,000 members in 1886.

Knox, Frank (1874-1944)—Republican vice-presidential candidate, 1936; secretary of the navy, 1940-44; opponent of New Deal.

Knudsen, William S. (1879-1948)—became president of General Motors in 1937; during the war served as director of industrial production for National Defense Commission, codirector of Office of Production Management, and lieutenant general in U.S. Army.

La Guardia, Fiorello H. (1882-1947)—Republican congressman elected in 1916 from New York City against Tammany Hall machine; served again 1923-33; cosponsored 1932 Norris–La Guardia Anti-Injunction Act that legally aided the right to strike; mayor of New York, 1934-44; known popularly as "Little Flower."

Landon, Alfred M. (1887-   )—banker and oil operator; governor of Kansas, 1933-37; 1936 Republican candidate for president against Roosevelt.

Lane, Layle—member of National Committee of March on Washington movement and a leader of Workers Defense League; later a vice-president of American Federation of Teachers.

Lend-Lease Act—passed in 1941; authorized unlimited military aid to any country that the president deemed vital to national defense; used to aid Britain and USSR.

Lewis, John L. (1880-1969)—president of United Mine Workers 1920-69; principal founder and leader of CIO from 1935 to 1940; withdrew from CIO in 1942; led successful miners' strikes in 1943.

Lynn, Conrad J. (1908-   )—civil rights lawyer and activist; joined CP in college; expelled in 1937; defended his brother Winfred Lynn and other political victims including the five Puerto Rican nationalists.

MacLaurin, Ben F.—regional director of Sleeping Car Porters Union; active in Workers Defense League; president of Household Workers Association, 1976; member of New York Board of Higher Education and other city and state committees.

MacLeish, Archibald (1892-   )—poet and supporter of New Deal; librarian of Congress, 1939-44; undersecretary of state, 1944-45.

McNutt, Paul V. (1891-1955)—Democrat, head of War Manpower Commission; governor of Indiana, 1933-37; known as "Hoosier Hitler" in labor circles for his strikebreaking role in 1935 Terre Haute general strike; U.S. commissioner in Philippines, 1937-39.

McWilliams, Carey (1905-   )—member of National Lawyers Guild; served on California Commission on Immigration and Housing, 1938-42; opposed internment of Japanese-Americans; editor of *Nation,* 1955-75.

Mannerheim, Baron Carl von (1867-1951)—responsible for suppression of Finnish workers' republic in 1918; in 1939 and 1941 commanded the Finnish army against Russia; president of Finland, 1944-46.

Marcantonio, Vito (1902-1954)—U.S. congressman for New York, 1935-37 and 1939-51; a leader of American Labor Party, he also ran at various times under Democratic, Republican, and Fusion tickets; followed the lead of Communist Party on many issues.

Marshall, Thurgood (1908-   )—became head of the legal staff of NAACP in 1936; argued 1954 school desegregation case before Supreme Court; appointed to Supreme Court, 1967.

Mitchell, Arthur W. (1883-1968)—Chicago lawyer; first Black Democratic congressman, 1935-43.

Murray, Philip (1886-1952)—born in Scotland, emigrated to U.S. in 1902, became coal miner; UMW vice-president 1920; CIO vice-president 1936; CIO president, 1940-52; headed organizing drive in steel and was USWA president, 1942-52.

National Association for the Advancement of Colored People (NAACP)—founded in 1908; became largest and most prominent civil rights organization in U.S.; early efforts focused against lynching.

National Negro Congress—organized in 1936 as coalition of over 500 groups; followed a People's Front line; split in 1940 and lost most of its influence after CP imposed its line of U.S. nonintervention in war; it was dissolved in 1947.

National Urban League—social service and civil rights group founded in 1910; predominantly geared toward legal action.

National Youth Administration—an agency established in June 1935 to provide part-time jobs, training, and placement for high school youths and sixteen- to twenty-four-year-olds who were members of families on relief.

New Deal—slogan of Roosevelt's 1932 election campaign and applied to social legislation enacted while he was in office; declared formally over at the end of 1943.

Nimitz, Chester W. (1885-1966)—appointed rear admiral in U.S. Navy, 1938; named commander in chief of Pacific fleet, 1941; chief of naval operations, 1945-47.

Office of Production Management (OPM)—established January 1941 to set policies and priorities for war production and to insure labor peace; replaced in January 1942 with War Production Board.

Patterson, Frederick D. (1901-   )—president of Tuskeegee Institute; founder of United Negro College Fund.

People's Front—policy adopted by Comintern in 1935 of forming coalition governments of workers' and liberal bourgeois parties; examples were Popular Front governments in France and Spain formed in 1936; in U.S., policy took form of backhanded support to Roosevelt as CP campaigned against his Republican opponent.

Pickens, William (1881-1954)—Black educator and author; field secretary of NAACP, 1920-42; appointed director of Interracial Section of Savings Bond Division of Treasury Department in 1941.

Powell, Adam Clayton, Jr. (1908-1972)—Black minister and Democratic politician; elected to New York city council, 1941; member of Congress, 1945-71; accused of misuse of House funds and expelled in 1967, an act declared unconstitutional by Supreme Court.

Prattis, Percival L. (1895-1980)—Black journalist for *Chicago Defender, Amsterdam News,* and *Pittsburgh Courier;* covered Europe and Middle East; editor and columnist for *Courier* during war.

Randolph, A. Phillip (1899-1979)—founded the *Messenger,* socialist antiwar magazine, 1917; founding president of Brotherhood of Sleeping Car Porters, 1925; president of National Negro Congress, 1936-40; head of March on Washington movement; became a vice-president of AFL-CIO in 1957.

Rankin, John (1882-1960)—right-wing Democrat, racist congressman from Mississippi, 1921-53.

Reuther, Walter (1907-1970)—former socialist, leader of Detroit auto workers in mid-1930s; became director of UAW General Motors department in 1939 and president of UAW in 1946; succeeded Philip Murray as president of CIO in 1952; helped engineer merger of AFL and CIO in 1955 but withdrew UAW from federation in 1968.

Roosevelt, Eleanor (1884-1962)—wife of Franklin Roosevelt; attempted to foster image as champion of labor, unemployed, women, and minorities; U.S. delegate to United Nations, 1945-53.

Roosevelt, Franklin D. (1882-1945)—Democratic president of U.S., 1933-45; after taking office, he sought, through reforms called the New Deal, to overcome the Great Depression while containing the militancy of the American workers.

Schuyler, George S. (1895-1977)—Black journalist; on the staff of A. Phillip Randolph's *Messenger,* replacing Randolph as editor, 1925-28; writer for *Crisis* magazine and longtime columnist for *Pittsburgh Courier.*

Scottsboro case—internationally known case of nine Black youths indicted in 1931 in Scottsboro, Alabama, for rape of two white women; sentenced to death or 75-99 years in prison; Supreme Court reversed convictions twice on procedural grounds; charges against five were dropped in 1937, three were freed in the 1940s, and the last escaped to Michigan in 1948; International Labor Defense played prominent role in defense effort.

Sforza, Carlo (1872-1952)—liberal Italian diplomat who went into exile in 1926 and served as foreign minister after World War II.

Smith, Ellison D. "Cotton Ed" (1866-1944)—organizer for Southern Cotton Association and field agent for cotton protective movement, 1905-08; Democratic U.S. senator from South Carolina, 1909-44; prominent racist.

Smith, Gerald L. K. (1898-1976)—advocate of fascism, anti-Black and anti-Semitic; launched "Committee of One Million" crusade against communism and the labor movement in 1930s; during and after the war, edited *The Cross and the Flag* newsletter and coordinated efforts of right-wing organizations nationally; headed the Christian Nationalist Crusade.

Smith Act (Alien Registration Act)—passed June 22, 1940, provided stiff jail terms for "teaching and advocating the overthrow of the United States government by force and violence" and conspiracy to do so; used to imprison eighteen leaders of SWP during war, and to fingerprint and register 3.6 million noncitizens in 1940; eleven CP leaders were convicted under it in 1949; a 1957 Supreme Court decision narrowed the act and made successful prosecutions under it almost impossible, by limiting it to advocacy of subversive actions, not just ideas.

Smith-Connally War Labor Disputes Bill—first federal antistrike law in U.S. history; gave War Labor Board power to subpoena union leaders and made it a felony to advocate strikes; authorized seizure of plants to break strikes; defied successfully by miners in 1943.

Stalin, Joseph (1879-1953)—became general secretary of Soviet Communist Party in 1922; Lenin called for his removal because Stalin was using post to bureaucratize party and state apparatus; after Lenin's death in 1924, Stalin gradually eliminated his major opponents, starting with Trotsky; became absolute dictator of the party and the Soviet Union in the 1930s.

Stimson, Henry Lewis (1867-1950)—Republican secretary of war, 1911-13, 1940-45; governor general of Philippines, 1927-29; secretary of state, 1929-33.

Talmadge, Eugene (1884-1946)—Democratic governor of Georgia, 1933-37 and 1941-43; arch segregationist.

Tanner, Väinö (1881-1966)—Finnish Social Democrat; prime minister, 1926-27; foreign minister at outbreak of war; took hard line against Soviets; held various cabinet posts throughout war; imprisoned, 1945-49; returned to parliament subsequently.

Tenerowicz, Rudolph G. (1890-1963)—Democratic member of House of Representatives, 1939-43; claimed to be "labor congressman"; initial supporter of Black effort to move into Sojourner Truth housing project;

doublecrossed Blacks and was declared a "betrayer of labor's interests" by the UAW; defeated for reelection in 1942.

Thomas, Norman (1884-1969)—leader of Socialist Party and its presidential candidate from 1928 to 1948.

Thomas, R. J. (1900-1967)—elected UAW vice-president in 1937; a leader of anti-Reuther bloc after World War II; defeated in 1947 UAW elections, he went on CIO staff; retired in 1964.

Tobin, Daniel J. (1875-1955)—reactionary head of Teamsters union; in 1941 collaborated with fellow Democrat Roosevelt in the Smith Act prosecution of leaders of Minneapolis Local 544 and Socialist Workers Party.

Townsend, Willard S. (1895-1957)—head of United Transport Service Employees Union, CIO; first Black vice-president of a union federation when his union was chartered and he went onto CIO executive board in 1942.

Truman, Harry S (1884-1972)—Democratic senator from Missouri, 1935-44; vice-president under Roosevelt; succeeded to presidency upon Roosevelt's death in April 1945; ordered atomic bombing of Hiroshima and Nagasaki; in spring 1947 announced Truman Doctrine of "containing" communism, implemented through the Marshall Plan (June 1947) to rebuild and rearm European capitalism, and through the creation of the North Atlantic Treaty Organization (NATO) in 1949.

Tubman, Harriet (c. 1820-1913)—American abolitionist and ex-slave; led over three hundred slaves to freedom; served in the Union army as a nurse and spy.

Turner, Nat (1800-1831)—led slave revolt in February 1831 in Virginia, for which he was executed.

Tuskegee Institute—Tuskegee, Alabama, state normal school founded in 1881 by Booker T. Washington, stressing vocational education and accommodation as the path for Blacks to follow; supported by many wealthy whites.

Vesey, Denmark (1767-1822)—a free Black, attempted to organize a slave uprising in Charleston, South Carolina, but was betrayed and hanged with thirty-seven others.

Wagner, Robert F. (1877-1953)—Liberal Democratic U.S. senator from New York, 1926-49; prominent New Dealer; author of 1935 National Labor Relations Act (Wagner Act), which established National Labor Relations Board (NLRB) and was referred to by many labor leaders as the "Magna Carta of labor."

War Manpower Commission—agency established April 1942 to formulate policies for recruiting and training workers in industry, agriculture, and government.

War Production Board—agency established January 1942 to replace Office of Production Management; set policies for production and purchasing of war material, established priorities for the national economy, and directed conversion and expansion of plants for war production.

Washington, Booker T. (1856-1915)—born a slave in Virginia; exponent of vocational training, self-improvement, and accommodation rather than struggle for Black rights; founded and directed Tuskegee Institute (1881) and National Negro Business League (1900).

Weaver, Robert C. (1907-   )—race relations officer of Department of Interior, 1933-37; special assistant in U.S. Housing Authority, 1937-40; held other posts related to housing and minority employment; NAACP board chairman in 1960; secretary of housing and urban development, 1966-69.

Weiss, Myra Tanner (1917-   )—a leader of SWP until 1960s when she withdrew from activity in the party; SWP vice-presidential candidate, 1952, 1956, and 1960.

White, Walter F. (1893-1955)—secretary of NAACP, 1931-55; served on several government commissions; author of several books.

Wilkins, Roy (1901-   )—managing editor of Kansas City Black newspaper, the *Call*, 1923-31; assistant executive secretary of NAACP and editor of its magazine, the *Crisis*, 1931-55; executive secretary, 1955-64, and executive director, 1964-77; helped organize 1963 march on Washington.

Willkie, Wendell (1892-1944)—industrialist; Republican candidate for president, 1940.

Workers Defense League—nonpartisan defense organization founded in 1936 mainly by forces in Socialist Party, "to deal with the business of injustice"; defended Odell Waller and other Black victims, the SWP, *Militant*, and wartime strikers.

Works Progress Administration (WPA)—government public works agency set up in 1935; included construction and repair work and work for artists; at its peak it had 3.5 million persons on payroll; name changed to Work Projects Administration, 1939; terminated in 1943.

INDEX

Abraham Lincoln Brigade, 30n
Africa, 30, 31-32, 218, 291-92. *See also* names of specific countries
Aikman, Duncan, 86
Aluminum Corporation of America, 230-31
America First Party, 333
American Civil Liberties Union, 156, 257n, 295, 348, 357g
American Federation of Labor (AFL), 16, 91-92, 211-13, 357g
American Labor Aid, 57
American Legion, 342
American Youth Congress, 114, 357g
America's Sixty Families (Lundberg), 81n
Amsterdam News (New York), 52, 55, 180
Anderson, William, 55
Anti-Black walkouts: at Hudson Naval Ordnance Arsenal, 182-85; at Mobile shipyards, 256n, 267; at Packard, 252-53; at Philadelphia Transportation Company, 302-7
Anti-Semitism, 19, 31
Arms industry, 176-77. *See also* Aviation industry
Associated Farmers, 342
Atlantic Charter, 224, 357g
Atom bomb, 19, 24, 354n
Attlee, Clement, 48, 357g
Attucks, Crispus, 104-5, 357g
Australia, 159
Auto industry, 75-78, 163-65, 178
Aviation industry, 95, 120-21, 252

Badoglio, Pietro, 291-92, 357g
Baldwin, Roger, 235, 357g

Baltimore Afro-American, 59, 105, 120, 129, 289, 351
Bankhead, John D., 196
Bass, Charlotta A., 220
Bedaux, Charles E., 230n
Bedaux system, 230
Belgium, 31
Bennett, Harry, 77, 333
Berry, A. W., 190
Bethune, Mary McLeod, 179, 328, 357g
Bevin, Ernest, 48, 357g
Biddle, Francis B., 153, 221n, 225, 274, 357g
Bilbo, Theodore G., 28, 88, 358g
Birmingham Age-Herald, 237
Black GIs: attacks on, 128-32, 161-62, 194-95, 196, 290-91, 326; in Australia, 159; in Britain, 248, 311-12, 323-24; and Detroit riot, 265, 290; in Germany, 310-11, 355; and Harlem rebellion, 281-82; protests by, 64-69, 133-35, 289, 296-97, 312-13, 321-23, 347-49; self-defense actions by, 93-94, 149, 156, 159-62; strikes by, 313-14, 341, 348; and World War I, 33-35. *See also* Black noncommissioned officers; Black officers; WACs; WAVES
Black Hundreds, 261n
Black leadership: and Harlem rebellion, 285-86; March on Washington movement and, 210; U.S. government and, 114, 202, 203-4, 239-41, 245-46
Black Legion, 266, 358g
Black nationalism, 16, 206
Black noncommissioned officers, 217-18

367

Black officers, 248, 297, 326, 340-41, 349-50
Black petty bourgeoisie, 41-45, 75-76, 101, 308-9
Black press, 111, 219-20, 253, 284-85, 289
Blacks, 16, 30n, 87, 274; and AFL, 16, 211-13; in Africa, 31-32, 36-37; attitudes of, 35-36, 180-82, 201, 241-42, 280-81; and CIO, 16, 137-39, 333; conditions of, 15-16, 97-99, 242-44, 282, 325-26; and India, 197-99, 200-201; and UAW, 75-78, 163-65, 254; and white workers, 39-40, 194, 210-11, 252, 280-81, 331-32; and World War I, 33-35, 61
Black women, 177, 226-27, 287. *See also* WACs; WAVES
Black Workers in the New Unions (Cayton and Mitchell), 76
Block, Emanuel, 316
Blood bank, 148-49
Bloodworth, Jack, 195
Blum, Leon, 47-48, 358g
Boston College, 40
Boston Evening American, 40
Breitman, George, 64n, 67, 221n, 222, 358g
Briar, James A., 55
Britain: and Africa, 31-32, 36, 44, 46, 47; and Asia, 37; Black GIs in, 248, 311-12, 323-24; and Greece, 334-35; and India, 197-98, 199-201, 222-23
Brookley Field (Alabama), 312-13
Browder, Earl, 344, 358g
Brown, Edgar G., 85
Brown, James R., 323-24
Buck, Pearl, 235
Bugas, John S., 265
Building Service Employees International Union, AFL, 67-68
Bulgaria, 23-24n
Burma, 200
Byrnes, James F., 339-40, 351, 358g

California Eagle, 51, 156, 220
Call, 175
Calloway, Ernest, 73, 74
Call-Post (Cleveland), 231
Camp, Lindley, 195
Camp Claiborne (Louisiana), 312
Camp Gordon (Florida), 313
Camp Lee (Virginia), 161, 217-18
Camp Stewart (Georgia), 288
Capitalism, 263, 328-30
Carlson, Grace, 254, 358g
Carney, Frank, 303, 304
Carter, Michael, 351
Cayton, Horace R., 76-77, 119
Censorship, 19, 23, 213, 219-26, 298-99, 323-24, 327, 328
Central Intelligence Agency (CIA), 20
Chamberlain, Neville, 47, 358g
Chicago Defender, 51-52, 113, 119, 284, 288
Chrysler Corporation, 178
Churchill, Winston, 200
Citrine, Walter, 48, 358g
Civilian Conservation Corps (CCC), 62, 358g
Civil Rights Defense Committee, 224
Civil War (U.S.), 38, 39, 40
Class struggle, 328-29
Clement, Turner, 187
Coakley, James F., 322
Cobbs, Hamner, 192
"Collective security," 24
Colman, William T., 290-91
Committee to Abolish Racial Discrimination (CIO), 318-20
Committee to Defend America by Aiding the Allies, 79
Communist Party (CP, U.S.), 24-25, 332-33; and atom bomb, 24; attacks "Double V" campaign, 157-58; and Detroit riot (1943), 262, 272-73; and discrimination in industry, 208, 230-31; and FEPC, 352; and Harlem rebellion, 282-

83; and Japanese-Americans, 153n; and labor conscription, 338n; and March on Washington movement, 123-24, 174-76, 207-8, 232, 233; and maritime industry, 316n, 317; on military segregation, 344; and miners' strikes, 239n; and National Negro Congress, 20; and no-strike pledge, 254; and Waller case, 189-91

Communist Party (Greece), 334n

Congress of Industrial Organizations (CIO), 358g; and Blacks, 16, 75-77, 137-39, 165-66, 348; Committee to Abolish Racial Discrimination, 318-20; and Detroit riots, 153-54, 262-64, 269-70; and South, 140-43

Congress Party (India), 199, 200

Conscientious objection, 73-75

Conscientious Objectors Against Jim Crow, 74

Cox, Edward E., 53, 358g

Cramer, Lawrence, 256

Crisis, 180

Crosswaith, Frank B., 96n, 358g

Curran, Joseph, 316n

Czechoslovakia, 23-24n, 30, 48

Daily Worker, 273, 344; and "Double V" campaign, 158; and FEPC, 244; and Harlem rebellion, 282; and March on Washington movement, 110, 123, 174-76; and Waller case, 189-91

Danzig, 32

Darden, Colgate W., Jr., 187, 190, 358g

Davis, Benjamin J., Jr., 174-75, 176, 189, 273, 358-59g

Davis, Benjamin O., Sr., 132, 160, 216, 350, 359g

Davis, H. L., 56

Davis, John P., 82

Dawson, William L., 249, 359g

Defend the Negro Sailors of the

U.S.S. Philadelphia (Parker), 64n

Democratic Party, 29, 142-43. *See also* Southern Democrats

Demonstrations, 170, 233-34, 235, 301. *See also* March on Washington; March on Washington movement

Department of Justice, 247

Detroit News, 264

Detroit riots: 1942, 151-54; 1943, 258-75

Dewey, Thomas E., 32, 359g

Dickerson, Earl B., 126

Discrimination in industry: and government policy, 92-93; and hiring, 17, 72-73, 84, 86-87, 92, 95, 98, 226-27, 302-5, 339-40; on the job, 97, 179, 230-31, 243, 293-94, 336-38; laws against, 91-92 (*see also* Executive Order 8802); Powell on, 345; UAW on, 127-28. *See also* Aviation industry; Fair Employment Practices Committee

Dixon, Frank M., 192, 196, 359g

Dobie, Gil, 40

"Double V" campaign, 157-58

Douglass, Frederick, 104-5, 359g

Dowell, C. M., 160

Draft: in World War I, 33; in World War II, 59-60. *See also* Conscientious objection

Drake, St. Clair, 74, 359g

Durtree, Carl T., 298

Dyer Bill, 52-54

Eastern Europe, 23-24n

Eastland, James O., 353

Economy, 23, 251

Editor and Publisher, 54

Education, 56

Egypt, 329

ELAS (National Popular Liberation Army, Greece), 334

Elections (presidential): 1940, 16, 54, 59n, 70, 333; 1944, 333

369

of, 105-6; cancellation of, 113-14; 118-19; CP and, 110; SWP on, 102-7, 110; *Pittsburgh Courier* and, 108-10

March on Washington movement, 20-21, 117-18, 210, 295; and CP, 207-8; demands of, 172; and India, 209; and mass actions, 164-65, 171-74, 176-77, 232-34; national gatherings of, 202-9, 276-79; and rank-and-file democracy, 103, 136, 202, 204, 206-7; and unions, 208-9, 278; on World War II, 104, 207, 276-77

Maritime industry, 316-18

Marshall, Donald J., 76, 77, 78

Marshall, Thurgood, 321, 362g

Marshall Plan, 23

Martin, Glenn L., 120-21

Martin, James W., 161

Marx, Karl, 328

Mass action, 333; vs. conscientious objection, 73-74; vs. individual action, 130-31, 167-69, 208; vs. letter-writing, 109-10

Mein Kampf (Hitler), 80, 168

Mekeel, H. Scudder, 327

Merchant Marine Act of 1936, 316n, 317

Merguson, R. Walter, 86

Merrick, Frank J., 226

Mexican-Americans, 254-55, 320

Migration to northern cities, 16, 87, 274

Militant, 25, 26, 283-84, 326; U.S. government suppression of, 23, 219-26

Military segregation: in air force, 98, 228-29, 248, 349-50; in army, 98, 294-95; Bethune on, 179; in coast guard, 248; government policy on, 17, 61-64, 85, 114, 162-63, 247-49, 326; in marines, 60, 248; in medical corps, 87, 98-99, 257-58; SWOC and, 137; in World War I, 61. *See also* Black officers; Black GIs; Blood bank

Miller, Dorie, 147n

Mine, Mill and Smelter Workers, CIO, 165-66, 230-31

Miners' strikes (1943), 239-41

Ming, Robert, 119

Mining industry, 141, 195, 239n

Minneapolis Sunday Tribune and Star Journal, 181

Mitchell, Arthur W., 113, 362g

Montgomery, Lou, 40-41

Morishege, Bob, 342

Morocco, 38

Murray, Philip, 126-27, 140-41, 186, 362g

Mussolini, Benito, 29, 39

Nation, 351

National Association for the Advancement of Colored People (NAACP), 20, 55, 67, 73, 131, 362g; Detroit demonstration of, 235; and Detroit riot (1943), 273-74; emergency conference of (1943), 252-54; and employment, 84, 300; and lynchings, 53, 54; and March on Washington movement, 21, 111-13, 119; and military segregation, 148, 218, 295, 321, 340, 347, 348; and Pickens, 90, 179-80; Powell on, 346; Rankin on, 156

National Association of Manufacturers, 52

National Colored Democratic Association, 351

National Council for a Permanent FEPC, 295

National Defense Council, 100

Nationalization, 107

National Maritime Union, CIO, 316n, 317

National Negro Congress (NNC), 20, 21, 74, 82, 124, 362g

National Urban League, 20, 21, 72-73, 81-82, 362g

National Youth Administration, 62, 179, 362g

373

100-102, 105, 106, 111-13; cancels march on Washington, 113, 114, 115-16, 118, 119; and March on Washington movement, 135-36, 173, 202-5, 232-34, 276; on U.S. politics, 278-79; and voting rights, 166; on World War II, 277

Rankin, John, 156, 225, 363g

Reco, Charles J., 194

Red-baiting: and invasion of Finland, 52; and NMU, 316n; and *Races of Mankind*, 298, 299; and Stalin-Hitler pact, 22

Red Cross, 148-49

Reed, Samuel, 217, 218

Rehabilitation centers, 310-11, 327

Relief, 17, 71, 97-98

Reuther, Walter, 127n, 235, 363g

Revolutionary party, 45, 50, 169

Rhodesia, 32

Richardson, James M., 167

Roosevelt, Eleanor, 112-13, 328, 363g

Roosevelt, Franklin D., 17n, 28, 59n, 350, 363g; and attacks on unions, 95, 239n, 263n; and Black leadership, 114, 202, 245-46; CP and, 190-91; and Executive Order 8802, 116, 118; and FEPC, 126-27; and Franco, 222; and Japanese-Americans, 153n; and labor conscription, 338n, 340; and March on Washington, 111, 114; on military segregation, 61-62, 85, 161, 162-63, 247-49; and poll tax, 214-15, 245; and "race riots," 270-71; and southern Democrats, 142; and Spain, 47-48; and wage freeze, 215n; and Waller case, 187-88

Russian revolution (1917), 39, 252

Ryder, Noble, 327

St. Paul Recorder, 217

Sarnoff, David, 127

Schuyler, George, 41, 79, 363g

Scott, Emmett J., 82

Scottsboro case, 24, 363-64g

Seabees, 347-48, 348-49

Seafarers International Union, AFL, 316-18

Self-determination, 63

Selfridge Field (Michigan), 290, 296, 297

Selway, Robert, 349

Seniority, 319

Sforza, Carlo, 292, 364g

Shipbuilding industry, 256, 336-38

Simmons, Eldridge, 308-9

Simmons, Isaac, 308-9

Simpson, Louise, 352n

Singapore, 200

Smith, Ellison D. "Cotton Ed," 28, 364g

Smith, Gerald L. K., 333, 364g

Smith, Jesse, 196

Smith, Oscar, 54

Smith Act, 23, 25, 364g

Smith-Connally War Labor Disputes Bill, 239n, 263n, 304, 364g

Socialism, 330-31

Socialist Appeal, 25

Socialist Party, 175, 279

Socialist Workers Party (SWP), 21-23, 64n, 257n, 333-34; on Black struggle and war, 210-11; and defense of USSR, 121-24; on Detroit riot (1943), 265-70; government attacks on, 22-23, 125-26; on March on Washington, 102-7, 110, 117-18; military policy of, 22, 60-64; program of, to end discrimination, 107

Somaliland, 291, 292

South Africa, 31

Southern Democrats, 245, 249, 298; and antilynching bill, 52-53; and FEPC, 244

Southern Regional Conference, 54

Southern whites, 86-87; Cobbs on 192; Ethridge on, 191-92, 236, 250; Graves on, 236-38; Pickens on, 89

Spain, 30, 47-48

Sparks, Chauncy, 327
Sports, 40-41
Stalin, Joseph, 29-30, 48, 158, 334n, 364g
Stalin-Hitler pact, 22, 24
Standard, William, 54
Steel industry 319
Steel Workers Organizing Committee (SWOC), CIO, 16, 137
Stewart, J. R., 88
Stimson, Henry L., 95, 113, 364g
Strikes: of Black GIs, 313-14, 341, 348; Ford, 75-78; miners', 239-41; North American Aviation, 95; truck drivers', 306. *See also* Anti-Black walkouts
Strong, George E., 235
Strong, Leonard, 235
Struggle for Negro Equality, The (Saunders and Parker), 251
Sullivan, Donald W., 167-69

Talmadge, Eugene, 196, 237, 364g
Tanner, Väinö, 51, 364g
Taxes, 97. *See also* Poll tax
Tenerowicz, Rudolph G., 154, 364-65g
Textile industry, 339
Thomas, Norman, 190, 365g
Thomas, R. J., 77, 154, 183, 252, 253, 271-72, 365g
Times-Dispatch (Richmond), 180
Tobin, Daniel J., 212, 365g
Townsend, Willard S., 262-63, 365g
Transport Workers Union, CIO, 302-5, 307
Trotsky, Leon, 22
Truman, Harry S, 350-51, 354-55, 365g
Tubman, Harriet, 104-5, 365g
Turman, Ned, 128-32
Turner, J. P., 305
Turner, Nat, 104-5, 365g
Tuskegee Institute, 53, 365g

Unemployment, 16, 17, 70-71, 243
Union control of military training, 22, 63, 69, 74, 107, 137

Union of Soviet Socialist Republics (USSR): defense of, 22, 121-24; and Ethiopia, 49-50; and Finland, 46; imperialist hatred toward, 19, 48; and World War II, 19
Unions: Blacks and, 16-17, 210-11, 252; and Blacks, 71-72, 211, 280-81; and the South, 238, 319. *See also* names of specific unions and labor federations
United Auto Workers (UAW), CIO: and Black workers, 71-72, 77-79, 127-28, 163-65, 178-79, 182-85, 252-53, 287; and Detroit NAACP demonstration, 235; and Detroit riot (1942), 151, 153-54; and Detroit riot (1943), 269-70, 271-72
United Mine Workers (UMW), 140, 141
United States: economy of, 23, 251; foreign policy of, 18-20, 46, 47, 48, 222, 223, 335. *See also* U.S. government
U.S. Army. *See* Military segregation
U.S. Army Air Force. *See* Military segregation
U.S. Aviation Corps. *See* Military segregation
U.S. Bureau of Education, 300
U.S. Coast Guard. *See* Military segregation
U.S. government: attacks by, on unions, 95, 267-68; attacks by, on SWP, 22-23, 125-26; and Black leadership, 114, 202, 203-4, 239-41, 245-46; and discrimination in industry, 92-93, 100 (*see also* FEPC); and Philadelphia Transportation Company strike, 304-5
U.S. Marine Corps. *See* Military segregation
U.S. Maritime Commission, 317
U.S. Navy. *See* Military segregation
U.S. Post Office, 219-26

New International
A MAGAZINE OF MARXIST POLITICS AND THEORY

IN ISSUE 7

Washington's Assault on Iraq
OPENING GUNS of WORLD WAR III

In the lead article of this issue of *New International,* Jack Barnes shows that Washington's bipartisan war against Iraq was no historical accident. U.S. imperialism is fighting for position in the declining old world order, not giving birth to a new one. $10.00

OTHER ARTICLES IN THIS ISSUE:

- **"The Working-Class Campaign against Imperialism and War"**
- **"Washington's Third Militarization Drive"**
- **"1945: When U.S. Troops Said 'No!'"**
- **"Communism, the Working Class, and Anti-Imperialist Struggle: An Example from the Iran-Iraq War"**

ALSO AVAILABLE

DISTRIBUTED BY PATHFINDER, 410 WEST ST., NEW YORK NY 10014.

BY AND ABOUT MALCOLM X

FROM PATHFINDER

Other titles from Pathfinder

U.S. Hands Off the Mideast!
Cuba Speaks Out at the United Nations
by Fidel Castro and Ricardo Alarcón
Introduction by Mary-Alice Waters, $9.95

Blacks in America's Wars
by Robert Mullen, $7.95

Cointelpro: The FBI's Secret War on Political Freedom
by Nelson Blackstock, $14.95

FBI on Trial
*The Victory in the Socialist Workers Party Suit
against Government Spying*
Edited by Margaret Jayko, $16.95

The Changing Face of U.S. Politics
The Proletarian Party and the Trade Unions
by Jack Barnes, $18.95

Out Now!
*A Participant's Account of the Movement in
the U.S. against the Vietnam War*
by Fred Halstead, $29.95

Nelson Mandela: Speeches 1990
'Intensify the Struggle to Abolish Apartheid'
by Nelson Mandela, $5.00

Thomas Sankara Speaks
The Burkina Faso Revolution 1983-87, $17.95

Che Guevara and the Cuban Revolution
Writings and Speeches of Ernesto Che Guevara, $20.95

In Defense of Socialism
by Fidel Castro, $12.95

The Communist Manifesto
by Karl Marx and Frederick Engels, $2.50

Cosmetics, Fashions, and the Exploitation of Women
by Joseph Hansen and Evelyn Reed
Introduction by Mary-Alice Waters, $11.95

Teamster Bureaucracy
The Trade Union Campaign against World War II
by Farrell Dobbs, $17.95